PREHISTORY AND HUMAN ECOLOGY OF

Kent V. Flannery and Joyce Marcus
General Editors

Volume 1   *The Use of Land and Water Resources in the Past and Present Valley of Oaxaca, Mexico*, by Anne V.T. Kirkby. Memoirs of the Museum of Anthropology, University of Michigan, No. 5. 1973.

Volume 2   *Sociopolitical Aspects of Canal Irrigation in the Valley of Oaxaca*, by Susan H. Lees. Memoirs of the Museum of Anthropology, University of Michigan, No. 6. 1973.

Volume 3   *Formative Mesoamerican Exchange Networks with Special Reference to the Valley of Oaxaca*, by Jane W. Pires-Ferreira. Memoirs of the Museum of Anthropology, University of Michigan, No. 7. 1975.

Volume 4   *Fábrica San José and Middle Formative Society in the Valley of Oaxaca*, by Robert D. Drennan. Memoirs of the Museum of Anthropology, University of Michigan, No. 8. 1976.

Volume 5   Part 1. *The Vegetational History of the Oaxaca Valley*, by C. Earle Smith, Jr. Part 2. *Zapotec Plant Knowledge: Classification, Uses and Communication*, by Ellen Messer. Memoirs of the Museum of Anthropology, University of Michigan, No. 10. 1978.

Volume 6   *Excavations at Santo Domingo Tomaltepec: Evolution of a Formative Community in the Valley of Oaxaca, Mexico*, by Michael E. Whalen. Memoirs of the Museum of Anthropology, University of Michigan, No. 12. 1981.

Volume 7   *Monte Albán's Hinterland, Part 1: The Prehispanic Settlement Patterns of the Central and Southern Parts of the Valley of Oaxaca, Mexico*, by Richard E. Blanton, Stephen Kowalewski, Gary Feinman, and Jill Appel. Memoirs of the Museum of Anthropology, University of Michigan, No. 15. 1982.

Volume 8   *Chipped Stone Tools in Formative Oaxaca, Mexico: Their Procurement, Production and Use*, by William J. Parry. Memoirs of the Museum of Anthropology, University of Michigan, No. 20. 1987.

Volume 9   *Agricultural Intensification and Prehistoric Health in the Valley of Oaxaca, Mexico*, by Denise C. Hodges. Memoirs of the Museum of Anthropology, University of Michigan, No. 22. 1989.

Volume 10   *Early Formative Pottery of the Valley of Oaxaca*, by Kent V. Flannery and Joyce Marcus, with ceramic analysis by William O. Payne. Memoirs of the Museum of Anthropology, University of Michigan, No. 27. 1994.

Volume 11   *Women's Ritual in Formative Oaxaca: Figurine-Making, Divination, Death and the Ancestors*, by Joyce Marcus. Memoirs of the Museum of Anthropology, University of Michigan, No. 33. 1998.

Volume 12   *The Sola Valley and the Monte Albán State: A Study of Zapotec Imperial Expansion*, by Andrew K. Balkansky. Memoirs of the Museum of Anthropology, University of Michigan, No. 36. 2002.

Volume 13   *Excavations at San José Mogote 1: The Household Archaeology*, by Kent V. Flannery and Joyce Marcus. Memoirs of the Museum of Anthropology, University of Michigan, No. 40. 2005.

Volume 14   *Excavations at Cerro Tilcajete: A Monte Albán II Administrative Center in the Valley of Oaxaca*, by Christina Elson. Memoirs of the Museum of Anthropology, University of Michigan, No. 42. 2007.

Volume 15   *Cerro Danush: Excavations at a Hilltop Community in the Eastern Valley of Oaxaca, Mexico*, by Ronald K. Faulseit. Memoirs of the Museum of Anthropology, University of Michigan, No. 54. 2013.

Volume 16   *Excavations at San José Mogote 2: The Cognitive Archaeology*, by Kent V. Flannery and Joyce Marcus. Memoirs of the Museum of Anthropology, University of Michigan, No. 58. 2015.

Related Volumes

Flannery, Kent V.
1986   *Guilá Naquitz: Archaic Foraging and Early Agriculture in Oaxaca, Mexico*. New York: Academic Press.

Flannery, Kent V., and Joyce Marcus
2003   *The Cloud People: Divergent Evolution of the Zapotec and Mixtec Civilizations*. Clinton Corners, New York: Percheron Press.

Marcus, Joyce, and Kent V. Flannery
1996   *Zapotec Civilization: How Urban Society Evolved in Mexico's Oaxaca Valley*. London: Thames and Hudson.

Jadeite statue placed below the floor of Structure 35, a temple of the Monte Albán II period (painting by John Klausmeyer).

Memoirs of the Museum of Anthropology
University of Michigan
Number 58

PREHISTORY AND HUMAN ECOLOGY OF THE VALLEY OF OAXACA
Kent V. Flannery and Joyce Marcus, General Editors
Volume 16

Excavations at San José Mogote 2

The Cognitive Archaeology

by
Kent V. Flannery
Joyce Marcus

with contributions by
Chris L. Moser
Ronald Spores
Dudley M. Varner
Judith Francis Zeitlin
Robert N. Zeitlin

Ann Arbor, Michigan
2015

©2015 by the Regents of the University of Michigan
The Museum of Anthropology
All rights reserved

Printed in the United States of America
ISBN 978-0-915703-86-9

Cover design by Katherine Clahassey

The Museum currently publishes two monograph series: Anthropological Papers and Memoirs. For permissions, questions, or catalogs, contact Museum publications at 1109 Geddes Avenue, Ann Arbor, Michigan 48109-1079; umma-pubs@umich.edu; www.lsa.umich.edu/ummaa/publications

Library of Congress Cataloging-in-Publication Data

Flannery, Kent V.
Excavations at San José Mogote 1 : the household archaeology / by Kent V. Flannery and Joyce
Marcus ; with a multidimensional scaling of houses by Robert G. Reynolds.
Excavations at San José Mogote 2 : the cognitive archaeology / by Kent V. Flannery and Joyce
Marcus ; with contributions by Chris L. Moser, Ronald Spores, Dudley M. Varner, Judith Francis Zeitlin,
Robert N. Zeitlin.
p. cm. -- (Memoirs ; no. 40, no. 58) (Prehistory and human ecology of the Valley of Oaxaca ; v. 13, v. 16)
Includes bibliographical references and index.
ISBN 0-915703-59-9 (Vol. 1)
ISBN 978-0-915703-86-9 (Vol. 2)
1. Indians of Mexico--Mexico--San José Mogote--Antiquities. 2. Indian pottery--Mexico--San
José Mogote. 3. Excavations (Archaeology)--Mexico--San José Mogote. 4. San José Mogote
(Mexico)--Antiquities. I. Title: Excavations at San José Mogote one. II. Marcus, Joyce. III.
University of Michigan. Museum of Anthropology. IV. Title. V. Series. VI. Memoirs of the Museum of
Anthropology, University of Michigan ; no. 40.
GN2.M52 no. 40
[F1219.1.S215]
306--dc22
                                    2005002562

The paper used in this publication meets the requirements of the ANSI Standard Z39.48-1984 (Permanence of Paper).

*dedicated to
the memory of
Chris L. Moser
1942–2003*

Contents

Illustrations

xiii

Tables

Acknowledgments

San José Mogote is a Formative archaeological site in the northern, or Etla, district of the Valley of Oaxaca. It was our privilege to excavate there for 15 years, from 1966 through 1980. We spent another twenty years, from 1981 through 2001, analyzing our discoveries. Our plan was to publish the results in three volumes, the first of which would cover the 35–40 Formative residences we recovered. That volume, *Excavations at San José Mogote 1: The Household Archaeology*, appeared in 2005.

In this, the second volume, we report on the 35–40 temples, men's houses, shrines, and ritual features discovered at San José Mogote. All that now remains is to publish the burials and tombs, which numbered more than 70.

Our best estimate is that the cognitive archaeology reported in this volume accounts for $200,000 worth of research. As we remarked in our 2005 volume, "that sounds like a lot of money, but spread out over 15 years of field work, it averages out to less than $14,000 per field season."

The acknowledgments section of our household archaeology volume filled three pages (Flannery and Marcus 2005: xxi–xxiii). This volume's acknowledgments will be shorter, since so many of the people who helped us were already thanked in *San José Mogote 1*. All the work reported here was supported by four grants from the National Science Foundation: GS-1616 (1967), GS-2121 (1968), GS-42568 (1974), and BNS-7805829 (1978). We made each grant last longer than expected by being as frugal as possible.

Permission to excavate was granted by Mexico's Instituto Nacional de Antropología e Historia (INAH). We thank former INAH Directors Ignacio Bernal, José Luis Lorenzo, Guillermo Bonfil Batalla, Ángel García Cook, Joaquín García Bárcena, and Eduardo Matos Moctezuma. The encouragement of our Mexican colleagues Linda Manzanilla, Teresa Rojas Rabiela, Mari Carmen Serra Puche, Ernesto González Licón, Lourdes Márquez Morfín, and Leonardo López Luján was greatly appreciated.

The staff of the INAH Regional Center in Oaxaca extended us every courtesy and made working in Oaxaca a delight. We are especially grateful to Manuel Esparza, María de los Angeles Romero Frizzi, Nelly Robles, Arturo Oliveros, Alejandro de Ávila, Roberto Zárate, Raúl Matadamas, and Enrique Fernández Dávila for their support.

At the village of San José Mogote, Heliodoro Jiménez and his extended family virtually let us turn their home into our field headquarters. We are eternally grateful to Heliodoro and Delfina, Armando and Isaac, Carlos and Rafaela, and all their hospitable relatives and in-laws. We felt great affection for our archaeological workmen at San José Mogote, and agree with veteran trowelman Irán Matadamas, who recently affirmed that those 15 years of excavation were *la época dorada . . . los mejores años de nuestra vida*.

Equally treasured were the days, weeks, and months spent with the graduate students who worked on various aspects of our University of Michigan project. Chris L. Moser, Susan Lees, Michael and Anne Kirkby, Silvia Maranca, Richard J. Orlandini, Suzanne K. Fish, Kathryn Blair Vaughn, Andrew Nickelhoff, William J. Parry, Jane C. Wheeler, Judith Smith, Suzanne Harris, Virginia Popper, Katherine M. Moore, Karen Mudar, Sonia Guillén, and Eloise Baker all contributed to our success.

Four archaeological colleagues excavated parts of the site for us and wrote chapters for this volume. Ronald Spores excavated Mound 3, Dudley Varner excavated Mound 8, Judith and Robert Zeitlin excavated Mound 9, and Chris Moser excavated the ballcourt. We dedicate this volume to Moser, who joined our project in 1966 and ran our photo lab for 10 years. Chris was taken from us prematurely while serving as Curator of Anthropology for the Riverside Municipal Museum in California.

In addition to the colleagues who wrote chapters for this volume, we were visited in the field by Frank Hole, Henry T. Wright, Richard I. Ford, James Schoenwetter, Joseph W. Hopkins, Richard

G. Wilkinson, and John W. Rick, all of whom stayed long enough to excavate ritual buildings or features. We appreciate their help. In addition, David C. Grove, the late Christine Niederberger, and the late Gareth W. Lowe helped us to identify foreign pottery types among our elite burial offerings. Jaime Awe immediately saw similarities between our Structure 31 and the circular "performance platforms" he was finding in Belize. We also acknowledge our project's two godfathers: the late Richard "Scotty" MacNeish and John Paddock.

We learned a great deal from neighboring archaeological projects in the Valley of Oaxaca. The work of Charles Spencer and Elsa Redmond at San Martín Tilcajete has provided us with data on the origins of the two-room temple and the temple precinct. Robert D. Drennan (at Fábrica San José) and Marcus C. Winter (at Tierras Largas) helped to firm up our horizon markers for the crucial Rosario phase. Denise C. Hodges determined the age and sex of all our burials. Michael Whalen (at Tomaltepec), Christina Elson (at Cerro Tilcajete), and Ronald K. Faulseit (at Cerro Danush) contributed important data on ritual at other Oaxaca sites. The monumental settlement pattern data assembled by Stephen A. Kowalewski, Gary M. Feinman, Laura Finsten, Richard E. Blanton, and Linda M. Nicholas helped us to put San José Mogote in its regional context.

This volume probably relies more heavily on illustrations than it does on text, and we are grateful to our talented artists and photographers. Two University of Michigan artists, John Klausmeyer and Kay Clahassey, executed hundreds of line drawings. David West Reynolds did many of the three-dimensional building reconstructions. Charles M. Hastings, John Clark, S. O. Kim, Eric Rupley, and David Mackres printed and enlarged hundreds of our field photographs. Most of our negatives were developed in the field by Chris Moser, whose photographic skills overcame our lack of a genuine darkroom.

Finally, we want to express our special thanks to the late José Luis Lorenzo for the advice he gave us during the period when he was in charge of INAH. Lorenzo visited us in the field just after our excavation of Structure 13 on Mound 1. In those days, an informal protocol directed excavators to consolidate any building with a stucco floor, no matter how little remained of it.

Lorenzo looked with disbelief at the unimpressive remnant of Structure 13, all dutifully repaired and consolidated with cement. "Do you really think that tourists will come to see that pathetic little patch of stucco floor?" he asked us. "And will you come back every 10 years, to keep repairing it as it erodes away?"

We told Lorenzo that nothing would please us more than to remove Structure 13 and continue downward, since our preliminary step trench (Appendix A) already showed that there were several earlier temples below it.

"Photograph it, draw it, remove it, and keep going down," said Lorenzo. "You've heard about taking a site back to its origins, right?"

Thank you, José Luis. Thank you for telling us to keep on digging, which enabled us to find Structures 35, 36, and 37. Without it, we would never have discovered that Monte Albán II temples were replaced every 52 years. An invaluable 50-cm statue of Motagua jadeite and a scene of noble Zapotec metamorphosis would still lie buried. Without your advice, we would never have found that our earliest Monte Albán II temple columns were baldcypress trees. Without you we would never have found Structure 37, our final Rosario phase temple, with its roof supported by posts set on volcanic tuff bases and its plus-sign-shaped masonry platform.

Lorenzo knew that we were concerned with Zapotec origins, and that one never gets back to the origins if he always consolidates the remnants of the final stage. He also knew that no one wanted to keep coming back for decades to repair a pathetic patch of stucco floor. Without his wisdom and authoritative advice, we would know much less than we do about the cognitive archaeology of the Zapotec state.

1 | San José Mogote and the Cognitive Archaeology of the Zapotec

San José Mogote is a Formative archaeological site in the northern, or Etla, subvalley of the Valley of Oaxaca. At its peak, the core village and its outlying residential wards covered 60–70 hectares (Fig. 1.1). We conducted excavations there from 1966 to 1980; our analysis of the recovered artifacts, plant remains, and animal bones lasted until 2001.

We published the first of three volumes on our research at San José Mogote in 2005. This monograph, *Excavations at San José Mogote 1: The Household Archaeology* (Flannery and Marcus 2005), describes the Early and Middle Formative residences so far excavated at the site. It also reports on the dooryards associated with the houses, as well as every midden, storage pit, hearth, earth oven, or other feature relevant to the activities of the household. Accompanying the description of each house is the complete inventory of all artifacts, carbonized plants, and animal bones found with it. *Excavations at San José Mogote 1* also describes the archaeological site and its environment in detail, making it unnecessary for those data to be repeated here. The reader who needs more information need only refer to our 2005 monograph.

Among the things *San José Mogote 1* did not cover were the public buildings we found, including men's houses, shrines, temples, and ritual features. We left all structures and features related to cosmology, ritual, religion, and ideology for the present volume, *Excavations at San José Mogote 2: The Cognitive Archaeology*.

We began our work at San José Mogote with the hope of finding houses and public buildings, but with no way to antici-pate how many we might find. Although we excavated less than two percent of the ancient village, we recovered all or part of 35–40 residences. That means that there may well be thousands of houses at the site. Such a figure is perhaps not unexpected for a 60–70 ha village that was occupied on and off for about 2000 years.

What surprises us is that we also recovered all or part of 35–40 public buildings. One reason may be that San José Mogote's public buildings were so much sturdier than the average wattle-and-daub house that their remains were more likely to survive. Another reason is that we spent more time excavating in the central core of the village than in the outlying residential wards. Whatever the case, we feel confident that San José Mogote witnessed the construction of hundreds of public buildings over the centuries. It would be hard to exaggerate the role of ritual in integrating Formative societies.

We should say something about the topics that will *not* be covered in this volume. For one thing, the total inventory of burials from San José Mogote will be left for a future volume, *Excavations at San José Mogote 3: The Mortuary Archaeology*. In this volume, we describe only those burials that were included in public buildings.

Likewise, this volume will not focus on the description of pottery types from our various Formative periods. We have already published in detail the pottery of the Espiridión complex, the Tierras Largas phase, and the San José phase (Flannery and Marcus 1994). The pottery of the Guadalupe and Rosario phases will be published in a future volume. In the meantime, we rely

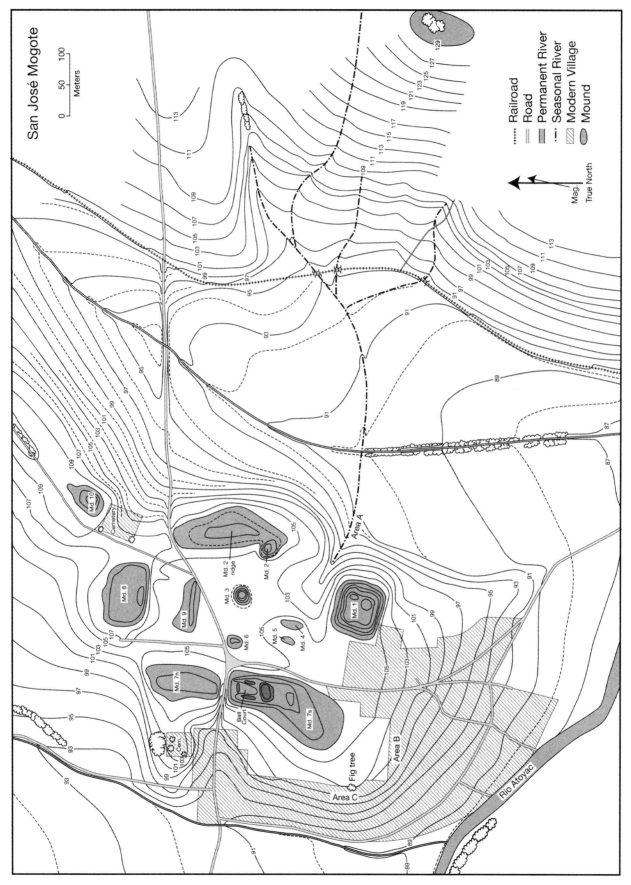

Figure 1.1. San José Mogote in the central Etla subvalley (contour map by M. J. Kirkby).

on useful descriptions of Middle Formative ceramics by Drennan (1976) and on brief summaries in Appendix A of Flannery and Marcus (2005). For the pottery of the Monte Albán I, II, and IIIa periods, we refer the reader to Caso, Bernal, and Acosta (1967).

The chipped stone tools from San José Mogote have been published in detail by Parry (1987). Pires-Ferreira (1975) has published the bulk of our obsidian, iron ores, and marine shell (see also Flannery and Marcus 2005). The figurines of all Formative phases have been the subject of a monograph by Marcus (1998).

Since all these volumes, as well as *San José Mogote 1*, are available in most libraries, it is unnecessary to reintroduce the site here. For the location of San José Mogote, the nature of its deposits, its artificial mounds, its residential neighborhoods, and the various grid systems used during our excavations, the reader need only consult Flannery and Marcus (2005). We repeat such data here only when it is necessary to place a public building in context.

A Note on Absolute Chronology

In this volume, we continue to present our radiocarbon dates in three different ways. "BP" refers to conventional radiocarbon years before the present; "b.c." refers to conventional radiocarbon years BC, derived by the 60-year-old tradition of subtracting 1950 from the BP date. (We continue to use b.c. because so much of Mesoamerica's Formative chronology is still based on old, uncalibrated dates.) Finally, "BC" refers to the two-sigma range of each date, once it has been converted to calendar years by dendrocalibration. The contrast between b.c. and BC is intended to eliminate any confusion about whether we are referring to conventional or dendrocalibrated ^{14}C dates.

Cognitive Archaeology

Cognitive archaeology is the study of all those aspects of ancient cultures and societies that are the product of the human mind: the perception, description, and classification of the universe (cosmology); the nature of the supernatural (religion); the principles, philosophies, ethics, and values by which human societies are led (ideology); the ways in which various aspects of the cosmos, the supernatural, or human values are conveyed in art (iconography); and all other forms of human intellectual and symbolic behavior that survive in the archaeological record.

Despite the fact that cognitive archaeology has its own definition, it should not be considered a separate branch of archaeology. Nor, for that matter, should cognitive archaeology be seen as some kind of postprocessual antidote to subsistence-settlement archaeology. The truth is that both cognitive and subsistence-settlement studies have always been part of *anthropological archaeology* (Flannery and Marcus 1976). Anthropology is holistic; it considers no aspect of human cognition or behavior inappropriate for study.

In the pages that follow, we look briefly at the cosmology, religion, and ideology of the Zapotec Indians of Oaxaca, described by the Spaniards who lived among them in the sixteenth and seventeenth centuries (Asensio 1905a [1580], 1905b [1580]; Balsalobre 1892 [1656]; Burgoa 1934a [1670], 1934b [1674]; Canseco 1905 [1580]; Córdova 1886 [1578], 1942 [1578]; Mata 1905 [1580]; Salazar 1945 [1581]). To be sure, we do not believe that sixteenth-century Zapotec cosmology, religion, and ideology can simply be projected back on the earlier peoples of the Valley of Oaxaca. We do believe, however, that if one starts with the archaeology of earliest times and moves slowly forward toward the centuries of the Spanish Conquest, one can document the long, slow evolution of the cosmology, religion, and ideology of the historic Zapotec. It took thousands of years for that complex of cognitive behaviors to take shape, and the ancient peoples of the Valley of Oaxaca left hundreds of small archaeological clues along the way. This volume does what it can to assemble those clues.

Cosmology

Like all the well-documented civilizations of sixteenth-century Mesoamerica, the Zapotec of Oaxaca saw the universe as divided into four great world quarters, each associated with a color. Whether a given quarter was associated with red, black, yellow, or white could vary from one community or region to another. The center of the world was associated with the sacred color blue-green, the hue of quetzal plumes and jadeite. The main axis along which the Zapotec world was divided was the east-west path of the sun, and the points where the sun rose and set during a solstice or equinox were well known.

The Zapotec had two calendars (Córdova 1886 [1578]). One was a solar year of 365 days; this was made up of 18 "months" of 20 days each, plus an extra 5-day period at the end. There was also a ritual calendar (or almanac) in which 20 hieroglyphic day signs were combined with 13 numbers, creating a total of 260 days (Alcina Franch 1993; Marcus 1976, 2003a). The ritual calendar was not keyed to solar or astral events; it was based on the Zapotec vigesimal counting system and the sacred number 13.

While the 260-day calendar was probably very ancient, its existence cannot be confirmed until we reach the Middle Formative period. At that point, we begin to see hieroglyphic day signs combined with numbers (Marcus 1976, 1980).

Religion

Zapotec religion was animatistic. Living things were distinguished from inanimate matter through their possession of a vital force called *pèe*, often translated "wind" or "breath." It was not only humans and animals that displayed *pèe*: anything that moved, such as a bolt of lightning, clouds traveling across the sky, a beating heart, corn tassels moving in the wind, or the effervescent foam on a cup of hot chocolate, was alive and therefore deserving of respect (Marcus 2003b).

As a result, the sixteenth-century Zapotec had two words for blood. *Rini* was dried, inanimate blood. *Tini* was flowing, moving, living blood, such as that emerging from a sacrificial victim, or drawn from one's own body by autosacrifice with an obsidian lancet, a stingray spine, or an agave thorn. One of the greatest sacrifices that one could make to the spirit world was a heart still beating and hence animated by *pèe*. The artifacts of ritual bloodletting, mentioned above, constitute some of our earliest evidence for the concept of *tini*.

The Zapotec recognized a supreme being "who created everything but was not himself created" (Córdova 1942 [1578]). This creator, however, was so remote and incorporeal that no images were ever made of him. Instead, the Zapotec made images of the great supernatural forces and beings with whom they came in contact on a regular basis. Most powerful and sacred of these forces was *Cociyo* or Lightning, the angry face of the Sky. *Cociyo*'s companions included *Zaa* (Clouds), *Niça Quiye* (Rain), *Pèe* (Wind), and *Quiezabi* (Hail). By AD 500, some Zapotec effigy vessels showed *Cociyo* carrying receptacles for those four companions on his back (Marcus and Flannery 1996: Fig. 10).

In Mesoamerican cosmology, Earth was the counterpart to Sky. To the Zapotec, Earth's angry face was *Xoo* or Earthquake, another great supernatural in the mold of *Cociyo*. There were a number of ways that Earth could be depicted in iconography (Marcus 1999)—in the form of four great world quarters; as an anthropomorphized Earth mask, with a cleft depicting the fissure opened by an earthquake; or as a crocodile's foot, an allusion to the belief that Earth was the back of a giant crocodile, floating on an endless sea.

Zapotec religion was run by full-time priests who had their own hierarchy. The supreme priest, described by the Spaniards as being "like our pope," was called a *uija-tào* or "great seer." Below him were high priests drawn from the nobility and assistant priests who were trained commoners. The standard Zapotec temple had two rooms, an outer (less sacred) chamber to which worshipers could come and an inner (more sacred) chamber in which priests alone performed rituals. The floors of both rooms had charcoal stains left by incense burners, and the inner room was often splattered with blood from the sacrifice of quail, turkeys, dogs, and human victims. Priests also offered up their own blood by drawing it from their tongues, earlobes, or other fleshy parts.

As we see in Chapter 3, the earliest ritual buildings at San José Mogote were not temples, but one-room men's houses. Actual temples did not appear until after 1000 b.c., and consisted of only one room at first. By 500 b.c., we see examples of incense burners and the sacrifice of human prisoners. Not until Monte Albán Ic (Late Monte Albán I) do we begin to see the addition of a second room to the temple. This second room, we suspect, served two purposes: (1) it provided a place where full-time priests could live, or pass virtually the entire day, and (2) it allowed the religious establishment to take some rituals out of the hands of commoners, restricting their performance to the less accessible inner room.

Ritual

For the late Roy Rappaport (1971, 1979), there were three principal components to religion. First came the *ultimate sacred propositions* that linked religion to cosmology. These propositions—believed to be true, despite the impossibility of verifying them—directed *ritual*, the second component of religion—and a key one for archaeologists. Because ritual involves repetitive performances and requires both artifacts and features, it leaves material traces to be found.

When performed correctly, ritual brings on the third of Rappaport's components: a *numinous* or *awe-inspiring experience*, during which strong human emotions validate the ultimate sacred propositions. While archaeologists normally cannot recover evidence for awe-inspiring experiences, the ancient Zapotec provided clues in the form of drugs that enhanced such experiences. Sixteenth-century Zapotec priests used plants such as jimson weed (*Datura* sp.), hallucinogenic mushrooms (*Psilocybe* sp.), morning glory (*Ipomoea* sp.), and strong wild tobacco (*Nicotiana* sp.) in their rituals. They also drank pulque, the fermented sap of the agave. Many of these plants were depicted in Zapotec art, increasing the likelihood that they were used in ritual.

As we indicate in Chapter 2, at least a few rituals can be traced back to the Archaic period in the Puebla-Oaxaca highlands. Included are (1) the creation of space for rituals such as dancing, games, or initiations, and (2) the sacrifice of children at times of harvest.

The Formative period at San José Mogote saw an explosion of ritual behavior, some possibly timed to solar events such as equinoxes and solstices. Men's and women's rituals had separate venues and artifact kits. Women engaged in divination, and communicated with recent ancestors using small solid figurines (Marcus 1998). Men built ritual houses, where they likely ingested a mixture of powdered lime and tobacco (Chapter 3). Autosacrifice involved the letting of one's own blood with obsidian lancets or stingray spines. Eventually, temples with standardized orientations replaced the earlier men's houses, and both Earth and Sky were depicted in ceramics (Marcus and Flannery 1994, 2004).

Political Ideology

Sixteenth-century Zapotec society was extremely hierarchical; the ruler's will was communicated to the commoners through several levels of nobles. No one doubted that this was the way the political system should operate, since monarchy was a shared ideal. The Zapotec believed that nobles and commoners had separate and unequal origins far back in time, making it appropriate for the former to direct the latter.

The Zapotec royal family was seen as having descended from semidivine ancestors who had long ago metamorphosed into "cloud people." Nobles ruled on earth, built temples, conquered enemies, protected their subjects, and were placed in elegant tombs after death. From there they, too, would ascend to the clouds, where they would be able to interact with Lightning.

0915703866

ISBN: 0 – 915703 – 86 – 6

Title: Excavations at San JosÚ Mogote
2 : the cognitive archaeology
/ by Kent V. Flannery, Joyce
Marcus ; with contributions by

Format: Paperback

P/O:

Supplier:

Returns:

Invoice:

Notes:

Commoners, on the other hand, were seen as descending only from earlier commoners; their remote ancestors were nameless.

The Zapotec king was referred to as a *coquitào* ("great lord"), while his principal wife was a *xonàxi* (Marcus 2006). The lineages of the greatest hereditary lords were called *tija coqui*; nobles of intermediate rank belonged to *tija joàna*; minor nobles belonged to lineages called *tija joànahuini*. Landowning commoners belonged to *tija pèniqueche*, "lineages of townspeople," but other commoners were landless serfs. Countless foreigners captured in war were turned into servants or slaves.

It is not clear, of course, how far back in Oaxaca prehistory this complex sociopolitical hierarchy existed. For example, we see no evidence in the Archaic period (Chapter 2) or the Tierras Largas phase (Chapter 3) for anything but an egalitarian ideology. Not until 1150 b.c., at the beginning of the San José phase, do we see clues that hereditary inequality had arisen (Chapter 4).

More than a thousand years later, during the Monte Albán II phase, we have abundant evidence for kings who lived in royal palaces and were buried in royal tombs; intermediate nobles of some kind, laid to rest in somewhat less elegant tombs; and commoners, buried in simple graves (Marcus and Flannery 1996:180–81). The task before us is to document each escalation of the sociopolitical hierarchy to the best of our ability.

Iconography

The prehistoric occupants of the Valley of Oaxaca conveyed many aspects of the cosmos, their ancestors, their deities, and their political hierarchy in art. Earth, Sky, and the four great world quarters were among the first topics to be depicted on ceramics (Flannery and Marcus 1994). A modest continuum of rank came to be reflected in the small, solid figurines of the San José phase (Marcus 1998). These figurines remained abundant until the end of the Rosario phase, about 500 b.c. At that point, a very interesting transition occurred. During the course of the Monte Albán I period, small solid figurines began to disappear from the archaeological record (Marcus 1998). At the same time, anthropomorphic urns and ceramic effigies of deceased ancestors began to emerge (Marcus 2009). We believe that this transition was related to the rise of hereditary aristocracy. Simply put, in the early Zapotec state, commoners' ancestors were no longer important; it was the ancestors of the hereditary nobles and the royal family who dominated the iconography.

The transition to state-authorized art seems to have been complete by AD 200, during the Monte Albán II phase. During this period, the depictions of supernatural forces and noble ancestors came to be linked. As we see in Chapter 13, ceramic effigies began to suggest that deceased nobles metamorphosed into "cloud people" and took on many attributes of Lightning. Zapotec culture, in other words, had moved several steps closer to that described by the sixteenth-century Spaniards, and those steps were reflected in the iconography of Monte Albán II.

2 | Ritual Life during the Archaic

In the past, the Archaic period has been defined as an era of hunting and gathering that took place under post-Pleistocene environmental conditions. That definition probably fits the Archaic of Texas and much of northern Mexico, but a different wrinkle is added when one travels south to Puebla and Oaxaca. In those parts of Mexico, the Archaic also included the first attempts at agriculture. In fact, the initial domestication of *Cucurbita pepo* squash appears to have taken place almost as soon as the Pleistocene ended (Smith 1997).

Our oldest radiocarbon dates for squash seeds and gourd rinds in Oaxaca are roughly 6950–6960 b.c., or 8035–7915 BC. The calibrated dates fall very near the transition from Pleistocene to Holocene (for a list of 40 dates relevant to early agriculture in Oaxaca, see Flannery 2009a: Table 1). Oaxaca's earliest specimens of runner beans have calibrated dates in the 6460–6220 BC range (Kaplan and Lynch 1999). The calibrated range for early maize in Oaxaca is 4355–4065 BC (Piperno and Flannery 2001).

Since the dates for early domesticates in the Tehuacán Valley are broadly similar (Byers 1967), we must alter our definition of the Archaic for the Puebla-Oaxaca highlands. In that region, the Archaic was an era of hunting, gathering, and the growing of early races of domestic crops.

Despite the addition of maize, beans, and squash to the diet, the rituals of the Archaic period continued to resemble those of ethnographically documented hunters and gatherers. Archaic groups in Puebla and Oaxaca changed their camps fairly often since the low productivity of early maize did not permit sedentary life. Not until genetic changes in maize had raised its yield to 200–250 kilograms per hectare could its harvests support year-round villages (Flannery 1973). This transition to sedentary life did not occur until 2000–1500 b.c. (Kirkby 1973).

During much of the Archaic period, the foragers of Puebla and Oaxaca spent the leanest seasons of the year dispersed over the landscape in groups the size of nuclear families. During seasons when localized resources were temporarily abundant, multiple families came together to form larger camps of perhaps 25–50 people. This annual cycle of dispersal and coalescence was typical of hunter-gatherers in the arid western United States, including many Uto-Aztecan speakers of the Great Basin (Steward 1938).

According to the ethnographic record, it was during times when 25–50 hunter-gatherers lived at the same camp that most rituals — including dances, games, initiations, courtship, and healing ceremonies — were held. Simply put, many rituals required participation by a group larger than the nuclear family. As a result, life in a multifamily camp was often the most exciting season of the year. For example, Woodburn (1972:200) reports that among the Hadza of Tanzania, social and ritual life in large camps could become so intense that hunting actually suffered.

Forager Camps and *Ad Hoc* Ritual

A great many hunter-gatherer rituals could be considered *ad hoc* activities. Rather than trying to schedule ceremonies months in advance, local groups simply held them whenever the food supply allowed large numbers of families to camp together.

Despite this lack of predictability, large camps were often laid out to accommodate ritual activity, and could even have ceremonial features. One of the most widespread patterns was to arrange the residential shelters in a circle or oval. The center of the camp then became an enclosed space devoted to communal activities. In many camps, this space was an area where bonfires were lit at night. Such bonfires kept wild animals at bay, made the darkness less frightening, and provided a place for conversation and storytelling.

Some foragers danced for hours around their central bonfire. For example, Yellen (1977) reports that the !Kung San of the Kalahari region arranged their huts in a circle, in the center of which they lit fires and danced. A sketch made by A. R. Radcliffe-Brown (1922) reveals that coastal foragers on the Andaman Islands likewise arranged their huts in an oval. Like the !Kung, they built bonfires in the enclosed area and there, on certain nights, many of the camp's 20–50 occupants danced.

This pattern of creating an enclosed ritual space within a circular or oval encampment goes back to very early times. Consider, for example, the case of M'lefaat, a camp near Mosul, Iraq, which was occupied almost 10,000 years ago (Kozlowski 1998). Its occupants first laid down a hard clay floor, 90–100 m long and 60–70 m wide. Upon this floor they then built 10 circular huts, arranged in an oval around a central space.

Comparable examples can be found in the Early Holocene New World. The Ring site near Ilo, Peru, was laid out in an almost perfect circle 26 m in diameter (Sandweiss et al. 1989). The Sapelo Island Shell Ring, occupied during the Archaic of coastal Georgia, had a similar layout (Thompson and Andrus 2011).

Ad Hoc Ritual at Gheo-Shih, Oaxaca

We do not know nearly as much as we would like to about the rituals of Archaic Oaxaca. We are fortunate, however, to have one radiocarbon-dated ritual feature from the open-air Archaic site of Gheo-Shih, 4 km northwest of Mitla in the eastern, or Tlacolula, subvalley of the Valley of Oaxaca.

Gheo-Shih is a 1.5 ha campsite on the floodplain of the Río Mitla, roughly 1660 m above sea level (Flannery and Spores 2003). Charcoal from the site has yielded two radiocarbon dates (Marcus and Flannery 2004), both of which came out to 6650 b.c. (Beta 190316 and 191398), with a dendrocalibrated two-sigma range of 7720–7560 BC.

Because of its location in the mesquite-grassland environment of the river floodplain, it seems likely that Gheo-Shih was occupied during the June-to-September rainy season, when wild foods such as mesquite pods and hackberry fruits would have been abundant. We also know that by that period, domestic gourds and squash had reached the Mitla area. These crops could have been grown on the floodplain of the Río Mitla during the rainy season.

Excavator Frank Hole recovered atlatl points of the Pedernales, La Mina, Trinidad, and San Nicolás types, metates and manos, scrapers, and choppers at Gheo-Shih. In the northern part of his excavation, he found higher than average numbers of tools for hunting and butchering. Also present were concentrations of ornaments made by drilling flat river pebbles (Marcus and Flannery 1996: Fig. 44).

Hole also uncovered an unusual feature near the center of the camp. It consisted of two parallel lines of boulders, stretching for 20 m and spaced 7 m apart (Figs. 2.1, 2.2). The 140 m² enclosed space had been swept clean of artifacts; the boulders had been set directly on a layer of indurated sand, determined by geomorphologist Michael J. Kirkby (pers. comm., 1967) to be the old Pleistocene alluvium of the Río Mitla. To either side of the boulder-lined feature were scatters of chert artifacts and fire-cracked rocks that may indicate the presence of activity areas in and around shelters (Fig. 2.3). For example, immediately to the northeast of the boulder-lined feature lay several crescent-shaped areas of debris that may have accumulated in or beside circular shelters.

We reconstruct Gheo-Shih as the rainy season encampment of a group numbering at least 25–30 persons. The boulder-lined area, which crossed the center of the camp from northwest to southeast, most resembles the kind of space that hunting-gathering groups of the Great Basin cleared for dances, initiations, or athletic competition (Lowie 1915; Steward 1938).

Guilá Naquitz Cave

In a volcanic tuff cliff 2.5 km to the north of Gheo-Shih sits Guilá Naquitz, a cave covering only 64 m² (Flannery 2009). Guilá Naquitz lies at 1926 m elevation in the midst of a deciduous thorn forest. At various points in the Archaic, families of 4–6 persons camped in Guilá Naquitz during the October-to-December dry season. There they harvested acorns and piñon nuts, baked the hearts of mature agaves, cooked the tender young stem sections of prickly pear, and collected a number of local fruits and berries. They also hunted deer, trapped cottontail rabbits, shelled runner beans, and roasted squash seeds.

Of all the Archaic living floors in Guilá Naquitz, the one closest in age to Gheo-Shih is Stratigraphic Zone B2. Charcoal from this stratum yielded a date of 6670 b.c. (SI-515) and a dendrocalibrated two-sigma range of 7995–7325 BC.

The family whose seasonal encampment produced Zone B2 engaged in a wide range of activities. They did not, however, leave behind any artifacts or features that can be linked to ritual behavior. There is also no evidence in the cave for the manufacture of ornaments from flat pebbles.

When we compare Guilá Naquitz and Gheo-Shih, therefore, the two sites reinforce the *ad hoc* nature of Archaic ritual. When

Figure 2.1. The boulder-lined "dance ground" in Area A of Gheo-Shih, viewed from the south. The vertical sticks mark small spots of colored soil to be investigated further; none proved to be postmolds. The irregular surface exposed by the excavation was analyzed by geomorphologist Michael J. Kirkby and declared to be indurated Pleistocene alluvium, left by an old stage of the Río Mitla.

foragers of the Mitla region were dispersed into small family groups of 4–6 persons, their ritual activity was minimal. When abundant wild resources allowed them to occupy multifamily camps of 25–30 persons, they sometimes created ritual space for dances, initiations, or games, and engaged in a number of activities (such as ornament manufacture) that were unrelated to subsistence.

The Question of Solar Alignment

The boulder-lined "dance ground" crossed Area A of Gheo-Shih at an angle of roughly 290°, relative to true north. Obviously, we are curious to know whether that alignment was simply one of convenience, or had actual cosmological significance.

In Chapter 3, we make the point that sedentary village societies often used solar events, such as equinoxes and solstices, to schedule rituals and align public buildings. Given the *ad hoc*

nature of most Archaic ritual, we suspect it might not have been practical to wait for solar or astral events when scheduling rituals. That having been said, we cannot rule out the possibility that the 290° alignment of the Gheo-Shih feature had some significance.

In 1991, a University of Michigan student, Jon Bryan Burley, examined the orientation of the Gheo-Shih "dance ground." He concluded that its alignment could be considered 69°45' west of true north (Burley, pers. comm., 1991). If it were indeed the case that the boulder-lined feature was aligned to the point of sunrise or sunset, Burley concluded that it must have been laid out between late May and early July, just before and after the summer solstice. This period falls in the summer rainy season—exactly the period when we suspect that Gheo-Shih was occupied.

We are reluctant to push these data too far. Since we have no other Archaic ritual features with which to compare Gheo-Shih's, we have no way of knowing whether its 69°45' alignment was unique or typical. None of our later ritual buildings have such an orientation, so the Gheo-Shih feature does not reflect an early

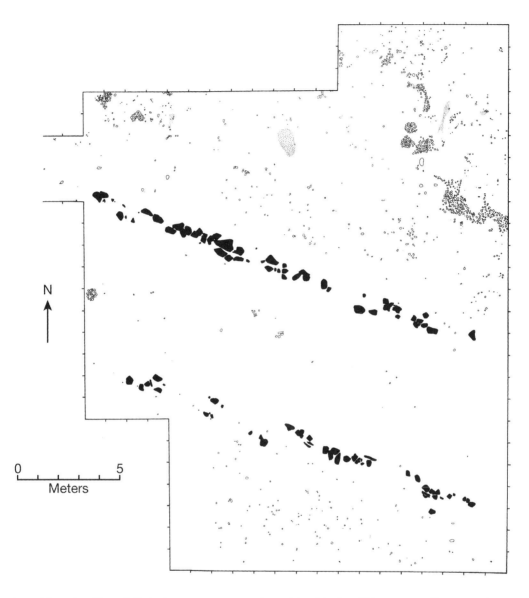

Figure 2.2. Plan view of Area A at Gheo-Shih. In the center we see a cleared, boulder-lined "dance ground" crossing the camp from northwest to southeast. At upper right we see areas of artifact scatter and fire-cracked rock that may represent the remains of perishable shelters. (Drawing by Frank Hole; the arrow indicates magnetic north.)

Figure 2.3. Area A of Gheo-Shih, seen from the north. The thickets of reeds and canes crossing the photo from left to right mark the course of the Río Mitla. In the left foreground are scatters of piece-plotted artifacts and fire-cracked rocks, possibly indicating places where perishable shelters disintegrated. Farther away one can see two lines of boulders, outlining what may have been a ritual space for dances, initiations, or athletic competition.

example of some longstanding solar alignment. Its orientation might simply be a product of the season during which it was used.

An Early Case of Human Sacrifice

Additional information on Archaic rituals in the Puebla-Oaxaca region comes from Coxcatlán Cave in the Tehuacán Valley (Fowler and MacNeish 1972:266–73). During the deposition of Zone XIV, a living floor occupied at 5000 b.c., two children under six years of age had been sacrificed and cannibalized.

One child had been decapitated and wrapped in a blanket and net; its skull had been placed in a basket nearby. A second decapitated child, also wrapped in a blanket and net, had its skull placed beside it. This skull had been burned or roasted, scraped to remove the flesh, and broken open so that the brain could be eaten. These two sacrificed children were accompanied by 9–10 baskets containing the desiccated remains of plants. The plant-filled baskets suggest that this act of sacrifice occurred at the time of a successful harvest, and may have been part of a ritual of thanksgiving.

The Zone XIV living floor reflects a large, multifamily encampment, analogous to the one seen earlier at Gheo-Shih. It provides further support for the idea that certain rituals were carried out on occasions when relatively large numbers of people were encamped together. The data from Coxcatlán Cave also suggest that Archaic foragers were already committed to the kind of child sacrifice seen later in Mexico. Such sacrifices continued to be held at harvest times by state-level Mesoamerican societies, although some Postclassic kingdoms substituted the eating of amaranth-dough figures of children whose heads had been lopped off (see, for example, Broda 1971).

Blood sacrifice is part of a reciprocal relationship with the celestial beings who control human destinies. In such rituals, humans offer their own blood (or the blood of others) in the belief that it encourages or rewards a favorable response from the supernatural world (Flannery and Marcus 2012). It would seem that this belief in ritual reciprocity was already present during the era of hunting, gathering, and incipient agriculture.

Implications for the Future

What our limited data on the Archaic show us is that two features of later Mesoamerican religion—human sacrifice and the setting aside of certain spaces for ritual activity—may have been established as long ago as the Early Holocene. These activities, to be sure, were not specifically Zapotec; they were features of a generalized Archaic culture that would one day give rise to multiple Mesoamerican societies. What is perhaps most interesting is the possibility that Archaic culture already included the concept of a reciprocal relationship with the spirit world, one in which sacrifices made by humans elicited supernatural favors.

3 | Men's and Women's Ritual in Early Segmentary Society

Sometime between 2000 and 1500 b.c., the early forager-gardeners of the Puebla-Oaxaca highlands began to create permanent villages of wattle-and-daub houses. Our data on this important transition from campsite to village are still inadequate.

Gradually, vessels of undecorated pottery began to replace the gourd containers of the Late Archaic. In Puebla's Tehuacán Valley, this drab pottery has been assigned to the Purrón complex (MacNeish, Peterson, and Flannery 1970). In the Valley of Oaxaca, equivalent pottery has been assigned to the Espiridión complex (Flannery and Marcus 1994: Chapter 7).

At San José Mogote, our data on the Espiridión complex are limited to the remains of one nuclear family residence, House 20 in Area C (Flannery and Marcus 2005:108–112). This house produced no radiocarbon samples. As a result, any date for the Espiridión complex can be no more than an estimate.

Our oldest date for the subsequent Tierras Largas phase (Beta-173807) is 3490 ± 80 BP, or 1540 b.c. The two-sigma calibrated range would be 2020–1620 BC (Flannery and Marcus 2005: Table 26.1). About all we can say about the Espiridión complex, therefore, is that it probably ended by 1800 BC.

We are on firmer ground when it comes to assessing the Tierras Largas phase, for which there are now 10 radiocarbon dates (Flannery and Marcus 2005:457–459). Based on the calibrated versions of these dates, we have estimated that the Tierras Largas phase lasted for half a millennium, from 1800 BC to 1300 BC.

Tierras Largas Phase Society

Our archaeological data suggest that villages of the Tierras Largas phase were egalitarian (no hereditary differences in rank) and politically autonomous (no village controlled by any other). Subsistence was based on a mixture of humid river bottomland farming, wild plant collecting, and hunting. Activities such as pottery making, weaving, and flintknapping were widespread, but there is little evidence for craft specialization. Trade for foreign resources such as obsidian and marine shell seems to have been negotiated at the level of the individual family, resulting in significant differences among households (Pires-Ferreira 1975).

Several lines of evidence indicate that Tierras Largas society had social segments larger than the extended family. First, its villagers built what appear to be men's houses—ritual buildings typical of village societies with clans or ancestor-based descent groups (Flannery and Marcus 2012). Second, San José Mogote seems to have been protected on its west side by a defensive palisade and produced evidence of raiding in the form of deliberately burned Tierras Largas phase residences and men's houses (Flannery and Marcus 2005:99–102). A study by ethnologist Raymond Kelly (2000) shows that the likelihood of intervillage raiding increases when societies have patrilineal, matrilineal, or ancestor-based cognatic descent groups. This raiding occurs because the "us vs. them" mentality of corporate social segments encourages group action against any other segment (or village) that is perceived to have committed an offense.

One behavior that probably helped to maintain the peace was the spacing of Tierras Largas phase villages at least 4–5 km apart. Maize productivity studies show that "villages in Oaxaca were leaving more space between themselves and their neighbors than their agricultural needs required. Their view of the world evidently included some notion of just how close their neighbors ought to live" (Flannery and Marcus 2005:7).

Worldwide Variation in Men's Houses

Men's houses are typical of societies where everyone begins life equal, but can ascend to a position of leadership by acquiring ritual knowledge, showing bravery in combat, or demonstrating entrepreneurial skill. Ethnographic data show that this practice provides talented and ambitious individuals with the opportunity to rise in prestige, while at the same time preventing them from becoming a hereditary elite. In a recent study (Flannery and Marcus 2012), we refer to these as "achievement-based societies." Such societies often build men's houses to help keep the venues for men's and women's ritual separate. Objects kept in men's houses frequently include relics of the ancestors.

Men's houses come in several contrasting types. The traditional Naga tribes of Assam built large, dormitory-style buildings in which all young men of a certain age went to live or sleep. The Mountain Ok of New Guinea, on the other hand, built smaller and more exclusionary men's houses, whose use was restricted to fully initiated ritual experts. Among the Siuai of Bougainville, aspiring Big Men built all-male "clubhouses" to host the powerful demons whose magic had helped them achieve renown.

For various reasons, we suspect that the early men's houses of San José Mogote were analogous to the small, exclusionary ritual buildings of the Mountain Ok. For one thing, our men's houses seem too small to have accommodated all the youths of the social segment building them. They consisted of one room only, sometimes flanked by a bench (or benches) on which men could sit and talk, and part of the already small floor space was taken up by a pit filled with powdered lime. As discussed below, we believe that this lime was intended for mixing with a ritual plant, such as tobacco, jimson weed, or morning glory. Lime speeds the release of nicotine or hallucinogens into the system.

It is also the case that certain middle-aged men, possibly community leaders, were buried near men's houses. The significance

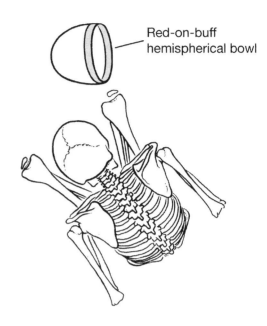

Red-on-buff hemispherical bowl

Figure 3.1. Burial 29 of San José Mogote, a man more than 40 years of age, buried in a seated position. This man was supplied with a typical Avelina Red-on-buff bowl of the Tierras Largas phase and interred near Structure 6, a men's house.

of such burials becomes evident if we look at the overall mortuary pattern of the Tierras Largas phase.

No Tierras Largas phase burials have as yet produced convincing sumptuary goods. Men and women were buried separately, rather than as marital pairs, and are usually found fully extended. However, three middle-aged men (one from the village of Tierras Largas and two from San José Mogote) were buried in the seated position, so tightly flexed as to suggest that they had been tied or bundled (Fig. 3.1). We believe these seated males to be men of relatively high achieved status—respected individuals who had passed through all the ritual levels typical of societies of this type. The two seated men from San José Mogote were buried near Structure 6, a men's house (discussed below).

While many achievement-based societies built only one men's house at a time, some (including the Mountain Ok) could maintain as many as four at a time, each dedicated to different rituals. Our evidence suggests that each residential ward at San José Mogote may have supported one men's house, and that such buildings were periodically razed and rebuilt. We cannot rule out the possibility that some wards had more than one ritual house at a time, but we found no convincing cases of multiple contemporary men's houses.

The implications of these buildings for Tierras Largas phase society are significant. Large, dormitory-style men's houses like those of the Naga confer no special privileges on the young men who live there. Small, exclusionary men's houses like those of the Ok divide communities or residential wards into a privileged ritual minority and an uninitiated majority. They set the stage, in other words, for the future creation of an elite.

Women's Ritual

While men's ritual was focused on the aforementioned lime-plastered buildings, women's ritual—including divination, healing, and communication with recently deceased ancestors—seems to have taken place in the household. And while men's ritual appears to have been *exclusionary* (privileging a subset of full initiates), women's ritual was essentially *inclusive*. The women of every household, no matter how humble, participated.

One of the ritual activities of Tierras Largas phase women was communication with the ancestors through the use of small, solid, handmade figurines (Marcus 1998). These small figurines appear mostly in the context of households and household middens, never in men's houses. Based on similar use of figurines in other egalitarian village societies, these small figures likely provided a solid venue to which the spirits of the ancestors could return during ritual. Figurines thus animated could be arranged in scenes, symbolically "fed," addressed, asked for favors, and even scolded for not having intervened with the spirit world on behalf of their descendants.

Because the figurines of the San José phase are so much more varied than those of the Tierras Largas phase, we will defer any substantial discussion of figurines until Chapter 4 (but see Marcus 1998: Chapter 9). All we will say here is that Tierras Largas phase figurines are predominantly female (for the contrast between male and females figurines, see Fig. 3.2). Clearly, the ancestor most frequently consulted during ritual was a female, such as a deceased mother, grandmother, aunt, or sister. Very few figurines are shown as pregnant, and those might represent ancestors who died in childbirth.

As explained in detail by Marcus (1998: Chapter 6), indigenous women's hairstyles in Oaxaca often reflect their social persona. Some of the most interesting figurines of the Tierras Largas phase have the elaborate hairdos that the Zapotec consider appropriate for young women of marriageable age. In some cases, a figurine's hairdo had been perforated in such a way that colored yarn or ribbons could be added to it (Fig. 3.2, right).

This brings us to another difference between men's and women's ancestor ritual—a difference that was once widespread in egalitarian, achievement-based societies. By the end of the Tierras Largas phase and the start of the San José phase, it seems clear to us that women were communicating with recent ancestors, while men were communicating with more remote

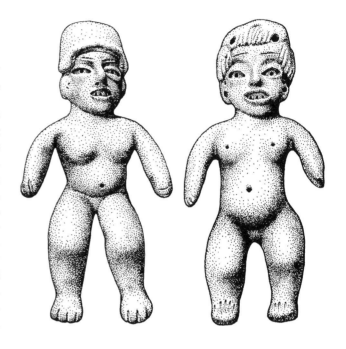

Figure 3.2. Two complete Tierras Largas phase figurines, found by Susana Ramírez at Site 1-1-16 near Hacienda Blanca, 4.5 km southeast of San José Mogote. The figurine on the left wears a cap usually seen on men. The figurine on the right depicts a woman whose hairdo has been perforated so that colored yarn or ribbons can be attached.

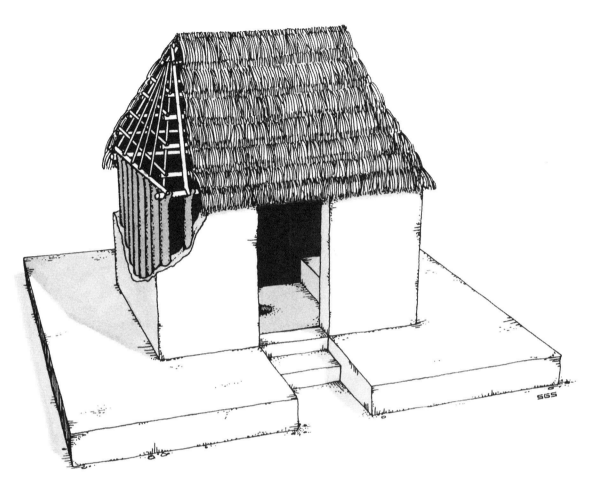

Figure 3.3. Artist's reconstruction of a typical men's house of the Tierras Largas or early San José phase. This drawing is based on details of Structures 3, 5, and 6 of San José Mogote, but is not intended to represent any specific building. The structure consists of a one-room wattle-and-daub building with a thatched roof, set on a low rectangular platform of crushed bedrock, clay, lime, and sand. The building and platform are coated with white lime plaster, and there may be an "apron" of white plaster surrounding the platform. The floor of the building is recessed 20–40 cm into the platform; there may be one step descending from the doorway into the room, and perhaps one to two steps (inset into the platform) descending from the door outside. The room usually has a pit in the floor for powdered lime. It may also have a sitting bench along one or more walls (drawing by David West Reynolds).

ancestors, perhaps even the mythological founders of ancestor-based descent groups. The small, solid figurines used by women look like everyday people. The objects associated with men's houses include grotesque masks that may have been used to impersonate mythological creatures.

The Tierras Largas Phase Men's Houses

Let us now look at the archaeological evidence for Tierras Largas phase men's houses at San José Mogote. Our best data come from Area C, on the west side of the village.

Roughly 300 m² of Area C was devoted to the building of men's houses. At any one moment, this area was the scene of a one-room ritual building no more than 4 × 6 m in extent (Fig. 3.3). Periodically, each of these buildings was razed and replaced with another, built not far away; in a few cases, later buildings were built directly over the ruins of earlier ones.

These men's houses differed from ordinary residences in several ways:

1. All were oriented roughly 8° north of true east, an orientation shared by later ritual buildings of the San José, Guadalupe, and early Rosario phases.
2. They contained 2–3 times as many pine posts as ordinary

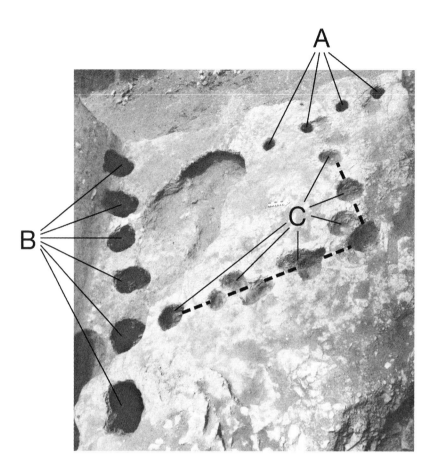

Figure 3.4. A patch of bedrock just west of the Area C profile, not far from the S31–S33 squares. The postholes from three overlapping Tierras Largas phase buildings can be seen. The four postholes marked A are from the earliest building, a small house. The six large postholes marked B are from the second building, probably a men's house. The shallow postholes marked C are from the corner of a later building of unknown function, whose posts barely reached bedrock.

houses, and the posts themselves tended to be larger (Fig. 3.4).

3. Their floors and walls (inside and out) were given multiple coats of white lime plaster.

4. Many were set on rectangular platforms, up to 40 cm high and lime plastered; in this case, the floors were recessed into the platform in such a way that one stepped down into the building.

5. Access to the door was via small steps, inset in the platform.

6. Surrounding each platform was a white-plastered floor whose outer limits, owing to later erosion, usually could not be determined (Fig. 3.5).

7. When preserved to a sufficient height, many men's houses appear to have had sitting or sleeping benches set along one or more walls.

8. When the central part of the floor was preserved, each building was found to have a lime-filled storage pit incorporated into the floor.

9. The usual household artifacts were missing from the floors of men's houses; at the same time, higher-than-average numbers of ceramic masks or mask fragments were associated with them. Such masks may have been worn by men dancing, or impersonating ancestors or spirit beings, during rituals.

The walls of each men's house were made from bundles of *carrizo* (*Phragmites* sp.) lashed together, daubed with clay, and plastered with lime. Roofs were thatched with reed canary grass (*Phalaris* sp.). This thatch may have been affixed to layers of reed matting, carbonized patches of which were sometimes preserved when the houses were burned (Figs. 3.6, 3.7).

Men's houses in many regions of the world were burned during raids because enemy villagers suspected that they were places where young men were instructed in the arts of war. We know that San José Mogote was concerned about raiding because of its aforementioned defensive palisade.

There is also a possible link between raiding and the use of

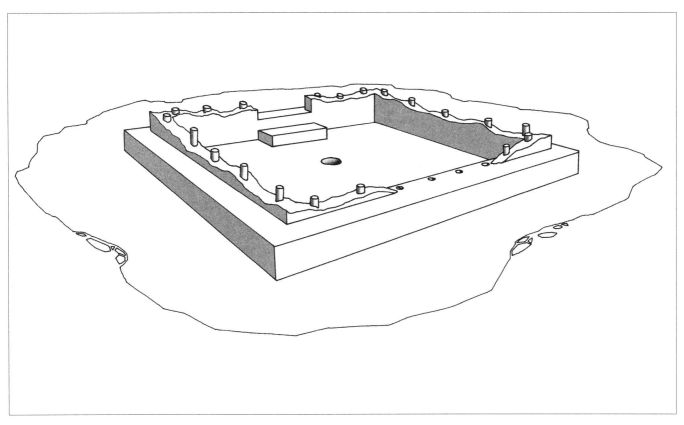

Figure 3.5. Artist's sketch of what a men's house like the one shown in Figure 3.3 looks like after having been razed to make way for a new one. The edges of the plaster "apron" surrounding it are damaged; the walls of the building have been broken down to the level at which the pine posts enter the platform. The recessed floor (including the interior step and the centrally placed pit for lime) is still intact, but rapidly becomes covered by fallen plaster, and eventually by destroyed wall chunks and other fill. This fill may enclose and trap sherds that can be used in dating the building (see Flannery and Marcus 1994).

powdered lime mixed with tobacco. The people of Oaxaca believed that strong wild tobacco had curative powers and could increase physical strength, making it an appropriate drug to use before raids. We believe that the tobacco was ritually ground in special boxlike metates with vertical walls and loop handles (Flannery and Marcus 2005: Fig. 4.20). These small metates, found only in the Tierras Largas and early San José phases, could be carried back and forth between one's home and the men's house. Their vertical walls would have prevented the tobacco from spilling, both during and after grinding.

Building Orientation and Calendric Ritual

One of the most significant changes between Archaic and Formative times was circumstantial evidence for calendric ritual. For the forager-gardeners of Gheo-Shih, a site described in Chapter 2, most rituals were probably held on an *ad hoc* basis. Owing to the unpredictability of wet, dry, and average years, Archaic foragers would have had difficulty knowing when food concentrations would permit large numbers of families to share the same camp. They were probably forced to defer certain rituals until the opportunities for multifamily camps presented themselves.

Once successful maize agriculture allowed Oaxaca's early farmers to live in villages year-round, it became possible to use solar or astronomical events to schedule some rituals. Many indigenous groups of Mesoamerica and the Southwest U.S. scheduled their rituals based on the shortest or longest days of the year (solstices) or the days when hours of daylight and darkness were equal (equinoxes). Assuming this to be true of Oaxaca as well, it meant that families could begin preparing well in advance of calendric rituals, stockpiling such items as food, costumes, and ritual paraphernalia.

Our best clue that Tierras Largas villagers were using solar or astral events to create ritual calendars is the fact that men's houses were consistently oriented 8° north of true east. We presume that

5 cm

5 cm

Figure 3.6. Fragment of carbonized *petate* (reed mat) from the ashy remains of a men's house. Area C, San José Mogote.

Figure 3.7. Two fragments of carbonized *petate* (reed mat) from the ashy remains of a men's house. Area C, San José Mogote.

this orientation had astrological (and/or cosmological) significance. It is also one of our earliest examples of an orientation that became widespread at later Formative sites. Complex A at La Venta, for example, was aligned 8° west of true north (Drucker, Heizer, and Squier 1959). That means that any building on the west side of Complex A, facing the plaza, faced 8° north of east.

We know that many early Mesoamerican groups were able to identify the vernal and autumnal equinoxes and the summer and winter solstices, any or all of which could have been used to orient ritual buildings. A number of Preclassic Maya sites have building complexes called "E Groups." Frans Blom (1924) was one of the first to speculate that these E Groups had astronomical significance.

E Groups are known from Calakmul, Nakbe, Tikal, El Mirador, Uaxactun, and Wakna (Chase and Chase 1995; Folan et al. 1995; Hansen 1998; Ricketson and Ricketson 1937). An E Group was made up of a large pyramid on the west side of a plaza, plus a long platform on the east side supporting three temples (E-I, E-II,

and E-III). The sun rose directly behind the middle temple (E-II) on the vernal and autumnal equinoxes (March 21 and September 23); it rose behind the north temple (E-I) on the summer solstice (June 21); and finally, it rose behind the south temple (E-III) on the winter solstice (December 21). Thus, Temples E-I to E-III served to mark the longest and shortest days of the year, as well as those times when the hours of day and night were of equal length.

We suspect that our Tierras Largas phase men's houses may have been laid out on a day when the sun rose at a point 8° north of east and set at a point 8° south of west. Once we begin trying to calculate on what day of the year that would have occurred, however, we discover that we get different answers, depending on the latitude and the century involved. Nowadays, at the latitude of Belize (latitude 16° N), the sun rises at a point 7.44° north of east during the summer solstice; this is close to the orientation we are seeking. However, at the Bay of Campeche (latitude 18° N), the sun might rise 5.44° north of east; in El Salvador (latitude 14° N) it might rise 9.44° north of east.

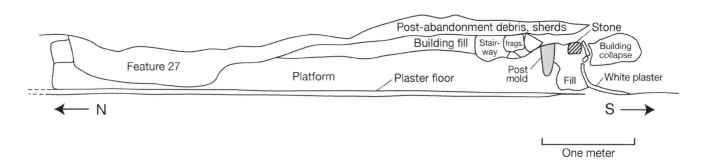

Figure 3.8. Simplified cross-section of the collapsed remains of Structure 3, as it appeared between Squares S21 and S25 of the Master Profile of Area C.

Another problem is that over time the earth's rotational axis undergoes changes, called *precessing* and *nutating* by astronomers. What this means is that during the Tierras Largas phase, the date on which the sun rose at a point 8° north of east was likely different from today's.

Neither of the University of Michigan astronomers we consulted (Douglas Richstone of the Department of Astronomy and Matt Linke of the Ruthven Museum Planetarium) felt that one could confidently specify the exact day on which the sun in Oaxaca would have risen at a point 8° north of east during the period 1800–1300 BC. Both agreed, however, that a date around the time of the summer solstice was a good working hypothesis.

Whatever the astronomical skills of the Tierras Largas villagers, we suspect that the process of creating Mesoamerica's solar and ritual calendars was underway by 1800 BC in "real" years. By early Monte Albán I times, we have hieroglyphic evidence for both the 365-day solar calendar and the 260-day ritual almanac (Caso 1928; Marcus 1976, 1980). By Monte Albán II times, as seen in Chapter 13, we have radiocarbon evidence that temples were being rebuilt as part of a 52-year ritual cycle.

The Sequence of Men's Houses at San José Mogote

The bulk of our men's houses were found in Area C of San José Mogote, a location described in *Excavations at San José Mogote 1* (Flannery and Marcus 2005: Chapter 6). The complete grid of 1 × 1 m squares for this area is given in Figure 6.2 of that volume, and can be consulted as needed. Two major parts of the grid were the Master Profile Sector (Squares S10A–S34F) and the Threshing Floor Sector (Squares S13G–S24Ō).

Let us now present our Tierras Largas phase men's houses in chronological order, beginning with Structure 3. Because each men's house was surrounded by an apronlike plaster floor that extended outward for several meters, its stratigraphic relationship

Figure 3.9. Working in Square S25A of the Area C Master Profile, Joseph W. Hopkins uses a paintbrush to expose the point where the lime-plastered apron around Structure 3 curves up to form the 40-cm vertical south face of the structure's platform. (The dark stains on the lower profile represent moisture from the severed roots of a modern tree.)

with other men's houses could often be determined even when the building itself was badly destroyed (see discussion in Flannery and Marcus 1994).

Structure 3

Structure 3 is the oldest men's house so far found at San José Mogote. It was discovered in the profile of Squares S21 through S25 of the Area C Master Profile (Figs. 3.8, 3.9).

The surviving remnant of Structure 3 suggests that this men's house once measured 4 m on a side (Fig. 3.10). Its floor was recessed 44 cm into the supporting platform, and bore several fragments of the plastered steps that had allowed initiates to enter the building.

Thirteen of the vertical posts incorporated into the eastern wall of Structure 3 had penetrated bedrock (Figs. 3.11, 3.12). Included was the post that defined the southeast corner of the building.

Flannery and Marcus (1994:123–126) have previously listed the ceramics whose deposition preceded and followed the use of Structure 3, as well as some 215 sherds trapped in the construction fill of the building. These sherds confirm a Tierras Largas phase date.

In addition, one radiocarbon sample was associated with Structure 3 (Flannery and Marcus 2005: Table 26.1). The date (Beta-190313) came out 3350 ± 40 BP, which converts to 1400 b.c. in radiocarbon years, or 1730–1520 BC when calibrated. This is currently our earliest known date for the building of men's houses in the Oaxaca highlands.

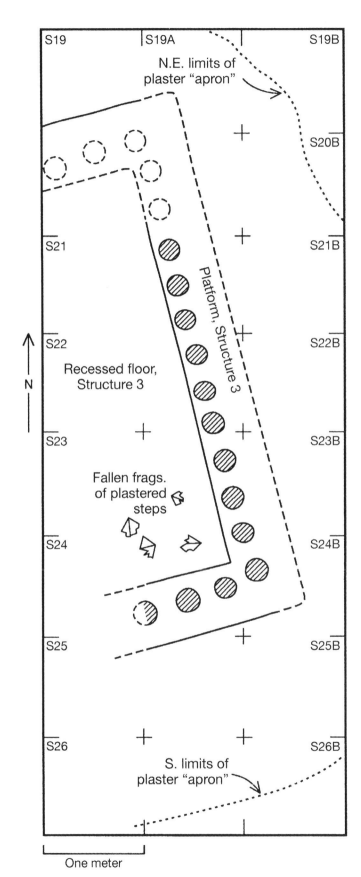

S19 S19A S19B

N.E. limits of
plaster "apron"

S20B

S21 Platform, Structure 3 S21B

S22 S22B

Recessed floor,
Structure 3

N

S23 S23B

Fallen frags.
of plastered
steps

S24 S24B

S25 S25B

S26 S26B

S. limits of
plaster "apron"

One meter

Figure 3.10. Plan view of Structure 3, the partial remains of a one-room men's house on a low platform surrounded by the plaster "apron" seen in Fig. 3.9. The hachured circles represent postholes in bedrock, whose cross-sections are shown in Fig. 3.12.

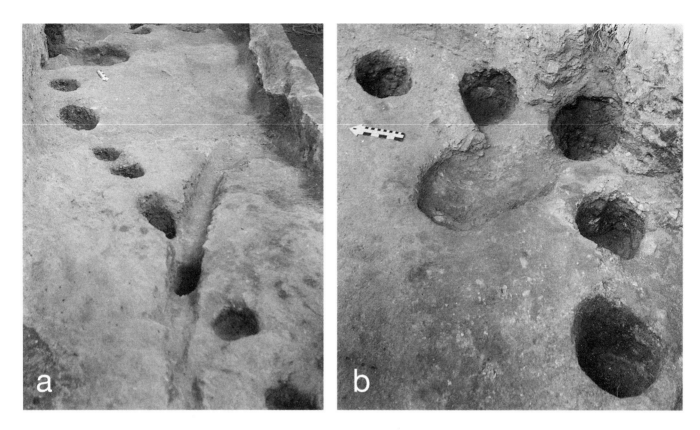

Figure 3.11. Two views of the postholes in bedrock left by Structure 3. *a*, postholes of the east wall, seen from the north. *b*, five postholes forming the southeast corner, seen from the west. (The cavity near the corner post is just a natural depression in bedrock.)

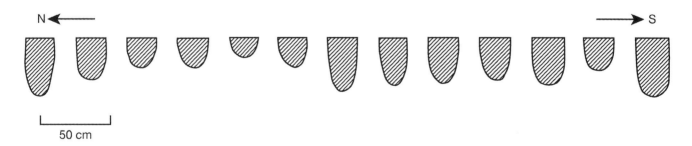

Figure 3.12. Cross-sections of the 13 best-preserved postholes in bedrock from Structure 3 (see Fig. 3.10 for locations). The northernmost lay in Square S21A and the southernmost at the border of Squares S24 and S24A. It should be remembered that each hole dug in bedrock was greater in diameter than the post itself.

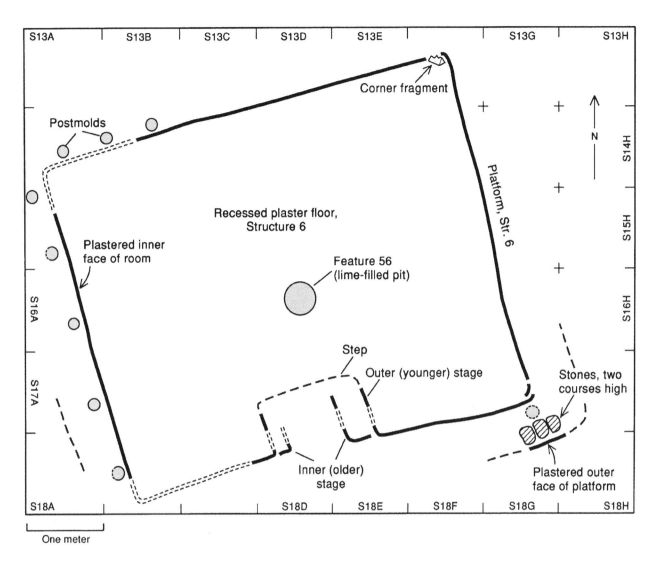

Figure 3.13. Plan view of Structure 6, within the grid system of Area C.

Structure 6

The second oldest men's house found in the Master Profile Sector of Area C was Structure 6 (Fig. 3.13). By opening up a 6 × 8 m area, delimited by Squares S13A–H and S18 A–H, we were able to recover virtually the entire recessed floor of the building (Fig. 3.14). The extent of that floor was 5.33 m east-west and 4.30 m north-south.

Structure 6 was built on a rectangular platform of crushed ignimbrite (volcanic tuff), lime, clay, and sand. The platform was too damaged to measure accurately, but it had apparently exceeded 8 × 8 m. Beyond the platform was the usual apronlike floor of lime plaster, traces of which could be seen in the stratigraphy of the Master Profile Sector. The stratigraphic placement of this apron indicated that Structure 6 was earlier than Structure 5 and later than Structure 3.

The vertical walls of the building were of wattle and daub (Fig. 3.15) and rose directly from the surface of the platform. In places, the wall foundations included uncut stones two courses high. Included within the wattle-and-daub walls were a series of vertical wooden posts, averaging 16 cm in diameter (Fig. 3.16). These posts went all the way through the platform and into bedrock. Posts were set 40–80 cm apart, which meant that there might be anywhere from 7 to 12 posts per wall.

There was an apparent doorway on the south side of the building. This doorway was 1.0–1.5 m wide and included remnants from two construction stages. Initiates would have entered by means of a step that had been placed 20 cm below the sill. This

Figure 3.14. Workmen build a protective stone wall around the surviving floor of Structure 6. At this stage of work, the floor has been swept clean of sherds and fallen plaster fragments; the interior step has been repaired with cement; and Feature 56, the central pit, has been emptied of its powdered lime. In this view from the northeast, one can see the way the floor of the room was recessed into the underlying platform.

Figure 3.15. Chunk of lime-plastered clay daub from one corner of Structure 6.

Figure 3.16. Fragment of clay daub with post impression, Structure 6.

Figure 3.17. Standing in Square S17A of Area C, Henry T. Wright works to expose the western side of Structure 6's recessed floor. In this view, looking south along the Area C Master Profile, the juncture between the horizontal plaster floor and the base of the west wall appears as a line running across the photograph from upper left to lower right. Wright is systematically following the vertical face of the west wall, coring out postmolds (like the one near his left elbow) and leaving fallen chunks of lime plaster on pedestals.

Figure 3.18. The northeast corner of the Structure 6 floor, including the broken corner fragment shown in Figure 3.15.

was halfway down to the floor, which was recessed 40 cm into the platform. There seems to have been a similar step on the outside, leading up to the door; it was too badly damaged to reconstruct.

The platform, step, floor, and wall surfaces inside and outside the building had all received multiple layers of lime plaster. Unlike the limey whitewash seen on typical Tierras Largas phase residences, this plaster resembled actual stucco. In some places, the walls appeared to have been plastered at least three separate times. Evidently it was important for the men's house to remain pure white, although we cannot be sure of the precise color symbolism.

Some clues to the construction of Structure 6 were provided by collapsed roof material, found among the pieces of fallen plaster on the floor. One fragment of fallen daub bore the impression of

what was probably a roof beam, 11 cm in diameter. Some 7 cm of clay daub had been applied to this beam, then given a half-centimeter coat of lime plaster.

We also found traces of reed matting. This substantiated our evidence from Structure 15, a later men's house, whose roof may have been burned in a raid (see below). It showed that roofs were constructed by lashing *petates*, or reed mats, over the roof beams, then thatching them with bundles of reed canary grass.

Figures 3.17 and 3.18 present some of the construction details of Structure 6. Figure 3.17 shows a few of the five postmolds running along the west wall of the building. Figure 3.18 shows a fallen fragment from the northeast corner of the recessed floor; this fragment is also indicated in Square S13F of Figure 3.13. The fragment had a flat upper surface, suggesting that there were built-in sitting benches along some walls of the men's house.

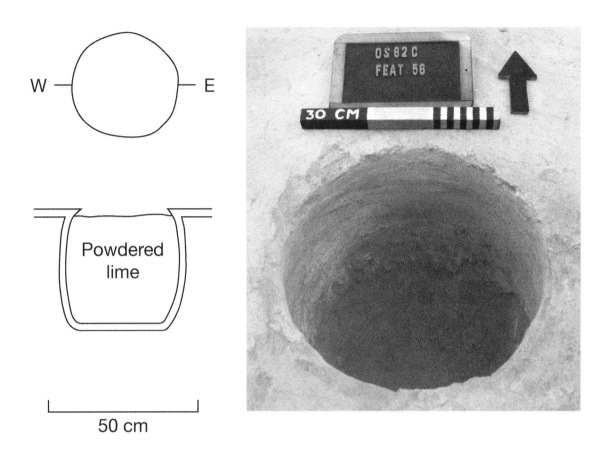

Figure 3.19. Two views of Feature 56, the lime-filled pit in the center of the floor, Structure 6. *Left*, plan and section drawings. *Right*, photograph (the black arrow points north).

Another built-in feature of Structure 6 was a cylindrical storage pit 36 cm in diameter and 38 cm deep, incorporated into the middle of the floor (Fig. 3.19). Designated Feature 56, this pit was part of the original construction rather than a later addition. When found, it was filled to the brim with powdered lime. As mentioned above, such lime may have been stored in the men's house to be mixed with a ritual plant such as wild tobacco (*quèeza* in Zapotec), jimson weed (*nocuàna còhui*), or morning glory. At the time of the Spanish Conquest, both the Zapotec and Mixtec of Oaxaca chewed wild tobacco mixed with lime during rituals (Furst 1978).

None of the ordinary houses at San José Mogote had such lime-filled pits. Occasionally, however, household units did produce box-shaped metates with loop handles like the one shown in Figure 3.20. We believe that these artifacts were men's ritual metates, and that the loop handles allowed them to be carried back and forth between the home and the men's house. Prior to rituals they could be used to grind wild tobacco, with the low walls of the metate preventing spillage. Structure 6 produced a one-hand mano small enough to be used for grinding lime, tobacco, or both, in a box-shaped metate (Fig. 3.21).

Some rituals held in men's houses evidently required masks; three examples are shown in Figure 3.22. Mask fragments were more common in or near men's houses than in and around ordinary residences. These masks were designed to cover only the lower half of the face. For the Zapotec, disguising the mouth was important, since it was from the mouth that *pèe* (wind, breath, or life force) left the body.

Structure 6 did not produce a radiocarbon sample. However, diagnostic Tierras Largas phase sherds were found trapped

2 cm

Figure 3.20. Reconstruction drawing of a boxlike, loop-handled ritual metate from Feature 65, Area B. Width, 14 cm. This type of metate may have been used for grinding tobacco into powder.

Figure 3.21. Combination one-hand mano and pestle, found in the fill above the plaster floor of Structure 6, northeast corner. Made from a white quartz cobble.

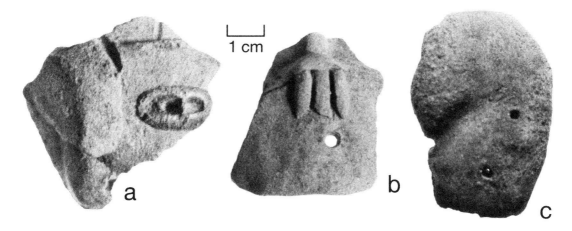

Figure 3.22. Fragments from three pottery masks, found in and around Structure 6. *a, b,* found in debris in the structure's southwest quadrant. *c,* found in debris just east of the structure.

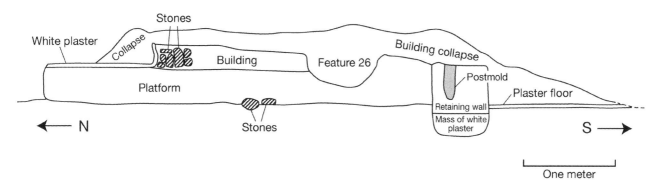

Figure 3.23. Simplified cross-section of the collapsed remains of Structure 5, a men's house, as it appeared between Squares S28 and S32 of the Area C Master Profile (see Flannery and Marcus 2005: Fig. 10.1).

between its original plaster floor, its second plaster floor, and its third or final plaster floor (Flannery and Marcus 1994:130). This final floor appeared to have been swept clean, as was typical with most ritual buildings. After Structure 6 fell into disuse, however, its walls and roof collapsed, and some 399 sherds accumulated among the bits of fallen plaster that came to cover its floor. All those postabandonment sherds belonged to the Tierras Largas phase (Flannery and Marcus 1994: Table 11.1).

Structure 5

Structure 5 was a later men's house in the Master Profile Sector. It was first detected in the profile of Squares S28–S32 (Fig. 3.23). Revealed in cross-section were (from north to south) a one-meter patch of recessed floor; the stone-reinforced juncture

where the floor plaster turned up to meet the vertical wall of a sitting bench; the postmold of an exterior post, set in a retaining wall of crushed volcanic tuff bedrock, clay, and lime plaster; and the plaster floor that had once formed an apron around Structure 5 (Fig. 3.24). Several meters of the platform that had once supported the men's house were also visible.

For convenience, our Master Profile had been laid out magnetic north-south. Since Structure 5 was oriented 8° north of east, the profile cut through it diagonally, making it difficult to estimate the true length of the building. Its recessed floor likely exceeded 4 m in its shortest dimension.

Two items recovered from the patch of recessed floor struck us as noteworthy. One was a fragment of carved conch shell, later identified as *Strombus galeatus*. Carved conchs of this species were traditionally used by the Zapotec as trumpets, blown to

Figure 3.24. Two views of the lime-plastered floor seen in the profile of Square S32, immediately south of Structure 5. In *a*, Rodolfo Sosa brushes the plastered vertical face created where the floor meets the south retaining wall of the platform supporting Structure 5. In *b*, Sosa brushes a patch of floor; a meter to the right, the cobble layer below the plaster has been exposed.

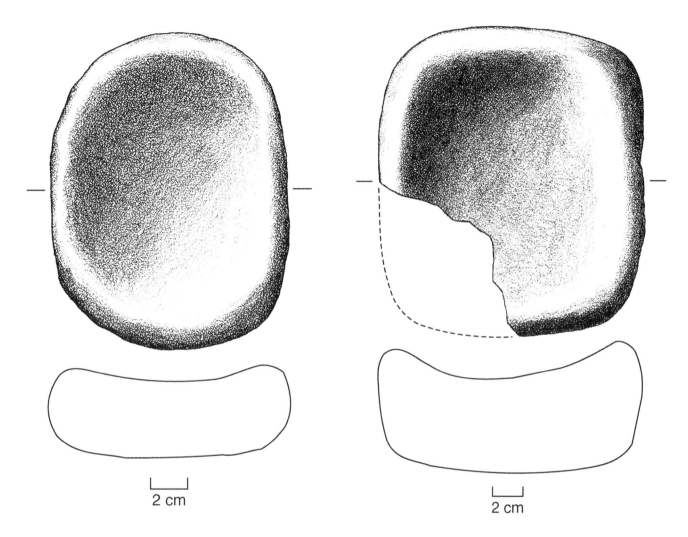

2 cm

2 cm

Figure 3.25. Small, basin-shaped metate of pink volcanic tuff, bearing residue from the grinding of powdered lime, found on the floor of Structure 5.

Figure 3.26. Small, basin-shaped metate of pink ignimbrite, found on the plaster apron just south of Structure 5.

2 cm

Figure 3.27. Polisher made of the vertebral centrum of an unknown fossil mammal, found on a patch of plaster apron just south of Structure 5.

summon participants to ritual or communal labor (de la Fuente 1949). For many societies of the American tropics, the trumpet-like sound made by the conch was thought to represent the voice of an ancestor (e.g., Goldman 1963:190–196).

The other noteworthy item in Structure 5 was a small, basin-shaped metate, bearing residue from the grinding of powdered lime (Fig. 3.25). This discovery suggests that had Structure 5 been more completely preserved, we would probably have found a pit in the floor containing powdered lime.

Two other artifacts were found on the apronlike floor stretching south from Structure 5. One was a second small, basin-shaped metate that might have been used for grinding lime (Fig. 3.26). The other was a small polisher made from the vertebral centrum of an unknown fossil mammal (Fig. 3.27). The latter is unique among Tierras Largas phase artifacts.

There were 829 sherds trapped in the fill of the platform and wall foundations of Structure 5; they have previously been published by Flannery and Marcus (1994:126–127). Some 808 sherds belonged to typical Tierras Largas phase types. The remaining 21 sherds were of types that made their first appearance toward the end of the Tierras Largas phase and then went on to

reach their maximum popularity during the San José phase. The 91 postabandonment sherds found lying among the bits of fallen plaster on the floor of Structure 5 had a similar mix of types (Flannery and Marcus 1994:127–128). We have therefore concluded that Structure 5 was built late in the Tierras Largas phase.

One charcoal sample from the fill of Structure 5 has been radiocarbon dated (M-2372). The conventional date was 3270 ± 160 BP, or 1320 b.c. (uncalibrated); the calibrated two-sigma range would be 1940–1140 BC.

Structure 9

Immediately below the ruins of Structure 5, we found the small remnant of an earlier lime-plastered building (Fig. 3.28). Called Structure 9, this remnant consisted of a fragment of recessed floor, a fragment of vertical face representing the east wall of the structure, and a fallen corner fragment. We suspect that Structure 9 may have been an earlier version of Structure 5, and that an effort had been made to superimpose Structure 5 almost directly on top of the earlier building.

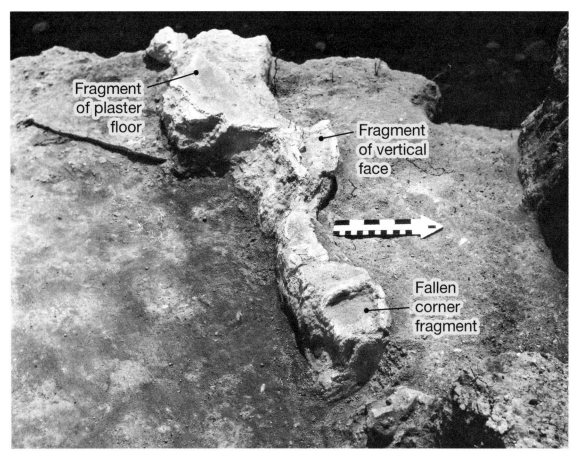

Figure 3.28. The lone surviving remnant of Structure 9, located in Squares S31 and S32 below Structure 5. The north arrow is marked in centimeters and in inches.

Figure 3.29. A surviving section of lime-plastered floor, Structure 15. Several chunks of fallen wall can be seen in the background (the black arrow points north).

Below: Figure 3.30. Two views of Feature 55, the lime-filled pit in the floor of Structure 15. *Left*, plan and section drawings. *Right*, photograph (the black arrow points north).

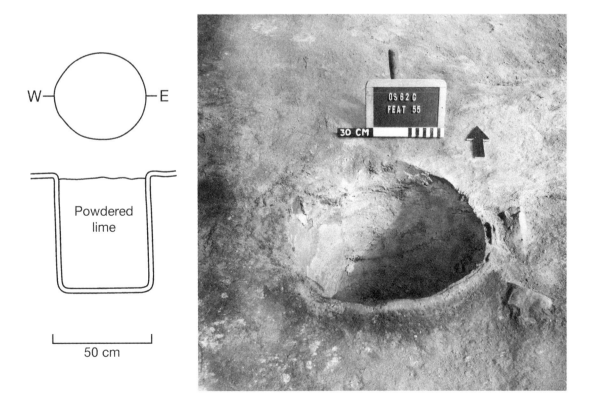

Structure 15

Structure 15 may have been the last men's house built in our Master Profile Sector. It had been badly damaged by later occupants of the site, and as a result we recovered no corners of the building. All that remained was a patch of the recessed plaster floor, occupying Squares S15C–E and S16C–E (Fig. 3.29).

Built into the center of the floor was Feature 55, a pit filled with powdered lime (Fig. 3.30). This cylindrical pit, 46 cm in diameter and 55 cm deep, was plastered with the same white stucco as the floor itself. It resembled Feature 56, the lime-filled pit in Structure 6.

Because it spanned Squares S15D and S16D, Feature 55 had intruded through the floor of Structure 6, barely missing Feature 56 (which fell wholly within Square S16D). In other words, Structure 15 had been built almost directly over the ruins of Structure 6. This was probably no accident.

A charcoal sample embedded in the floor of Structure 15 (Beta-190315) yielded a conventional radiocarbon date of 3270 ± 40 BP, or 1320 b.c. (uncalibrated), and a calibrated two-sigma range of 1630–1440 BC.

After Structure 15 had been abandoned, it had been deliberately leveled, with fragments of its thatched roof and lime-plastered wattle-and-daub walls left lying on the recessed floor. We discovered that an offering of imported marine shell had been placed among the fragments of collapsed plaster, near the presumed center of the abandoned men's house. This offering (Fig. 3.31) appears to have been a necklace made from 11 shells of *Cerithium stercusmuscarum*, a horn shell that lives in sand flats, estuaries, and mangrove swamps on Mexico's Gulf Coast. This was, as we shall see, not the only case in which a probable necklace of seashells was left atop the remains of an abandoned and razed men's house.

Structure 10 (and Earlier Buildings)

As our excavations moved east from the Master Profile, we came upon the remains of additional Tierras Largas phase men's houses. These remains were too fragmentary to be interdigitated stratigraphically with the remains of Structure 5, the nearest of the other men's houses.

The most extensive of these remains were those of Structure 10, located in Squares S31–S31B and S32–S32B (Figs. 3.32, 3.33). We recovered what appears to have been the northeast corner of the building; 5 postmolds; and the fragment of a possible bench from the east wall.

Structure 10 had been built relatively early in the Tierras Largas phase, not far above the Zone G midden layer (see Flannery and Marcus 2005 for a discussion of Zone G). Excavator James Schoenwetter cross-sectioned all the postmolds (Fig. 3.34) and proceeded to excavate down to bedrock. There he discovered 3 more sets of postholes, 11 of which may be from an earlier version of Structure 10.

Figure 3.35 shows a plan view of the volcanic tuff bedrock

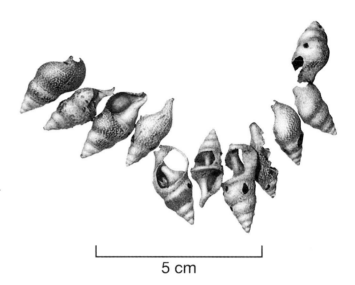

5 cm

Figure 3.31. This necklace of horn shells (*Cerithium stercusmuscarum*) was left atop the remains of Structure 15 after it had been razed.

in Squares S31 through S33C. The 4 postholes labeled Series A were small, and probably came from an ordinary wattle-and-daub residence. The 6 large postholes labeled Series B almost certainly outline the northeast corner of a destroyed men's house. One of them contained the rounded end of a carbonized pine post, suggesting that the building had been burned (Fig. 3.36). One of the Series B postholes was a double hole (Fig. 3.37), suggesting that a corner post had become loose or damaged and had to be replaced.

The 11 postholes labeled Series C so closely approximate the postmold pattern of Structure 10 that they may well have come from an earlier version of the same men's house. It looks as if the Series C building had also needed to have a few of its wall posts replaced over time. Unfortunately, it proved impossible to determine the order in which the 3 sets of posts had been driven into bedrock.

Structures 11 and 12

Men's houses had also been built in the Threshing Floor Sector of Area C (Flannery and Marcus 2005: Fig. 6.2). A deep sounding in Squares S16H through S18H exposed two men's houses that had been built one after another, just to the north of the Tierras Largas phase residence referred to as House 18 (Fig. 3.38).

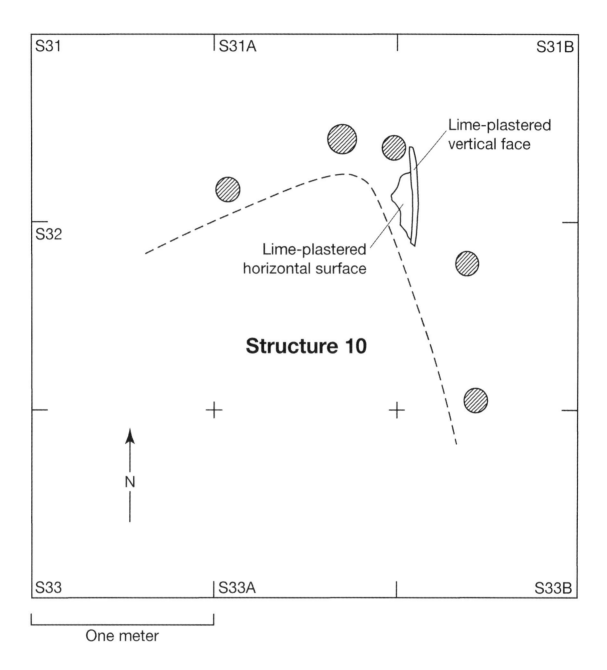

Figure 3.32. Remains of Structure 10, a lime-plastered men's house in Squares S31–S33B of Area C. The hachured circles are postmolds. The dashed line indicates the break between the sunken floor and the sitting bench. The lime-plastered horizontal surface may have broken off the latter.

Figure 3.33. Structure 10 after the postmolds had been excavated and the loose chunk of plastered bench had been removed.

Very little remained of these two men's houses beyond patches of their sunken plaster floors. Fortunately, these patches sometimes included the juncture between the floor itself and a wall or bench. Such junctures were indicated by a vertical upturn of the floor plaster.

Structure 11, to the east, was the most deeply buried of the two buildings and presumably the first built. Resting on its floor was the wall corner fragment shown in Figure 3.39.

Structure 12 was the less deeply buried of the two men's houses, and presumably the second built; it might have served to replace Structure 11 when the latter fell into disrepair. Two discoveries in Structure 12 indicated that the grinding of powdered lime and/or tobacco for ritual had gone on there. First, a fragment of a small, rectangular, boxlike metate was found in the fill of the building (Fig. 3.40). Second, we recovered the base of a circular pit filled with powdered lime, built into the floor of Structure 12 (Fig. 3.41). The base of this pit had penetrated bedrock, creating the irregular cavity seen in Figure 3.38. In short, Structure 12 provides further evidence for the use of powdered lime in men's houses.

Structure 18

One other men's house, Structure 18, was discovered in the south profile of Squares S18H–S18N in the Threshing Floor Sector (Fig. 3.42). Structure 18 must have been built relatively early in the Tierras Largas phase, because it lay stratigraphically below a house (House 18) and a midden layer (Zone F) of that phase (see Flannery and Marcus 2005: Figs. 7.1, 7.2). We were able to expose very little of Structure 18. We did, however, recover evidence that it had been burned.

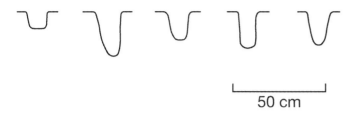

Figure 3.34. Cross-sections of the postmolds associated with Structure 10. The postmold at far left is the westernmost; from there the sequence proceeds clockwise (refer to Fig. 3.32). (Original drawing by James Schoenwetter.)

Figure 3.35. Plan view of Squares S31–S33C, Area A, showing postholes in bedrock below Structure 10. The four postholes of Series A appear to be from an ordinary residence. The eight postholes of Series B are probably from a razed men's house. The eleven postholes of Series C may be from an earlier version of Structure 10. (Feature 48 was a Tierras Largas phase cistern; see Flannery and Marcus 2005:118.)

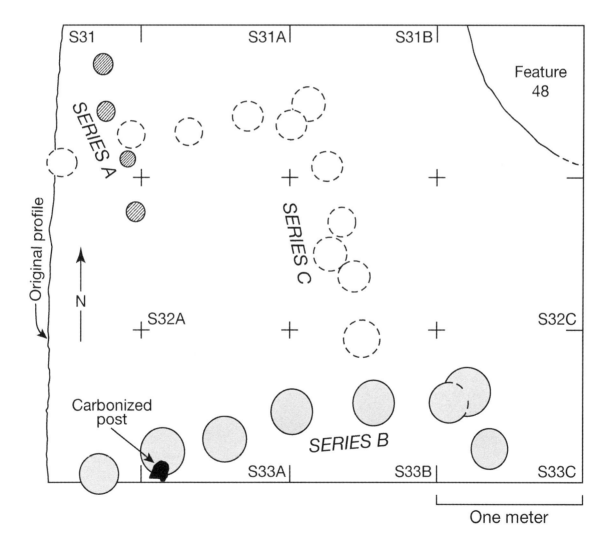

Right: Figure 3.36. The rounded end of a carbonized pine post from Series B, found in a posthole in bedrock. (See Fig. 3.35 for location.)

2 cm

Below: Figure 3.37. Sample cross-sections of postholes in bedrock below Structure 10. *Top row*, all 4 postholes of Series A. *Middle row*, 7 postholes from the east-west line of Series B. *Bottom row*, 5 postholes from the east-west line of Series C. (Refer to Fig. 3.35)

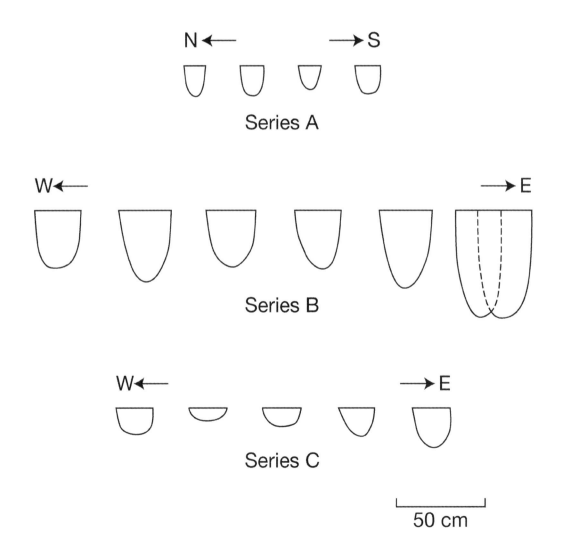

N ←   → S

Series A

W ←   → E

Series B

W ←   → E

Series C

50 cm

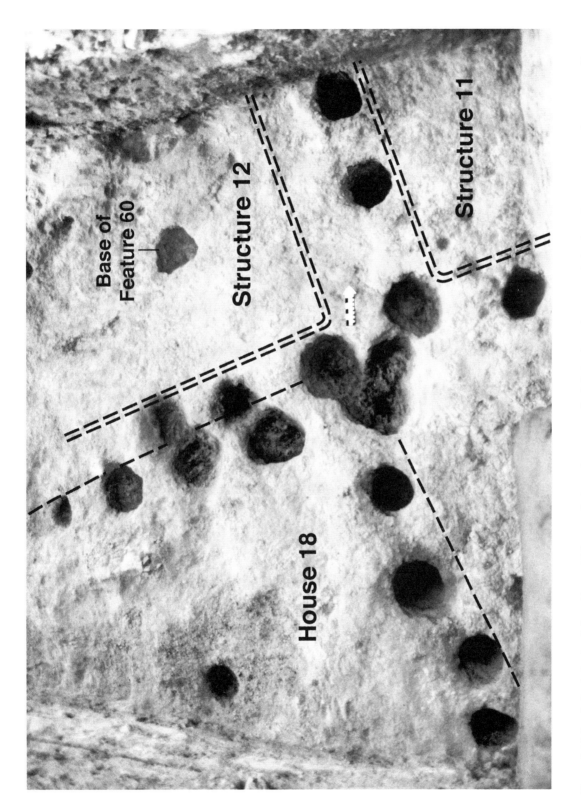

Figure 3.38. Postholes in bedrock from House 18 form an L-shaped corner on the left. To the right are postholes from Structures 11 and 12, two small lime-plastered men's houses. (Structures 11 and 12 were built at different times, after the abandonment of House 18.) Feature 60 was a lime-filled pit in Structure 12.

Figure 3.39. Corner fragment from the lime-plastered wall of Structure 11.

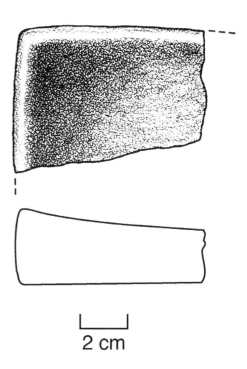

Figure 3.40. A fragment of small, basin-shaped, rectangular metate, found in the fill of Structure 12. The metate had once been used to grind lime.

Figure 3.41. Feature 60, a circular pit in the floor of Structure 12, shown after the powdered lime had been removed. The north arrow is marked in both centimeters and inches.

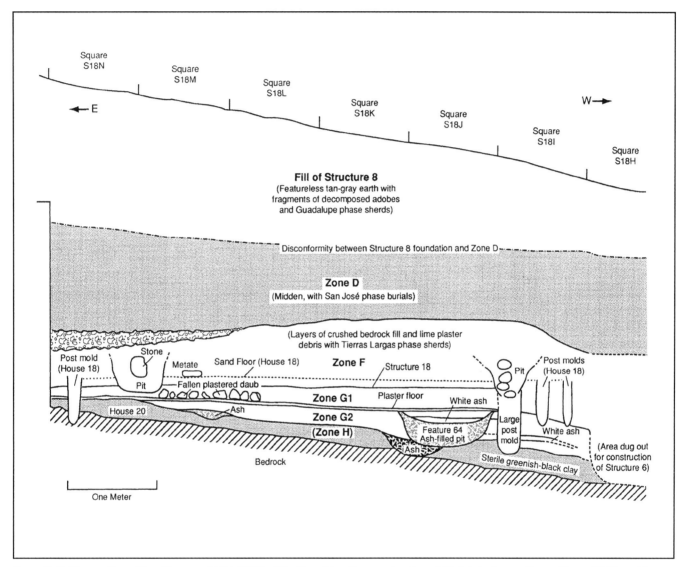

Figure 3.42. The south profile of Squares S18H–S18N of the Threshing Floor sector, Area C. Visible in the profile are House 20 (Zone H); Stratigraphic Zone G, here divided into building collapse (G1) and a midden (G2) facies; Structure 18 in Zone F; and House 18 in Zone F.

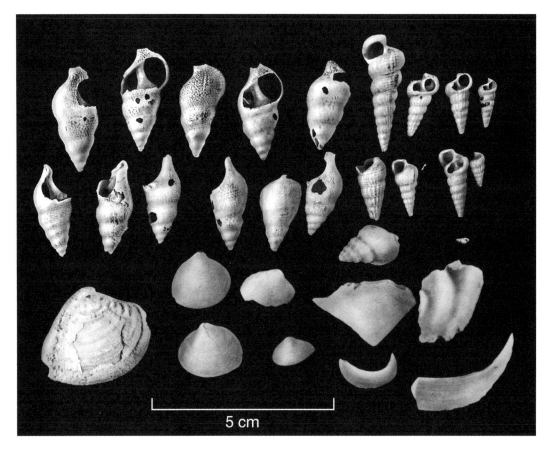

Figure 3.43. Collection of marine shells and trimmings from shell ornaments, left atop the remains of Structure 18 after it had been burned.

Atop the collapsed remains of Structure 18, someone had left an offering of imported marine shell (Fig. 3.43). The bulk of the molluscs probably represent the remains of a necklace of horn shells (a dozen *Cerithium stercusmuscarum* and eight *Cerithidea mazatlanica*). These univalves were accompanied by miscellaneous examples of *Chione subrugosa*, *Polymesoda* sp., and trimmed-off pieces of larger molluscs.

This discovery provides us with a second example of a horn shell necklace, left as an offering above the ruins of a men's house (see Structure 15, above). One example could be dismissed as a random event, but two cases suggest a pattern.

Obviously, we would like to know what the postabandonment offering of a seashell necklace meant. We suspect that shell necklaces were more likely to be offerings to ancestors than to deities. We say this because during later periods at San José Mogote, offerings to deities tended to involve the sacrifice of birds or mammals rather than ornaments. During later stages of the Formative, for example, jade beads were left with burials, while quail were sacrificed in temples.

4 | The San José Phase and the Cognitive Archaeology of Early Rank Society

The Tierras Largas phase was followed by the San José phase, for which we currently have fifteen radiocarbon dates (Flannery and Marcus 2005:459–462). A sixteenth date (M-2331) is believed to fall at or near the transition from Tierras Largas to San José. That transition took place between 1200 and 1150 b.c., and the San José phase then lasted until 900 or 850 b.c.

When the ¹⁴C dates for the San José phase are dendrocalibrated, however (Flannery and Marcus 2005: Table 26.2), it appears that the phase may actually have lasted 350 to 400 years. In "real" years, it probably began by 1350/1300 BC and ended by 1000/950 BC. The gradual changes in pottery allow us to divide the San José phase into early, middle, and late subphases, but our ¹⁴C dates are not precise enough to provide calendar years for those subphases.

Changes in Society

Perhaps a dozen lines of evidence suggest that San José phase society was characterized by a continuum of hereditary rank. This continuum can be detected in the escalating use of sumptuary goods; in the differing ways that individuals were buried; in the

way rank was communicated in art; in the way elite children were treated; in the restriction of certain ornaments to elite individuals; in the differences in elegance among houses and their contents; and so on. Let us look at some of these lines of evidence.

1. While most adults of the San José phase were buried fully extended and prone, a small percentage of adult men were buried in a very tightly flexed (probably bundled) position. These flexed men were more likely than most to have multiple offerings of jadeite ornaments; more likely to have pottery vessels with carved Earth or Lightning motifs; and more likely to have had secondary burials (perhaps wives or siblings) added to their graves (Marcus and Flannery 1996:96–99).

2. The children of certain families had their heads artificially deformed, presumably as a sign of rank (Marcus and Flannery 1996:105–106).

3. Symbols of authority and subordination became common (Marcus and Flannery 1996:96). Along with the handmade figurines of the phase, we found miniature four-legged stools, like those on which sixteenth-century Central American chiefs sat. The mat motif—later used as an authority symbol throughout Mesoamerica—appeared for

the first time on San José phase pottery.

4. The small, solid figurines of the San José phase seem to reflect both positions of authority and positions of subordination (Marcus and Flannery 1996:99). Some depict men and women standing erect, arms folded across their chest, in what looks like a stereotyped "obeisance posture." A smaller number of figurines depict men seated crosslegged with their hands on their knees, looking authoritative and chiefly.

5. While ornaments of iron ore seem to have been restricted to elite individuals, other sumptuary goods displayed a gradient from higher to lower rank. Among the latter were jadeite, pearl oyster (*Pinctada* sp.), spiny oyster (*Spondylus* sp.), pearly freshwater mussels, and mica.

   Many men and women were buried with a single jadeite bead placed in the mouth. Burial 18 at San José Mogote, however, was buried with two jadeite earspools and three jadeite beads in her mouth (Flannery and Marcus 2005: Fig. 18.4*h*). The situation with regard to imported mollusc shell is even more variable. Some households seem to have had little or no access to shell. Some had access to freshwater mussels, but not marine shells; still others had abundant access to mother-of-pearl and spiny oyster. Some families show signs of having been involved in ornament manufacture, while others do not (Flannery and Marcus 2005:79–81).

6. Differences in house construction also displayed a gradient in rank (Marcus and Flannery 1996:103–106). House 13 at San José Mogote was roughly 3 × 5 m in size and poorly made, with slender posts and no coating of whitewash. Its occupants had left behind little jadeite, few deer bones, and only modest evidence of craft activity.

   At the other end of the gradient was the multistructure household known as Houses 16–17. This was a well-made, heavily whitewashed residence with an attached lean-to (Flannery and Marcus 2005: Fig. 18.2). It was well supplied with jadeite, *Spondylus* shell, and pottery imported from the Basin of Mexico, the Gulf Coast, and the Tehuacán Valley. Its occupants had engaged in chert biface manufacture, woodworking, sewing, basketmaking, and the production of mother-of-pearl ornaments.

7. Many other signs of rank appear to have formed a continuum, rather than a series of steps or strata. One possibility is that individuals descended in rank as their genealogical distance from the most highly ranked member of their society increased. The strong association of male burials with ceramics featuring Lightning or Earthquake motifs, discussed below, suggests that the male line was emphasized. On the other hand, a number of San José phase burials consist of a man and woman buried together, presumably a husband-wife pair. Perhaps, as among the historic Zapotec and Mixtec, men of rank sought to marry women of rank, and such advantageous marriages were emphasized by laying couples to rest side by side.

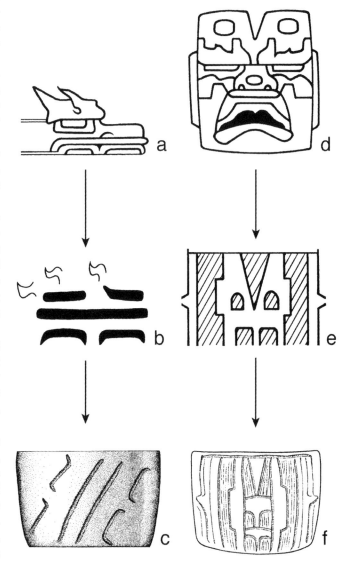

Figure 4.1. Motifs representing Sky in its angry form, Lightning (*a-c*), and Earth in its angry form, Earthquake (*d-f*), dominated the iconography of the San José phase. *a* and *d* are realistic versions that show up all over southern Mexico. *b* and *e* are the stylized versions used on San José phase pottery (*c* and *f*).

8. We note that sixteenth-century Zapotec kinship was of the bilateral Hawai'ian type, which was true for most Oto-manguean speakers (Spores and Flannery 2003:339–342). In this system, both parents' ranks are important. Birth order was also taken into account when sixteenth-century Zapotec offspring were ranked (Córdova 1886 [1578]; Marcus 1992, 2003a, 2006). The latter fact may help explain why ordinal numbers appear in some of our earliest Zapotec hieroglyphic texts.

9. While various wards at San José Mogote continued to build men's houses during the early San José phase, we believe that our first temples appeared during this phase as well. In an earlier work (Flannery and Marcus 2012), we presented worldwide evidence that a shift from men's houses to temples often accompanies the appearance of hereditary rank. However, in the history of some rank societies (on the island of Tikopia, for example, or during the Halaf period in northern Mesopotamia), there was a transitional period during which men's houses and temples coexisted. Such seems to have been the case at San José Mogote.

Cosmology and Iconography

The pottery of the San José phase provides us with more information on cosmology and iconography than did the pottery of the Tierras Largas phase. One reason is that several pottery types of the San José phase were carved and/or incised with motifs that had a virtually pan-Mesoamerican distribution (Flannery and Marcus 2000). We believe that these motifs reflect not only greater social complexity in Oaxaca, but also greater interregional interaction throughout Mexico, with emerging elites exchanging gifts and borrowing value-laden motifs.

Because this is a topic on which we have already written extensively, we will keep our comments brief and refer the reader to our monograph on the Early and Middle Formative pottery of the Valley of Oaxaca (Flannery and Marcus 1994:135–286). In that volume, we make the following points:

1. Many of the freestanding motifs of the San José phase seem to refer to Earth or Sky, which were major provinces of the cosmos for most historic speakers of Otomanguean languages.

2. These two parts of the cosmos were usually shown in their "angry" forms, Earthquake and Lightning. Earth might be shown as a grotesque human with a snarling feline mouth and a cleft in his skull, opened by an earthquake (Fig. 4.1*d–f*). Alternatively, he might be depicted as having two oval eyes with four clefts and four world quarters in his open mouth (Fig. 4.2). Lightning (Cociyo in the Zapotec language) was pictured as a serpent of fire in the sky. In its most stylized version, the serpent's face was shown as a series of excised bars, with upside-down U motifs representing his gums, and sine curves depicting the flames that rose from his eyebrows (Fig. 4.1*a–c*).

Figure 4.2. Not all representations of Earth depict it as Earthquake. On this incised vessel from San José Mogote, we see a series of dots representing the four world quarters and multiple clefts, apparently placed inside the mouth of this being. (See Flannery and Marcus 2005: Fig. 18.14.)

3. Symbols of Earth and Sky were more likely to be found in residential areas than around public buildings, suggesting an association with families or descent groups rather than public institutions (Marcus 1999).

4. Within residential wards, these two supernatural forces were almost mutually exclusive. Areas A and C of San José Mogote were dominated by Sky or Lightning motifs. Area B was dominated by Earth or Earthquake motifs. The implication is that certain families or descent groups were more strongly associated with one cosmic symbol than the other.

5. Among the adult burials at San José Mogote, we found funerary vessels with Earthquake or Lightning motifs associated exclusively with men. This is the opposite of the situation at Tlatilco in the Basin of Mexico, where

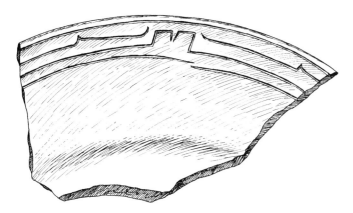

Figure 4.3. It was once thought that most incised "double-line-break" motifs were iconographically neutral. This Atoyac Yellow-white sherd from San José Mogote, however, suggests that the double-line-break is a stylized version of Earthquake's cleft head (see discussion in Flannery and Marcus 1994: Chapter 12).

(according to Tolstoy 1989b:290) such vessels tended to occur with women. Tolstoy (1989a:117) believes that there were two intermarrying groups at Tlatilco, and that "the in-marrying spouse was often a male." At San José Mogote, on the contrary, we see evidence that the in-marrying spouse was most often a female (Flannery and Marcus 1994:136). Since San José Mogote had perhaps its most intense foreign relations with the Basin of Mexico, we wish we had more detailed information on who married in, and from where.

6. Some children (too young to have their sex determined accurately) were buried with Earthquake or Lightning vessels like those buried with men. Other children were buried with bowls and jars like those found most often in the burials of adult women. We suspect, therefore, that one's relationship to Earth or Sky was present from the moment of birth, and was gender-specific to males (Flannery and Marcus 1976).

7. A series of incised motifs on white-slipped pottery, called "double-line-breaks" (Coe 1961), were common from the very beginning of the San José phase (Plog 2009, n.d.). Several of our incised white vessels at San José Mogote suggest that the double-line-break was not an iconographically neutral motif, but a stylized version of Earthquake's

cleft head (Fig. 4.3). That being the case, we can say that Lightning motifs were more numerous at the start of the San José phase (1150 b.c.), but came to be outnumbered by Earthquake motifs by the time of the Guadalupe phase (850 b.c.).

Conclusions

Thus it appears that one of the major concerns of the San José phase was the assertion of one's relationship to Sky (Lightning) or Earth (Earthquake), and that such relationships were thought to be present from birth. This concern may date from the emergence of rank, and could suggest that San José Mogote's elite claimed descent from the powerful spirits of Earth or Sky.

It is clear from the widespread circulation of Earth and Sky motifs that Formative societies in the Basin of Mexico, Puebla, Morelos, Guerrero, the Gulf Coast, and the Pacific Coast of Chiapas shared many of these same concerns. We suggest that Mexico's circulation of pottery with Sky and Earth motifs was analogous to the circulation of heraldic crests among the Tlingit, Haida, Tsimshian, and other chiefly societies of the Pacific Northwest (de Laguna 1990). Such circulation usually results in

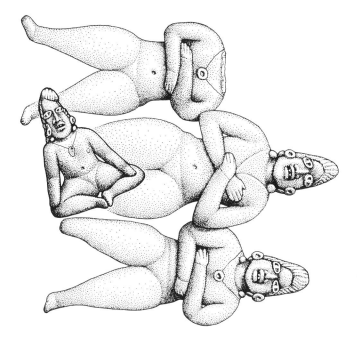

Figure 4.4. The makers of San José phase figurines sometimes depicted social inequality by placing some figures in a position of authority while others were shown in a position of obeisance. Feature 63 at San José Mogote contained a scene in which one seated authority figure rested upon three figures in positions of obeisance (see Flannery and Marcus 2005: Chapter 18).

a great deal of shared iconography, which is what we see between 1150 and 850 b.c.

Women's Ritual

During the early San José phase, men's and women's ritual continued the same spatial separation seen in the preceding phase. The household remained the primary venue for women's ritual. There, women continued to communicate with recent ancestors through the use of small, solid figurines.

During the excavation of Houses 16–17, a multistructure residence in Area B of San José Mogote, we came upon a buried scene of four figurines (Fig. 4.4). Called Feature 63, this scene involved three figurines in positions of obeisance: fully extended, supine, with their arms folded across their chests and their heads pointing slightly north of east.

The fourth figurine appears to have been seated upright originally, resting on the bodies of the three supine figures before slumping under the weight of the overburden. This figure depicted a man seated in a position of authority, with his hands on his knees, wearing what appear to have been jadeite earspools

and a shell pendant. This scene may represent an ancestor of high rank, buried atop three of his subordinates. Such evidence of rank should not surprise us, given that the scene was buried in the residence of a relatively high status family (Flannery and Marcus 2005: Chapter 18).

We know that sixteenth-century Zapotec women participated in divination rituals, usually oriented toward the affairs of the family (Marcus 1998:11–15). Such divination might be aimed at determining the cause of a family member's illness; selecting a name for a newborn child; predicting the outcome of a marriage or pregnancy; or determining whether a given day was auspicious for a certain activity.

One form of Zapotec women's divination can be shown to have had San José phase precursors. This was *tiniyaaya niça*, or "water divination." In this ritual, a woman knelt on a reed mat facing a water-filled basin (Fig. 4.5, top). She then cast maize kernels onto the surface of the water, noting the number of kernels that remained floating. Alternatively, she might divine the answer to her query by observing whether the kernels floated in groups of three, five, or thirteen. This divination served to take the responsibility for decision-making out of the hands of the woman and assign it to the spirit world.

Figure 4.5. Above we see a Zapotec woman practicing divination by tossing maize kernels into a water-filled basin. Below we see the remains of a basin suitable for water divination, found in the dooryard of Household Unit C3 at San José Mogote.

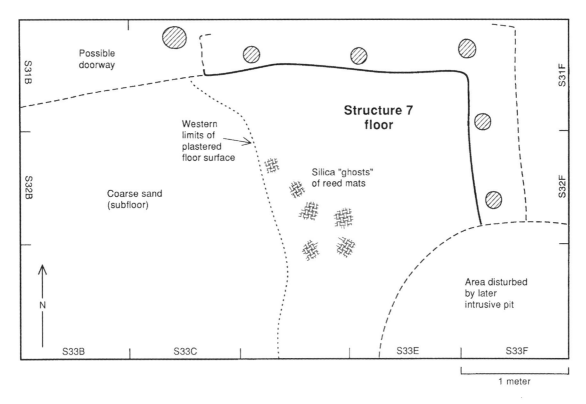

Figure 4.6. Partial plan of Structure 7, an early San José phase men's house from Area C. Like the Tierras Largas phase men's houses seen earlier, this was a lime-plastered, one-room public building with its floor recessed into a low platform.

Household Unit C3, a residential unit in Area A of San José Mogote, yielded two features that could have served as water-filled basins for *tiniyaaya niça* (Marcus 1998: Fig. 3.2). Feature 3 was a circular basin 1.2 m in diameter and 5 cm deep, excavated into the dooryard east of the house (Fig. 4.5, bottom). This basin had been mud-plastered, given a coat of waterproof lime stucco, then painted red with specular hematite.

Three meters to the south was a second circular basin, called Feature 8. It, too, had been waterproofed with stucco, but this basin had been painted yellow instead of red (Flannery and Marcus 2005:273–279).

The lime-plastered interiors of these basins would have allowed them to retain water long enough to perform the divination rite (Marcus 1999). We find it significant that each basin was painted with one of the colors associated with Mesoamerica's four world quarters. Unfortunately, we were unable to excavate the entire dooryard to determine whether there had once been four basins, each painted a different color.

Household Unit C3 produced two radiocarbon dates: one from charcoal found on the dooryard surface and another from the charcoal found in a cooking pit called Feature 2 (Flannery and Marcus 2005:459–462). The date from the dooryard (SI-464)

came out to 1170 b.c.; its dendrocalibrated two-sigma range would be 1650–1030 BC. The date from Feature 2 (Gx-0875) came out to 930 b.c.; its calibrated range would be 1375–825 BC.

Circumstantial evidence, therefore, suggests that by 1000 b.c., the occupants of San José Mogote had both water divination and ritual color symbolism. That evidence comes from the dooryard of a San José phase residence, a setting that ethnohistoric data identify as a likely venue for women's ritual.

Men's Ritual

For at least the first part of the San José phase, the men of the village continued to build small one-room men's houses for their ritual activities. One of these, Structure 7, was built in the Master Profile Sector of Area C, not far from the earlier men's houses of the Tierras Largas phase. Another, however, was built just above sterile soil on Mound 1. This second ritual structure may have served the men of Area A, a residential ward newly founded during the San José phase (Flannery and Marcus 2005: Chapter 13). Let us now look at these San José phase men's houses.

Figure 4.7. The northeast corner of Structure 7, showing the lime-plastered walls rising vertically from the lime-plastered floor. The north arrow is marked in both centimeters and inches.

Structure 7

The remains of Structure 7 were discovered in Squares S31B–S33F of the Master Profile Sector, Area C (Fig. 4.6). Structure 7 was sandwiched stratigraphically between House 1 and House 7 of the San José phase (Flannery and Marcus 1994:357–362).

Structure 7 continued the same ritual alignment seen in our Tierras Largas phase men's houses: 8° north of east. It differed from those earlier men's houses in the color of its lime plaster. Rather than being pure white, the plaster covering Structure 7 was the same color as the yellowish cream slip on Atoyac Yellow-white pottery.

We recovered only the northeast quadrant of Structure 7 (Figs. 4.7, 4.8). Its floor was sunk 20 cm below the surface of the platform on which it had been built. Postmolds left by at least six of

its vertical wall posts were found in the stubs of the north and east walls. These posts appear to have been 16 cm in diameter and spaced 70–100 cm apart.

Owing to the way Structure 7 had deteriorated after its abandonment, we know many of the details of its construction (Figs. 4.9, 4.10). While the lime-plastered floor surface was still intact in the northeast corner, it had been eroded away at a point 2.0–2.5 m to the west. This allowed excavator James Schoenwetter to see that the underlying platform had a cementlike mixture of crushed volcanic tuff bedrock, clay, sand, and lime. The builders began the floor by laying down a layer of coarse sand. Over this came a layer of packed clay, then a layer of much finer orange sand. Finally came the floor surface, a thick layer of stucco the color of Atoyac Yellow-white slip.

On the surviving patch of stucco surface, Schoenwetter found

Figure 4.8. View of Structure 7 from the east, showing the northeast corner. Two of the postmolds in the north wall had been excavated at this point. The north arrow rests on the recessed floor.

a number of silica exoskeleton "ghosts" from patches of reed matting. We do not know whether these patches were from mats placed on the floor of the building, or fragments that fell to the floor when the mat-and-thatch roof collapsed. Schoenwetter also recovered a grinding stone bearing traces of powdered lime (Fig. 4.11); it was found in the fill just above the floor.

Some 255 sherds were found in the coarse sand layer exposed by erosion; they have already been published by Flannery and Marcus (1994:359–362). These sherds indicate a San José phase date, consistent with the building's stratigraphic placement.

A Men's House on Mound 1

Mound 1, the tallest and most pyramidal of all the mounds at San José Mogote, is actually a natural hill whose height was increased by the addition of buildings (Flannery and Marcus 2005:396). The hill overlooks Area A of the site, making it a logical place for residents of that ward to construct public buildings.

We have no evidence that the summit of Mound 1 had ever been used before the early San José phase. One of the first buildings placed there was House 13, a modest wattle-and-daub residence built directly on sterile soil (Flannery and Marcus 2005: Chapter 22).

In addition to House 13, it appears that the people of the San José phase built a small, lime-plastered building with many characteristics of a men's house on Mound 1. This was the first of a series of Formative public buildings on that spot. Those public buildings culminated with Structure 28, a Rosario phase temple, which we describe in Chapter 8.

We found traces of the aforementioned San José phase men's

Figure 4.9. The northeast corner of Structure 7 seen from the south, showing the recessed floor, the vertical faces of the north and east walls, and several postmolds. James Schoenwetter places his left hand against the north wall. At this point, the surviving patch of plaster floor had been cut through to expose the various subfloor levels. Schoenwetter's feet rest on the surface left after removal of the lowermost coarse sand. What appears to be a raised bench (some 10 cm east of his left hand) is actually a remnant of the original floor, complete even to the uppermost lime plaster. The dark stain on the profile is not a feature; it represents moisture that leaked from the severed root of a modern tree.

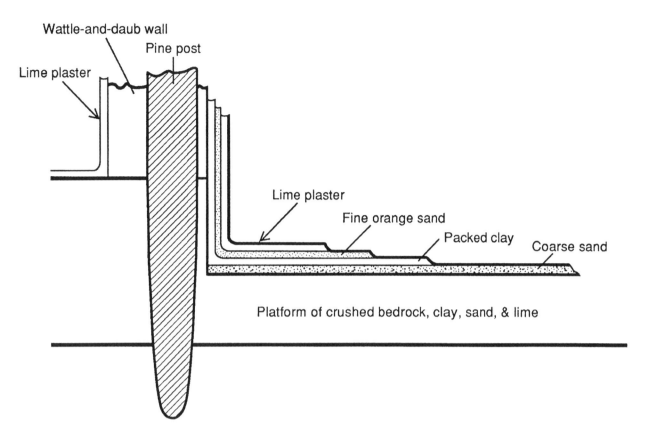

Figure 4.10. Cross-section drawing of the surviving remnant of Structure 7, showing the various layers of construction. First came a series of pine posts, which gave the building its outline. Around this was built a platform of crushed bedrock, clay, sand, and lime; above this, the walls of the building were of wattle and daub. The area that was to be the floor of the building was left recessed 20 cm or more below the upper surface of the platform. The floor was built up of successive layers of coarse sand, hard packed clay, and fine orange sand. Over this went a layer of white lime plaster that covered the platform and the building. Each stage of construction offered opportunities for diagnostic sherds to become trapped in the various layers of the building.

Figure 4.11. Grinding stone showing traces of having been used to grind lime into a fine powder. Found in the fill just above the floor of Structure 7 (Square S32E).

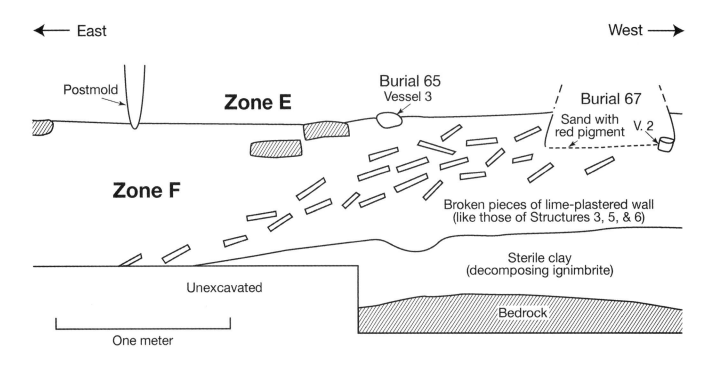

← East   West →

Postmold

Zone E

Burial 65
Vessel 3

Burial 67
Sand with
red pigment   V. 2

Zone F

Broken pieces of lime-plastered wall
(like those of Structures 3, 5, & 6)

Sterile clay
(decomposing ignimbrite)

Unexcavated

Bedrock

One meter

Figure 4.12. East-west profile of Squares S5E9 and S5E10, Mound 1, at the level of Zones E and F below Structure 28. Zone F contained broken fragments of the lime-plastered wall of a building similar to Structures 3, 5, and 6 in Area C.

house while excavating the stratigraphic sequence below Structure 28. All that remained of the building by then were eroded patches of its white stucco floor and fallen pieces of its plastered walls. Every fragment we found, including the joints where the floor plaster merged with the base of a wall or a sitting bench, suggested that the building resembled Structure 7 in Area C (see above). So little of the building's plan was recovered, however, that we did not give it a structure number.

The site chosen for this men's house was near the center of the hilltop, and may have been its original high point. The building had been constructed on a layer of sterile greenish clay, the decomposition product of the volcanic tuff bedrock below it (see Fig. 4.12). During the course of the building's collapse, it came to be incorporated into a layer of early San José phase midden called Zone F.

The grid of 2 × 2 m squares designed for the excavation of this part of Mound 1 is discussed in Chapter 8. For the purposes of this chapter, the reader need only note that traces of the San José phase men's house were scattered over an area roughly 6 × 4 m in extent, confined to Squares S5E8–S5E10 and S6E8–S6E10 of our grid. One fragment of lime-plastered wall is shown in Fig. 4.13.

Near the border between Squares S5E8 and S5E9, we found the spider monkey skull shown in Figure 4.14. It lay below the level of the fallen lime-plastered daub, at the level of the floor of the badly destroyed men's house. The monkey's skull appeared to have had its features covered with the same lime plaster used for the building; it was then painted red with ocher (Marcus 1998:50). This object, unique at San José Mogote, may have been a trophy or offering kept in the men's house.

Spider monkeys (*Ateles geoffroyi*) are not native to the Valley of Oaxaca, but were once abundant in the tropical forests of the Isthmus of Tehuantepec. The people of the San José phase were clearly familiar with them, since they made accurate figurines of spider monkeys (Fig. 4.15). This monkey was later used as the hieroglyph for the eleventh of the twenty day signs used in the Zapotec ritual calendar (Marcus 1992: Fig. 4.20, Table 4.13).

Figure 4.13. Fragment from the wall of a probable lime-plastered men's house found in Stratigraphic Zone F, Mound 1.

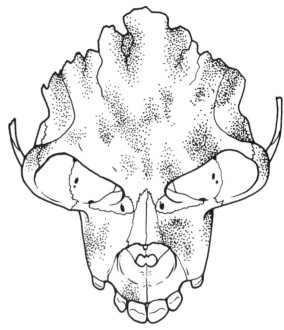

Figure 4.14. Partial remains of the skull of a spider monkey (*Ateles geoffroyi*), found in Square S5E8 (near the border of S5E9), Zone F. This monkey skull, with its features coated in lime plaster and painted red, was eventually crushed by the weight of the overlying earth; the areas of stipple indicate smears of red pigment. From its location, this skull was probably an offering or trophy associated with the lime-plastered men's house whose collapsed remains were found around it.

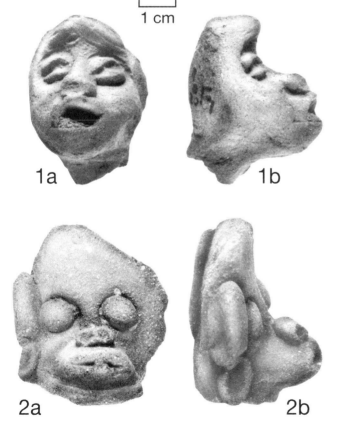

Figure 4.15. Front and side views of two heads from spider monkey figurines. Specimen 1 was found in the earthen fill of Structure 4 of Barrio del Rosario Huitzo. Specimen 2 was found on the surface of Area A at San José Mogote.

Figure 4.16. Possible fragment of a lime-plastered, red-painted water divination basin, found in Stratigraphic Zone F.

In the debris near the collapsed remains of the Zone F men's house we recovered San José phase sherds; a lump of unworked iron ore; a fragment of a weakly magnetic iron ore mirror; pieces of pearl oyster, spiny oyster, and conch shell; fish spines that had perhaps been used for ritual bloodletting; and other remains typical of the San José phase. We also found one fragment of red-painted lime plaster that could have come from a basin for water divination (Fig. 4.16).

A Possible Secular Public Building in Area A

During the San José phase, public architecture was not necessarily limited to ritual or religious structures. There were occasional enigmatic buildings that may reflect secular social institutions. One such building was Structure 16 in Area A at San José Mogote. Structure 16 was a one-room building on a puddled adobe platform, partially destroyed by the later construction of the stone-and-adobe platform we called Structure 2 (see below).

To provide a context for Structure 16, let us begin by describing the only other building in the Valley of Oaxaca that resembled it. That building was Structure 11 at the site of Santo Domingo

Tomaltepec, excavated by Michael Whalen (1981:38–43).

During the San José phase, Tomaltepec was a 1.2 ha village in the piedmont east of the city of Oaxaca. Structure 11 was a puddled adobe platform measuring roughly 4 m by 6 m and standing 1 m high (Fig. 4.17). Its long axis was oriented 16–17° east of true north, rather than showing the 8° orientation of ritual buildings. No evidence of a staircase was found, but that might be because the extensive overburden prevented Whalen from clearing all sides of the structure.

Structure 11 was built upon a layer of large foundation stones, followed by alternating layers of adobe—sometimes puddled and sometimes in the form of circular, planoconvex adobes and fist-sized stones, set in a puddled adobe matrix (Whalen 1981:38). The exact placement of Structure 11 within the San José phase is not clear; it was built stratigraphically above an early San José phase household (Unit ESJ-1), and therefore does not date to the very beginning of the phase. The circular, planoconvex adobes used in Structure 11 resemble those used in Structures 1 and 2 at San José Mogote (see below).

One of the most interesting features of Structure 11 was a large clay-plastered cell, possibly for storage, positioned so as to lie below the floor of any structure placed on the platform.

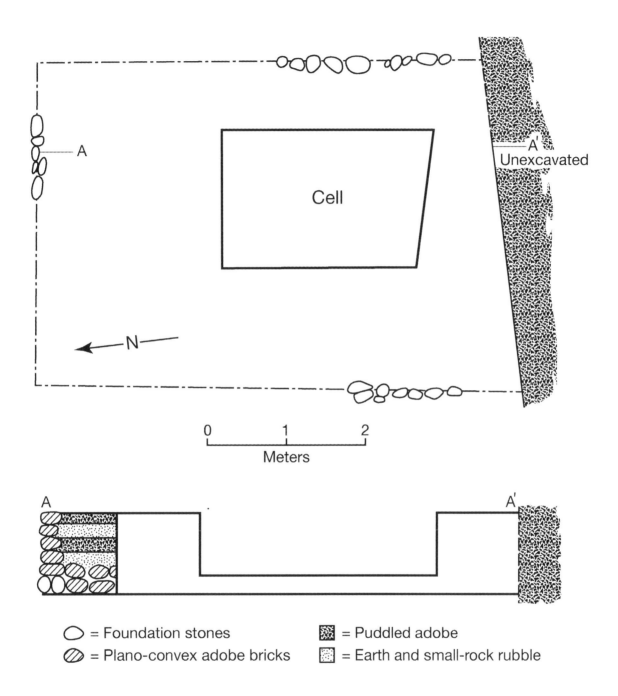

Cell

N

| 0 | 1 | 2 |
Meters

A'
Unexcavated

A

A'

○ = Foundation stones
⊘ = Plano-convex adobe bricks
▓ = Puddled adobe
▒ = Earth and small-rock rubble

Figure 4.17. Plan view (above) and cross-section (below) of Structure 11 at Santo Domingo Tomaltepec in the western Tlacolula subvalley. The south end of the structure was not recovered (redrawn from Whalen 1981: Fig. 10).

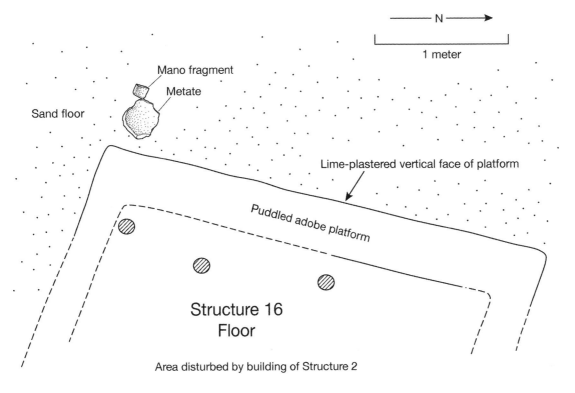

Figure 4.18. Plan view of Structure 16, a one-room building on a puddled adobe platform surrounded by a sand floor. This building was partly destroyed by the later construction of Structure 2, which both covered Structure 16 and incorporated it within its fill.

This cell was several meters on a side and more than half a meter deep, with well-defined vertical walls. The material originally stored there could not be determined, since the cell was filled with postabandonment debris when discovered.

Whalen was uncertain—as are we—exactly how to label Structure 11. On the one hand, it did not have the typical orientation of a San José phase ritual building. On the other hand, it seems unlikely that a residence would have had such a large area of its floor taken up with a plastered storage cell. Tentatively, therefore, we consider Structure 11 to be a special-purpose building of some kind, possibly a communal or chiefly storage facility.

Now let us turn to Structure 16 of San José Mogote, which came to light while we were investigating Structure 2 in Area A (see below). Structure 16 appears to have been built roughly at

the level of Household Unit C3 (the residence whose dooryard produced the two water divination basins mentioned above).

Structure 16 was a puddled adobe platform about 1 m high, oriented roughly 21° east of true north (Fig. 4.18). It measured 3.45 m north-south; its east-west dimension could not be recovered because it had been damaged by the builders of Structure 2. Like Structure 11 at Tomaltepec, Structure 16 had been built of alternating layers of puddled adobe clay, fist-sized stones, and bits of what may have been burnt daub or adobe fragments. Its nearly vertical west face (Fig. 4.19) had been given a coating of adobe clay, followed by a solution of lime resembling whitewash.

Covering the upper surface of the platform was a floor of stamped clay with a light coating of sand. This floor began 25–40 cm in from the edge of the platform, and its maximum

Figure 4.19. Two workmen expose the nearly vertical west face of the puddled adobe platform supporting Structure 16. Owing to the height of this platform, the building must have had a staircase on one of its destroyed sides.

north-south dimension was 2.85 m. Three postmolds, each 10–12 cm in diameter, were found along the west edge of the floor. In other words, the available evidence suggests that Structure 16 was the platform for a small, one-room building with a roof of some kind and a clay floor covered with sand.

In the portion of Structure 16 that had been damaged by the builders of Structure 2, we found traces of a lime-plastered storage cell like the one recovered by Whalen in Structure 11 at Tomaltepec. Because of the extensive destruction it was not possible to recover the dimensions of this cell. All we can say is that Structure 16 appears to have been another special-purpose building like Structure 11 at Tomaltepec, perhaps a communal or chiefly storage facility.

Surrounding Structure 16 on the south and west was a level floor of stamped earth, with an overlying layer of fine sand from the Atoyac River. A mano, a metate, and a sample of 37 sherds were found lying on this floor near the base of the platform. The metate and mano are shown in Fig. 4.20. The sherds have been published by Flannery and Marcus (1994:363–367) and date to the San José phase.

If the metate and mano found nearby were associated with Structure 16, it raises the possibility that maize was one of the resources stored in the cell, and that it was ground as needed. That is, of course, only one possibility. What seems more certain is that both Structure 16 of San José Mogote and Structure 11 of Tomaltepec had storage capacities beyond that of a typical household.

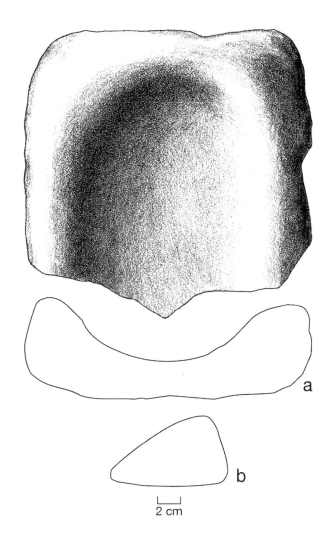

Figure 4.20. Ground stone tools found on the sand floor just west of Structure 16. *a*, broken basin-shaped metate. *b*, cross-section of broken mano with airfoil cross-section.

2 cm

The Beginnings of Adobe Architecture, Stone Masonry, and the Pyramidal Platform

Both Areas A and C were the scenes of impressive San José phase public buildings, platforms far too large to have been built for men's houses like Structure 7.

We know much less about the platform in Area C, which was discovered at a depth of 1.6 to 3.4 m in Test Pit 2 of the Threshing Floor Sector (Flannery and Marcus 2005: Fig. 8.1). Time and resources did not permit removing enough overburden to trace out this platform. We could see, however, that it had completely buried House 15, our oldest San José phase residence.

The fill of the Area C platform was dense, crushed volcanic tuff bedrock. The surface of the platform was smoothed clay, covered by a sand floor. There were enough adobe bricks associated with the platform to indicate that the interior retaining walls of the platform, used to stabilize the basketloads of fill, were of adobes. These adobes were of the same circular, planoconvex

type used in Structure 11 at Tomaltepec. We would later learn that the unusual shape of these early adobes resulted from their having been molded in the lower halves of broken storage jars (see Chapter 5).

Structures 1 and 2

We know more about the San José phase public buildings in Area A. We assigned them two names, Structure 1 and Structure 2, even though both buildings may once have been part of a single integrated complex (Fig. 4.21). Both structures were terraced to a gentle slope, coming down off the piedmont spur on which most of the later ceremonial architecture of San José Mogote was built. This slope descended from west to east and was bracketed by a pair of arroyos. These two arroyos established the northern and southern limits of Structures 1 and 2; since the arroyos lay 18 m apart, neither structure could be more than 18 m in width.

Each of the two structures was a rough-and-ready platform,

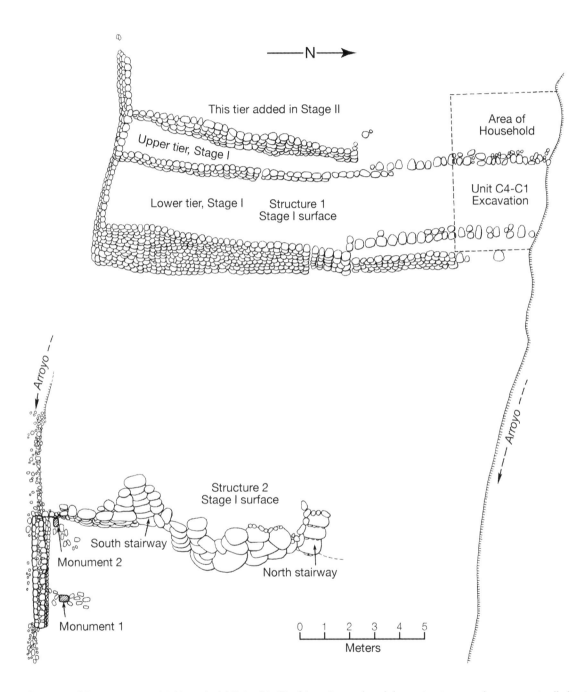

Figure 4.21. Plan view of Structures 1 and 2. Household Units C4–C1 of Area A antedated these structures and were eventually buried beneath them.

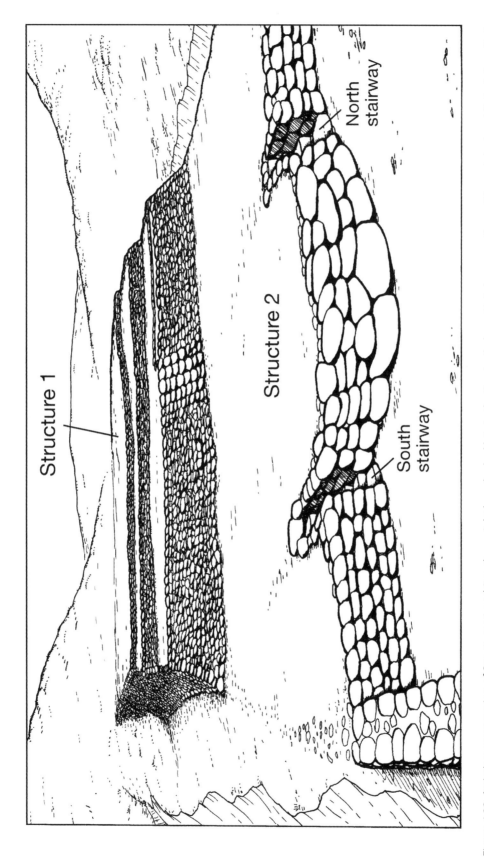

Figure 4.22. Artist's reconstruction of Structures 1 and 2 as they might have looked late in the San José phase. Not shown are the wattle-and-daub public buildings that once stood atop them but were eventually eroded away, leaving only traces of their clay floors (drawing by David West Reynolds).

Figure 4.23. Workmen expose the east face of Structure 2. The South Stairway appears in the right foreground.

adapted to the gentle slope without much concern for bilateral symmetry. To be sure, the perishable buildings that the platforms had once supported may have been symmetrical, but those buildings had long since eroded away. All that remained of them were a few patches of hard-packed, almost burnished, puddled-adobe floor surface to indicate where they once had stood. The walls were likely to have been wattle and daub.

Let us begin with Structure 2, the eastern half of the architectural complex (Figs. 4.22, 4.23). It had been preserved to a height of 1 m, and may once have occupied the full 18 m span between the two arroyos. Its façade, or eastern face, was built of carefully fitted but untrimmed boulders.

Built into the façade were our two earliest examples of inset stone staircases, designated the North and South Stairways. Each had once consisted of 3–7 stone steps and was so narrow (60–75 cm) that it could have accommodated only one person at a time.

One of the most interesting features of the Structure 2 façade is that it contained both local and nonlocal stones. While many of the stones were of the same volcanic tuff that constitutes bedrock at San José Mogote, others were of limestone from the quarries of Rancho Matadamas, 5 km to the west and on the opposite side of the Atoyac River. Still others were of travertine from Fábrica San José, 5 km to the east of San José Mogote.

The presence of these nonlocal stones suggests that San José Mogote could now call upon smaller villages in its hinterland to contribute stones and labor when it wanted to erect public buildings. This is tangible evidence that the 12–14 smaller communities within a half-day's walk of San José Mogote probably did, indeed, take orders from that chiefly center (Marcus and Flannery 1996:108–109).

Let us consider what this says about the buildings atop Structures 1 and 2. It implies that they served an area larger than San José Mogote; their significance, in other words, was regional. That makes it likely that they were early temples, at least in the generic sense of the term, because our men's houses seem to have had little significance beyond their respective residential wards. We are disappointed that the buildings atop Structures 1 and 2 were too badly destroyed to yield ground plans.

Beneath its patches of puddled-adobe floor, Structure 2 had been built up of basketload upon basketload of earthen fill. This fill was strengthened by somewhat informal-looking retaining walls of circular, planoconvex adobes.

As Figure 4.21 makes clear, a relatively well made stone masonry wall ran almost due east from the façade of Structure 2, beginning at the point where it reached the arroyo on its southern border. This wall ran for more than 4 m; its full length

Figure 4.24. The wall running east from Structure 2, during excavation. In the background, one can see a mass of stones that had fallen from its upper courses after abandonment. Monuments 1 and 2 were found near the bottom of this mass of fallen stones.

was unrecoverable, owing to erosion. Because this wall formed a corner with the façade of Structure 2, it would have made anyone standing in front of the South Stairway feel as if he or she were standing in a rectangular court. We would like to know if, as seems plausible, there was once a comparable wall extending out from the north end of the façade. Unfortunately, the erosion caused by the north arroyo would have destroyed it long ago.

In the course of exposing the east-west wall flanking the south arroyo, we were forced to remove a mass of stones that had fallen from its upper courses (Fig. 4.24). Within this mass of stones we found two carved monuments, Monuments 1 and 2, that had likely been part of the original wall (their locations are given in Figure 4.21).

Monument 1 seems to represent the head of a large cat, perhaps a jaguar or mountain lion (Fig. 4.25). It was carved on a volcanic tuff boulder. Monument 2 seems to represent the head of a large bird with a caruncle on its beak, possibly a vulture (Fig. 4.26). It was carved on a slab of volcanic tuff.

We are struck by the fact that Monuments 1 and 2 seem to have been executed in a local Oaxaca carving style, one that does not resemble the style of other chiefly centers such as Chalcatzingo (Grove 1987) or San Lorenzo (Coe and Diehl 1980). The jaguar or puma later became a day sign in the Zapotec calendar (Marcus 1992), so its depiction during the San José phase should not be surprising.

Since excavating Area A of San José Mogote, we have had an opportunity to see first-hand the Recinto, or sunken court, at the important site of Teopantecuanitlán in Guerrero (Martínez Donjuán 1985, 2010). While unique in many ways, the Recinto does have similar narrow, single-file staircases, and stone masonry walls with carved stones set in their upper courses. It is also terraced to the gentle slope coming down from a hill. In other words, although different in its details, the Recinto shares a number of features with San José Mogote's earliest stone-and-adobe ritual complex.

Let us move now to Structure 1, which lies 9–11 m upslope from Structure 2 (Fig. 4.21). Structure 1 was a pyramidal platform, faced with stone slabs laid in place like bricks (Fig. 4.27). The platform had originally been at least 18 m wide north-south, and ran east-west for more than 9 m before it was truncated by erosion.

One could detect at least three architectural levels in Structure 1 (Fig. 4.21). Its earliest level, designated Stage I, had two tiers. The lower tier stood 1.5 m high; the upper tier increased the building's height by another half meter. At a slightly later date, another tier (Stage II) was superimposed on Stage I, adding yet another half meter to its overall height. There had been a final thick cap of clay (Stage III) added to the structure, but this last enlargement was so badly eroded that its dimensions could not be determined.

Figure 4.25. Two views of Monument 1. *a*, the carved stone as it was found beneath the fallen stones of Structure 2. *b*, an artist's rendering of the stone.

Figure 4.26. Monument 2 and its location. *a*, Isaac Jiménez crouches in front of the wall running east from Structure 2, exactly where Monument 2 was found. *b*, an artist's rendering of the stone.

San José Mogote 2

Figure 4.27. Structure 1 seen from the southeast.

Figure 4.28. Two views of Structure 1. *a*, patches of the original puddled clay surface of the lower tier, Stage I, can be seen to either end of the north arrow. In *b*, workmen are removing several meters of black alluvial clay that had covered up the east face of the lower tier, Stage I.

On the upper surface of the lower tier of Stage 1 we found patches of a puddled-adobe clay floor, not unlike the one associated with Structure 2 (Fig. 4.28*a*). It is not clear what sort of building went with this floor; it is even possible that the lower tier was a kind of porch or veranda, with the main part of the building lying upslope (to the west).

We found 52 sherds lying on the patches of puddled-adobe floor associated with Stage I. These sherds have been published by Flannery and Marcus (1994:370), and all belong to San José phase types. In addition, Structure 1 had been built directly above Household Unit C4 of Area A, whose ceramics we have analyzed (Flannery and Marcus 1994: Table 14.1). The building's stratigraphic position, therefore, places it late in the San José phase. After their abandonment, Structures 1 and 2 came to be buried under several meters of black alluvial clay (Fig. 4.28*b*). None of the sherds from this black clay would have been out of place in a typical San José phase household (Flannery and Marcus 1994:371).

Conclusions

Structures 1 and 2 of San José Mogote represent an important escalation in ritual architecture. For the first time, we see a construction effort large enough to involve multiple work gangs, some of which may have brought nonlocal stone from satellite communities. Public buildings now required hundreds of basketloads of earthen fill, which was stabilized with retaining walls built of adobes. These early adobes were circular and planoconvex, as the result of having been molded in the lower halves of broken storage jars. The outer facing of each pyramidal platform was made from drylaid stone masonry, left slanting or stepped to prevent collapse.

The perishable buildings atop these late San José phase platforms would have been relevant to a much wider audience than the men's houses of earlier times. We believe that they were temples, and that they served all or most of the territory controlled by the hereditary leaders of San José Mogote. Although these buildings were badly eroded, none of their surviving clay floors bore traces of sitting benches or pits filled with powdered lime, two features that characterized our earlier men's houses.

Two novel features of Structure 2 were its carved stone monuments and single-file staircases of up to seven stone steps. There are suggestions that the steps ascended from a rectangular court, now largely eroded. The single-file nature of the staircases suggests that even though Structures 1 and 2 may have had regional significance, many of their rituals might have been accessible only to a privileged minority of spectators. In other words, although these pyramidal platforms may have supported early temples, we have little evidence that large audiences were allowed access to them. The same observation, to be sure, could be made for the Recinto at Teopantecuanitlán.

5 | Guadalupe Phase Ritual and Sociopolitical Cycling

Sometime around 850 b.c., the San José phase came to an end. What followed was a Middle Formative period called the Guadalupe phase. We have assigned this phase a date of 850–700 b.c., with the caveat that our sample of radiocarbon dates for the Guadalupe phase still needs to be increased (Flannery and Marcus 2005: Chapter 26).

Absolute dating is not the only unresolved aspect of the Guadalupe phase. This phase was originally defined in the Etla, or northern arm of the Valley of Oaxaca, and the diagnostic types, vessels, and motifs of the Guadalupe phase are most abundant in that subvalley. As one moves into the Zimatlán and Tlacolula subvalleys, those diagnostics diminish in frequency to the point where one could argue that each subvalley featured its own regional variant.

We believe that this lack of stylistic uniformity reflects the fact that 850–700 b.c. was a period of dynamic sociopolitical cycling. Almost all long-lived chiefly centers experience moments when rival centers arise to challenge their position in the administrative hierarchy (Anderson 1994). For San José Mogote, the Guadalupe phase appears to have been such a moment. One of San José Mogote's Middle Formative rivals was Barrio del Rosario Huitzo, a village 16 km to the northwest. While never as large as San José Mogote, Huitzo put up its own impressive

public buildings. Its pottery decoration also suggests that it reached outside the Valley of Oaxaca to establish economic or sociopolitical ties with villages in the Valley of Nochixtlán, some 50 km to the north (Marcus and Flannery 1996:113).

As a result, Huitzo's Atoyac Yellow-white pottery shares a number of incised motifs with Yucuita, a chiefly center near Nochixtlán. In the design inventory of Plog (n.d., 2009), these motifs include Elements 35–38 on Atoyac Yellow-white bowls (see Flannery and Marcus 1994: Table 12.1 and Fig. 12.19). Huitzo also shares fewer design elements with San José Mogote than predicted by Plog's gravity model, given the relatively short distance between the two sites (Plog 2009).

In addition to the weakening of San José Mogote's influence on other villages' pottery styles, other lines of evidence suggest that San José Mogote had lost some of its political clout. During the Guadalupe phase, for example, San José Mogote seems to have lost access to two of its principal iron ore sources: Loma de la Cañada Totomosle, north of Huitzo, and Loma los Sabinos, not far from the emerging chiefly center of San Martín Tilcajete (Flannery and Marcus 2005:87). The Guadalupe phase would thus appear to represent a downturn in San José Mogote's cycles of waxing and waning political power.

Sociopolitical Alliance Building

It should be noted that San José Mogote did not remain passive during this period of challenges to its sociopolitical dominance. It engaged in a number of strategies designed to prevent its satellite communities from shifting their allegiance to a rival chiefly center.

Hypogamous Marriage

One method used by chiefly lineages to strengthen their alliances with subordinates was hypogamy, or "marrying down." This was the strategy of sending a high-status woman from a chiefly center to marry the leader of a subordinate community. Hypogamy raises the prestige of the subordinate community leader while obligating him to the donor of the bride. The Aztec leaders of Tenochtitlán, for example, often sent their daughters or sisters to marry the leaders of subordinate communities (Carrasco 1974, 1984; Marcus 1992).

Many of our Middle Formative figurines show us that elite women of the Guadalupe phase used sumptuary goods to communicate their rank. Figure 5.1, a reconstruction drawing based on numerous broken fragments, depicts an elite woman with large, multicomponent jadeite ear ornaments. On her chest is an equally complex multicomponent pectoral, probably of spiny oyster or mother-of-pearl. On the woman's feet are sandals, with the lacing of straps shown in great detail. In many Mesoamerican societies, wearing sandals was a mark of high status because it meant that one's feet never touched the ground.

Fábrica San José, a two-hectare village in the piedmont some 5 km east of San José Mogote, was almost certainly one of the latter village's satellite communities. The resources of Fábrica San José included saline springs, used as a salt source since Tierras Largas times, and travertine quarries, the source of some of the stones in Structure 2 of San José Mogote. This would have been an important satellite for San José Mogote to retain.

According to excavator Robert D. Drennan (1976), the richest Guadalupe phase burials at Fábrica San José were those of women, suggesting that elite families at San José Mogote may have been practicing hypogamy with the leaders of this salt-producing village. Burial 39 of Fábrica San José, shown in Figure 5.2, is a good example. This burial was associated with House LG-1, Fábrica San José's most elaborate Guadalupe phase residence.

Burial 39 was a woman 40–60 years of age, laid to rest fully extended and prone. In her mouth were a jadeite pendant, 53 jadeite beads, and 1 brown stone bead. The pottery vessels with her included 2 yellow-white bowls, a red storage jar, and a Delia White beaker. The Delia White beaker, an imported vessel made somewhere outside the Valley of Oaxaca, is the region's earliest example of an elite drinking vessel; it likely held 600–800 cc of hot chocolate or pulque, enough for one high-status individual. We suspect that Burial 39 may have been a hypogamous bride from San José Mogote.

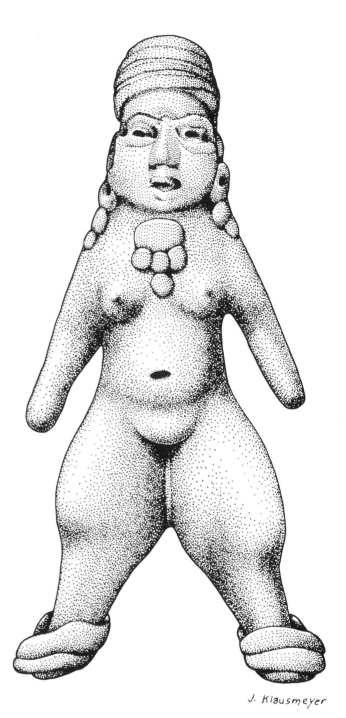

J. Klausmeyer

Figure 5.1. Figurines of the Guadalupe phase suggest that elite women wore elaborate, multicomponent jadeite ear ornaments, complex shell pectorals, and well-made sandals that kept their feet from touching the ground.

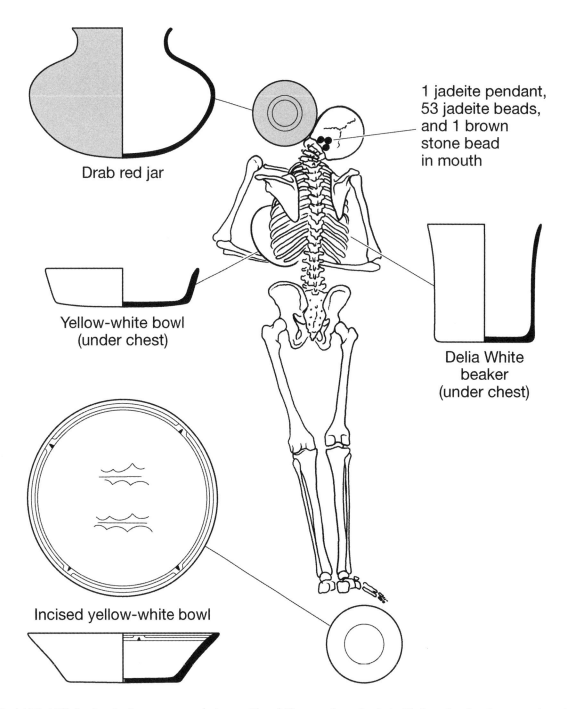

Drab red jar

1 jadeite pendant,
53 jadeite beads,
and 1 brown
stone bead
in mouth

Yellow-white bowl
(under chest)

Delia White
beaker
(under chest)

Incised yellow-white bowl

Figure 5.2. Burial 39 at Fábrica San José was a woman between 40 and 60 years of age, buried with three local pottery vessels and an imported Delia White beaker. Inside her mouth were 53 jadeite beads and a jadeite pendant. This woman may be a hypogamous bride from San José Mogote.

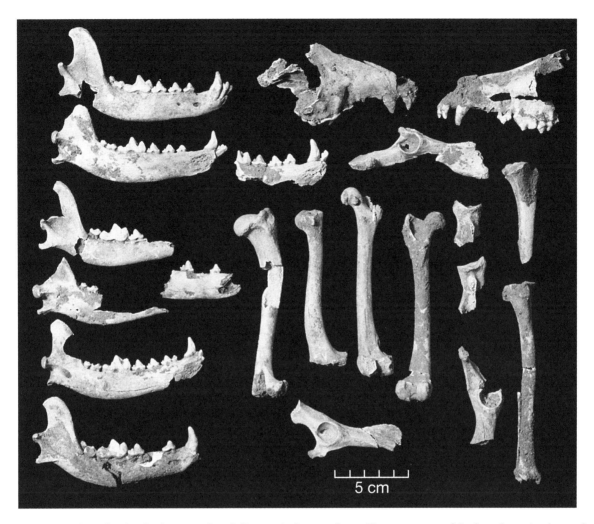

Figure 5.3. Guadalupe phase families built sociopolitical alliances by hosting feasts. These are some of the faunal remains from a feast at which at least 50 kilograms of dog meat were consumed.

Feasting

Another strategy for building alliances was the sponsoring of feasts. To be sure, the Guadalupe phase was not our first period to yield evidence of feasting. House 4, a San José phase residence in Area C of San José Mogote, produced evidence for a feast at which five dogs had been butchered (Flannery and Marcus 2005:189–190, Fig. 9.39).

Our clearest evidence for a Guadalupe phase feast comes from Feature 99 at Tierras Largas, another village that was likely subordinate to San José Mogote. Feature 99, an abandoned storage pit used for refuse disposal, contained the remains of at least five dogs (Fig. 5.3). These dogs had all been butchered in the same systematic way. A number of forelegs were found together, a number of hind legs were found together, and a number of skull elements were found together, suggesting that the meat had been divided in such a way that certain individuals could be provided with specific parts of the animal. All the scapulae had been smashed in the same way, as if a single butcher had been assigned the task of freeing the foreleg.

At least 50 kg (110 pounds) of meat had been butchered, cooked, and eaten at this feast. What we do not know is whether the participants included guests from another community or if they were all residents of Tierras Largas.

Temple Building

Leaders of the Guadalupe phase also sought to impress their followers by building temples larger than any seen previously. Our two best examples are Structure 8 of San José Mogote and Structure 3 of Barrio del Rosario Huitzo.

These two Middle Formative temples shared a number of construction details. Both were one-room structures whose

Figure 5.4. The use of planoconvex adobes in Structure 8. In *a*, the workman on the left exposes a retaining wall of planoconvex adobes. An outer wall of boulders can be seen in the background. In *b*, we see an unfinished adobe in the bottom of a broken jar, showing how the latter was used as an adobe mold.

wattle-and-daub walls were ultra-thick and had been given extra layers of clay plaster coated with lime whitewash. Both sat on platforms built of earthen fill and circular planoconvex adobes, over a foundation of untrimmed fieldstones. In both cases, the earthen fill of the platform had been strengthened with crisscrossing adobe retaining walls, which essentially created a series of rectangular cells to be filled with basketloads of earth. Both temples were aligned 8° north of east, evidently still an important ritual orientation in the Guadalupe phase. Both also had wide staircases, in contrast to the single-file stairways of earlier periods. This fact suggests that rituals were now performed for larger audiences.

Structure 8

Structure 8 of San José Mogote was built in Area C, stratigraphically above the San José phase residences, men's houses, and middens of that ward. This temple lay so close to the present land surface that it had endured both erosion and post-Conquest plowing. As a result, we will never know Structure 8's full

Figure 5.5. A view of the northern part of Structure 8 during excavation. The workman in the foreground (in Square S13N) is sitting on the puddled clay surface of the platform; his left hand is inside a posthole from the temple that once stood there. Near his right knee, the puddled clay surface has been removed to show an underlying retaining wall of planoconvex adobes. (This view is from the east.)

dimensions. All we can be sure of is that its east wall ran for more than 20 m north-to-south.

It was while we were investigating the interior of Structure 8 that we discovered how Oaxaca's early planoconvex adobes had been made. At various places in the earthen fill, the builders had discarded fragments of broken storage jars with unfinished adobes still in them (Fig. 5.4). This told us that the lower portions of broken Fidencio Coarse storage jars had been used as molds for making circular adobes.

The retaining walls within the building's fill sometimes had as many as four courses of these adobes, stacked flat side down and surrounded with clay mortar. Four courses was apparently the limit of wall height, because we typically found traces of the temple floor above that level. The floor was of thick, puddled adobe clay and bore occasional postmolds from the wall posts. Such was the case with the adobe wall shown in Figure 5.5, which appeared in Squares S13K–S15N of the one-by-one meter grid established for Area C (Flannery and Marcus 2005: Fig. 6.2).

While the interior retaining walls for the fill of Structure 8 were of adobe, the outer walls were of drylaid stone masonry

Figure 5.6. The southern end of Structure 8, seen from the northeast. In the foreground are the stone foundations for the eastern margin of the platform. In the background are two retaining walls for the earthen fill, each composed of planoconvex adobes. Each workman kneels in a compartment from which the earthen fill has been removed. (The area shown occupies roughly Squares S22K through S25Q.)

several courses high (Fig. 5.6). The shape of the eastern wall left no doubt that it had included a staircase, and a wide one at that. As can be seen in Figures 5.7 through 5.10, the total width of the staircase was about 9 m. Of this width, about 6.5 m were the stone foundation for the lowest step of the stairway itself, and the remaining 2.5 m were made up by the stone foundations of the flanking "balustrades" (for want of a better term). Judging by what we know of Structure 3 at Huitzo (see below), the "balustrades" themselves were most likely heavy adobe blocks whose real purpose was to keep the stairway from collapsing

under the weight of foot traffic.

Whatever the case, there was a striking difference between the 6.5-meter-wide steps of Structure 8 and the narrow, single-file stairways of Structure 2 (compare Fig. 4.20). Clearly, by the Guadalupe phase, the builders of temples were expecting a larger audience to ascend the steps and witness ritual performances.

Despite its badly eroded condition, Structure 8 yielded some artifacts that contributed to our understanding of Guadalupe phase ritual. Two complete figurines were found in the earthen fill of Structure 8. To be sure, neither can be considered to be in

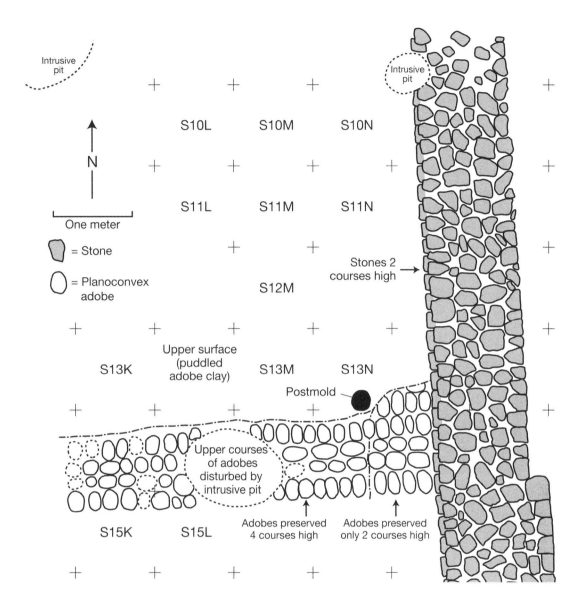

Figure 5.7. Plan view of the northern third of Structure 8. The additional row of stones appearing in Squares S14P and S15P/S15Q is believed to reflect the north side of the staircase.

situ, since they were part of the building's fill rather than resting on the floor. These figurines are Guadalupe phase Specimens 1 and 2 of Marcus (1998:247).

Specimen 1 (Fig. 5.11, left) is the nearly complete figure of a standing woman wearing a noseplug, earspools, and a circular pendant or pectoral. She has a large cloth headwrap, held in place by what appears to be a string of spherical beads. There are traces of white paint on her face, and she seems to be wearing a pubic apron made from some kind of fiber.

Specimen 2 (Fig. 5.11, right) is the nearly complete figure of a

woman with her legs extended straight out in front of her, hands on her knees. She, too, has prominent earspools and a circular pendant or pectoral. Her hairdo consists of a cloth headband, plus what may be a prominent chignon quadrille and two smaller Zulu knots (see Marcus 1998: Fig. 6.7).

In Figure 5.12 we see a large obsidian blade that was discovered on a sand layer in Square S24N. That sand layer seemed to represent all that was left of the eroded temple floor in that part of Structure 8. This very long blade, superficially resembling obsidian from the Otumba source in the Basin of Mexico, may

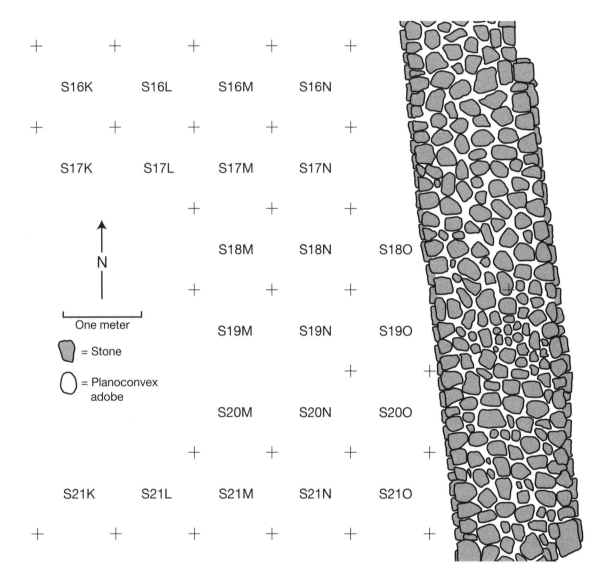

S16K S16L S16M S16N

S17K S17L S17M S17N

N

One meter

⬠ = Stone

◯ = Planoconvex
adobe

S18M S18N S18O

S19M S19N S19O

S20M S20N S20O

S21K S21L S21M S21N S21O

Figure 5.8. Plan view of the central third of Structure 8. The additional row of stones beginning in Square S16P and ending in Square S22Q is believed to be the foundation for the lowermost step of the staircase.

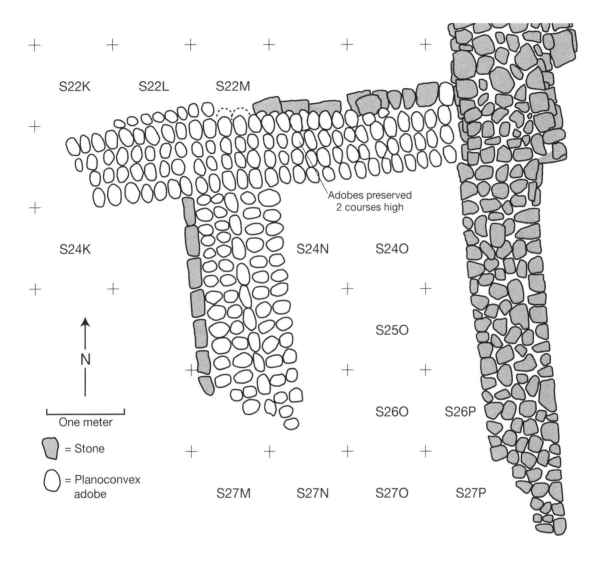

Figure 5.9. Plan view of the southern third of Structure 8. The additional row of stones appearing in Squares S22Q and S23Q is believed to reflect the south side of the staircase.

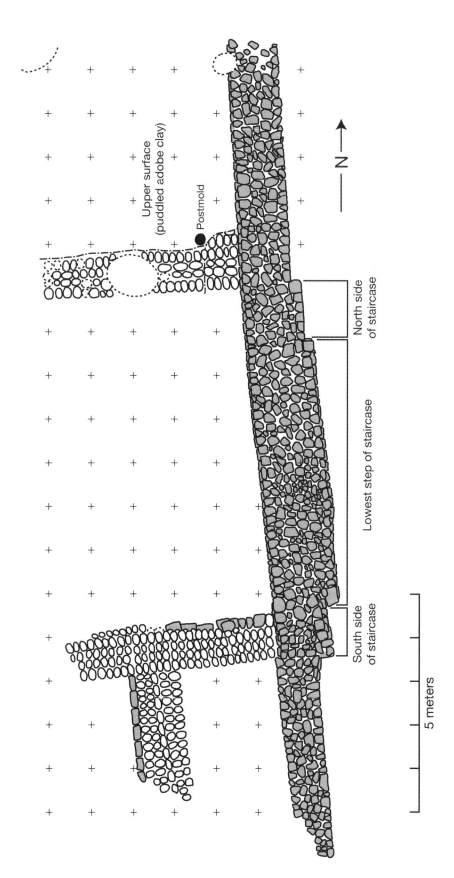

Upper surface
(puddled adobe clay)

Postmold

North side
of staircase

Lowest step of staircase

South side
of staircase

N

5 meters

Figure 5.10. Overall view of the surviving remnant of Structure 8, the stone and adobe foundation for a Guadalupe phase temple. The full dimensions of the building are unknown, but it appears that the staircase was 7.28 m wide, while the lowest step was at least 6 m wide.

Figure 5.11. Two figurines found in the earthen fill of Structure 8, Area C. Specimen 1 is on the left, Specimen 2 on the right.

have been used in the temple for bloodletting; when found, it had been broken into three pieces that could be refitted.

In Figure 5.13 we see a 98-gram piece of black mica, found just above the stone foundations of Structure 8. Its stratigraphic position suggested that it might have been left behind when the temple floor eroded away. Although black mica is native to the Valley of Oaxaca (Flannery and Marcus 2005:88), a piece this large was a rare find at San José Mogote. We do not know what role mica might have played in temple activities.

Finally, test excavations elsewhere in Area C suggest that Structure 8 may have occupied the west side of a small patio, and that the north, south, and east sides of that patio may have

had similar temples. Unfortunately, time ran out before we could confirm this possibility.

The Guadalupe Phase Temple of a Rival Chiefly Center

As previously mentioned, one of San José Mogote's biggest Guadalupe phase rivals was the chiefly center now buried beneath the Barrio del Rosario of San Pablo Huitzo. Barrio del Rosario Huitzo was already occupied during the San José phase, but was likely only a hamlet of 5–10 extended families at that time (Flannery and Marcus 2003d:60).

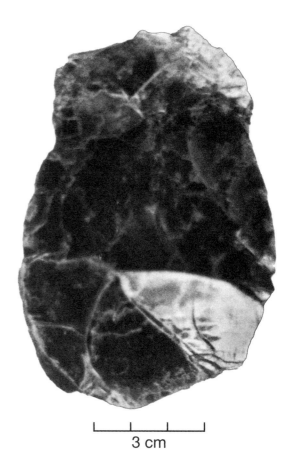

2 cm

3 cm

Figure 5.12. Large obsidian blade from Structure 8. This blade, broken into three pieces, was found on a sand layer that may represent all that was left of the temple floor (Square S24N).

Figure 5.13. A 98-gram piece of biotite (black mica) found just above the stone foundation of Structure 8.

Figure 5.14. Two views of Structure 4, Barrio del Rosario Huitzo. In *a*, workmen expose the multi-tiered edge of the pyramidal platform. In *b*, we see a nearly vertical retaining wall in the interior of the platform.

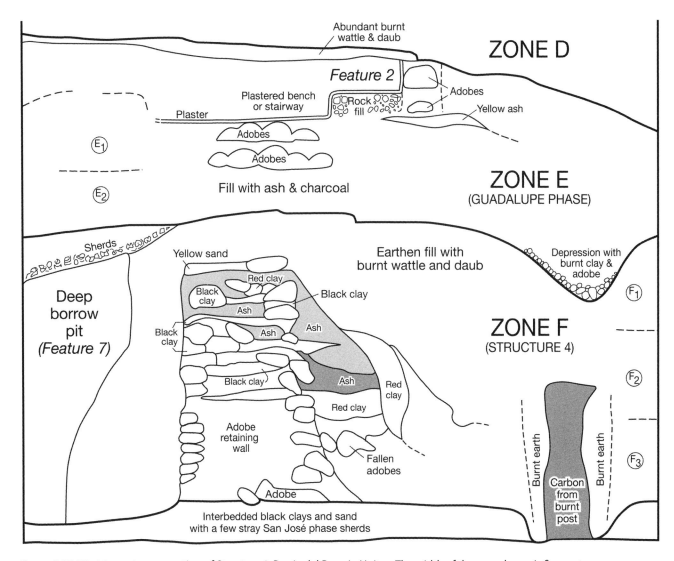

Figure 5.15. West to east cross-section of Structure 4, Barrio del Rosario Huitzo. The width of the area shown is five meters.

During the Guadalupe phase, Barrio del Rosario Huitzo grew to cover at least 2.7 ha, of which 3500 m² (about 13 percent) were taken up by an artificial mound. That mound represents the accumulated remains of a series of superimposed public buildings, spanning most of the Middle Formative period (Flannery and Marcus 2003d). During its rise to prominence, as previously mentioned, the chiefly center at Huitzo shared more ceramic motifs with the rank societies of the Nochixtlán Valley than expected, while sharing fewer motifs with San José Mogote than would have been expected (Plog 2009).

Structure 4

The first of the public constructions built at Huitzo was Structure 4 in Stratigraphic Zone F (Figs. 5.14, 5.15). Structure 4 was the original pyramidal platform that supported all the

later Middle Formative structures built in that area. We were unable to determine the full dimensions of Structure 4 because it is now buried beneath a series of present-day houses. Only through the generosity of landowner Josefina Bolaños was the University of Michigan team allowed to excavate in the space between these houses (Fig. 5.14a).

Structure 4 was 2 m high. It rose in a series of tiers and was built of earthen fill with an outer facing of undressed fieldstones. As was typical of the Guadalupe phase, this fill was strengthened with retaining walls, oriented 8° north of true east. Some of these retaining walls were of undressed stones (Fig. 5.14b), while others were of planoconvex adobes set in clay mortar of different colors (Fig. 5.15). The varied soil colors involved suggest that more than one ward of the village participated, each bringing its own basketloads of fill.

Figure 5.16. A team of masons begins to stabilize and repair the surviving remnant of Structure 3. Perhaps 80 percent of the temple had been made into adobes prior to excavation.

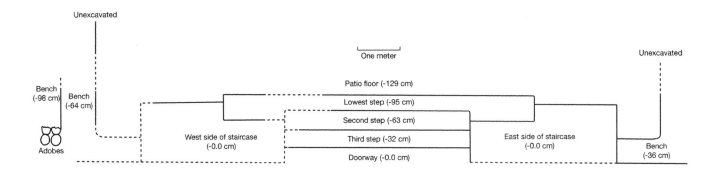

Figure 5.17. Plan of the surviving remnant of Structure 3, showing the staircase and the L-shaped benches that probably connected this temple to two others on the same patio. Structure 3 faced 8° west of true north.

Included in Structure 4 were a series of pine posts up to 30 cm in diameter. We found two that had been burned. One of these carbonized posts (shown in Fig. 5.15) yielded a conventional radiocarbon date of 850 b.c. (M-2102). The dendrocalibrated two-sigma range would be 1390–760 BC.

The conventional date of 850 b.c. falls right at the transition from the San José phase to the Guadalupe phase. It fits well with two facts: (1) Structure 4 seems to have been built directly on a layer of interbedded black clays and sand containing only San José phase sherds, and (2) the earthen fill of Structure 4 contains more redeposited San José phase sherds than Guadalupe phase sherds. We therefore suspect that Structure 4 was built either right at the end of the San José phase or very early in the Guadalupe phase.

Feature 2

Superimposed above Structure 4, in Stratigraphic Zone E, we found traces of a later building (Fig. 5.15). Referred to simply as Feature 2, the remains consisted of a piece of plastered patio floor and a section of lime-plastered step from a staircase. Both the patio and the step had been reinforced with planoconvex adobes. We now suspect that Feature 2, which we were unable to trace for any distance, had once been part of a plastered staircase on the west side of a Guadalupe phase temple.

Structure 3

Of all the subsequent Guadalupe phase temples, built one above another in the stratigraphic sequence at Huitzo, the one we know the most about is Structure 3 in Zone C (Figs. 5.16–5.21). Even Structure 3 could not be fully excavated, however, because at least 80 percent of the building had been destroyed by twentieth

-century adobe makers prior to our arrival. We did manage to investigate the entire north side, which included a wide staircase.

Because of its partial destruction, we were able to investigate much of the internal construction of Structure 3. Its fill consisted of basketloads of two different types of earth, black alluvial clay and gritty yellow loam. This fill was strengthened by retaining walls of circular planoconvex adobes, like those used in Structure 8 at San José Mogote. The outer casing of the structure was composed of similar adobe walls, consolidated with mortar made from the same clay as the adobes. Over the entire structure went a thick layer of smoothed and burnished clay, covered with white lime plaster. The finish was like that applied to Structure 28 at San José Mogote, a Rosario phase temple (described in Chapter 8).

The only part of Structure 3 that had survived to be measured was the north side (Fig. 5.17). From this side, we learned that the structure had been 1.3 m high and 11.5 m wide east-west. In the center of the north side was a staircase consisting of three steps, held in place by two heavy "balustrades" that we simply referred to as the east and west sides of the staircase. Such construction was typical of Middle Formative Oaxaca; the architects of that era had not yet learned how to keep the steps of their staircases from spreading laterally under the weight of foot traffic, so they encased the steps between heavy adobe blocks. These blocks could be considered the forerunners of the true balustrades that graced later Zapotec staircases. The architects of Structure 3 had strengthened each step by building it of planoconvex adobes, encasing it in hard clay, and coating it with lime plaster.

Structure 3 was essentially the substructure of a temple whose floor lay only 32 cm above the third, or topmost, step of the stairway (Fig. 5.17). That temple had walls of thick wattle and daub, surfaced with a heavy coating of adobe clay and multiple layers of lime plaster. Only traces of this temple remained because it had later been leveled and replaced with another. As we cleared

Figure 5.18. Work in progress on the Structure 3 staircase, only part of which had been freed from its matrix. The postholes in the foreground are intrusive from a later building.

Figure 5.19. The staircase of Structure 3, as it looked after careful repairs had been made with mud plaster. By this time, a protective roof had been built over the surviving remnant of the temple.

the upper surface of Structure 3, we encountered postholes that we thought at first might be from its north wall (Fig. 5.18). We eventually concluded that they were intrusive, having been made by the posts of the later temple.

Because Structure 3 was our best-preserved example of a Guadalupe phase public building, we had our masons reconstruct the damaged parts of its staircase and north façade (Fig. 5.19). For a decade following our excavation, the reconstructed façade was left open for viewing but protected from rain by a roof. After that, realizing that there would be no funds to maintain the roof after our project ended, we covered the building with plastic sheets and backfilled the excavation to prevent looting.

One of the most interesting features of Structure 3 was the fact that it had low benches running north from its east and west ends. Both benches are shown in our plan drawing (Fig. 5.17), and the eastern bench appears in one of our photographs (Fig. 5.20). Owing to the huge amount of overburden that would have

to be removed, we were unable to trace these benches for more than a few meters.

With the wisdom of hindsight, we now believe that these benches were designed to connect Structure 3 to similar temples on the east and west sides of the same patio. In other words, Guadalupe phase Huitzo may have featured a small rectangular patio with temples on its north, south, east, and west sides. Only additional excavation could confirm this, and unfortunately, the overburden cannot be removed without destroying a number of later buildings.

Structure 3 faced 8° west of true north—an orientation shared by most of the Tierras Largas, San José, and Guadalupe phase public buildings so far discussed, as well as Complex A at La Venta on the Gulf Coast (Drucker, Heizer, and Squier 1959).

Figure 5.20. Architectural evidence that Structure 3 was one of several temples facing onto the same patio. In the lower left corner of the photo we see the east side of the staircase. Running east from the staircase is a low bench that turns a corner and runs north, probably to connect with the staircase of a west-facing temple. Unfortunately, its northward course was interrupted by a later pit.

Conclusions

The Guadalupe phase was a period of sociopolitical cycling in the Valley of Oaxaca. San José Mogote lost its monopoly on impressive public buildings and its access to some of its most useful iron ore resources. Barrio del Rosario Huitzo—and perhaps also San Martín Tilcajete—seems to have become a rival of San José Mogote, competing for the support of subordinate villages and hamlets. As a result, San José Mogote may have resorted to a whole series of allegiance-building strategies, including feasting and chiefly hypogamy.

Despite this competition among chiefly centers, there seems to have been broad agreement on the layout and construction of religious buildings. Temples were raised above the rest of the village on pyramidal platforms of drylaid stone masonry. The temples themselves had thick wattle-and-daub walls and were reached by stairways wide enough to allow five or more worship-

pers at a time to ascend side by side. This may mean that many rituals were public performances, presented to larger audiences than those of the San José phase.

Continuity with earlier periods was evident in building orientation, which still featured a deviation of 8° from true north or true east. This orientation was widespread in Mexico, characterizing public buildings as far south as Tabasco. The fact that the 8° orientation was used in Oaxaca as early as 1500 b.c., however, makes it impossible to attribute it to influence from some other region. No area of Mexico can be shown to have used the 8° orientation earlier than Oaxaca.

Structure 8 of San José Mogote and Structure 3 of Huitzo both show signs of having shared a patio with three other temples. If so, the Guadalupe phase provides us with our first example of a ritual patio with temples on all four sides. We do not know the purpose behind such a four-temple unit, but it anticipates later temple patios at Monte Albán. It also suggests a complexity of

Figure 5.21. Artist's reconstruction of Structure 3 at Barrio del Rosario Huitzo, including the benches that probably connected it to other temples sharing the same patio (drawing by David West Reynolds).

ritual activity that might require trained priests, whether full-time or part-time.

The circular planoconvex adobes used for late San José and early Guadalupe phase buildings are currently unique to Oaxaca. We do not doubt that, with further excavation, we will find that they were in use elsewhere. So far, however, they have not shown up in Puebla, Morelos, Chiapas, or the Gulf Coast. Eventually, San José Mogote's architects would replace these circular adobes with the rectangular type so common in Rosario phase Oaxaca, Chiapa de Corzo, La Venta, and other Middle Formative sites.

6 | The Reburial of Elite Middle Formative Youths on Mound 1

In Chapter 4 we described the remains of a likely San José phase men's house on Mound 1 of San José Mogote. Pieces of that building were found in Stratigraphic Zone F below Structure 28, a Rosario phase temple. Zone F was a layer of San José phase debris that accumulated before any Guadalupe or Rosario phase structures had been built on Mound 1.

In the course of exploring Zone F, we found a series of Middle Formative burials intrusive into that stratum. All were the secondary burials of individuals who had originally been buried elsewhere, only to be exhumed later and reburied in the upper part of Zone F. We do not know why that particular spot was chosen to receive these burials. It might have been considered a ritually significant place, either because it had once been the scene of a men's house or because it had already been chosen as the venue for a future temple.

These secondary burials date to the period of transition between the late Guadalupe phase and the early Rosario phase (somewhere in the neighborhood of 700 b.c.). In the course of

describing the offerings left with them, we refer to two previously published studies of Formative Oaxaca ceramics: (1) an analysis of the attributes of Guadalupe and Rosario phase pottery from Fábrica San José by Drennan (1976); and (2) an analysis of the incised design elements on Early and Middle Formative pottery by Plog (2009, n.d.; for the complete inventory of Plog's design elements, see Flannery and Marcus 1994: Figs. 12.19–12.21).

Burial 65

Preparations for Burial 65 included digging an oval pit into Zone F and covering the floor of the pit with a layer of clean river sand (Figs. 6.1, 6.2). Added to the sand layer was a circular patch of red pigment that contained several disarticulated human bones. The only other human remains found were some skull fragments and a few finger bones, making it impossible to assess the age and sex of the individual involved.

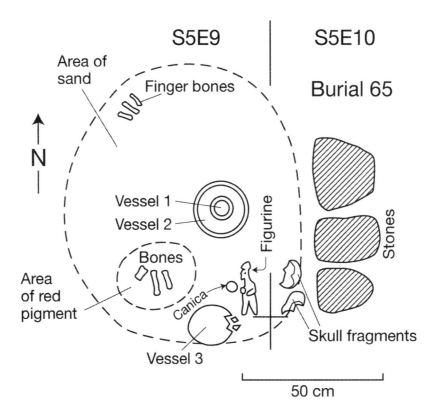

Figure 6.1. Plan view of Burial 65, a secondary burial intrusive into Stratigraphic Zone F.

Figure 6.2. A view of Burial 65 from the west at the moment of discovery. In the center of the photo one can see Vessel 1 inside Vessel 2. On the right, near the north arrow, are the figurine and limestone *canica*. In the background are the tops of two stones in Square S5E10.

The burial pit fell mainly in Square S5E9 but extended a short distance into three adjacent squares. An alignment of three stones in Square S5E10 may have been associated with Burial 65. The offerings consisted of three pottery vessels, a complete figurine, and a limestone *canica* or pecked stone ball.

The figurine (Fig. 6.3) belongs typologically to the Guadalupe phase (Marcus 1998: Fig. 16.1). It has the typical elaborate sandals, pubic apron, prominent navel, eyes, earspools, and nose ornament found on figurines at Barrio del Rosario Huitzo and other Guadalupe phase sites. Pottery Vessels 1 and 2 (found stacked one inside the other) are also typical of the Guadalupe phase (Fig. 6.4). Vessel 1 is an undecorated Josefina Fine Gray beaker; Vessel 2 is an undecorated Socorro Fine Gray deep bowl.

Vessel 3 (Fig. 6.5) does not belong to any of our usual Oaxaca Formative pottery types, and is likely a foreign import. It is a highly burnished, mahogany brown bottle whose neck may have been broken when the skeleton was exhumed and reburied. We showed this bottle to David C. Grove and he suspects that it may be a Valley of Morelos pottery type, Madera Coarse (Brown variety).

Figure 6.3. Offerings from Burial 65. On the left is a typical Guadalupe phase figurine with a prominent navel and sandals. On the right is a limestone *canica* or pecked stone ball.

Figure 6.4. Offerings from Burial 65. On the right is Vessel 1, a Josefina Fine Gray beaker. On the left is Vessel 2, a Socorro Fine Gray deep bowl.

We wish that Burial 65 had included enough skeletal elements to allow its sex to be determined. In our experience, individuals in Formative Oaxaca who were buried with a "female ancestor" figurine tended to be women, and we would like to have been able to confirm this by skeletal criteria. We are also curious about the possible vessel from Morelos. The Middle Formative was a time when high-status women were exchanged as brides (Marcus and Flannery 1996:114–115, 134–135) and we would like to know whether such exchanges linked Morelos and Oaxaca.

Burial 66

Burial 66 was found in an irregularly shaped pit, intrusive into Zone F in Squares S5E11 and S5E12 (Fig. 6.6). The skeletal remains, although widely dispersed throughout the pit, included enough key elements so that Hodges (1989:87) was able to detect the presence of two individuals. One of those individuals was 16–18 years of age and possibly male. The other was a child of indeterminate sex, 10–11 years old. We do not know whether these two young people had originally been buried together, or whether their remains had simply been combined when they were reburied. It appeared that several offerings had been broken when one or both skeletons were exhumed.

Dispersed through the Burial 66 pit were five pottery vessels, plus two fragments of marine shell that may once have been part of a shell vessel. The shell fragments appear to belong to *Malea ringens*, the same cask shell modified to serve as a bowl in the case of Burial 71 (see below).

Vessel 1, reconstructed from scattered fragments, was a large

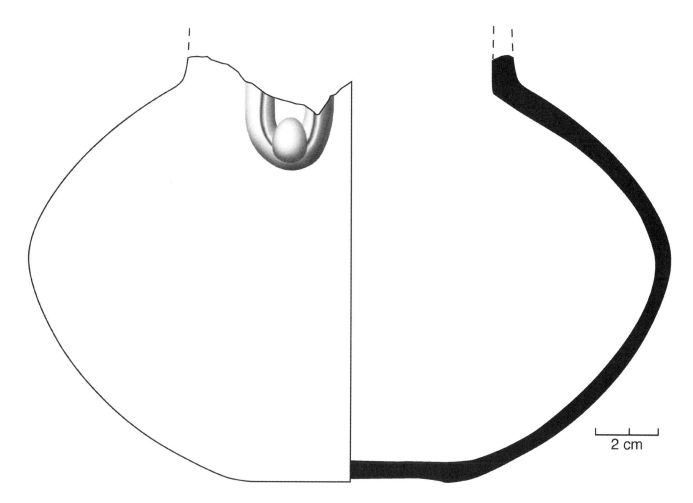

Figure 6.5. Vessel 3, an offering found with Burial 65. This highly burnished, mahogany brown bottle (broken in antiquity) is foreign to the Valley of Oaxaca, and may be Madera Coarse (Brown variety) from the Valley of Morelos.

Socorro Fine Gray bowl with a flat base and outcurved walls (Fig. 6.7). On the exterior of its base this bowl bore a simulated *petate* or mat impression, created through the use of postfiring incisions. Vessel 2, also badly broken, was a Socorro Fine Gray bowl with flat base and outleaned walls (Fig. 6.8*a*).

Vessel 3 was a Delfina Fine Gray bowl with a flat base and outcurved walls (Fig. 6.9). Vessel 4 was a Josefina Fine Gray bowl with a flat base and outcurved walls (Fig. 6.8*b*).

Vessel 5 was a tall Josefina Fine Gray beaker, displaying both fine-line incising and negative or "resist" white decoration (Fig. 6.10). Displayed twice, on opposing sides of the beaker, we see a motif that Grove (1984:126) and Marcus (1999:79) have identified as "the crocodile's foot." This is one of several symbols that Formative potters used for Earth, which some ancient Mesoamerican people thought of as the back of a giant

crocodile. The use of the foot was a *pars pro toto* reference to the mythical crocodile.

Two fragments of a possible cask shell bowl that may have been broken during exhumation of the original burials are shown in Figure 6.11. Finally, in Figure 6.12, we see two large sherds that were included in the earthen fill of Burial 66. Both sherds appear to have come from fine grayware beakers, decorated with a combination of fine-line incising and negative white. One sherd is Socorro Fine Gray, the other Josefina Fine Gray.

Typologically, the pottery vessels from Burial 66 suggest a date somewhere near the transition from the Guadalupe phase to the Rosario phase. While Vessels 2, 3, and 4 would not seem at all out of place if found in a Guadalupe phase house, the use of "resist" white-on-gray decoration does not occur until roughly 700 b.c. and is considered a Rosario phase attribute (see Chapter 7). What

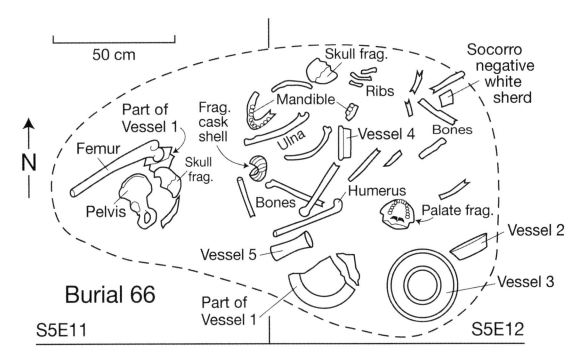

Figure 6.6. Plan view of Burial 66, a secondary burial intrusive into Stratigraphic Zone F.

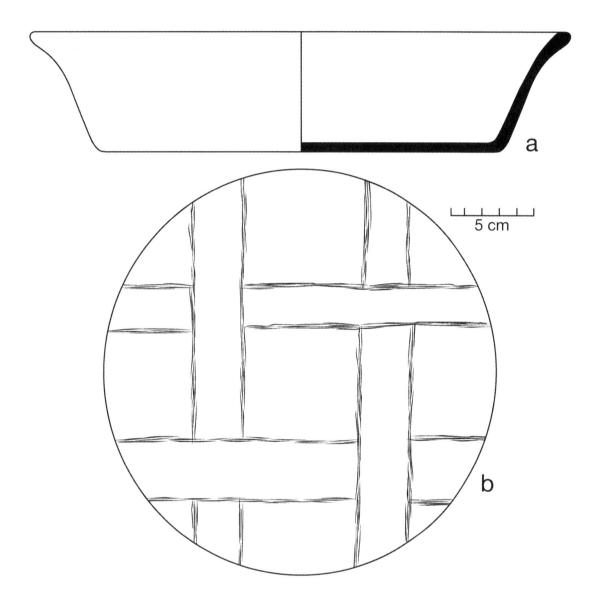

Figure 6.7. Reconstruction drawing of Vessel 1 from Burial 66, which was badly broken. This was a large Socorro Fine Gray bowl with flat base and outcurving wall. On the exterior of its base the vessel bore an imitation of a mat impression, made by post-firing incisions and scratches. *a*, cross-section. *b*, exterior of base.

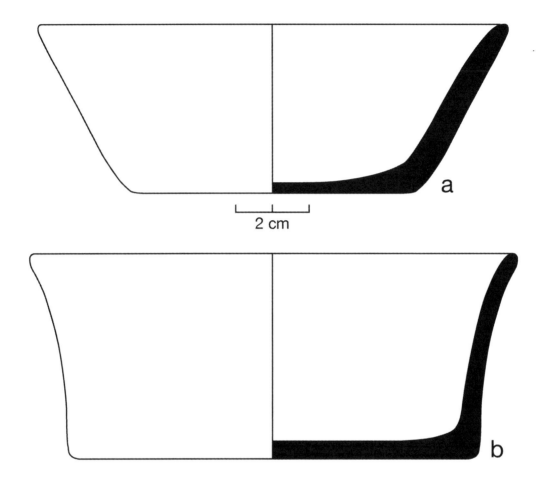

Above: Figure 6.8. Reconstruction drawings of Vessels 2 and 4 from Burial 66, both of which were badly broken. Vessel 2 (*a*) was a Socorro Fine Gray bowl with flat base and outleaned wall. Vessel 4 (*b*) was a Josefina Fine Gray bowl with flat base and outcurved wall.

Below: Figure 6.9. Vessel 3 from Burial 66, a Delfina Fine Gray bowl with flat base and outcurved wall.

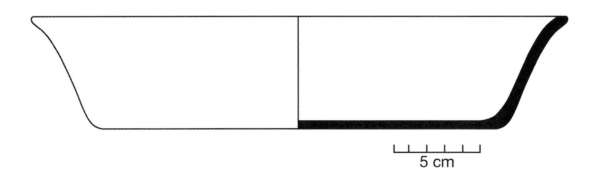

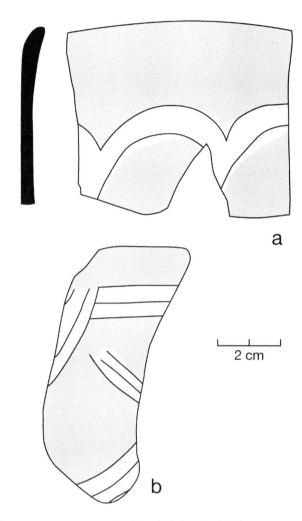

Above: Figure 6.10. Reconstruction drawing of Vessel 5 from Burial 66, a Josefina Fine Gray beaker with fine-line incising and negative white decoration. The "crocodile's foot" motif appears twice, on opposite sides of the vessel. Height, 17.5 cm.

Above: Figure 6.12. Two sherds included in the fill of Burial 66. *a*, rim of Socorro Fine Gray beaker with fine-line incising and negative white decoration. *b*, body sherd of Josefina Fine Gray with fine-line incising and negative white decoration.

Left: Figure 6.11. Two fragments of cask shell from Burial 66.

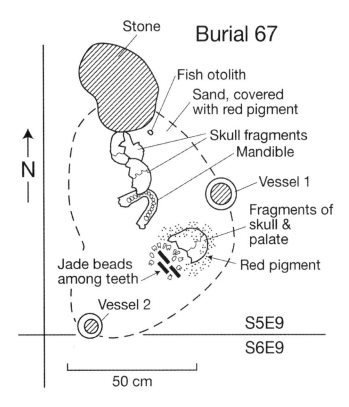

Figure 6.13. Plan view of Burial 67, a secondary burial intrusive into Stratigraphic Zone F.

Figure 6.14. Workman Genaro Luis cleans a skull fragment, part of Burial 67. In the foreground, Vessel 1 can be seen projecting up from the sand-filled matrix of the burial.

makes any secondary burial difficult to date precisely is the fact that decades (or even centuries) can elapse between the original burial and its exhumation and reburial. This allows for the possibility that some vessels were added at the time of reinterment.

Burial 67

Burial 67 was found in an irregularly shaped pit in Square S5E9 (Fig. 6.13). The bottom of the pit was covered with a layer of sand, heavily infused with red pigment (Fig. 6.14). A stone found at the edge of the pit may have been associated.

Although the skeletal remains in Burial 67 were few in number, they included most of a broken skull. Hodges (1989:87) considers this individual to be a young woman, 15–17 years of age. Three tubular jadeite beads were found among her teeth, suggesting that the beads may have been placed in her mouth. The placement of jadeite beads in the mouth of a burial was a longstanding pattern in Early and Middle Formative Oaxaca (Flannery and Marcus 2005: Figs. 5.18, 18.4h). While most individuals received only one small circular bead, high-status individuals might be given a cluster of elegant beads like those found with Burial 67 (Fig. 6.15).

The offerings found with Burial 67 included two pottery vessels (Fig. 6.16) and a fish otolith. Vessel 1 was a small Socorro Fine Gray jar (Fig. 6.17a). Vessel 2 was a small Socorro Fine Gray *tecomate* or neckless jar (Fig. 6.17b). The rim of this *tecomate* had been decorated with a band of fine-line incising and "zoned toning," the alternation of burnished and matte areas.

When one examines the entire band of zoned toning on Vessel 2,

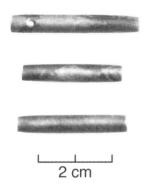

Figure 6.15. Three tubular jadeite beads from the mouth of Burial 67. The bead at the top, biconically drilled at one end, is mottled green and white; so is the bead in the center. The bead at the bottom of the photo is apple green.

Figure 6.16. Vessels 1 (left) and 2 (right) from Burial 67.

one can see the evolution of a common Guadalupe phase motif ("diamond-in-a-box") into a common Rosario phase motif ("pennant"). It appears that when the burnished, diamond-shaped area was stretched horizontally (Fig. 6.17*c*) it lost its diamond shape, and the matte areas to either side of it began to look like incised pennants or small naval flags.

As for the fish otolith (Fig. 6.18), it may have been one of this young woman's personal possessions, kept as a kind of amulet or charm. This particular otolith comes from a drum or croaker (Family Sciaenidae) and was one of many otoliths imported from the Pacific Coast, along with the fish spines used for bloodletting in Formative Oaxaca (Flannery and Marcus 2005:96).

Our impression of Burial 67 is that it probably dates either to the late Guadalupe phase or the Guadalupe-Rosario transition. The small jar and *tecomate* strike us as very typical of the offer-

ings found with San José and Guadalupe phase women, and the three elegant jadeite beads from the area of her mouth suggest that she was a young woman of relatively high status.

Burial 68

The pit for Burial 68 was circular and fell entirely within Square S5E11 (Fig. 6.19). Its floor had been covered with a layer of sand and sprinkled with red pigment; two stones at the edge of the pit appeared to have been associated. The skeletal elements recovered were insufficient to determine the sex of the reburied individual, but Hodges (1989:87) found enough evidence to suggest an age of 18–25 years.

The offerings found with Burial 68 are unique. They consist

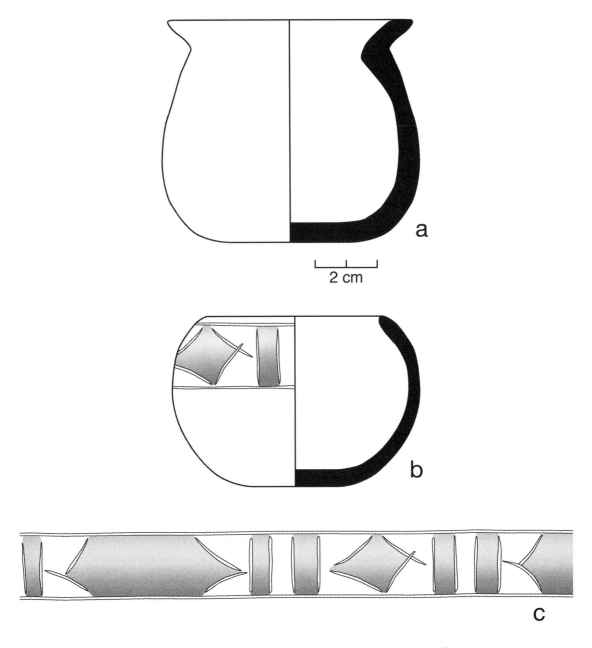

Figure 6.17. Vessels 1 and 2 from Burial 67. *a*, Vessel 1, a small Socorro Fine Gray jar. *b*, Vessel 2, a small Socorro Fine Gray *tecomate*, decorated with a band of fine-line incising and zoned toning. *c*, a rollout of the decorative band on Vessel 2, showing the way the Rosario phase "pennant" motif developed out of the Guadalupe phase "diamond-in-a-box" motif. Areas shown as white are matte; areas shown as gray are burnished.

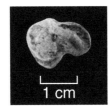

Figure 6.18. Otolith of drum (Family Sciaenidae) found with Burial 67.

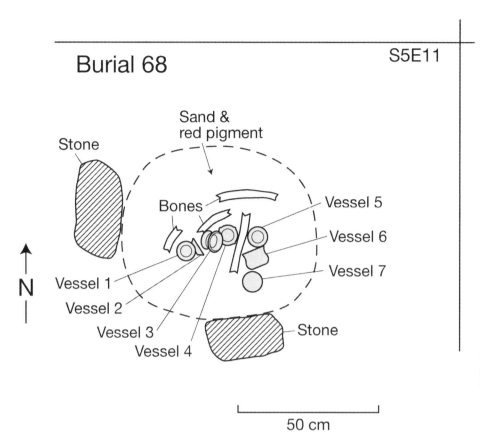

Figure 6.19. Plan view of Burial 68, a secondary burial intrusive into Stratigraphic Zone F.

Figure 6.20. Burial 68 at the moment of discovery, showing isolated human bones amid the cluster of miniature Socorro Fine Gray vessels. The arrow points north and is marked in centimeters and inches.

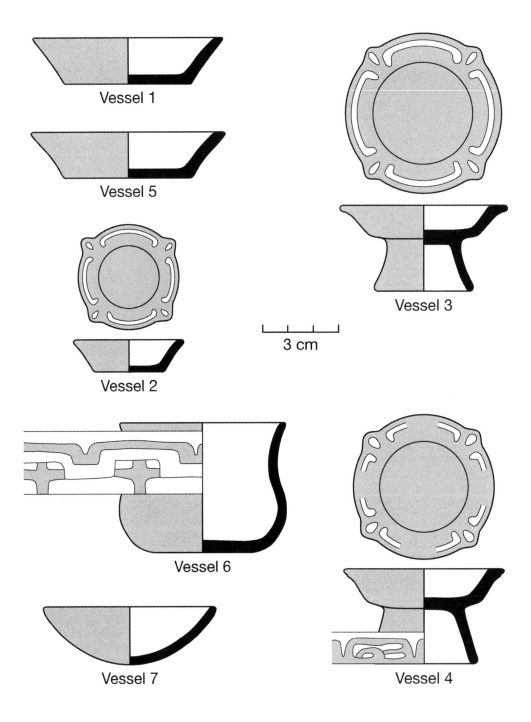

Figure 6.21. Vessels 1–7 from Burial 68, a miniature "table setting" of Socorro Fine Gray pottery. Vessels 2, 3, 4, and 6 display incising and negative or "resist" white decoration. Note the "crocodile's foot" motif on Vessel 4.

Burial 71

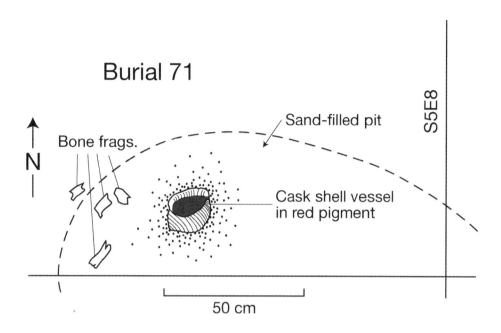

Figure 6.22. Plan view of Burial 71, a secondary burial intrusive into Stratigraphic Zone F. This burial was only partially excavated owing to time constraints.

of a set of seven miniature pottery vessels, all belonging to the Socorro Fine Gray type (Figs. 6.20, 6.21). Once we had removed and cleaned these vessels, we had the impression that we were looking at a miniature "table setting" for an individual of high status. We were used to seeing full table settings from Classic tombs at Monte Albán (Marcus and Flannery 1996:214), but had never expected to see a Middle Formative example.

Two of the vessels (Vessels 1 and 5) were flat-based bowls with outleaned walls; one (Vessel 7) was a hemispherical bowl. Vessel 2 was a flat-based bowl with Drennan's (1976) Rim Form 1 and Eccentricity 3 (see Chapter 7). Its rim had been decorated with a design motif similar to Element 80 of Plog (2009), done with fine-line incising and negative white.

Vessel 6 was a composite silhouette bowl, also decorated with fine-line incising and negative white. The design combines crosses or plus signs with an upside-down version of Plog's (2009) Design Element 31.

Finally we come to Vessels 3 and 4. Both were flat-based bowls featuring Drennan's Rim Form 9 (see Chapter 7) and a flaring pedestal base. The rims of these vessels were decorated with the same motif seen on Vessel 2, executed in fine-line incising and negative white. The pedestal base of Vessel 4 was

also decorated with the crocodile's foot motif, seen on Vessel 5 of Burial 66.

Chronologically, we would assign this miniature table setting to the beginning of the Rosario phase. Many of the vessel shapes would be at home in the Guadalupe phase, but the combination of fine-line incising and negative white decoration is considered a Rosario phase attribute (see Chapter 7). The fact that someone would create such an elegant miniature table setting for an individual 18–25 years of age suggests that he or she was born into a family of high rank.

Burial 71

It was not possible to expose Burial 71 in its entirety because it extended into several 2 × 2 m squares that we did not have time to excavate further. The pit had been partially filled with the same kind of sand seen in previous burials (Fig. 6.22). Unfortunately, our sample of human bone fragments was too meager to allow Hodges (1989) to determine the age and sex of the individual.

The only burial offering found in the area we excavated was a bowl carved from marine shell, resting in a deposit of red

Figure 6.23. Two views of a vessel made from the cask shell *Malea ringens*, found with Burial 71. The upper photo shows how the parietal wall of the aperture was cut away to make the shell into a bowl.

pigment. The species involved is the cask shell *Malea ringens*, sometimes referred to as "the grinning tun" (Keen 1958). This large gastropod frequents the Pacific Coast from Sonora to northern Peru. Figure 6.23 shows how the parietal wall of the aperture was trimmed away to convert the shell into a bowl.

Overview

The secondary burials intrusive into Zone F provided us with a number of insights. First, all the individuals whose age could be established were relatively young; they therefore cannot have been village elders. Second, we know of no late Guadalupe or early Rosario houses on Mound 1, so these young people lived (and presumably were buried) elsewhere in the village. Third, someone chose to exhume them and rebury them in the debris from a ritual building atop Mound 1; this was done not long before a Rosario temple (Structure 28) was built on the same spot.

Fourth, several of the burial pits were prepared with a layer of sand and a good deal of dry red pigment, and many of the burial offerings were unusual, even unique.

Since these individuals were presumably too young to have earned the right to such unusual offerings through community service, it is likely that they were entitled to them by birth. Perhaps by moving these highly ranked youths to a place where their remains would forever be covered by an important temple, their families sought to honor them (and by extension, their entire lineage). Some of the offerings found with these burials were broken in antiquity, perhaps when they were exhumed and moved. What we do not know is whether additional offerings were added at the time of their reburial.

It would seem that the stage was now set for the construction of the most important temple of the Rosario phase: Structure 28, which stood on a masonry platform known as Structure 19B (Chapter 8).

7 | An Introduction to the Rosario Phase

The Guadalupe phase was followed by the Rosario phase, which was a period of population increase. There were now between 70 and 85 communities in the Valley of Oaxaca, and our estimate for the valley's population is 3500–4000 persons (Marcus and Flannery 1996:124). Ten Rosario phase radiocarbon samples suggest a date of 700–500 b.c., and when those dates are calibrated, the phase spans the period 900 to 600 BC (Flannery and Marcus 2005).

We believe that during this period at least three rank societies were competing for political supremacy within the valley. The northernmost of those societies had San José Mogote in the Etla subvalley as its paramount chiefly center. It occupied the top position in a three-tiered administrative hierarchy; at least 18–23 villages and hamlets occupied the second and third tiers of the hierarchy. Our population estimate for this society was about 2000 people. Perhaps 1000 of them lived at San José Mogote itself, a sprawling village of 60–65 hectares.

The southernmost of the three rank societies lay in the Zimatlán subvalley, with its paramount center at San Martín Tilcajete. This polity had an estimated 700–1000 persons.

Finally, the easternmost of the valley's major rank societies occupied the Tlacolula subvalley, with its paramount center at Yegüih. This polity had an estimated 700–1000 persons, 200–500 of whom lived at Yegüih.

So intense was the political rivalry among these three rank societies that a nearly unoccupied 80 km^2 buffer zone had been created in the center of the valley. A gap of more than 9 km separated the southernmost of San José Mogote's satellite communities from the northernmost of Tilcajete's satellites (see Marcus and Flannery 1996: Fig. 128). Buffer zones of this type appear to be common in regions with competing chiefly societies. Hally (1999) describes comparable buffer zones between Late Mississippian rank societies in Georgia, and Kopytoff (1987) found similar zones separating indigenous African rank societies. Such buffer zones, Kopytoff adds, serve as convenient places for ambitious leaders to found new chiefly societies when the opportunity presents itself.

The Rank Society Headed by San José Mogote

During the Rosario phase, San José Mogote did everything it could to regain its position as the most powerful chiefly center in the Valley of Oaxaca. Among other things, it appears to have had the largest concentration of highly ranked families. Surface collections carried out at the site suggest that it featured at least seven areas of elite residence, as defined by the presence of sherds from elegant burnished gray vessels like those we found with Burials 66 and 68 (Chapter 6). These seven elite residential areas covered 33.7 ha and were occupied by an estimated 564 persons. When one combines these elite neighborhoods with the areas of known Rosario phase public buildings, the total "downtown" district of San José Mogote covered at least 42 ha, or about two-thirds of the village. It was in the outlying barrios and hamlets surrounding San José Mogote that most Rosario families of commoner status lived.

In the administrative hierarchy below San José Mogote were small villages such as Fábrica San José (an estimated 50–80 persons living in 10–16 households) and Tierras Largas (an estimated 50 persons living in 9–10 households). Fábrica San José was probably a second-tier village, under the control of an elite extended family with sociopolitical ties to San José Mogote.

One of the Rosario phase burials at Fábrica San José was a young woman in her teen years, her skull having been deformed as a sign of rank (Drennan 1976: Fig. 89). Her burial offerings included a large hollow figurine in fine gray pottery (perhaps representing an important ancestor); six more fine gray vessels; and an imported marine shell. She represents the richest Rosario phase burial found at Fábrica San José, and may have been a hypogamous bride sent from San José Mogote to marry a man from the highest-ranked family at Fábrica San José. This continues a pattern we saw in the Guadalupe phase (Chapter 5).

In contrast to Fábrica San José, whose ties to San José Mogote are believed to have kept the latter supplied with salt and travertine (Drennan 1976), the village of Barrio del Rosario Huitzo seems to have remained autonomous during the Rosario phase. Huitzo, located in the far north of the Etla subvalley, erected its own impressive public buildings. Structure 2 at Huitzo was a large temple platform with retaining walls of stone and adobe. Under one of its retaining walls we found an apparent sacrificial victim, a man 35–40 years of age, who lay crushed beneath the weight of the wall (Flannery and Marcus 2003d:62).

The residence of the most highly ranked Rosario phase family so far discovered lay in Stratigraphic Zone B of the Structure 19 overburden on Mound 1 at San José Mogote (Flannery and Marcus 2005:417–443). We have reconstructed the Zone B Residence as a rectangular building 14–15 m on a side. In its center was an open 8 × 8 m patio. Under the patio floor we found a two-chambered stone masonry tomb. This central patio was surrounded by adobe walled rooms, some of which had been destroyed by erosion. One room, on the west side, was a semi-subterranean storage room whose walls extended down more than a meter below those of the other rooms.

Although the individual buried in the central patio tomb had been removed in antiquity, several other burials were discovered in the Zone B Residence. One of these was a woman 25–35 years of age, whose cranial deformation resembled that of the aforementioned hypogamous woman at Fábrica San José. The

woman buried in the Zone B Residence at San José Mogote was accompanied by jadeite ornaments even more elegant than those found with Burial 67 (Chapter 6).

We have previously compared and contrasted the Zone B Residence at San José Mogote with the earliest known Zapotec royal palace, Structure 7 at San Martín Tilcajete (Flannery and Marcus 2005:419). Perhaps the most important difference is that the Zone B Residence was built with one uniform size of adobe brick throughout, while the Tilcajete palace was constructed with adobes of at least three different sizes, colors, and soil proveniences, suggesting that it had been built by corvée labor gangs (Spencer and Redmond 2001:221–222). Thus, in the dichotomy of chiefdoms and monarchies proposed by Sanders (1974), the Zone B Residence at San José Mogote looks more like a "chiefly residence," while Structure 7 of Tilcajete has the evidence of corvée labor necessary to qualify as a "royal palace."

Dating Buildings to the Rosario Phase

The Rosario phase was a crucial period in the sociopolitical history of the Valley of Oaxaca. It witnessed the kind of intense competition between rank societies that frequently sets the stage for the emergence of a pristine monarchy, or first-generation state (Flannery and Marcus 2012: Chapter 17). In the case of the Valley of Oaxaca, it seems to have been the centuries-long competition between San José Mogote and San Martín Tilcajete that led to the virtual abandonment of San José Mogote and the founding of Monte Albán (Flannery and Marcus 2003c). By moving to the more easily defended summit of a nearby 400 m mountain, the leaders of San José Mogote and at least 2000 of their followers had put themselves in a better position to wage war on their rivals.

To chronicle this period, it is necessary to be able to date Rosario public buildings with precision. We need to know when the typical one-room temple of Rosario society was replaced by the typical two-room temple of the Zapotec state. We need to know when chiefly residences gave way to royal palaces. We need to know when the leaders of Oaxaca society began to use hieroglyphic writing as part of their competitive strategy. We need to know when the longstanding 8° north of east orientation used for Early and Middle Formative public buildings gave way to the true east-west or north-south orientation used by the later Zapotec state.

Thanks to the work of Bernal (1946) and Caso, Bernal, and Acosta (1967), we know exactly what Monte Albán Ia ceramics—the pottery used by the earliest residents of that city—look like. In this chapter, we focus on the ceramics of the Rosario phase, including the attributes used to date Structures 19, 28, 14, 37, and 31 of San José Mogote (Chapter 8).

The Rosario phase takes its name from the type site of Barrio del Rosario Huitzo (Flannery and Marcus 2003d). In the stratigraphy of that site, public buildings of the Guadalupe phase gave way to public buildings of the Rosario phase, and these in turn gave way to buildings with many of the pottery types of Monte

Albán Ia. Unfortunately, public buildings are not the ideal venue for defining ceramic phases; their fill often features basketloads of earth containing redeposited sherds from earlier periods. That fact makes it difficult to tell exactly when a particular pottery type disappears from the record because fragments of it keep showing up in the fill of later buildings.

Despite these problems, we learned several facts about Rosario phase pottery during our work at Huitzo. For one thing, Socorro Fine Gray replaced Atoyac Yellow-white as the dominant bowl ware. Josefina Fine Gray, while less abundant than in the Guadalupe phase, was also present in Rosario. While composite silhouette bowls in graywares continued to be popular, there was an explosion of bowls with flat bases and outleaned or outcurved walls.

Several decorative attributes of gray bowls characterized the Rosario phase. One of the most distinctive of these was a form of "negative" or "resist" decoration that appeared white against the natural gray of the sherd. Our project ceramicist, William O. Payne, concluded that this negative white effect was achieved by coating certain areas of the vessel with resin (or even a thin layer of clay that could be flaked off after firing). In the oxygen-deprived atmosphere of a reducing kiln, this coating prevented the surface of the vessel from turning its usual gray color.

A second Rosario attribute, originally defined on the Middle Formative pottery of the Tehuacán Valley, was "zoned toning" (MacNeish, Peterson, and Flannery 1970). This attribute resembles the more widespread technique of pattern burnishing, in which the decoration relies on the contrast between matte and burnished areas of the vessel. In the case of zoned toning, however, the matte and burnished areas are separated into zones by incised lines.

A third Rosario attribute was the use of the incised "pennant motif," done either in negative white, zoned toning, or both. We have already pointed out in Chapter 6 that the Rosario phase pennant motif evolved out of the Guadalupe phase "diamond-in-a-box" motif (see Fig. 6.17).

In the 1970s, we showed pottery with all these attributes to the late Ignacio Bernal, whose master's thesis pioneered the subdivision of the Monte Albán I period into phases Ia, Ib, and Ic (Bernal 1946). Bernal told us emphatically that he had seen no negative white, zoned toning, or pennant incising on Monte Albán I grayware. To be sure, he did see other sherds in our Rosario collections that reminded him of Monte Albán Ia. In the end, it became clear to us, and to him, that the highly burnished *gris* wares of Monte Albán I must have evolved out of Socorro Fine Gray pottery of the Rosario phase.

When Drennan (1976) was excavating at Fábrica San José, only 5 km east of San José Mogote, he found houses and features dating to the Guadalupe and Rosario phases. Like San José Mogote, Fábrica San José was abandoned at the end of the Rosario phase. Fortunately, Caso, Bernal, and Acosta's (1967) illustrations of Monte Albán I pottery are comprehensive enough so that Drennan could see what the similarities and differences between Rosario and Monte Albán I ceramics were.

Drennan decided to design a multidimensional scaling program that would place all of the houses at Fábrica San José in chronological order and provide quantitative criteria for the definition of each Middle Formative phase. As of 2014, Drennan's study is still the most useful reference work for anyone attempting to date buildings from the Middle Formative era of the Etla subvalley. We will review some of his most important findings here.

During the Rosario phase, flat-based bowls with outleaned or outcurved walls were the most common vessels in Socorro Fine Gray. Drennan identified a series of rim forms for these bowls, the most common twelve of which are shown in Figure 7.1. Four of these rim forms (numbers 6, 7, 8, and 12) did not last beyond the Rosario phase; the other eight lasted into Monte Albán Ia.

Drennan also identified a number of eccentricities on the rims of these bowls, seven of which are shown in Figure 7.2. Five of these eccentricities (numbers 2, 3, 4, 6, and 7) did not last beyond the Rosario phase; the other two lasted into Monte Albán Ia.

Drennan also identified nine incised motifs (a–i) on the rims of Socorro Fine Gray bowls at Fábrica San José (see Figs. 7.3 and 7.4). His pennant and crescent motifs (c, d, and e) did not last beyond the Rosario phase, and only the most elaborate versions of his scallop motif (a, b) lasted into Monte Albán Ia. Of his "line-break" motifs (g, h, and i), many were present already in the San José and Guadalupe phases; only the most elaborate versions lasted into Monte Albán Ia. It was Drennan's hachure motif (f) that came to the fore in Monte Albán Ia—for example, on the vessels defined by Caso, Bernal, and Acosta (hereafter CBA) as belonging to Type G16.

Parenthetically, we should add that Drennan's list of motifs on Socorro Fine Gray bowls at Fábrica San José is somewhat shorter than the motif inventory at San José Mogote. Such a difference is to be expected when a 65 ha chiefly center is compared with a 3 ha satellite community. Simply put, we recovered Socorro Fine Gray vessels at San José Mogote that have never been found at Fábrica San José, and still others whose frequency at the chiefly center were almost certainly higher than at any of its second-tier villages.

Figure 7.5 illustrates two already mentioned attributes of the Rosario phase: zoned toning and negative (or resist) white decoration. Figure 7.5*b* is a rim sherd from a composite silhouette bowl, a vessel found in both the Guadalupe and Rosario phases (see Fig. 7.6). In Figure 7.7 we show yet another Socorro Fine Gray composite silhouette bowl, one that combines both negative white decoration and pattern burnishing. This diagnostically Rosario phase vessel is one that helped us to date Structure 19 at San José Mogote (Chapter 8).

Another item that helped us to distinguish the Rosario phase from Monte Albán Ia was the Suchilquitongo tripod dish, a vessel named for a site near Huitzo where it was particularly abundant (Fig. 7.8). During the Rosario phase, these dishes were undecorated and appeared in two utilitarian wares, Lupita Heavy Plain and Guadalupe Burnished Brown. Beginning in Monte Albán Ia, potters began decorating these dishes either with red paint

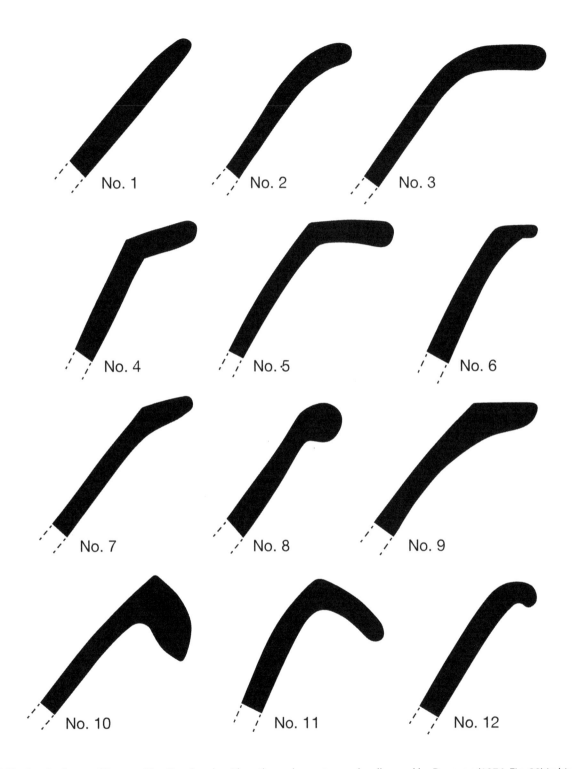

Figure 7.1. Twelve rim forms of Socorro Fine Gray bowls with outleaned or outcurved walls, used by Drennan (1976: Fig. 28) in his multidimensional scaling. Numbers 6, 7, 8, and 12 did not last beyond the Rosario phase. The other eight rim forms lasted into Monte Albán Ia.

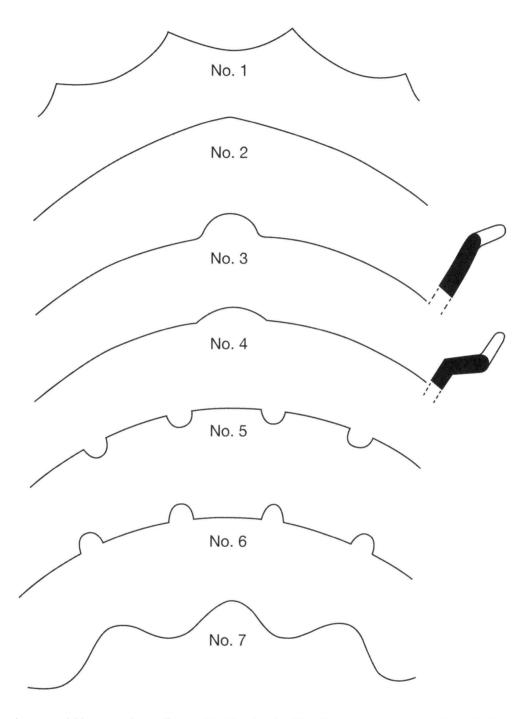

Figure 7.2. Seven rim eccentricities appearing on Socorro Fine Gray bowls with outleaned or outcurved walls, used by Drennan (1976: Fig. 29) in his multidimensional scaling. Numbers 2, 3, 4, 6, and 7 did not last beyond the Rosario phase; numbers 1 and 5 continued into Monte Albán Ia.

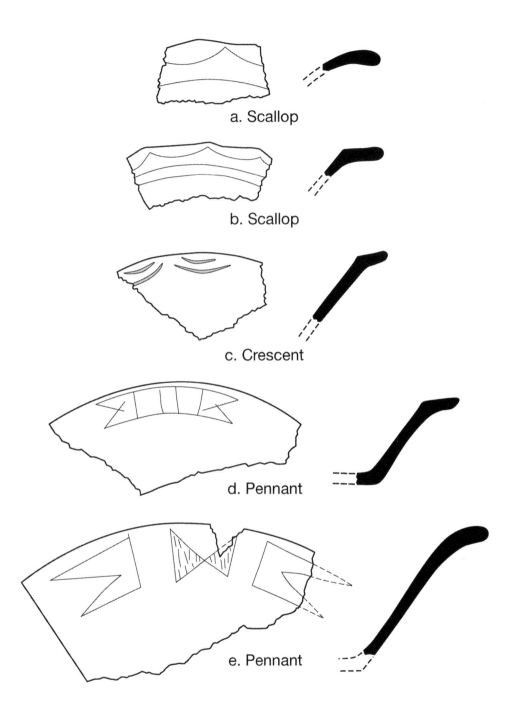

Figure 7.3. Incised Motifs a–e from the rims of Socorro Fine Gray bowls with outleaned walls (redrawn from Drennan 1976: Fig. 32). Motifs c, d, and e did not last beyond the Rosario phase.

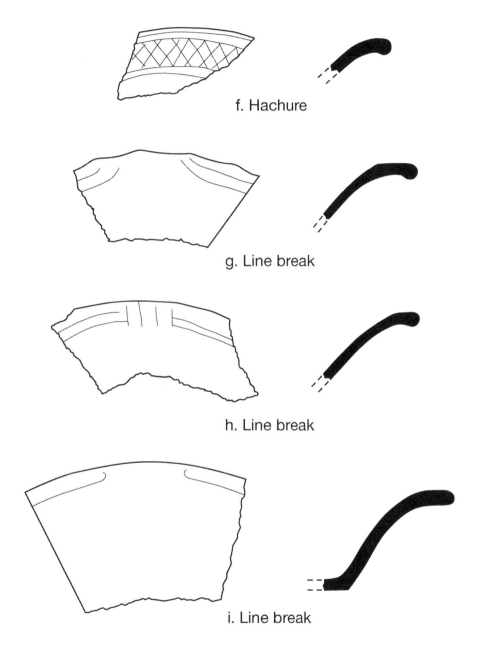

f. Hachure

g. Line break

h. Line break

i. Line break

Figure 7.4. Incised Motifs f–i from the rims of Socorro Fine Gray bowls with outleaned or outcurved walls (redrawn from Drennan 1976: Fig. 32). Motif f appeared during the Guadalupe phase, fell out of favor in the Rosario phase, and reappeared in Monte Albán Ia.

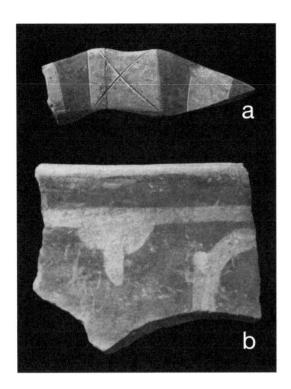

Figure 7.5. Two attributes of Socorro Fine Gray pottery, both typical of the Rosario phase. *a*, zoned toning. On this incised bowl rim, burnished zones appear dark gray; zones left matte appear light gray. *b*, negative (resist) white decoration. On this unincised bowl, the white motifs were produced by covering certain areas with clay or resin during firing.

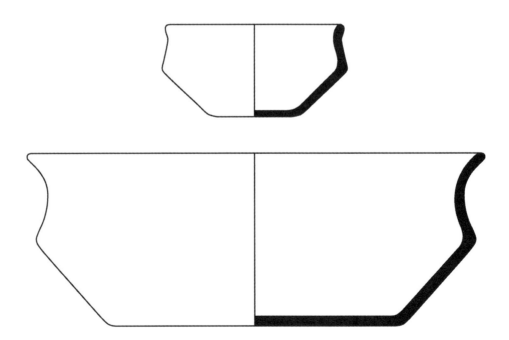

Figure 7.6. Composite silhouette bowls of the Rosario phase (redrawn from Drennan 1976: Fig. 14).

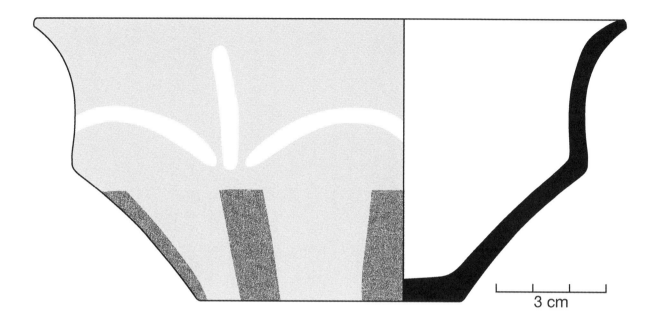

Figure 7.7. A Socorro Fine Gray composite silhouette bowl displaying two Rosario phase attributes. Above the carination it has a crescent and vertical line motif in negative white. Below the carination it has pattern burnishing in the form of alternating bands of burnished (lighter gray) and matte (darker gray) surfaces. This bowl, reconstructed from roughly 50 percent of the vessel, was found in the fill between Structures 19 and 19A (see Chapter 8).

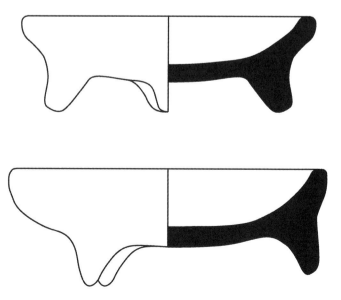

Figure 7.8. Suchilquitongo tripod dishes (redrawn from Drennan 1976: Fig. 16). Undecorated versions of these dishes were present in the Rosario phase. During Monte Albán Ia, they were decorated with red paint or fillet bands.

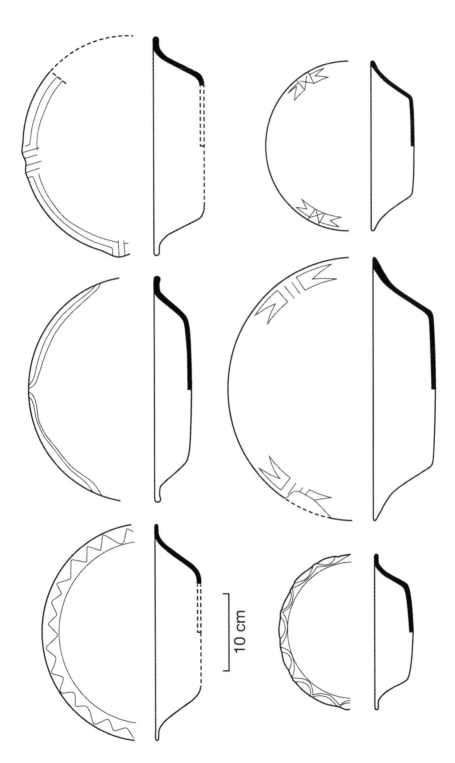

10 cm

Figure 7.9. Six Socorro Fine Gray bowls from Feature 36 at Tierras Largas (redrawn from Winter 1976: Fig. 3).

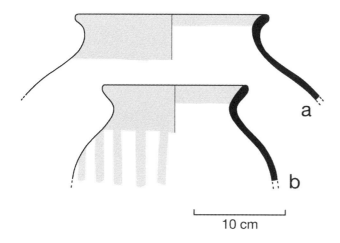

10 cm

Figure 7.10. Two Fidencio Coarse jars from Feature 36 at Tierras Largas. *b* displays the finger-width stripes of weak red paint characteristic of the Guadalupe and Rosario phases. *a* has weak red wash on the rim, an attribute of the Rosario phase that endures into Monte Albán Ia. There it appears on jars of CBA Type C2. (Redrawn from Winter 1976: Fig. 4.)

or with an appliqué fillet band. Often a garnet red band at the rim identifies these vessels as belonging to the CBA Type C4. Drennan found that undecorated Suchilquitongo dishes did not last into Monte Albán Ia; the *crema* type called C4, on the other hand, is diagnostic of Period Ia (see Chapter 10).

The Rosario Phase at Tierras Largas

Tierras Largas was a 3 ha hamlet some 10 km south of San José Mogote; it probably occupied the third tier in the hierarchy below San José Mogote. During the Rosario phase, residences at Tierras Largas appear to have been simple, one-room wattle-and-daub houses, flanked by dooryards with bell-shaped storage pits (Winter 1972). When they had ceased to be useful as storage features, many of the bell-shaped pits at Tierras Largas became convenient receptacles for trash from the nearest house. This happened both to Feature 36 in Excavation Square 2186 and to Feature 130 in Excavation Squares 2984 and 3037. So many large sherds and reconstructable vessels of the Rosario phase were present in Features 36 and 130 that Winter (1976) decided to publish them as a snapshot of the Rosario phase ceramics at Tierras Largas.

To be sure, no trash-filled pit constitutes a primary deposit. In addition to its Rosario phase vessels, Feature 36 at Tierras Largas contained redeposited sherds from earlier periods, including such types as Atoyac Yellow-white, Leandro Gray, and Xochiltepec White. Nor could any trash pit be seen as containing the whole spectrum of Rosario phase vessels. Feature 36 gives us only a glimpse of the Rosario phase pottery from a third-tier hamlet.

In Figure 7.9 we see six Socorro Fine Gray bowls from Feature 36. All have flat bases and outcurved walls. Drennan's Rim Forms 2, 3, and 9 are recognizable. The incised designs on the rims include pennants, line breaks, and scallops.

Figure 7.10 shows two Fidencio Coarse jars from Feature 36. One displays the finger-width stripes of weak red paint characteristic of the Guadalupe and Rosario phases. The other has a weak red wash on the rim; this is an attribute of the Rosario phase that lasted into Monte Albán Ia, where it would be found on CBA Type C2.

Winter (1976) correctly notes that during the San José phase, Fidencio Coarse was most often made from brown clay. During the Guadalupe phase, it could be made either from brown clay or pale buff (*crema*) clay. By the Rosario phase, this type was most often made from the same pale buff clay later used for the

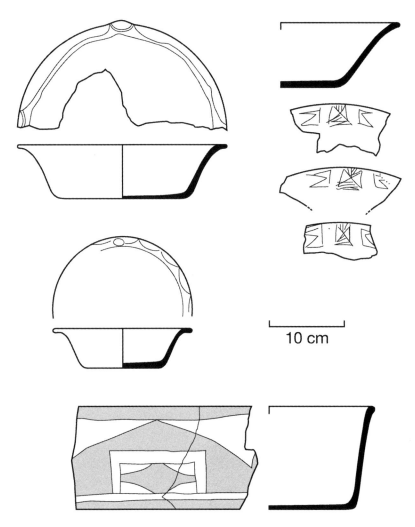

10 cm

Figure 7.11. Six Socorro Fine Gray vessels from Feature 130 at Tierras Largas (redrawn from Winter 1976: Fig. 6).

crema wares of Monte Albán Ia. To put it another way, Fidencio Coarse of the Rosario phase evolved gradually into the Monte Albán Ia pottery type known as C2. Such "morphing" of Rosario phase types into CBA types can make it difficult to distinguish Rosario and Monte Albán Ia using surface-collected sherds alone (see Chapter 11).

Let us now look at Feature 130, the second bell-shaped pit from Tierras Largas. Although dominated by Rosario phase pottery, this feature also contained redeposited sherds of the Tierras Largas, San José, and Guadalupe phases. Figure 7.11 shows six Socorro Fine Gray vessels from Feature 130. Among the flat-based, outcurved-rim bowls we see Drennan's Rim Forms 2 and 3; one example of Drennan's Eccentricity 3; one incised scallop design; and three examples of Drennan's Motif e pennant. We also see a cylindrical bowl with the "diamond-in-a-box" motif done in zoned toning.

Figure 7.12 illustrates two charcoal braziers from Feature 130. One specimen has a band of red wash at the rim, identifying it as Fidencio Coarse. The undecorated brazier below it is classified by Winter as Lupita Heavy Plain.

Finally, Winter gives us his opinion on which incised motifs on burnished grayware were characteristic of the Rosario phase, and which did not appear until Monte Albán Ia. While we are happy to have Winter's assessment, it is also clear that Tierras Largas—a third-tier Rosario phase hamlet—had an impoverished repertoire of motifs when compared to either San José Mogote or Fábrica San José.

Figure 7.13 illustrates some of the motifs that Winter assigns to Monte Albán Ia. We agree with Winter that his Motifs e, f, and g were typical of Monte Albán Ia; however, his Motifs a, b, c, and d were all used during earlier periods. Based on our much larger sample of pottery from San José Mogote, Motifs a and

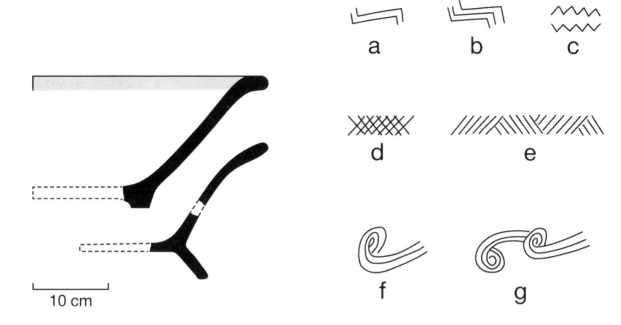

Figure 7.12. Charcoal braziers from Feature 130 at Tierras Largas (redrawn from Winter 1976: Fig. 7).

Figure 7.13. Incised motifs on Middle Formative pottery in Oaxaca. While *a–d* do occur on Monte Albán Ia pottery, all those motifs existed in earlier periods. *e–g* were all popular during Monte Albán Ia (redrawn from Winter 1976: Fig. 8).

b can be found on Leandro Gray pottery made during the San José phase, and Motifs c and d can be found on Atoyac Yellow-white pottery made during the Guadalupe phase (Flannery and Marcus 1994:150–152). Our point is that some of these motifs had a long history in Oaxaca, often appearing, then vanishing, then later reappearing. Thus it would be wiser for us to base our chronologies on full pottery assemblages rather than on isolated sherds or motifs.

Dating Rosario Buildings

There are useful Rosario phase collections from at least four sites in the Etla subvalley: San José Mogote, Barrio del Rosario Huitzo, Fábrica San José, and Tierras Largas. San José Mogote has the largest collection, the greatest variety, and the largest

number of unique pieces, many of them made for elite burials or offerings. Thanks to Drennan, however, it is his Fábrica San José monograph that provides us with the most rigorous program for placing collections of rim forms, eccentricities, and design motifs in chronological order. Tierras Largas confirms most of Drennan's observations, but lacks the variety of vessels and attributes seen in the larger collections from San José Mogote and Fábrica San José.

In our dating of Rosario phase buildings and monuments, which follows, we list every diagnostic sherd. It should be clear that we have been careful, to the point of meticulousness, in using all the Rosario ceramic attributes on which Drennan (1976), Winter (1976), and Flannery and Marcus (2005) agree. Using those criteria, the following archaeological units at San José Mogote date to the Rosario phase:

1. Stratigraphic Zones B, C, D, and E of the Structure 19 overburden on Mound 1.
2. Structures 19, 19A, and 19B.
3. Structure 28.
4. The initial building stage of Structure 14 on Mound 1.
5. Structure 37.
6. Monument 3 in the corridor between Structures 14 and 19.
7. Structure 31.

Why have we been so painstaking in our dating of every Rosario building? Because we need to know exactly what the social organization, religion, and political ideology of the Valley of Oaxaca were during the last two centuries leading up to the founding of Monte Albán. Only then can we identify the changes leading to the first Zapotec state.

In none of the archaeological units listed above did we find so much as a single sherd of Monte Albán Ia (or later) pottery.

(The reader who wants to see what unequivocal Monte Albán Ia pottery looks like need only flip the pages ahead to Chapter 10.) If Household Units R-1 and R-2 at Fábrica San José and Features 36 and 130 at Tierras Largas belong to the Rosario phase, then so do all the stratigraphic zones, structures, and monuments listed above, because at San José Mogote we relied on exactly the same ceramic attributes that Drennan and Winter did.

Because we were so careful in our dating of Rosario buildings and features, we are able to propose the following scenario: the stone masonry, adobe masonry, burnished gray pottery, building orientation, tomb construction, and hieroglyphic writing of the late Rosario phase provided the template for all those same activities during Monte Albán Ia. We also propose that the bulk of Monte Albán's founders came from the Etla subvalley, whose Rosario phase ceramic diagnostics provide better precursors for Monte Albán Ia pottery than do the diagnostics of the Tlacolula or Zimatlán subvalleys.

8 | The Conversion of Mound 1 into a Rosario Phase Acropolis

Prior to 700 b.c., all the most impressive temples at San José Mogote had been built at the level of the village itself. Test pits made in the cornfields east of our Area C stratigraphic profile (Flannery and Marcus 2005) suggest that this pattern continued into the early Rosario phase. Then, sometime early in the seventh century b.c., the leaders of San José Mogote decided to build their biggest temple ever on the summit of Mound 1. There it would tower 12–13 m above the rest of the village, visible from a distance of several kilometers.

The spot chosen for this temple had a long history of ritual use. During the San José phase it had been the scene of a likely men's house (Chapter 4). During the Middle Formative, this same area was considered appropriate for the secondary burials of elite youths from the late Guadalupe and early Rosario phases (Chapter 6).

The first stage of Rosario construction on Mound 1 was the building of Structure 19B, the stone masonry platform on which the temple would stand. Structure 19B measured 17 m on a side and was oriented 8° north of east. The stones used were a mixture of volcanic tuff bedrock and large limestone blocks, the latter having been transported across the Atoyac River from the quarries of Rancho Matadamas. These quarries had long served

the area as a source of limestone and chalcedony (Whalen 2009: Figs. 7.3, 7.4).

The second stage of construction was the building of Structure 28, the adobe and wattle-and-daub temple itself. This temple shared the 8° north of east orientation of the Structure 19B platform beneath it.

It appears that over time, the walls of Structure 19B began to buckle under the weight of Structure 28. To keep them from collapsing, San José Mogote's architects surrounded Structure 19B with a still larger platform whose outer walls were buttressed with sloping piles of stones. This larger building, which we have designated Structure 19A, measured 25.5 m east-west and 20 m north-south.

Structure 19A's orientation was true east-west, which represented a change in building orientation. What is most significant about this change is that it represents the abandonment of an orientation used for all public buildings in Oaxaca since at least 1500 b.c., in favor of a new orientation that would now be used for all subsequent public construction. We do not know whether this change was an arbitrary choice or was necessitated by a natural phenomenon, such as an actual shift in the point where the sun rose on a specific day of the year.

Figure 8.1. Aerial oblique photo of Mound 1 at San José Mogote, showing the location of Structures 14, 19, 21 and 22, as well as House 13. Areas A (to the east) and C (to the west) are also visible. (Photograph courtesy of Tonny Zwollo.)

Figure 8.2. Isaac Jiménez stands on the southeast corner of Structure 19, facing north. To the right of him is the huge mound of overburden that covered Structure 19 when it was first discovered.

Unfortunately, Structure 19A did not provide a final solution to the problem of keeping the walls of the platform upright. It eventually became necessary to create a still larger version of the same building, measuring 28.5 m east-west and 21.7 m north-south. This final version of the building—the first version we discovered, and hence the first one given a number—has been designated Structure 19. Its construction involved much larger and heavier stones than before, some of them set vertically and others horizontally. The sherds in the fill, as well as a burnt post used for a radiocarbon sample, date this final stage of the platform to the second half of the Rosario phase.

Excavation of the Structure 19 Overburden

To prepare for our description of the various construction stages of Structure 19, the reader should refer to Figure 8.1. This aerial photograph shows the location of Structure 19 relative to other landmarks on Mound 1.

Figure 8.2 shows Structure 19 as it looked when it was first discovered. At that time, only its final stage was visible because the platform was covered with a huge mound of overburden left by the collapsed remains of later buildings. Figure 8.3 shows the grid of 2 × 2 m squares that we created above the final stage of the building and its overburden.

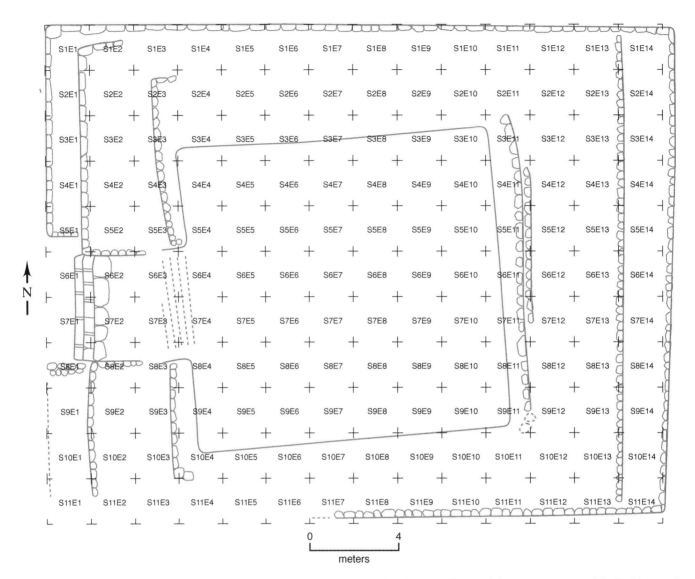

Figure 8.3. The grid of 2 x 2 m squares established above Structure 19, providing horizontal control during excavation of the building and its overburden.

We found an official geodesic benchmark on the highest point of the Structure 19 overburden when we arrived. This benchmark became the northwest corner of Square S6E9 of our grid, and we used it as the datum point from which we established the depths and horizontal locations of all the buildings and features we encountered. Figure 8.4 shows our crew breaking ground on the overburden by excavating the first of the 2 × 2 m squares.

Our strategy for excavating the Structure 19 overburden was modeled on the excavation of Tepe Gawra, Iraq, by E. A. Speiser of the University of Pennsylvania (Speiser 1935). Early on, Speiser realized that he did not have to settle for the usual narrow step trench. The conical summit of Tepe Gawra was small enough so that each stratigraphic level could be excavated in its entirety. One half of each stratum could be excavated first, leaving a "witness section." Once this long cross-section had been drawn, the second half of the stratum could be excavated.

We decided to excavate the southern half of the Structure 19 overburden first, allowing the cross-section left by the removal of Squares S6E1–S6E14 to become our "witness section" (Figs. 8.5–8.7). Once this section had been drawn, the northern half of the overburden could be excavated. In the course of excavating down from the geodesic benchmark we encountered seven superimposed strata, as follows:

Zone A was the uppermost stratum. In the central squares of

Figure 8.4. Work beginning on the first 2 x 2 m squares laid out on the mound of overburden above Structure 19. The crew is exposing Stratigraphic Zone A. (View from the northeast.)

the grid, this stratum was thick enough to be divided into two layers, A1 and A2. Zone A1 dated to Monte Albán II and contained the partial remains of Structure 29 (Chapter 14). Zone A2 dated to Monte Albán Ia and contained the remains of Structures 23 and 24, two small ritual buildings (Chapter 10). Outside the grid's central squares, Zone A was too thin to be subdivided.

Zone B dated to the Rosario phase and contained the remains of an elite residence. This residence and its diagnostic ceramics have been described in Flannery and Marcus 2005:417–443.

Zone C dated to the Rosario phase and contained the remains of two buildings: Structure 27, a residence (Flannery and Marcus 2005:411–417) and Structure 31, a circular "performance platform" (Chapter 9).

Zone D dated to the Rosario phase, and its major component was the earthen fill of the Structure 28 temple (see below).

Zone E dated to the Rosario phase, and its major component was the earthen fill from all three building stages of the Structure 19 platform (19B, 19A, and 19).

Zone F dated to the San José phase and contained the likely remains of a lime-plastered, wattle-and-daub men's house (Chapter 4).

Sterile soil was reached at depths varying from 4.5 m to 4.8 m below the geodesic benchmark. It consisted of the type of greenish-gray clay that forms above decomposing ignimbrite bedrock.

The Excavation of Structure 19's Three Construction Stages

As mentioned above, Structure 19 was built in three stages: Structure 19B (the oldest), Structure 19A (the second), and Structure 19 (the third and final stage). Figure 8.8 shows the relationship of all three building stages to each other and to Structure 28. Two photographs show the surviving walls from all three building stages: Figure 8.9 covers the west end of the building, and Figure 8.10 covers the east end.

The Structure 19 Staircase

The main staircase for Structure 19 was built into its west wall. The earliest version of the staircase (19B) had been too affected by later remodeling to allow us to consolidate it. The Structure 19A staircase, however, was still 50 percent intact, and can be seen in Figure 8.11. Its treads and risers were composed of Matadamas limestone, interdigitated with smaller volcanic tuff stones.

The Rosario phase architects were evidently so satisfied with this staircase that they decided not to replace it when Structure 19 was built. Instead, they interrupted the west wall of Structure 19 as it neared the old staircase, then gave the wall a 90° angle so that it turned back into the west wall of Structure 19A. Through

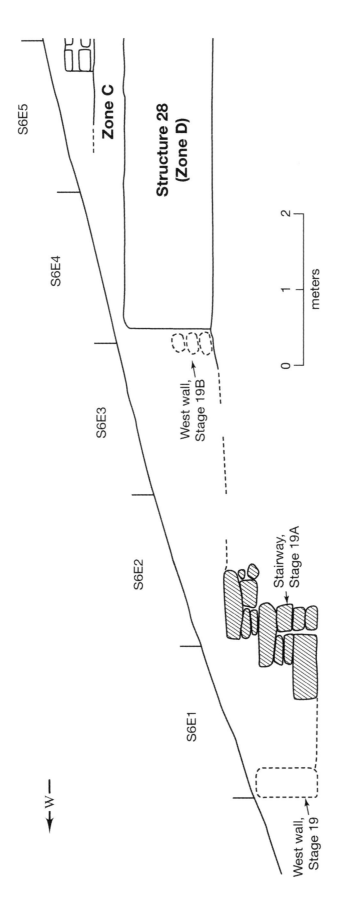

Figure 8.5. West-to-east cross-section of Structure 19 and its overburden, Part 1 of 3. Objects drawn with a solid line appeared in the S6 row of squares. Objects drawn with a dashed line appeared in adjacent squares, and have been added just to show their position relative to the solid-line objects.

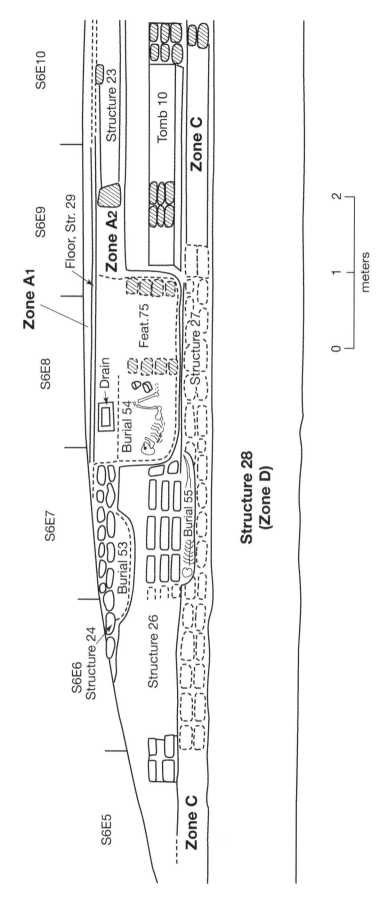

Figure 8.6. West-to-east cross-section of Structure 19 and its overburden, Part 2 of 3. Objects drawn with a dashed line were in squares adjacent to the S6 row.

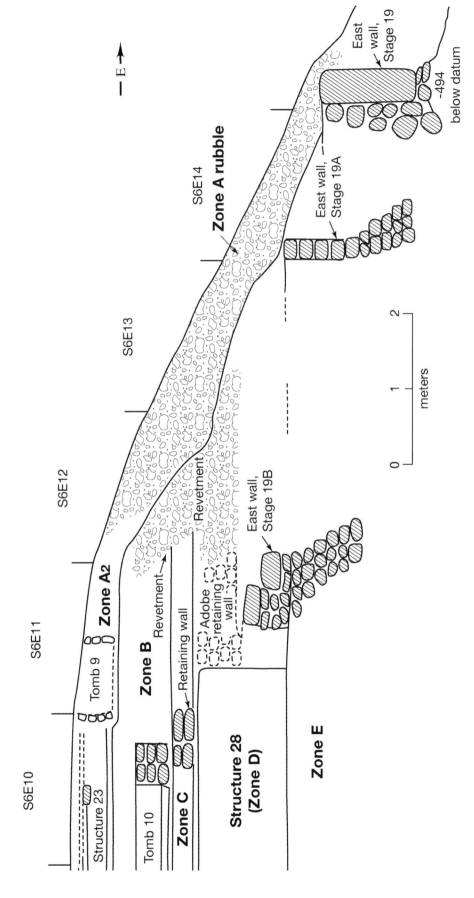

Figure 8.7. West-to-east cross-section of Structure 19 and its overburden, Part 3 of 3. Objects drawn with a dashed line were in squares adjacent to the S6 row.

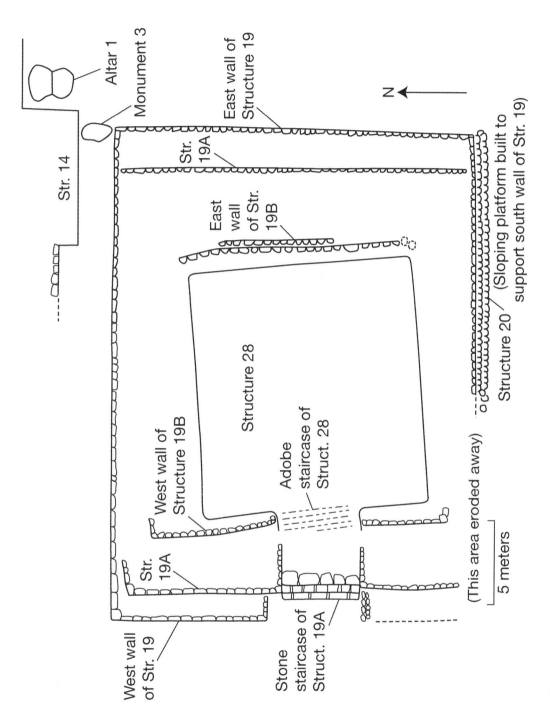

Figure 8.8. Plan view of Structure 19 showing its earlier stages, Structures 19A and 19B. Structure 19B was originally built to support Structure 28, a Rosario phase temple with an adobe staircase. Nearby structures are discussed in the text.

Figure 8.9. A view of Structure 19 from the northwest, showing the west side after its 19, 19A, and 19B stages had been partially exposed. Also shown is the flagstone pavement later added to brace the north wall.

Figure 8.10. The east walls of Structures 19, 19A, and 19B as seen from the north. The workman with the ranging pole stands beside Structure 28, the adobe substructure for a Rosario phase temple.

Figure 8.11. Details of the staircase and west wall of Structures 19 and 19A. In *a*, Isaac Jiménez stands at the northern limit of the stone masonry staircase on the west side of Structure 19A. The west wall of Structure 19 lies to his right (extreme left of the photo). In *b*, we see how the architects of Structure 19 made a right angle in its west wall, directing it back into the wall of Structure 19A so that they could continue to use the pre-existing staircase.

this architectural device, they allowed the Structure 19A staircase to continue to serve even after Structure 19 had been built (see Figs. 8.8, 8.11*b*).

The South Wall of Structure 19 and the "Structure 20" Fieldstone Platform

Before excavating Structure 19, we decided to expose its perimeter completely. This strategy allowed us to consolidate all four walls of Structure 19 with cement, preventing its collapse while we explored its earlier construction stages.

It appeared to us that the most vulnerable part of Structure 19 was its south wall, which had already suffered from erosion. In Figure 8.12 one can see our workmen cleaning the orthostats at the base of that wall. These orthostats were nonuniform and the irregular spaces between them had been filled with smaller stones, stacked one upon another like the rungs of a ladder.

Below the orthostats, we came upon a sloping fieldstone platform that projected out farther to the south. As can be seen in Figure 8.13, the construction style of this fieldstone platform could not have been more different from that of the orthostatic wall above it. It reminded us of the fieldstone foundations of Structure 8, the Guadalupe phase temple platform we had discovered in Area C (Chapter 5).

Initially, we saw two possibilities for this fieldstone structure: it could be the wall of an earlier building, or it could simply be

a rough platform created to support the weight of Structure 19's orthostats. We tentatively labeled it Structure 20 and continued to investigate it. Eventually we decided that it had been created simply so that the south wall of Structure 19 would have a solid foundation to rest upon.

In the course of our work along the south wall, we saved all the sherds that had been used as chinking among the wall stones. Fourteen of these sherds were rims from Socorro Fine Gray outleaned/outcurved-wall bowls. When coded in Drennan's system (see Chapter 7), their attributes were as follows:

Rim Form 2, no decoration: 3
Rim Form 2, scallop in negative white: 2
Rim Form 2, Eccentricity 3, no decoration: 1
Rim Form 3, no decoration: 2
Rim Form 4, fineline incised pennant and negative white: 1
Rim Form 5, horizontal band in zoned toning: 2
Rim Form 5, horizontal lines in negative white: 1
Rim Form 5, fine horizontal incised lines and negative white: 1
Rim Form 9, scallop in negative white: 1

Two additional diagnostic sherds, both belonging to the Rosario phase (Fig. 8.14), were found in the foundations of the south wall.

Dating the Fill of Structure 19

Once the perimeter of Structure 19 had been consolidated

Figure 8.12. Excavating the south wall of Structure 19. In *a*, workmen have cleaned the orthostats at the base of the wall and are beginning to expose Structure 20, the sloping platform that served as footing for the orthostats. In *b*, workmen clean the southeast corner of Structure 19. In this view, one can see how the gaps between the orthostats were filled with ladder-like stacks of smaller stones, placed one above another.

with cement, we began removing the fill added between Structures 19A and 19. Figures 8.15 and 8.16 show two stages in the removal of this fill, and Figure 8.17 presents a cross-section of the area. In addition to recovering hundreds of sherds from this fill, we found charcoal from a burned construction post in Square S2E14. Once we felt that we had an adequate sample of sherds to date the fill, we backfilled the area. We included modern soft drink bottles in our backfill so that any future archaeologists would know that the area had been excavated.

Ceramics from the Fill between Structures 19A and 19

Some 79 of the sherds found in the fill between Structures 19A and 19 were diagnostics. They were as follows:

ROSARIO PHASE DIAGNOSTICS

rims of Socorro Fine Gray outleaned/outcurved-wall bowls: 34

rims of Socorro Fine Gray composite silhouette bowls: 9 (4 plain; 2 incising only; 1 zoned toning only; 1 negative white only; 1 zoned toning and negative white)

rim of Socorro Fine Gray beaker: 1

rims of Socorro Fine Gray hemispherical bowls: 2

rims of Guadalupe Burnished Brown bowls: 8

fragment of Lupita Heavy Plain potstand/brazier: 1

rim of Fidencio Coarse jar: 1

rim of Fidencio Coarse *tecomate*: 1

DIAGNOSTICS OF THE GUADALUPE PHASE OR EARLIER PERIODS

rims of Josefina Fine Gray outleaned-wall bowls: 3

rims of Josefina Fine Gray composite silhouette bowls: 2

fragment of Josefina Fine Gray squash effigy: 1

rims of Atoyac Yellow-white bowls: 3

rims of Atoyac Yellow-white cylinders: 2

rim of Atoyac Yellow-white jar: 1

rim of Leandro Gray bowl with bolstered rim: 1

rim of Leandro Gray *tecomate*, excised: 1

fragments of Coatepec White: 2

fragments of Xochiltepec White: 2

rims of Avelina Red-on-buff hemispherical bowls: 2

rims of hemispherical bowls, Matadamas Orange inside, Atoyac Yellow-white outside: 2

We coded all 34 rims of Socorro Fine Gray outleaned/outcurved-wall bowls in Drennan's system. The attributes were as follows:

Figure 8.13. The south wall of Structure 19, looking east. In the foreground a *media cuchara*, or mason's assistant, cleans between the stones of Structure 20. In the background, a mason consolidates the Structure 19 wall with cement.

Rim Form 1, no decoration: 1

Rim Form 2, no decoration: 4

Rim Form 2, fineline incised pennant: 1

Rim Form 2, wideline incised Motif i: 1

Rim Form 2, horizontal band in zoned toning: 1

Rim Form 2, crescents in negative white: 2

Rim Form 2, vertical lines in negative white: 2

Rim Form 2, horizontal lines in negative white: 1

Rim Form 2, negative white, motif unclear: 1

Rim Form 2, wide horizontal incised lines and negative white: 1

Rim Form 3, no decoration: 2

Rim Form 3, fine horizontal incised lines and zoned toning: 1

Rim Form 3, crescents in negative white: 1

Rim Form 3, Eccentricity 3, wideline incised crescents: 1

Rim Form 3, Eccentricity 3, wideline incised crescents and negative white: 1

Rim Form 3, Eccentricity 7 (?), crescents in negative white: 1

Rim Form 4, Eccentricity 1 (?), fineline incised crescent: 1

Rim Form 4, Eccentricity 7, fine horizontal incised lines and zoned toning: 1

Rim Form 4, Eccentricity 7, horizontal lines in negative white: 1

Rim Form 5, no decoration: 1

Rim Form 5, fineline incised pennant: 1

Rim Form 5, fine horizontal incised lines: 2

Rim Form 5, horizontal band in zoned toning: 1

Rim Form 5, crescents in negative white: 1

Rim Form 5, horizontal line in negative white: 1

Rim Form 5 (?), Eccentricity 5, wideline incised scallop: 1

Rim Form 10 (?), fine horizontal incised lines: 1

In sum, the sherd sample from the final construction stage of Structure 19 was a mixture of Rosario phase diagnostics and

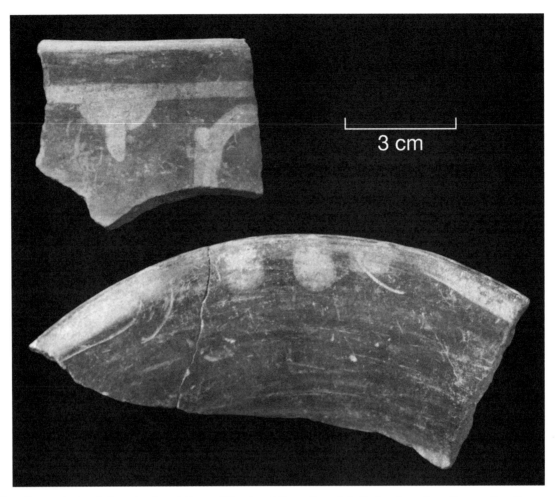

Figure 8.14. Two diagnostic sherds from the foundations of Structure 19's south wall. Both sherds are from Socorro Fine Gray vessels of the Rosario phase, decorated with negative white motifs.

redeposited sherds from earlier periods. Some of the diagnostic sherds suggested a date in the second half of the Rosario phase.

A Radiocarbon Date from Structure 19

As mentioned above, we recovered charcoal from a construction post in Square S2E14. This charcoal became radiocarbon sample Beta-179876. The conventional date came out 2560 ± 180 years before the present, or 610 b.c. When dendrocalibrated, the two-sigma range of this date is 1110–350 BC. We consider the date of 610 b.c. to confirm the Rosario phase age of Structure 19.

Other Ceramics Used to Date Structure 19

1. Sherds from among the Foundation Stones of the East Wall
We exposed the eastern wall of Structure 19 to the depth of the wall foundation stones. We hoped that the sherds trapped in the clay mortar between these stones would help us to date the final construction stages of Structure 19. All the pottery we recovered dated to the Rosario phase or earlier periods.

ROSARIO PHASE DIAGNOSTICS
rims, Socorro Fine Gray outleaned/outcurved-wall bowls: 19

rims, Socorro Fine Gray composite silhouette bowls with negative white alone: 2

rim, Socorro Fine Gray composite silhouette bowl with incising and negative white: 1

rim, Socorro Fine Gray bowl, exterior incising: 1

rim, Socorro Fine Gray incurved-rim bowl, exterior incising: 1

rim, Socorro Fine Gray bowl like those used to dedicate Structure 28 (see below): 1

possible Socorro Fine Gray bowl with pedestal base, with incising and zoned toning: 1

rims, Guadalupe Burnished Brown outleaned-wall bowls: 18

rim, Guadalupe Burnished Brown hemispherical bowl: 1

fragments, Lupita Heavy Plain undecorated Suchilquitongo tripod dishes: 3

fragments, Lupita Heavy Plain pot stands or charcoal braziers: 10

rims, Fidencio Coarse jars: 12

rim, Fidencio Coarse *tecomate*: 1

Figure 8.15. The east end of Structure 19 during the removal of the earthen fill between the Structure 19A stage and the Structure 19 stage. The workman with the ranging pole stands at the profile left by removal of the north half of the fill. On the right one can see the sloping stones supporting the vertical east wall of Structure 19A.

Figure 8.16. The east end of Structure 19 during the removal of earthen fill between the Structure 19A stage (left) and the Structure 19 stage (right). In this view, facing north, the south half of the fill has been removed. On the left, one can see the sloping stones supporting the vertical east wall of Structure 19A.

DIAGNOSTICS OF EARLIER PERIODS
   rim, Josefina Fine Gray outleaned-wall bowl in Guadalupe
      phase style: 1
   rims, Atoyac Yellow-white outleaned-wall bowls: 4
   rim, Atoyac Yellow-white hemispherical bowl: 1
   giant macrorims, Atoyac Yellow-white: 2
   rim, Delia White beaker: 1
   rim, Xochiltepec White outleaned-wall bowl: 1
   rim, Xochiltepec White cylinder, excised: 1
   rim, Matadamas Orange hemispherical bowl: 1
   rim, Tierras Largas Burnished Plain bowl: 1

We coded all 19 rims of Socorro Fine Gray outleaned/

outcurved-wall bowls in Drennan's system. The attributes were
as follows:
   Rim Form 2, no decoration: 3
   Rim Form 2, fine horizontal incised lines: 1
   Rim Form 2, wide diagonal incised lines: 2
   Rim Form 2, crescents in negative white: 2
   Rim Form 2, negative white, motif unclear: 1
   Rim Form 2, Eccentricity 2, wide horizontal incised lines and
      negative white: 1
   Rim Form 3, fine horizontal incised lines: 1
   Rim Form 3, crescents in negative white: 1
   Rim Form 4, no decoration: 1
   Rim Form 5, horizontal bands in zoned toning: 2

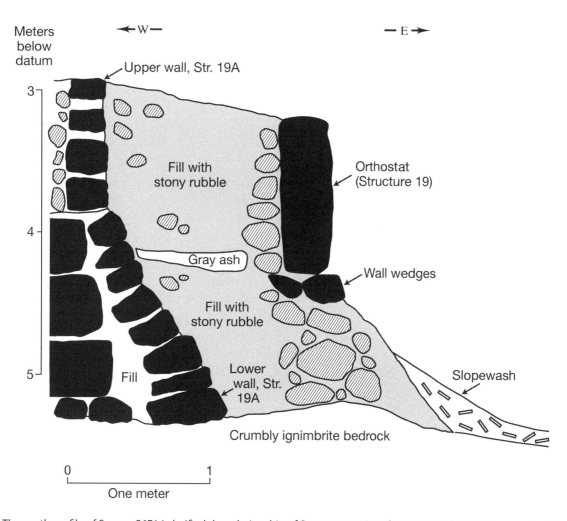

Figure 8.17. The north profile of Square S6E14 clarified the relationship of Structures 19A and 19. We see that the lower part of the east wall of Structure 19A had a slope, suggesting that one of its roles was to prevent earlier stages of the building from collapsing. Considerable fill was piled against Structure 19A when Structure 19 was built. On the right we see one of the basal orthostats from the east wall of Structure 19 (many stones from the upper wall were missing).

Rim Form 5, triangles in zoned toning: 1
Rim Form 5, fine horizontal incised lines with zoned toning: 1
Rim Form 6, fine horizontal incised lines: 1
Rim Form 7, no decoration: 1

2. Sherds from among the Foundation Stones of the North Wall

We were able to recover a sample of diagnostic sherds from the clay mortar between the foundation stones of the north wall of Structure 19. Included were 5 rims from Socorro Fine Gray outleaned/outcurved-wall bowls that we coded as follows:

Rim Type 2, no decoration
Rim Type 5, no decoration
Rim Type 5, Eccentricity 5, no decoration

Rim Type 5, Eccentricity 6, no decoration
Rim Type 9, Eccentricity 7, no decoration

The sample also included 5 rims from Socorro Fine Gray composite silhouette bowls. Two had plain rims, 2 were incised, and 1 had crescent motifs in negative white. The remaining sherds were from an undecorated Suchilquitongo tripod dish in Lupita Heavy Plain ware; 2 charcoal braziers of Lupita Heavy Plain; 4 outleaned-wall bowls of Guadalupe Burnished Brown; 2 jar rims of Fidencio Coarse; and 2 redeposited Early Formative sherds.

Figure 8.18. The east end of Structure 19 during the investigation of Stage 19B. In this view from the northeast, the workman in the foreground is cleaning the east wall of Structure 19B with a whisk broom. The workman in the background points to the sloping reinforcement wall created when the Structure 19B wall began to buckle under the weight of Structure 28. (At this point, the fill between the Structure 19B and Structure 19A walls has been removed.)

3. *Sherds from just above Sterile Soil in Square S6E14*

No traces of Stratigraphic Zone F were encountered in Square S6E14. In that area, Zone E—the earthen fill of Structure 19—simply rested on a layer of yellow, sandy, nearly sterile soil at a depth of 450 to 480 cm below datum. We recovered a total of 105 sherds lying on this yellow soil. The 44 diagnostic sherds were as follows:

rims, Socorro Fine Gray outleaned/outcurved-wall bowls: 13
rims, Socorro Fine Gray composite silhouette bowls: 4
rim, Socorro Fine Gray beaker: 1
fragment of annular base, Socorro Fine Gray: 1
rims, Guadalupe Burnished Brown bowls: 16
fragments, Lupita Heavy Plain undecorated Suchilquitongo tripod dishes: 2
fragments, Lupita Heavy Plain potstands or charcoal braziers: 3
rims, Fidencio Coarse jars: 4

We coded all 13 rims of Socorro Fine Gray outleaned/outcurved-wall bowls in Drennan's system. The attributes were as follows:

Rim Form 1, no decoration: 1
Rim Form 2, no decoration: 1
Rim Form 2, crescents in negative white: 2
Rim Form 2, Eccentricity 3, crescents in negative white: 2
Rim Form 3, crescents in negative white: 3
Rim Form 4, no decoration: 1
Rim Form 5, horizontal band of pattern burnishing: 1
Rim Form 9, wideline incised scallop: 1
Rim Form 10, Eccentricity 5, wideline incised scallop: 1

In sum, no sherd found in the walls of Structure 19 appeared to be later than Rosario phase in date.

4. *Feature 53*

Feature 53 was a deep, irregular, ash-filled pit that occupied most of Square N10E16. Its most notable contents were dozens of fragments of Lupita Heavy Plain charcoal braziers;

we suspected that the large amounts of ash found in the pit had come from these braziers. Included in the ash was a gray obsidian blade more than 10.5 cm long.

Feature 53 also produced 3 sherds from a Socorro Fine Gray outleaned-wall bowl featuring Drennan's Rim Form 11, Eccentricity 2, incised on the rim with two wide parallel lines.

Our suspicion is that during the filling of Structure 19 with basketloads of earth, someone saw an opportunity to get rid of a mass of ash-filled braziers by adding them to the fill.

Exposing Structure 19B

The procedure we used for exposing Structure 19B—the earliest construction stage of Structure 19—was the same one we had used to expose Structure 19A. We carefully removed all the fill between the east wall of Structure 19A and the east wall of Structure 19B (Fig. 8.18). No sherds in this fill were later in age than the Rosario phase. Once all the sherds had been removed from the fill, the area was backfilled, and we added modern soft drink bottles to the fill.

Dating Structure 19B with Ceramics

We were initially limited in our efforts to remove the fill from Structure 19B by the fact that it lay directly beneath the Structure 28 temple, and we did not want to undermine the temple and its contents. Fortunately, the northwest corner of Structure 19B (parts of Squares S2E4–S2E6 and S3E4–S3E6) was exposed, which allowed us to recover more than 200 sherds from the fill. The 39 diagnostic sherds from this collection—which suggest an early Rosario phase date—were as follows:

  rim of Socorro Fine Gray outleaned-wall bowl, Rim Type 2, undecorated: 1
  rim of Josefina Fine Gray outleaned-wall bowl: 1
  rims of Lupita Heavy Plain bowls: 2
  fragments of Lupita Heavy Plain charcoal braziers, one with a mat-impressed floor: 2
  rims of Fidencio Coarse jars: 4
  rims of Atoyac Yellow-white bowls: 2
  rim of Leandro Gray cylinder: 1
  rim of Matadamas Red hemispherical bowl: 1
  miscellaneous body sherds of Rosario, Guadalupe, and San José phase types: 25

This Structure 19B sherd sample is small, but it contains no sherd dating to a period later than the Rosario phase.

A Cross-Section of Structure 19B

Once we had fully explored Structure 28, the Rosario phase temple built upon Structure 19B, we were finally able to excavate to sterile soil in Squares S5E9–S5E13. This gave us a stratigraphic cross-section of Structure 19B and clarified its relationship to Structure 28 (Figs. 8.19, 8.20).

An unexpected bonus of this stratigraphic excavation was that it showed us very clearly the way that Structure 19B had begun to collapse under the weight of the Structure 28 temple. As Figure 8.19 shows, some of the limestone blocks forming the east wall of Structure 19B had fallen outward and slid downslope in Squares S5E12 and S6E12. The Rosario phase architects responded to this problem by piling ignimbrite rubble against Structure 19B to keep it from collapsing further. They then encased Structure 19B inside a new building, Structure 19A.

Dating the Structure 19B Fill (Zone E) with Ceramics

One byproduct of our stratigraphic excavation in Squares S5E9–S5E13 was that we recovered a large sample of sherds from the fill of Structure 19B (Stratigraphic Zone E). The 255 diagnostic sherds from this fill were a crucial discovery because that sherd collection provided us with a *terminus ante quem* for the beginning of construction on the platform.

The diagnostic sherds in our sample lead to the conclusion that Structure 19B was built early in the Rosario phase. Many of the Socorro Fine Gray and Josefina Fine Gray diagnostics we found would not be out of place in the late Guadalupe phase. Even in the case of those Socorro Fine Gray outleaned-wall bowl rims with Rosario phase attributes, the Structure 19B fill collection contains mainly the simpler rim forms, eccentricities, and motifs found early in the Rosario phase. Almost none of the more complex attributes seen in late Rosario are present.

Rosario phase diagnostics are, in fact, greatly outnumbered in our sample by San José phase and Guadalupe phase diagnostics. This may mean that the leaders of San José Mogote called upon every residential ward of the village to contribute basketloads of fill to the construction of Structure 19B. Some of those wards had abundant San José and Guadalupe phase middens that could be turned into fill.

The diagnostic sherds from the Structure 19B fill were as follows:

TIERRAS LARGAS BURNISHED PLAIN
  hemispherical bowls, rims: 5
  jars, rims: 4
  tecomate body sherd, interrupted rocker stamping: 1

AVELINA RED-ON-BUFF
  hemispherical bowls, rims: 6

MATADAMAS RED
  hemispherical bowl, rim: 1
  jars, rims: 2

MATADAMAS ORANGE
  hemispherical bowls, rims: 2
  outleaned-wall bowls, rims: 2
  jars, rims: 8

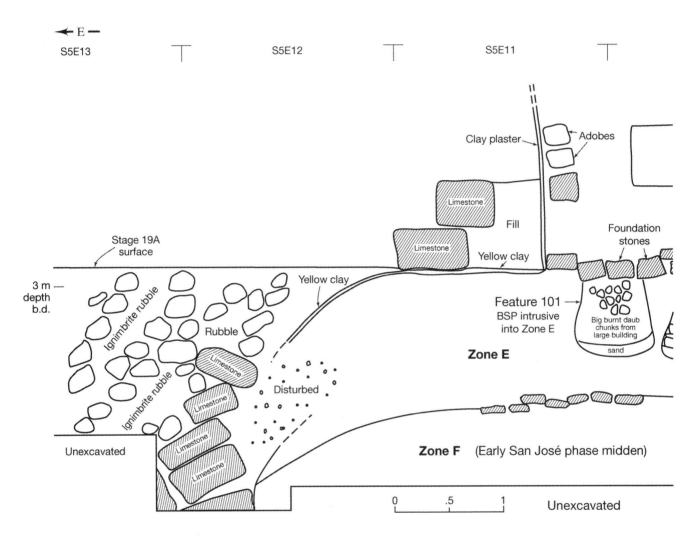

Figure 8.19. East-west cross-section through the S5 row of squares, Structures 19B and 19A, showing Stratigraphic Zones E and F below Structure 28. Part 1 of 2. (BSP = Bell-shaped pit)

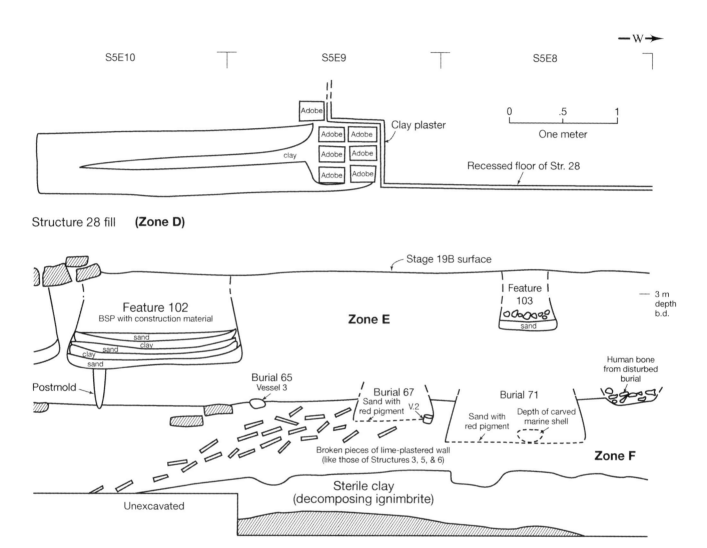

Figure 8.20. East-west cross-section through the S5 row of squares, Structures 19B and 19A, showing Stratigraphic Zones E and F below Structure 28. Part 2 of 2. (BSP = Bell-shaped pit)

FIDENCIO COARSE
    jars, rims: 10
    tecomate sherd: 1

LEANDRO GRAY
    cylinders, plain rims: 6
    outleaned-wall bowls, plain rims: 4
    outleaned-wall bowl, excised: 1
    bowls with bolstered rim: 2
    giant macrorim: 1

ATOYAC YELLOW-WHITE
    cylinders, plain rims: 3
    cylinders, incised rims: 11
    outleaned-wall bowls, plain rims: 25
    outleaned-wall bowls, incised rims: 13
    bowls with bolstered rim: 2
    giant macrorims: 4
    jar with tall cylindrical neck: 1
    incurved-rim bowl, incised rim: 1
    tecomate body sherd, zoned: 1

SAN JOSÉ RED-ON-WHITE
    hemispherical bowl, rim: 1

LUPITA HEAVY PLAIN
    outleaned-wall bowl, plain rim: 1
    tecomate, brushed below rim: 1
    hemispherical bowls, plain rims: 3
    potter's bat(?): 1
    potstand, reused as pigment dish: 1
    charcoal braziers, rims: 13
    charcoal brazier, annular base: 1
    Suchilquitongo tripod dish, undecorated: 1

XOCHILTEPEC WHITE
    body sherd: 1

DELFINA FINE GRAY
    cylinder, plain rim: 1
    outleaned-wall bowl, plain rim: 1

COATEPEC WHITE-RIMMED BLACK
    outleaned-wall bowl, plain rim: 1

DELIA WHITE
    beaker, plain rim: 1
    cylinder, plain rim: 1
    base of cylinder or beaker: 1
    hemispherical bowls, rims: 2
    outleaned-wall bowl, basal sherd: 1
    body sherds: 2

GUADALUPE BURNISHED BROWN
    outleaned-wall bowls, rims: 16
    outleaned-wall bowl, base: 1

SOCORRO FINE GRAY
    outleaned/outcurved-wall bowls, rims: 29
    composite silhouette bowls, plain rims: 4
    composite silhouette bowls, collared rims: 3
    composite silhouette bowl, incised rim: 1
    composite silhouette bowls, zoned toning: 2
    composite silhouette bowl, negative white: 1
    composite silhouette bowls, basal sherds: 2
    composite silhouette bowls, body sherds: 2
    cylinder base, incised: 1
    cylinder base, incising and negative white: 1
    beakers, plain rims: 5
    incurved-rim bowl, incised rim: 1
    shallow dish, plain rim: 1
    shallow dish, incising and negative white: 1

JOSEFINA FINE GRAY
    outleaned-wall bowls, plain rims: 3
    outcurved-wall bowls, plain rims: 6
    composite silhouette bowls, plain rims: 4
    composite silhouette bowl, negative white only: 1
    composite silhouette bowls, incising and negative white: 7
    composite silhouette bowls, bases: 2
    beakers, plain rims: 4
    beaker, base: 1
    bowl with beveled rim: 1
    oval bowls with pinched-in sides: 3

We coded all 29 rims of Socorro Fine Gray outleaned/outcurved-wall bowls in Drennan's system. The attributes were as follows:
    Rim Form 1, no decoration: 1
    Rim Form 2, no decoration: 18
    Rim Form 2, fineline incised pennant: 1
    Rim Form 2, fineline incised pennant and zoned toning: 1
    Rim Form 3, no decoration: 1
    Rim Form 3, fineline incised horizontal lines and zoned toning: 1
    Rim Form 5, no decoration: 1
    Rim Form 5, fineline incised pennant: 1
    Rim Form 5, Eccentricity 1, fineline incised Motif h and zoned toning: 1
    Rim Form 7, undecorated: 1
    Rim Form 7, fineline Motif c: 1
    Rim Form 12, undecorated: 1

The Chronology of Structure 19B

Based on the ceramics in its earthen fill, we conclude that

Structure 19B was built early in the Rosario phase. When it began to collapse under the weight of Structure 28, it was shored up by having Structure 19A built around it. The final stage of the platform, Structure 19, was added in the latter part of the Rosario phase. That means, presumably, that the shift to a true east-west orientation occurred in middle or late Rosario times.

Features 101–104

In the course of excavating Squares S5E8–S5E11, we found four interesting features in the upper part of Stratigraphic Zone E. Features 101–103 were bell-shaped pits that appeared to contain leftover construction material (see Figs. 8.19, 8.20). Feature 104 was a unique offering.

Feature 101 spanned Squares S5E10, S6E10, S5E11, and S6E11. Its mouth was roughly 60 cm in diameter, while its basal diameter expanded to 74 cm. This pit was 88 cm deep, and its lower 10 cm contained fine sand. Above this we found numerous chunks of burnt daub from the destruction of a relatively large building.

Feature 102 lay mostly in Squares S5E10 and S6E10. Its mouth was roughly 1.4 m in diameter, while its base expanded to 1.64 m. Its depth was 90 cm, and its lower half was filled with alternating layers of fine sand and clay. The presence of a postmold just below (and partially truncated by) Feature 102 suggests that Structure 19B might not have been the first building constructed in that area. Unfortunately, we have no clue what that earlier building might have been.

Feature 103 lay within Squares S5E8 and S6E8. Its mouth was roughly 46 cm in diameter, while its base expanded to 58 cm. Its depth was 54 cm, and there was a layer of fine sand in the bottom of the pit. Above that, we found more chunks of burnt daub like those in Feature 101.

The fine sand and winnowed clay in these bell-shaped pits resembled the ingredients for clay mortar. The presence of Features 101–103 suggests that the masons who built Structure 19B kept their construction materials close at hand in bell-shaped pits and swept the leftover material into those pits when the work was done. The daub fragments hint that an earlier building might have been destroyed to make way for Structure 19B, but we have no idea what that building may have been.

Feature 104 was a cylindrical pit intrusive into Stratigraphic Zone E, and may represent an offering buried there before construction began on Structure 28. The pit was 13 cm in diameter and more than 30 cm deep; it occupied parts of Squares S5E11 and S5E12 (Fig. 8.21). In it we found the remains of 5 vessels, only 3 of which were ceramic.

Vessel 1 (Fig. 8.22a) was a small rust-colored jar only 5.9 cm tall.

Vessel 2 (Figs. 8.22b, 8.23) was an oval bowl carved from the shell of *Ancistromesus mexicanus*, the largest known limpet. This Pacific gastropod is native to rocky coasts from Sinaloa south to Peru. The bowl has a maximum length of 14.5 cm and is unique

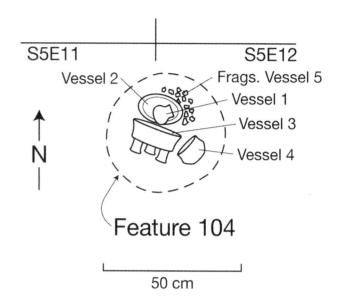

Figure 8.21. Plan view of Feature 104, a cylindrical pit intrusive into Stratigraphic Zone E below Structure 28. This feature spanned the border between Squares S5E11 and S5E12.

in the Formative of Oaxaca.

Vessel 3 (Figs. 8.24a, 8.25 *left*) was a Socorro Fine Gray bowl with three hollow supports. It displays the typical negative white decoration of the Rosario phase.

Vessel 4 (Figs. 8.24b, 8.25 *right*) was a Socorro Fine Gray composite silhouette bowl with negative white decoration.

Vessel 5 (Figs. 8.26, 8.27) was, we suspect, a gourd vessel covered with lime stucco and decorated with painted motifs. Because the gourd itself had decomposed, only fragments of the painted stucco had survived. As far as we can tell, the design motifs included a double-line-break, flower petals, swirls, and a symbolic representation of Earth in which the four world quarters are shown as dots.

Other Items Found in Zone E

Two small ceramic jars (Figs. 8.28, 8.29) were found in Square S5E8 of Zone E. Both are crudely made and have the same clay body as the pottery type Fidencio Coarse. It is probably significant that these small jars were found directly below the Structure 28 temple; they might have contained a liquid offering of some kind.

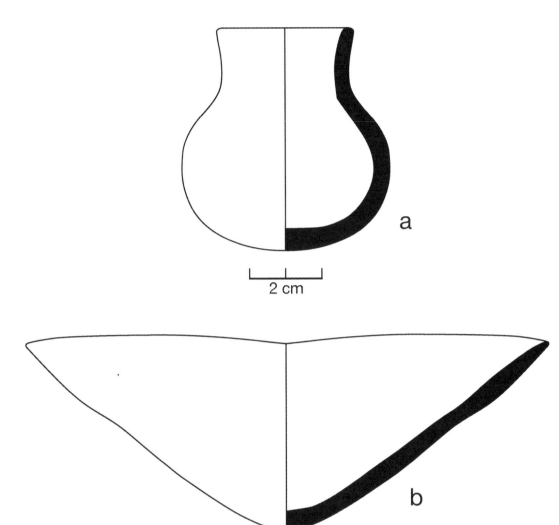

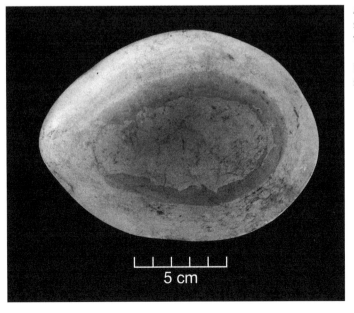

Above: Figure 8.22. Two vessels from Feature 104. *a*, Vessel 1, a small rust-colored jar. *b*, Vessel 2, a bowl carved from the shell of the limpet *Ancistromesus mexicanus*.

Left: Figure 8.23. Vessel 2 from Feature 104, a large carved limpet shell. Maximum length, 14.5 cm.

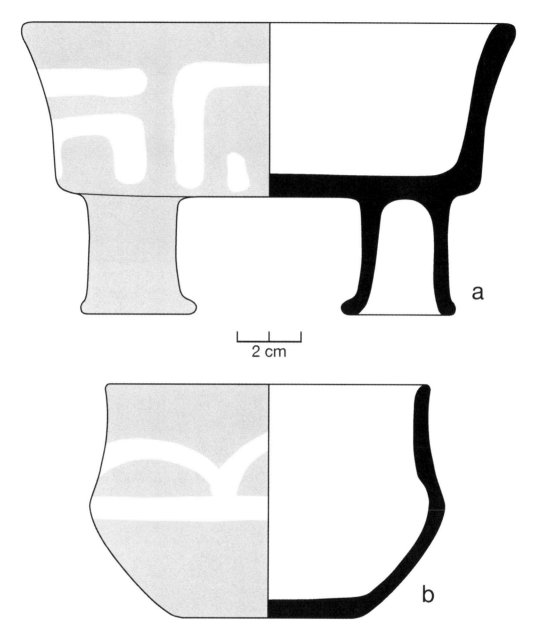

Figure 8.24. Two Socorro Fine Gray vessels from Feature 104. *a*, Vessel 3, a tripod bowl with negative white decoration. *b*, Vessel 4, a composite silhouette bowl with negative white decoration.

Figure 8.25. Vessel 3 (*left*) and Vessel 4 (*right*) from Feature 104. Both are Socorro Fine Gray vessels with negative white decoration.

Below left: Figure 8.26. Fragments of the lime plaster coating on Vessel 5, Feature 104. *a* and *b* display double-line-break motifs in white against a dark background. *c* shows part of a flower petal motif. *d* displays a crumbling Earth motif with small circles for the four world quarters.

Below right: Figure 8.27. Motifs painted on Vessel 5 of Feature 104, reconstructed from plaster fragments. *a*, double-line-break. *b*, petals. *c*, swirl. *d*, Earth with four world quarters.

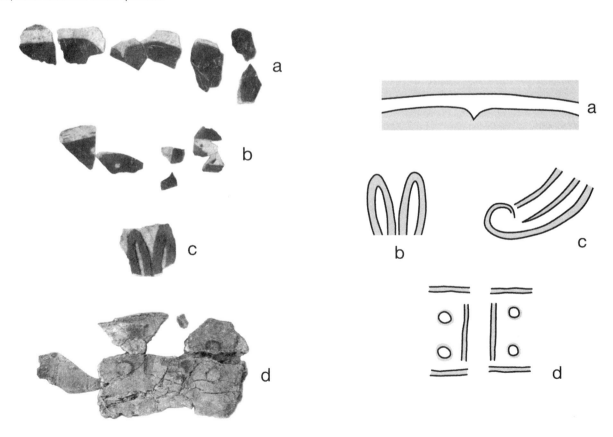

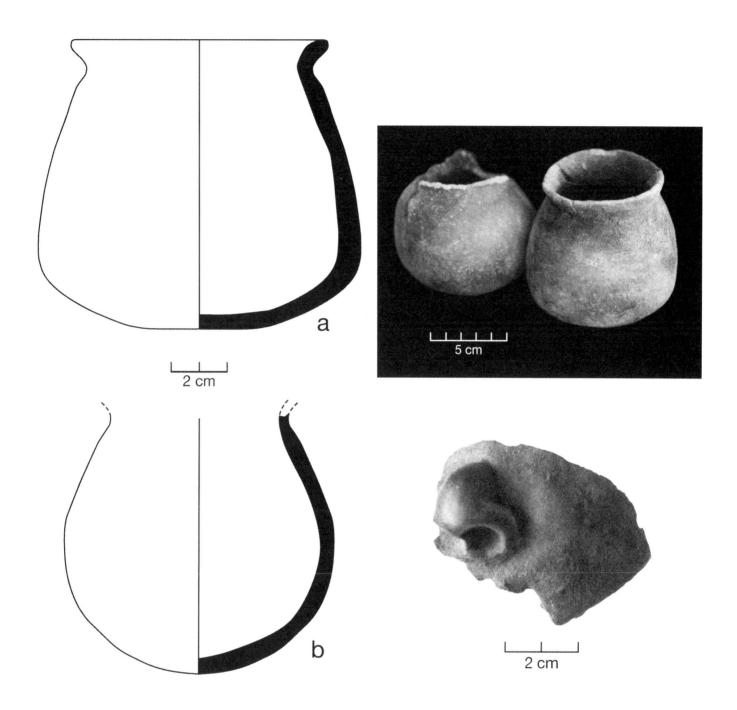

Left: Figure 8.28. Two small jars found in Zone E below Structure 28. These vessels, found in Square S5E8, have the same clay body as Fidencio Coarse. *a*, Vessel 1. *b*, Vessel 2.

Upper right: Figure 8.29. Two small jars from Square S5E8, Stratigraphic Zone E, below Structure 28. Vessel 1 is on the right.

Lower right: Figure 8.30. Fragment of ceramic mask recovered from Zone E below Structure 28.

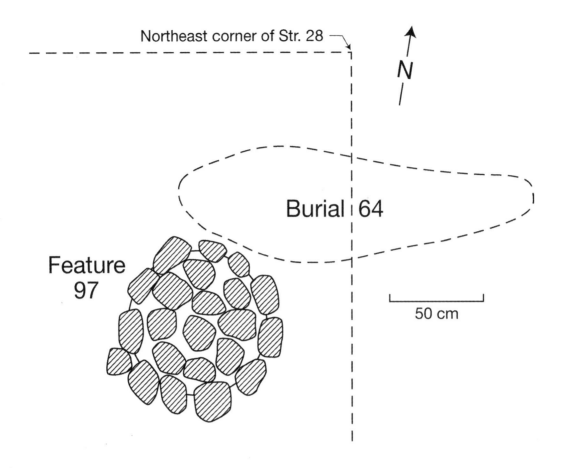

Figure 8.31. Feature 97 and Burial 64 were discovered beneath the northeast corner of Structure 28 and may have been part of a dedication ritual. Feature 97 was a storage silo of some kind; Burial 64 was a fully extended adult skeleton. Both had been buried in Zone E, the fill of Structure 19B.

A large fragment of ceramic mask (Fig. 8.30) was found in Zone E below the Structure 28 temple. Whether it represents debris from a ritual, or simply one more object included in the fill, is unknown.

Feature 97 and Burial 64: Possible Dedicatory Offerings

Two more discoveries made in the fill of Structure 19B are worthy of mention. Feature 97 was a small storage silo; Burial 64 was a fully extended adult skeleton. Both were intrusive into Structure 19B at the very spot where the northeast corner of the Structure 28 temple would later be placed. These features have the look of dedicatory offerings, but their stratigraphic position makes it uncertain which building they were designed to honor. They could be either post-construction offerings for Structure 19B or pre-construction offerings for Structure 28. Their location is given in Figure 8.31.

Feature 97 was a cylindrical storage silo, 1.1 m high and 70 cm in diameter. Its walls were lined with clay, and its domed roof was made of stones held in place with clay mortar (Fig. 8.32). One of the most interesting aspects of this silo was that it had been sealed so completely that when our workmen began removing the stones of the roof, they found it virtually empty; no later fill had managed to enter. There were signs, however, that an animal of some kind had burrowed in from the side in ancient times, perhaps eating the silo's contents and using it as a burrow.

On the floor of the silo we found hundreds of small rodent and songbird bones, almost certainly the contents of disintegrated owl pellets. It is possible, therefore, that an owl had established its home base in the silo at some time in the past, perhaps entering through the animal burrow. The complete list of small animal species found in Feature 97 is as follows:

Sorex sp. (shrew): 1 left mandible
Sylvilagus floridanus (cottontail rabbit): 1 left ulna
Liomys irroratus (spiny pocket mouse): 4 right mandibles, 6 left mandibles, 1 maxilla
Reithrodontomys fulvescens (fulvous harvest mouse): 3 mandibles
Reithrodontomys sp.: 2 mandibles

cf. *Reithrodontomys*: 19 mandibles
Peromyscus cf. *melanophrys* (white-footed mouse): 6 mandibles
Peromyscus sp.: 22 mandibles
cf. *Peromyscus*: 1 left mandible
Cricetid rodents: 461 limb bones
Unidentified lizard: 1 dentary bone
Miscellaneous bones of Icteridae (orioles), Thraupidae (tanagers), Emberizidae (grosbeaks), and other songbirds

We have no idea what material might originally have been stored in this silo; possibly it was food of some kind, since this might be what encouraged the animal to burrow into it. Given that it looks like a miniature version of the central Mexican *cuexcomatl*, or corn storage silo, it is possible that it once held a dedicatory offering of maize for the temple. Once buried in the fill of Structure 19B, it appears never to have been opened until the temple above it was abandoned and an animal burrowed into it.

We are not sure whether Burial 64 was intended as a dedication for the Structure 28 temple or the Structure 19B platform beneath it. The alignment of the skeleton matched that of both structures, which was 8° north of east. Burial 64 was fully extended face down, with its head to the west (Fig. 8.33). Because certain key skeletal elements were not well preserved, Hodges (1989:87) was unable to determine the sex of this adult individual; given that Burial 64 measured almost 5'8" in the ground, however, it is likely to have been a man. Between the individual's thighs someone had placed 2 deer bone awls, or *piscadores*, and 5 dog canines perforated for suspension (Fig. 8.34).

The dedicatory rituals associated with the Structure 28 temple and its Structure 19B platform, in other words, went through many stages. First came the building of Structure 19B; then came the interment of Burial 64, the Feature 97 storage silo, and Feature 104; then came the building of Structure 28 and the interment of four offering vessels below the corners of its recessed floor (see below). It is no surprise to learn that Rosario phase ritual was diverse and multistage. What frustrates us is that there is no way to deduce the subtle nuances of that ritual and the sacred propositions that motivated it.

Structure 28

Let us now turn to the actual Rosario phase temple supported by the Structure 19B masonry platform. This temple has been designated Structure 28, and it lay completely within Stratigraphic Zone D of the Structure 19 overburden.

As Figure 8.35 reveals, the orientation of Structure 28 was 8° north of east. That fits with the evidence that it was designed to stand upon Structure 19B, which displayed the same orientation. Figure 8.36 presents a view of Structure 28 from the northeast. In the photo, one can see the very top of the east wall of Structure 19B, separated from Structure 28 by no more than a meter. One can also see the north wall of Structure 19, the final stage of the

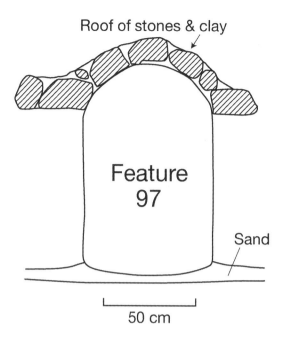

Figure 8.32. Two views of Feature 97, a storage silo with a roof of stones and clay, buried beneath Structure 28. *Above*, we see a cross-section of the feature. *Below*, we see a photo of the feature at the point at which excavations had broken through the roof. The arrow points north.

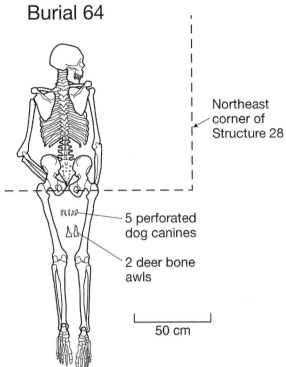

Burial 64

Northeast
corner of
Structure 28

5 perforated
dog canines

2 deer bone
awls

50 cm

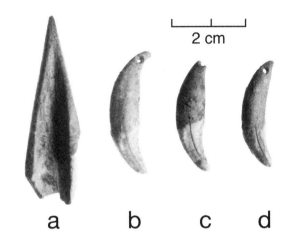

2 cm

a   b   c   d

Figure 8.33. Plan view of Burial 64, an individual buried in Zone E below the northeast corner of Structure 28. Identified as an adult, this individual would have been 170 cm tall and is therefore likely to have been a male. His burial may have been part of the dedication of either Structure 28 or Structure 19B, since his body was aligned with both structures (8° north of east; head to west, face to north).

Figure 8.34. Burial 64 was accompanied by five perforated dog canines (possibly part of a necklace) and two deer bone awls. Here we see one of the awls (*a*) and three of the perforated canines (*b–d*).

platform, as well as a low pavement of flagstones that was added later to keep that wall from collapsing outward (see Chapter 14).

While Structure 28 was too damaged to measure precisely, our best estimate is that its original substructure measured 14.2 m east-west and 13.4 m north-south. The best-preserved corner of that substructure (on the northeast) stood 1.52 m tall. As shown in Figure 8.37, its outer walls were of rectangular adobe bricks; its interior consisted of earthen fill, divided into discrete cells by a series of regularly spaced adobe retaining walls. The substructure's exterior had been given several coats of white lime plaster.

As the preceding paragraph implies, 1.52 m did not constitute the total height of the temple—only the height of its adobe substructure. Above the adobes, the temple had once had extra thick wattle-and-daub walls, coated on both their interior and exterior surfaces with lime plaster. This wattle-and-daub superstructure

had long since collapsed, but we found evidence of it in the form of burnt daub. The cane impressions in this daub were larger in diameter than those found in ordinary residential debris.

The reason the temple had been provided with such a strong adobe substructure was so that its floor could accommodate a recessed or sunken central area, which we estimate to have measured 9.2 m north-south and 5.6 m east-west. The recessed part of the floor was framed by adobes (Fig. 8.38). On the east, these adobes formed such a wide horizontal expanse as to suggest the presence of a bench, by means of which one could step down onto the recessed floor. The depth to which this sunken floor was recessed could not be measured with precision, but it seems to have extended down at least 70 cm below the rest of the temple floor. There were traces of bricks on the west side that suggested two step-downs of 35 cm each.

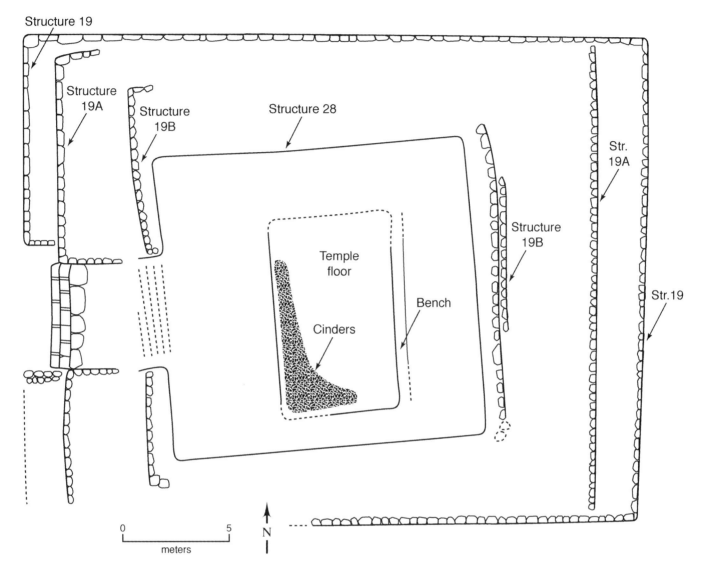

Figure 8.35. Plan view of the Structure 28 temple and its Structure 19B platform. Also shown are two later enlargements of the platform, Structures 19A and 19.

The Structure 28 temple also had a staircase on its west side. This staircase was made of adobes like the rest of the temple and occupied only the central third of the wall. Figure 8.39 shows how the wall of the substructure turned west at a 90° angle to create the south side of the staircase. We tried our best to work out the details of the adobe staircase, but it had been too badly destroyed during later modifications of the building. We did discover, however, that small stone slabs had been used to reinforce the riser of each step at the point where it met the tread (Fig. 8.40).

Given that the adobe staircase had the same 8° north of east orientation as the rest of Structure 28, we wondered what adjustment the architects might have made when the underlying platform's orientation shifted to true east during its Structure 19A stage. Figure 8.41 shows what we learned about this transition. When the orientation of the platform changed, the masons

covered Structure 28's adobe staircase with stony rubble; over this rubble, they built a staircase of stone slabs with a different orientation. Unfortunately, owing to subsequent erosion, only a few stone slabs from this new staircase had survived.

The Dedication of Structure 28

In the course of our work we discovered that four complete pottery vessels—later crushed by the weight of the overburden— had been buried under the four corners of Structure 28's recessed floor (Figs. 8.42, 8.43). It appeared that considerable thought had gone into the vessels chosen and their placement; the bowls in the northwest and southeast corners were both Socorro Fine Gray, while the bowls in the northeast and southwest corners were both Guadalupe Burnished Brown.

Above: Figure 8.36. Structure 28 seen from the northeast. The ranging pole is marked in 10 cm units and measures 2 m in height.

Below: Figure 8.37. This cross-section of the western edge of Structure 28 (at a point just north of the stairway) shows the way the west wall of Structure 19B was raised in order to keep the substructure of Structure 28 from bulging outward.

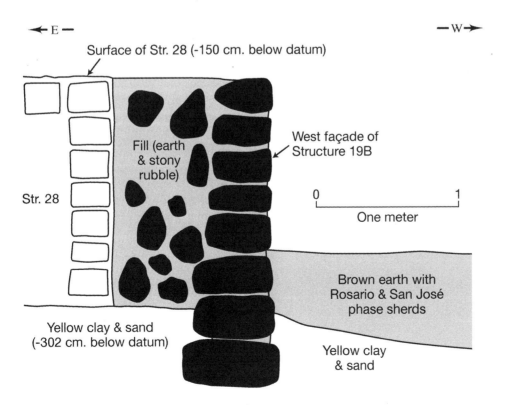

Figure 8.38. Two views of the recessed floor of Structure 28. On the left, Irán Matadamas squats on the recessed floor, cleaning some of the adobe brickwork exposed by the burning of the temple's west side. On the right, a workman standing in the northwest corner of the recessed floor holds a ranging pole at the spot where Vessel 4 (a subfloor offering) was later found. On the floor behind him are adobes dislodged by fire.

Figure 8.39. The original staircase on the west side of Structure 28 was made of adobes. This view from the south shows how the west wall turned west at a 90° angle to produce the south side of the staircase. (The stones on the left were added at a much later date.)

Above: Figure 8.40. Two views of the original adobe staircase on the west side of Structure 28. Both views show that small stone slabs were used to reinforce the point where the riser of each step met the tread. The view on the left is from the north; that on the right is from the south.

Below: Figure 8.41. An east-west cross-section through Structures 19A and 28, along the north profile of Squares S6E1–S6E4. This drawing shows how the stone staircase of Structure 19 once led to the adobe staircase of Structure 28. (Adobes are shown as white; construction stones are shown as black; stony rubble added later is hachured.)

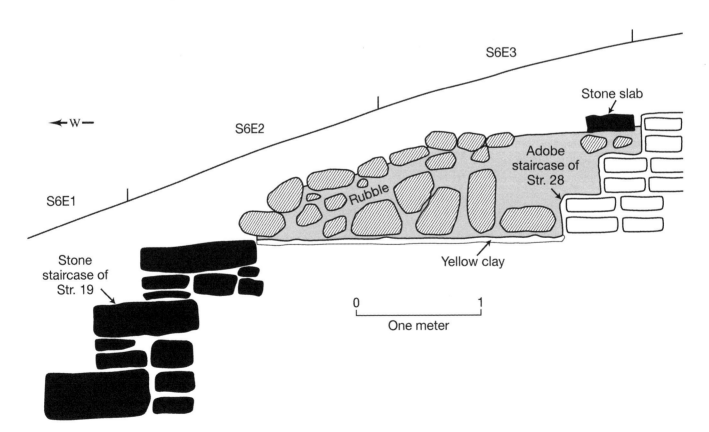

Figure 8.42. Artist's reconstruction of the recessed floor of the Structure 28 temple, showing the locations of the buried dedicatory vessels. From left to right, they are Vessel 1, Vessel 3, Vessel 2, and Vessel 4 (not drawn to scale).

1. Vessel 1 (in the southeast) was a Socorro Fine Gray composite silhouette bowl with a rim diameter of 64 cm and an estimated height of 27.5 cm.
2. Vessel 2 (in the northeast) was a Guadalupe Burnished Brown outleaned-wall bowl with a rim diameter of 37 cm and a height of 10 cm (Fig. 8.44).
3. Vessel 3 (in the southwest) was a Guadalupe Burnished Brown outleaned-wall bowl with a rim diameter of 38 cm and a height of 12 cm.
4. Vessel 4 (in the northwest) was a Socorro Fine Gray bowl with a flat base and flaring walls; the exterior of the base bore a *petate* or reed mat impression. The estimated rim diameter of this bowl was 47 cm and the height was roughly 16 cm.

All four of these bowls are large enough to have been serving vessels for multiple individuals. We suspect that the vessels may have been used to serve food to the participants during a dedication ritual for the temple, after which they were buried under the four corners of the recessed floor. Their placement hints at a reference to the four great world quarters of the Mesoamerican cosmos.

Items Left Behind on the Recessed Floor

To expose the recessed floor of the Structure 28 temple, we of course had to remove lots of the usual post-abandonment earthen fill. We considered any items we encountered in this fill to be in tertiary context. Eventually, however, we came upon large intact patches of the lime-plastered floor itself. Three objects were found lying in direct contact with this floor, and all were items that could potentially have been related to temple activities. Their locations are shown in Figure 8.45.

In the southeast corner of Square S5E8 we found a broken obsidian artifact that appears to be an imitation stingray spine (Fig. 8.46*a*). This artifact was most likely used for bloodletting.

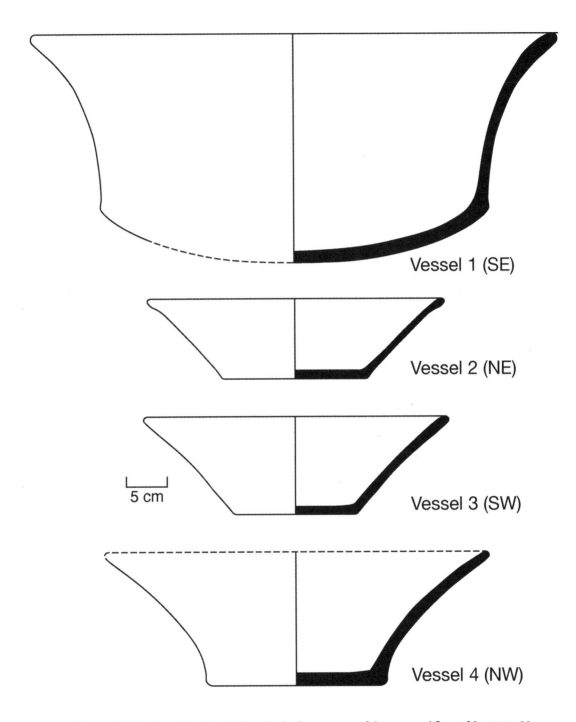

Figure 8.43. The large bowls buried under the four corners of the recessed floor of Structure 28.

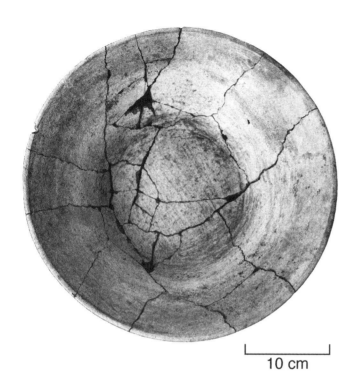

Figure 8.44. Vessel 2, a Guadalupe Burnished Brown vessel buried beneath the northeast corner of the recessed floor, Structure 28. This large bowl had been broken by the weight of the overburden.

10 cm

In Square S8E9 we found a human clavicle showing deliberate cut marks (Fig. 8.46*b*). This object could constitute evidence for ritual cannibalism.

Finally, in Square S7E9 we found the ulna of a bobwhite quail (*Colinus virginianus*). Elderly Zapotec informants told us that quail were likely chosen for sacrifice because one can observe them drinking from dewdrops. As a result of their apparent refusal to drink dirty water, quail are considered "clean" or "pure" birds by the Zapotec, making them appropriate offerings (Marcus and Flannery 1994). This was our first of many discoveries of quail bones in temples.

The Burning of Structure 28

As far as we know, Structure 28 was the most important temple at San José Mogote during the Rosario phase. Its lofty position on Mound 1 was only enhanced by its placement on the Structure 19B platform; it would have been visible for many kilometers.

Despite the size and defensive manpower of San José Mogote, the Structure 28 temple eventually became the target of a raid. Late in its history, it was the scene of an intense fire that destroyed its wattle-and-daub superstructure and left thousands of fragments of burned daub lying on its recessed floor. So intense was the fire that much of this clay daub was vitrified, turning to masses of grayish, glassy cinders (Figs. 8.45, 8.47).

Experimental burning of wattle-and-daub buildings has shown it to be unlikely that so destructive a fire was accidental. Gary D. Shaffer (1993), who has conducted such experiments, examined our cinders and reports that since temperatures of at least 1100° to 1200° C are needed for clay vitrification, it is unlikely that our cinders could have been produced without intentional burning. Mirjana Stevanović (1995) also examined our cinders and found them similar to those from deliberately burned wattle-and-daub houses in Neolithic Eastern Europe; she, too, sees evidence for temperatures in excess of 1000° C. Alison E. Rautman (1983) undertook a petrographic analysis of our cinders and pointed out

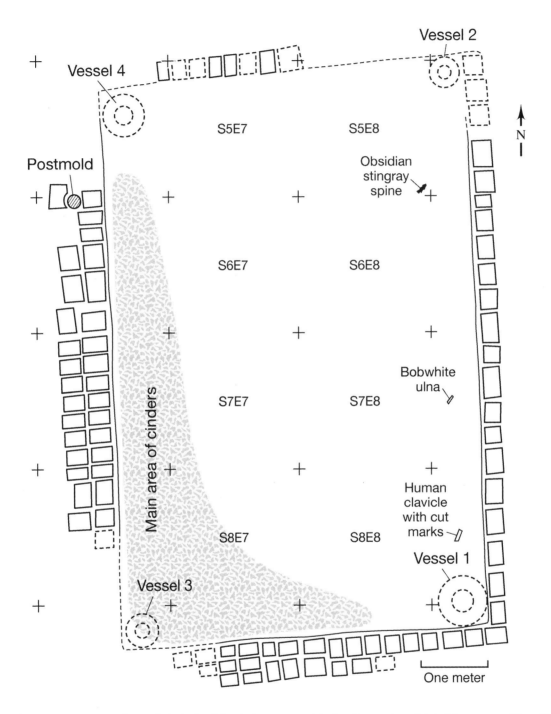

Figure 8.45. When Structure 28 was burned, the bulk of the cinders accumulated on the western third of the recessed floor. Vessels 1–4 were unburned because they were buried below the floor. An obsidian stingray spine, a quail ulna, and a human clavicle with cut marks were found on intact patches of the eastern floor.

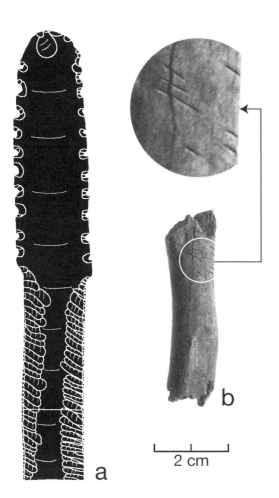

Figure 8.46. Two objects found lying on the recessed floor of the Structure 28 temple. *a* is an imitation stingray spine chipped from an obsidian blade (its point was broken off). *b* is a fragment of human clavicle with deliberate cut marks.

that even the quartz grains in the clay were melted, which could reflect temperatures as high as 1700° C. In sum, the Structure 28 temple seems to have been deliberately burned at a very high temperature.

Dating Structure 28 with Ceramics

We recovered ceramics from three different contexts relevant to Structure 28. First, there were sherds in the adobe substructure of the temple; second, there were sherds in the fill above the recessed floor; and third, there were sherds in the fill heaped around Structure 28 after its abandonment.

Let us begin with the substructure itself. As described earlier, adobe walls had been used both to outline this substructure and to divide it into cells that could then be filled with basketloads

of earth. Those basketloads of earth contained sherds of Socorro Fine Gray composite silhouette bowls that would not be out of place in the Guadalupe phase or the early Rosario phase (Figs. 8.48, 8.49). Many of the outleaned- or outcurved-rim bowls displayed Drennan's Rim Eccentricity 7, which did not last beyond the Rosario phase (Figs. 8.49, 8.50). A number bore incised crescent or scallop motifs, with or without pattern burnishing, while others featured the pennant motif, with or without negative white decoration (Fig. 8.50). There were also Josefina Fine Gray sherds that would not be out of place in the Guadalupe phase or early Rosario phase (Fig. 8.51).

In addition, many of the diagnostic sherds in the Structure 28 fill belonged to pre-Rosario periods, and had presumably been introduced into the fill of the structure via the basketloads of earth. Many sherds were Tierras Largas phase types, and might

5 cm

Figure 8.47. A sample of vitrified cinders from the recessed floor of Structure 28.

have been brought from as far away as Areas B and C of the village. Included were fragments of Tierras Largas Burnished Plain, Avelina Red-on-buff, and Matadamas Orange. There were also dozens of Atoyac Yellow-white sherds with incised motifs like those found in the houses and middens of Area A (Flannery and Marcus 2005:252–294). Our suspicion, therefore, is that every residential ward of San José Mogote might have contributed its share of earthen fill during the construction of Structure 28. This would have given the temple community-wide significance, justifying its lofty position on Mound 1.

The figurine fragments in our sample also suggested that the fill dirt had come from many different proveniences. Included

were several diagnostic San José phase heads, a foot with a typical Guadalupe phase sandal, and a few fragments from Rosario phase figurines.

Let us turn next to the basketloads of earth used to cover the burnt recessed floor. We concluded that this fill had been added after the destruction of the temple, and that its purpose was to level the area so that Structures 27 and 31 (two buildings of Stratigraphic Zone C) could be built above the ruins of Structure 28. We saved all the sherds from this earthen fill, hoping that they would provide a general date for the abandonment of Structure 28 and the reuse of the area for new buildings. The diagnostic ceramics from this provenience were as follows:

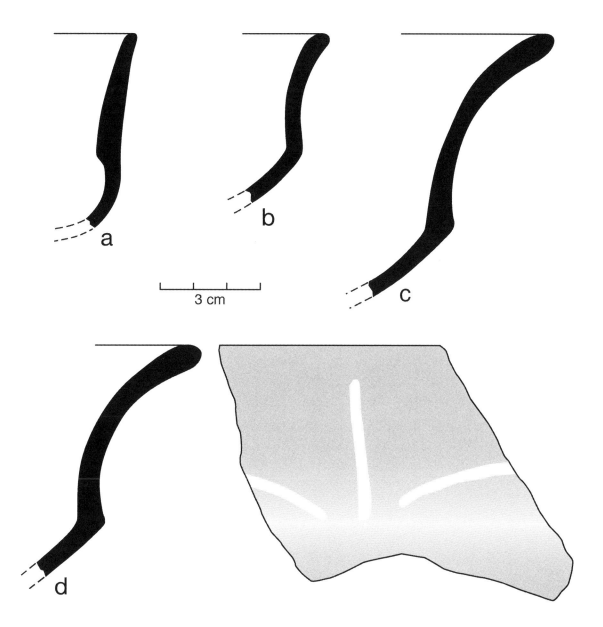

Figure 8.48. Socorro Fine Gray composite silhouette bowls from the fill of Structure 28. *a–c* are undecorated; the motif on *d* is done in negative white. *a* and *b* would not be out of place in a Guadalupe phase assemblage, while *d* has Rosario phase attributes. All our evidence suggests that Structure 28 was built relatively early in the Rosario phase.

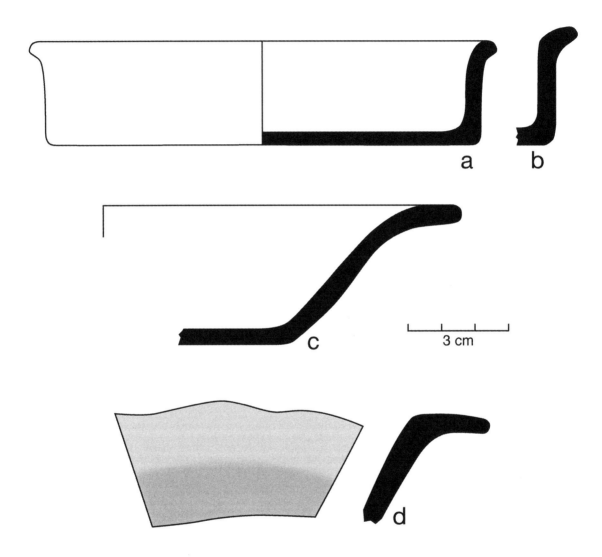

Figure 8.49. Undecorated Socorro Fine Gray sherds from the fill of Structure 28. *a, b*, shallow dishes with slightly everted rims (*a* is reconstructed from sherds). *c*, outcurved-wall bowl with Drennan's Rim Form 3. *d*, outcurved-wall bowl with Rim Form 5 and Eccentricity 7. This eccentricity did not last beyond the Rosario phase.

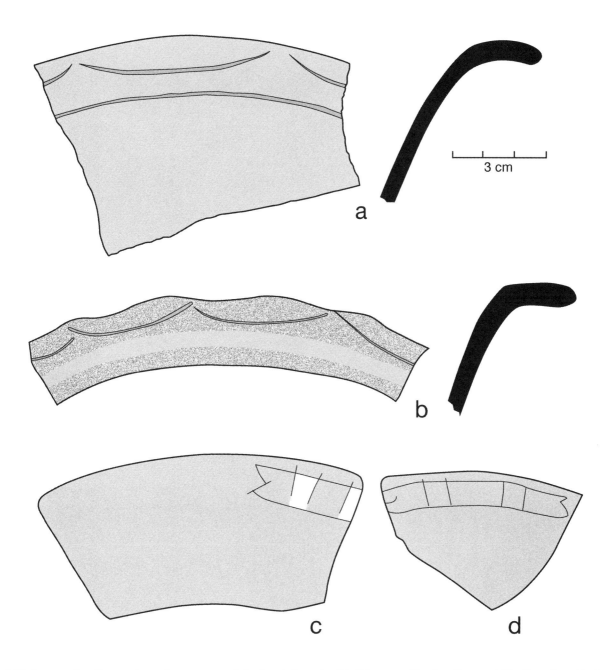

Figure 8.50. Socorro Fine Gray outleaned- or outcurved-rim bowls from the fill of Structure 28. *a* has Drennan's Rim Form 3 and incised crescents. *b* has Rim Form 5, Eccentricity 7, crescent incising, and pattern burnishing. *c* and *d* have incised pennants; *c* also has negative white.

GUADALUPE BURNISHED BROWN
  outleaned-wall bowls, rims: 9

SOCORRO FINE GRAY
  outleaned/outcurved-wall bowls, rims: 50
  composite silhouette bowls, plain rims: 16
  composite silhouette bowls, rims, incising only: 4
  composite silhouette bowls, rims, negative white only: 4
  composite silhouette bowls, rims, incising and negative white: 5
  composite silhouette bowls, rims, pattern burnishing: 3
  composite silhouette bowls, zoned toning: 2
  miniature composite silhouette bowls, rims: 4
  bowl body sherds: 8
  incurved-rim bowls, rims: 2
  shallow dishes, rims: 5
  convex-walled bowls, rims: 5
  "ashtrays": 2
  very large bowl, like Vessel 1 of Fig. 8.43: 1 rim

JOSEFINA FINE GRAY
  composite silhouette bowls, rims: 6
  sherds from beakers: 2

LUPITA HEAVY PLAIN
  fragments of undecorated Suchilquitongo tripod dishes: 3

FIDENCIO COARSE
  jar rims: 15
  jar shoulders with plastic decoration: 2
  tecomate sherd: 1

TIERRAS LARGAS BURNISHED PLAIN
  body sherds: 2

AVELINA RED-ON-BUFF
  hemispherical bowls, rims: 5
  jar shoulders with plastic decoration: 2

MATADAMAS RED
  jar rim: 1

MATADAMAS ORANGE
  body sherds: 3

LEANDRO GRAY
  body sherds: 6

ATOYAC YELLOW-WHITE
  fragments of cylinders and outleaned-wall bowls: 15

SAN JOSÉ RED-ON WHITE
  body sherd: 1

XOCHILTEPEC WHITE
  body sherd: 1

DELIA WHITE
  body sherd: 1

COATEPEC WHITE
  body sherds: 3

SAN JOSÉ SPECULAR RED
  body sherd: 1

We coded all 50 rims of Socorro Fine Gray outleaned/outcurved-wall bowls in Drennan's system. The attributes were as follows:
  Rim Form 1, no decoration: 3
  Rim Form 2, no decoration: 7
  Rim Form 2, fineline incised pennant: 1
  Rim Form 2, fineline incised crescent: 1
  Rim Form 2, wide horizontal incised lines: 3
  Rim Form 2, fineline incised pennant with negative white: 2
  Rim Form 2, vertical lines in negative white: 2
  Rim Form 2, crescent in negative white: 1
  Rim Form 2, Eccentricity 3, fineline incised crescent: 1
  Rim Form 2, Eccentricity 4, wide vertical incised lines and negative white: 1
  Rim Form 3, no decoration: 1
  Rim Form 3, fine horizontal incised lines: 1
  Rim Form 3, horizontal stripes in zoned toning: 3
  Rim Form 3, crescent in negative white: 1
  Rim Form 3, Eccentricity 3, undecorated: 1
  Rim Form 3, Eccentricity 3, fine horizontal incised lines: 1
  Rim Form 3, Eccentricity 4, wideline incised crescent: 1
  Rim Form 3, Eccentricity(?), wideline horizontal incised lines: 1
  Rim Form 4, no decoration: 1
  Rim Form 4, fine horizontal incised lines: 1
  Rim Form 5, no decoration: 1
  Rim Form 5, fine horizontal incised lines: 3
  Rim Form 5, fineline incised scallops: 2
  Rim Form 5, horizontal lines in negative white: 4
  Rim Form 5, vertical lines in negative white: 2
  Rim Form 7, fineline incised pennant: 1
  Rim Form 12, Eccentricity 3, horizontal lines in negative white: 1
  Rim Form (?), Eccentricity 3, wideline incised crescent: 1
  Rim Form (?), Eccentricity 7, wide horizontal incised lines: 1

We conclude that the earth used to cover the burnt recessed floor of Structure 28 contained a mixture of Rosario phase sherds and redeposited ceramics from even earlier periods. This was no surprise, since the buildings found in Stratigraphic Zone C (above Structure 28) also dated to the Rosario phase (see Flannery and Marcus 2005: Chapter 23).

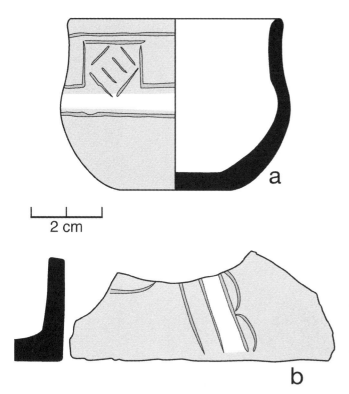

2 cm

Figure 8.51. Josefina Fine Gray pottery from the fill of Structure 28. *a*, small composite silhouette bowl with incised motif and negative white stripe (reconstructed from sherds). *b*, cylinder with motif combining incising and negative white. Both vessel forms occur in the Guadalupe phase; the negative white is a Rosario phase attribute.

Let us now turn to our third ceramic sample from the vicinity of Structure 28. Sometime after the abandonment of that burned temple, the leaders of San José Mogote oversaw the heaping of thousands of basketloads of fill around it, leveling the area so that Structures 27 and 31 could be built. Our sample of sherds from this postabandonment fill consisted of more than 500 diagnostic sherds of the Tierras Largas, San José, Guadalupe, and Rosario phases. In addition, we recovered more than 1500 nondiagnostic body sherds. All these sherds, of course, were in tertiary context.

We coded all 112 rims of Socorro Fine Gray outleaned/outcurved-wall bowls in Drennan's system. The attributes were as follows:

Rim Form 2, no decoration: 24
Rim Form 2, fine horizontal incised lines: 5
Rim Form 2, fineline incised crescents: 2
Rim Form 2, fineline incised pennant: 1
Rim Form 2, wide horizontal incised lines: 4
Rim Form 2, wideline incised crescents: 1
Rim Form 2, wide horizontal incised lines and zoned toning: 2
Rim Form 2, fine horizontal incised lines and negative white: 3

Rim Form 2, fineline incised crescents and negative white: 2
Rim Form 2, crescents in negative white: 10
Rim Form 2, vertical stripes in negative white: 2
Rim Form 2, Eccentricity 3, undecorated: 1
Rim Form 3, no decoration: 4
Rim Form 3, fine horizontal incised lines: 5
Rim Form 3, wide horizontal incised lines: 1
Rim Form 3, fine horizontal incised lines and zoned toning: 1
Rim Form 3, horizontal lines in zoned toning: 1
Rim Form 3, horizontal lines in negative white: 4
Rim Form 3, Eccentricity 3, wideline (?) incised crescents: 1
Rim Form 3, Eccentricity 4, wideline dot motif: 1
Rim Form 3, Eccentricity 6, wideline incised sine curves: 1
Rim Form 3, Eccentricity 6, horizontal lines in negative white: 1
Rim Form 3, Eccentricity 7, undecorated: 1
Rim Form 3, Eccentricity 7, fine horizontal incised lines: 2
Rim Form 3, Eccentricity 7, fineline incised pennant and zoned toning: 1
Rim Form 4, no decoration: 2

Rim Form 4, fineline incised pennant: 1
Rim Form 4, wideline incised sine curves: 1
Rim Form 5, no decoration: 2
Rim Form 5, fine horizontal incised lines: 2
Rim Form 5, fineline incised crescents: 1
Rim Form 5, fineline incising and negative white: 1
Rim Form 5, horizontal stripes in zoned toning: 1
Rim Form 5, vertical lines in negative white: 1
Rim Form 5, crescent in negative white: 1
Rim Form 5, horizontal lines in negative white: 2
Rim Form 5, Eccentricity 4, wide horizontal incised lines: 1
Rim Form 5, Eccentricity 4, wideline incised sine curves: 1
Rim Form 5, Eccentricity 4, fineline (?) incised crescents with negative white: 1
Rim Form 5, Eccentricity 5, wide horizontal incised lines: 1
Rim Form 5, Eccentricity 6, fineline incised sine curves: 1
Rim Form 5, Eccentricity 7, undecorated: 4
Rim Form 5, Eccentricity 7, fineline incising (?): 1
Rim Form 7, fine horizontal incised lines: 1
Rim Form 9, no decoration: 3
Rim Form 10, Eccentricity 6, wide horizontal incised lines: 1
Rim Form 12, fine horizontal incised lines: 1

In addition to the 112 outleaned/outcurved-wall bowl rims, the Zone D fill contained the following Socorro Fine Gray sherds:
composite silhouette bowls, plain: 30
composite silhouette bowls with negative white alone: 7
composite silhouette bowl with incising and negative white: 1
composite silhouette bowls with incising and zoned toning: 6
composite silhouette bowl, incised with crescent motif: 1
composite silhouette bowls with plain everted rims: 3
composite silhouette bowls, miniature: 4
rims from cylindrical or hemispherical bowls: 4
bowl with rim flange, incised, with negative white: 1

rims of "ashtrays": 4
rims of very large bowls, similar to the buried offerings in the corners of Structure 28: 2
rims of globular ollas, plain: 4
fragment of bird effigy: 1

Given the hundreds of Rosario phase sherds found in the construction fill of Structure 28, the earth used to cover up its recessed floor, and the tons of earth heaped around it to level the area for future construction, there can be no doubt about the temple's date. Not one single sherd found in association with the building—not even in its postabandonment fill—was later in age than Rosario.

Dating Structure 28 with Radiocarbon

Lying among the masses of vitrified cinders from the burning of Structure 28, we found what appeared to be a fallen roof beam. This carbonized wooden beam became radiocarbon sample Beta-177624. The conventional date came out 2550 ± 60 years before the present, or 600 b.c. When dendrocalibrated, this date has a two-sigma range of 820–500 BC.

The conventional date for this sample falls in the middle of the Rosario phase, but we should bear in mind that the roof beam was presumably part of the original construction of the temple. Beta-177624 therefore dates the moment at which the temple was built, not the moment at which it was destroyed. We suspect that the actual burning of Structure 28 took place somewhat later than 600 b.c., and may have been one of a series of events convincing the leaders of San José Mogote that their chiefly center did not occupy a sufficiently defensible location. This realization was probably one of the factors leading to their eventual relocation to the summit of Monte Albán.

9 | Architecture and Writing in the Service of the Chief

The burning of Structure 28 temporarily deprived the residents of San José Mogote of their most prominent temple. Soon, however, their architects set about building a replacement. The spot chosen for the new Rosario phase temple was only a few meters north of Structure 19, the final stage of the masonry platform supporting Structure 28.

Structure 14

The first phase of the new temple's construction was the building of Structure 14, its supporting masonry platform. Structure 14 originally had the shape of a giant plus sign (Fig. 9.1). Because this platform was extensively modified during the Monte Albán II period, however, it proved difficult to calculate its original Rosario phase dimensions. As nearly as we can tell, the east-west arm was about 24 m long, while its north-south arm was closer to 21 m. The platform originally had a wide staircase on its east side, overlooking Area A of San José Mogote (Fig. 9.2). Its rear wall, in other words, would have been on the west.

Later Modification of Structure 14

The modifications imposed on Structure 14 during Monte Albán II were extensive. The architects of that period wanted a staircase on the west side, in preparation for which they destroyed the original west wall of the building. They did not need a staircase on the east, so they removed many of the stones in the original Rosario phase staircase and used them elsewhere. They also enlarged the building by creating a new north wall (see Fig. 9.1 and Chapter 13).

Despite the best efforts of the Monte Albán II architects, however, some parts of the original Rosario platform survived. For example, we found the fieldstone footing for its original north wall, albeit deeply buried by later fill (Fig. 9.1). Best preserved of all was the Rosario phase south wall, which still retained one of the jogs that had given the original building its plus-sign shape. The surviving jog in the south wall, in fact, turned out to be the best place to work out the stratigraphic relationship of the Rosario phase and Monte Albán II versions of Structure 14.

The Stratigraphy of the Jog in the South Wall

Figure 9.3a shows our crew beginning to excavate the jog in the south wall. We discovered that the Rosario phase version of the south wall had been built with large blocks of limestone from the Matadamas quarries. The Monte Albán II masons added new courses of smaller stones to this wall until they had virtually doubled its height (Fig. 9.3b).

The fill inside the jog was almost 2 m deep (Fig. 9.4). The

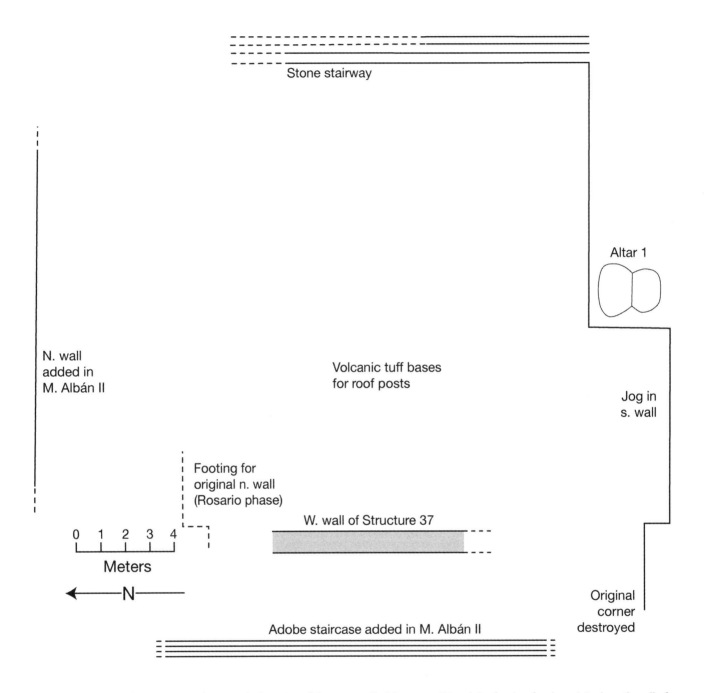

Stone stairway

N. wall
added in
M. Albán II

Volcanic tuff bases
for roof posts

Altar 1

Jog in
s. wall

Footing for
original n. wall
(Rosario phase)

W. wall of Structure 37

0 1 2 3 4

Meters

◄——N——►

Original
corner
destroyed

Adobe staircase added in M. Albán II

Figure 9.1. Plan view of Structure 14, showing the location of the west wall of Structure 37 and the footing for the original north wall of Structure 14.

Figure 9.2. The east side of Structure 14. Surviving courses of stones from the original late Rosario phase stairway (now badly destroyed) have been consolidated with cement.

deepest 50 cm (from 1.5 m depth down to sterile soil) yielded about 250 sherds; roughly 20 percent of the diagnostics belonged to the Rosario phase, and 80 percent consisted of redeposited Tierras Largas, San José, and Guadalupe phase types. As was the case with Structure 19, the diversity of Formative sherds hinted that every residential ward of the village had been called upon to contribute basketloads of fill.

At depths of 1.1 m to 1.5 m, the fill was less dense. This level yielded more than 100 redeposited-looking sherds of the Rosario, Guadalupe, and San José phases. Among the diagnostics were Socorro Fine Gray bowls with attributes that included Drennan's Rim Form 5 with 2 parallel incised lines on the rim and possible zoned toning; Drennan's Eccentricity 7; Drennan's Rim Form 5 with fineline crescents; and outleaned rims with crescents in negative white. We also found 2 outleaned-wall bowls in Gua-

dalupe Burnished Brown, a Lupita Heavy Plain charcoal brazier, 2 Atoyac Yellow-white bowls, a Fidencio Coarse jar shoulder, and a typical San José phase figurine leg.

At depths of 90 cm to 1.1 m, we recovered more than 150 redeposited Rosario, Guadalupe, San José, and Tierras Largas phase sherds. Included among the diagnostics were sherds of Socorro Fine Gray, Fidencio Coarse, Atoyac Yellow-white, San José Specular Red, and Avelina Red-on-Buff.

The transition from the fill of the original Rosario building to the fill of the later Monte Albán II building took place at a depth of 80–90 cm. Among the Monte Albán II diagnostics in this level were 2 CBA Type G21 rims, a G21 base, a subtype G12b base, 3 fragments of C12 bowls, a C11 sherd, a C7 sherd, and an A11 bowl rim. At least 30 redeposited sherds of the Rosario and San José phases were also present.

Figure 9.3. Stratigraphic excavation of Structure 14. *a*, beginning excavation of the jog in the south wall. *b*, Irán Matadamas points to one of the smaller stones added to the south wall during Monte Albán II. The larger Rosario phase stones can be seen at the level of his waist. (View from inside the jog.)

Figure 9.4. Excavation inside the jog in the south wall of Structure 14. *a*, view from the west, showing the big wedging stones used to level the Rosario stage of the wall. The smaller stones of the Monte Albán II stage can be seen above. *b*, view from the northeast as the workmen reach sterile soil.

Above: Figure 9.5. Structure 14. Maestro Genaro Luis consolidates the jog in the south wall to prevent its future collapse.

Right: Figure 9.6. *a*, A workman pedestals the footing stones from a remnant of the Rosario phase north wall of Structure 14. This wall, which appears to have had a jog in it similar to the one in the south wall, was badly destroyed during Monte Albán II, and later completely engulfed by the fill of the adobe staircase built for Structure 36. *b*, This broken Formative loaf-shaped mano was reused as construction stone in Structure 37, not far to the south of the wall remnant shown in *a*.

For some reason, the density of sherds in the fill was sparser at depths of 60–80 cm. However, from a depth of 60 cm up to the highest in situ wall stone of the jog, the density of sherds was greater and left no doubt that we were in the Monte Albán II stage of Structure 14.

Based on these results, we conclude that the original plus-sign-shaped Rosario phase version of Structure 14 stood about 1.0 to 1.1 m high. The Monte Albán II masons raised its south wall by at least 90 cm.

After completing our stratigraphic excavation, we backfilled the jog in the south wall with earth (and occasional soft drink bottles from the modern era) and consolidated it with cement to prevent its collapse (Fig. 9.5).

Structure 37

Just as Structure 19B had been built to support the Structure 28 temple, the original Rosario phase version of Structure 14 had been built to support the temple we called Structure 37. In contrast to Structure 28, however, this new temple was given the true east-west orientation we saw in Structures 19A and 19.

It took us a long time to reach Structure 37 because it had been buried beneath three or four Monte Albán II temples. The collapse of those temples had left more than 2.5 m of overburden atop Structure 14 (see Appendix A). Not until we had thoroughly documented and removed all those Monte Albán II temples were we finally able to uncover Structure 37, sitting atop the ruins of the Rosario phase stage of Structure 14 (Fig. 9.6).

Structure 37 lay at a depth of 3.0–3.5 m below the arbitrary

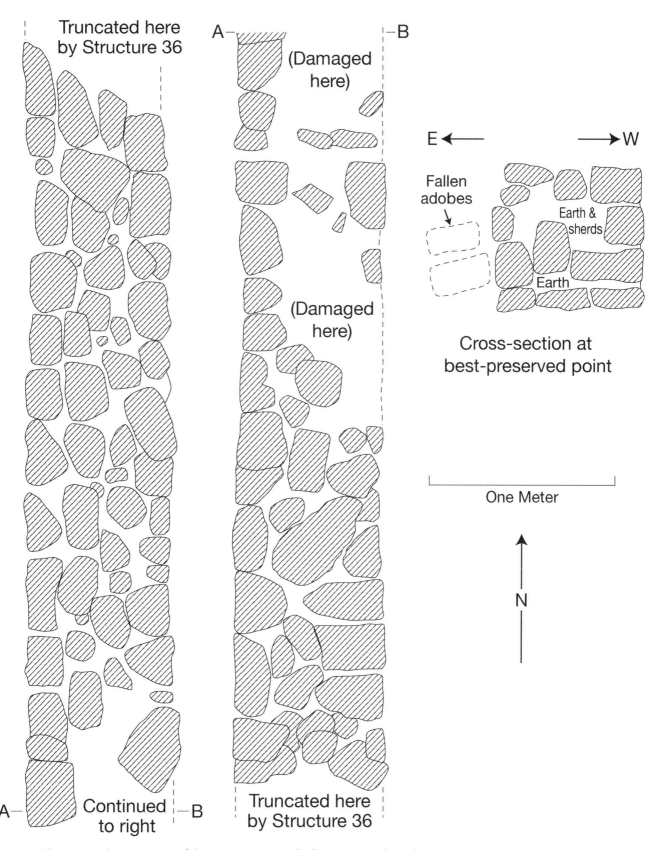

Figure 9.7. Plan view and cross-section of the surviving west wall of Structure 37, the earliest temple placed on Structure 14 (3.0–3.5 m below datum). Late Rosario phase.

Figure 9.8. View (from the southwest) of the best-preserved stretch of outer façade on the west wall of Structure 37. It is from this area that the cross-section shown in Fig. 9.7 was taken.

datum established for the Structure 14 overburden (see Appendix A). We could not determine the temple's precise dimensions because it had been extensively damaged during the building of Structure 36, a Monte Albán II temple. We did, however, recover an intact 8 m section of Structure 37's west wall (Figs. 9.7–9.9), which allowed us to see that the temple's walls had been made of adobe brick, placed on a masonry foundation consisting of four courses of stones. Incorporated into the wall was a segment of burnt post.

Structure 37 also provided us with evidence for an architec-

tural feature seen in no previous temple. Still sitting in place, in what would once have been the center of Structure 37, were 2 cut stones that appeared to be the volcanic tuff bases for a pair of roof-support columns (Fig. 9.10). More of these conical, flat-topped stones came to light in the earthen fill of Structure 36, and others had been reused in a flagstone pavement created during Monte Albán II (Fig. 9.11). We even found 2 unfinished examples of these column bases in the fill of a later building.

Only in Structure 37, however, did we find such column bases in situ; in all other contexts, they had been reused as fill. Our

Figure 9.9. Two views (from the north) of the surviving west wall of Structure 37. The north arrow is marked in both centimeters and inches.

Figure 9.10. Volcanic tuff bases for wooden roof-support columns. The two at far left were found in association with Structure 37. The remaining examples were found in the fill of later buildings. The two at far right in the back row were never finished. The ranging pole is marked in 10-cm sections.

suspicion, therefore, is that the roof of Structure 37 was supported by a number of wooden columns set on volcanic tuff bases, their conical lower ends having been driven into the platform below. Given this unique architectural feature, we are disappointed that Structure 37 was not better preserved.

Dating Structure 37 with Ceramics

Since the stone masonry foundation of the west wall was the best preserved part of Structure 37, we drew it and photographed it, then took it apart carefully, saving every sherd incorporated into its construction. Some 140 of the sherds were diagnostics, and none belonged to a period more recent than the Rosario phase. The diagnostics from Structure 37 were as follows:

SOCORRO FINE GRAY
    rims of outleaned/outcurved-wall bowls: 46
    rims of composite silhouette bowls: 10 (5 plain; 2 incised
        only; 3 negative white only) (Fig. 9.12*a*)
    bases of composite silhouette bowls: 2
    bases of shallow dishes, slightly everted lip: 4 (2 plain; 1
        incised only; 1 pennant incised plus negative white)

rim of "ashtray": 1
rim of miniature outleaned-wall bowl: 1

JOSEFINA FINE GRAY
    rims of composite silhouette bowls: 3
    rims of vertical-walled bowls: 2
    rim of bowl with pennant incising and negative white: 1
        (Fig. 9.12*c*)
    rim of outleaned-wall bowl: 1
    body sherds with incising or negative white: 2

GUADALUPE BURNISHED BROWN
    rims of outleaned/outcurved-wall bowls: 10
    rims of bowls with trace of white wash: 2

FIDENCIO COARSE
    rims of jars: 2
    rim of *tecomate*: 1

LUPITA HEAVY PLAIN
    fragments of undecorated Suchilquitongo tripod dishes: 2
        (Fig. 9.12*d*)

Figure 9.11. Close-up view of the flagstone pavement added to the north wall of Structure 19 (see Fig. 8.9). The black arrow points to a circular base for a roof-support column, reused as a flagstone. The flagstone pavement dates to Monte Albán II and used stones robbed from Structure 37 and an earlier stage of Structure 14.

fragments of charcoal braziers: 2
mat-impressed potstand base: 1
rim of *tecomate*: 1
rim of outleaned-wall bowl: 1

ATOYAC YELLOW-WHITE
    rims of cylindrical bowls, plain: 3
    rim of cylindrical bowl, incised: 1
    rims of outleaned-wall bowls, plain: 3
    rims of outleaned-wall bowls, incised: 8
    rims, too small to tell shape: 2
    giant macrorim: 1
    body sherd of *apaxtle* (basin): 1
    tecomate body sherd, rocker stamped: 1

COATEPEC WHITE-RIMMED BLACK
    rim of outleaned-wall bowl: 1

COATEPEC WHITE
    incised body sherds: 2

DELIA WHITE
    rim of beaker: 1

LA MINA WHITE
    rim of incurved-rim bowl: 1

AVELINA RED-ON-BUFF
    rims of hemispherical bowls: 8

MATADAMAS RED
    rim of jar: 1
    rim of hemispherical bowl: 1

MATADAMAS ORANGE
    rims of jars: 2
    rim of outleaned-wall bowl: 1

FIGURINE FRAGMENTS
    heads with slit eyes: 2
    head with 2 ploughing-stroke eyes: 1
    torso of seated figure: 1
    heads with Guadalupe or Rosario phase punched-pupil eyes: 3

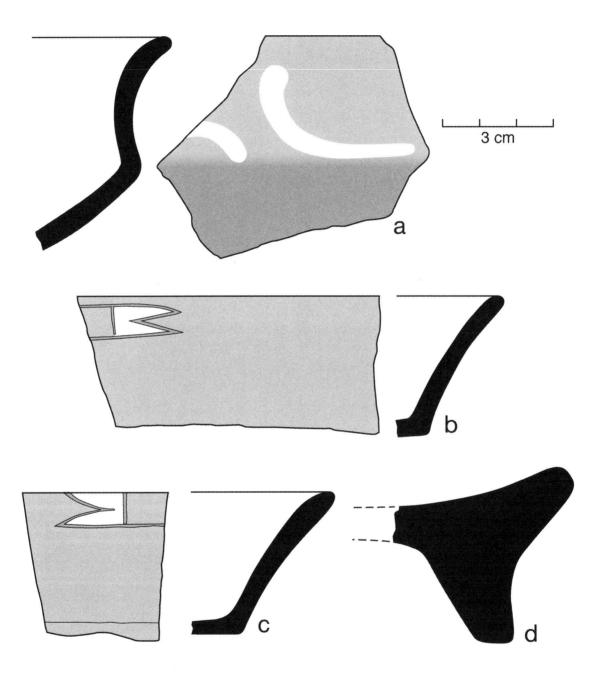

Figure 9.12. Sherds from the fill of Structure 37. *a*, Socorro Fine Gray composite silhouette bowl with negative white crescents. *b*, Socorro Fine Gray bowl incised with Drennan's Type d pennant in negative white. *c*, Josefina Fine Gray bowl incised with Drennan's Type d pennant in negative white. *d*, undecorated Suchilquitongo tripod dish, Lupita Heavy Plain ware.

We coded all 46 rims of Socorro Fine Gray outleaned/outcurved-wall bowls in Drennan's system. The attributes were as follows:

Rim Form 1, pennant incising, negative white: 1 (Fig. 9.12*b*)
Rim Form 2, no decoration: 2
Rim Form 2, fine horizontal incised lines: 2
Rim Form 2, fineline incised scallop: 2
Rim Form 2, fineline incised pennant: 1
Rim Form 2, wide horizontal incised lines: 4
Rim Form 2, fine horizontal incised lines and zoned toning: 1
Rim Form 2, fineline incised pennant and negative white: 1
Rim Form 2, fineline incising pennant and blob of negative white: 1
Rim Form 2, crescents in negative white: 2
Rim Form 2, negative white, motif unclear: 1
Rim Form 2, Eccentricity 1, fineline incised scallop: 1
Rim Form 2, Eccentricity 3, fineline incised crescents: 2
Rim Form 3, no decoration: 3
Rim Form 3, fine horizontal incised lines: 3
Rim Form 3, fineline incised scallop: 1
Rim Form 3, wide horizontal incised lines: 1
Rim Form 3, fine horizontal incised lines and zoned toning: 2
Rim Form 3, horizontal band of pattern burnishing: 2
Rim Form 3, horizontal line in negative white: 1
Rim Form 3, crescent in negative white: 1
Rim Form 5, no decoration: 2
Rim Form 5, fine horizontal incised lines: 1
Rim Form 5, horizontal band of pattern burnishing: 3
Rim Form 5, horizontal lines in negative white: 1
Rim Form 5, Eccentricity 4, horizontal band of pattern burnishing: 1
Rim Form 9, no decoration: 1
Rim Form 9, fineline incised bowtie (probably a version of the pennant motif): 1
Rim Form (?), fine horizontal incised lines and zoned toning: 1

A Radiocarbon Date from Structure 37

Charcoal from the burnt post fragment found in the wall of Structure 37 became radiocarbon sample Beta-177626. The conventional date came out 2540 ± 90 years before the present, or 590 b.c.; the calibrated two-sigma range would be 840–400 BC. We consider this to be a late Rosario phase date, and we suspect that Structure 37 may have been the last major temple built before the bulk of San José Mogote's population left to participate in the founding of Monte Albán.

In building Structure 37 and its original plus-sign-shaped platform, the leaders of San José Mogote were sending a very clear message to the rival society who had burned Structure 28:

> You may have destroyed our temple, but you have not defeated us. We have now built an even more impressive temple only a few meters away. Bring it on.

Monument 3 and the Iconography of Chiefly Power

By building Structure 14 right next to Structure 19 and giving it the same orientation, the architects of San José Mogote had created an east-west corridor between the two stone masonry platforms. In the vicinity of the jog in the south wall of Structure 14, that corridor was only 2 m wide (Fig. 9.13).

When we first turned our attention to this corridor in 1975, it was filled with slopewash from the post-Rosario phase overburden of both Structure 14 and Structure 19. We first became aware how deep this slopewash was when we were clearing the so-called "*laja* porch," a flagstone pavement built during Monte Albán II to brace the slumping north wall of Structure 19 (see Fig. 8.9).

Once we had exposed the flagstone pavement, we could see traces of at least two white stucco floors in the profile of the corridor fill. We suspected that these two floors might be somehow related to the temples built on Structures 14 and 19. We decided, therefore, to create a grid of 1 × 1 m squares for the corridor and excavate it carefully, searching for features. As can be seen in Fig. 9.13, this grid consisted of 26 squares labeled C1 through C26, with "C" standing for "corridor." We decided not to tie this grid to either of the ones created for Structures 14 and 19, since those were both 2 × 2 m grids, and we did not know how any features we found in the corridor would relate to either of them.

Among other things, we did not know how deep the corridor excavation would be. We therefore decided to measure all depths in the corridor from the highest in situ stone of the jog in the south wall of Structure 14. Since the depth of that stone below the arbitrary datum point established for the Structure 14 overburden had already been measured, we could easily tie any item to that datum if it seemed appropriate.

The Stratigraphy of the Corridor Fill

For the first 50 cm or so of the excavation, we found ourselves in featureless slopewash that had filled the corridor to the level of the grassy 1975 land surface. This slopewash had some ancient sherds in it, but also pieces of Colonial or modern glass.

At a depth of roughly 50 cm, the nature of the deposit changed. Now we were clearly in a layer that was the decomposition product of adobe walls. With the wisdom of hindsight, we later realized that the source of this material was most likely the adobe walls of the temples built atop Structures 14 and 19 during Monte Albán II (Chapters 13 and 14); centuries of rain had washed the clay from those walls into the corridor.

At a depth of 1.43 m, we came upon a badly deteriorating stucco floor that ran the length of the corridor. We now suspect that this floor had once been connected to the adobe staircase added to Structure 14 during Monte Albán II times (Chapter 13). Unfortunately, the floor was not preserved well enough to be traced north or west of Square C1. We had equally bad luck trying to find the eastern limits of the floor; just east of Squares C25 and C26, it had been destroyed by a huge trash pit. This pit, obviously intrusive from above, was filled with broken incense

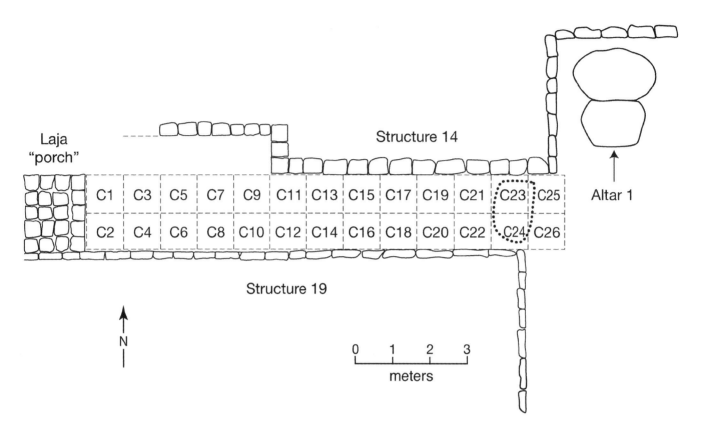

Figure 9.13. The corridor between the north wall of Structure 19 and the jog in the south wall of Structure 14 was divided into a grid of 26 1 × 1 m squares (C1–C26). An unexpected bonus of our corridor excavation was the discovery of Monument 3, which lay mostly in Squares C23 and C24 (heavy dotted line).

braziers and effigy urns from the Monte Albán II period. (See Chapter 13 for a discussion of this pit, which we eventually labeled Feature 20.)

As for the poorly preserved stucco floor at a depth of 1.43 m, we swept it clean and then removed it, saving all the sherds trapped beneath it. Included were diagnostics of both Monte Albán II (such as Types G21 and C11, and subtype C12b) and the Rosario phase (such as Socorro Fine Gray with negative white decoration).

Continuing downward, we came upon another stucco floor at a depth of 1.51 m. This second floor had deteriorated much like the first; it was filled with root hairs and cracks that left it more gray than white. It, too, had been truncated on the east by the same huge pit, and the floor petered out before it could be connected to any feature on the west.

In Squares C13–C17, however, this second floor not only reached the wall of Structure 14 but curled up against it, as often happens when a floor is laid against a preexisting wall. The same was true in Squares C14–C18, where the stucco floor curled up against the north wall of Structure 19. We concluded that the

entire corridor between those two platforms had been given a series of stucco floors during a period when Monte Albán II temples were being built atop Structures 14 and 19. As we had done with the first floor, we swept this second floor and then removed it, saving all the sherds trapped beneath it. Once again, the subfloor sherds suggested a Monte Albán II date for the floor.

As our excavation proceeded downward, we came upon a very firm earthen surface at a depth of 1.57 m. This surface, which ran the length of the corridor, did not appear to be a floor. Rather, it appeared to be an old land surface, and therefore a natural feature rather than anything man-made. In profile, its uppermost layer appeared to be an "A" soil zone—that is, an organic layer that had once supported vegetation. At first we thought that we might have reached the original land surface on which Structures 14 and 19 had been built, but we soon realized that we were still some distance above that point. Obviously, therefore, the A zone we found must have formed during a hiatus in the use of Structures 14 and 19—a hiatus lasting long enough for vegetation to grow in the corridor.

We swept the old land surface carefully, saving all the sherds

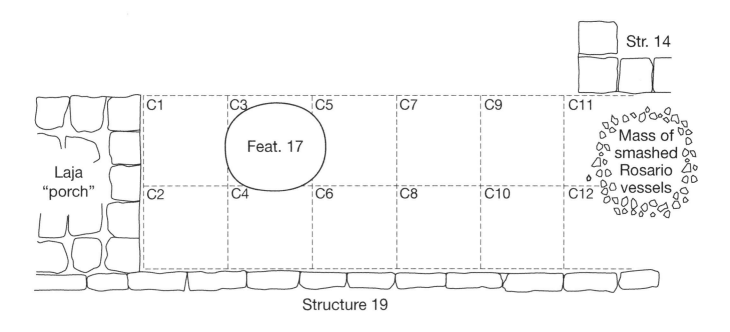

Figure 9.14. Feature 17, a Rosario phase pit, was found mostly in Square C3 of the corridor between Structures 14 and 19. About 3.5 m to the east was a mass of smashed Rosario phase braziers/incense burners.

that were in contact with it. None were later in age than the Rosario phase. Also, as we swept we began to find man-made features intrusive into the old land surface.

The first of these features was a cylindrical pit, oval in plan and largely restricted to Square C3 (Fig. 9.14). Designated Feature 17, this pit varied between 95 cm and 1.12 m in diameter and was 1.14 m deep (Fig. 9.15). It had been dug down from the level of the old land surface, and its earthen fill yielded ash, a dog vertebra, a cottontail rabbit pelvis, and a few sherds of the late Guadalupe and early Rosario phases.

About 3.5 m east of Feature 17, we found a mass of smashed Rosario phase vessels lying on the old land surface (Fig. 9.14). Virtually all these vessels were charcoal braziers or incense burners, but too many sherds were missing to allow them to be reconstructed.

Still farther to the east, in Square C17, we came upon Feature 18 (Fig. 9.16), a stone-lined hearth roughly 70 cm in diameter and 12 cm deep. It was well made, with 4 large stones and more than a dozen smaller stones outlining it. It had been dug down into the A zone of the old land surface, and it was filled with white

ash and small bits of charcoal from slender branches.

Still farther to the east we came upon a second hearth, which we designated Feature 19 (Fig. 9.17). This hearth lay mainly in Square C23, although it intruded a bit into C21 and C24. Roughly 65 cm in diameter and 12 cm deep, it was outlined by 15 to 16 medium-sized stones. This hearth had also been dug down into the A zone of the old land surface. It contained white ash and substantial chunks of fuel, some of which looked to us like prepared pine charcoal, the kind still made today by the *carboneros* who fell and burn pine trees in the mountains east of San José Mogote.

Dating Features 18 and 19 with Radiocarbon

We submitted charcoal samples from the 2 stone-lined hearths, Features 18 and 19, to Beta Analytic. The sample from Feature 18 became Beta-173808; its conventional date was 2510 ± 40 years before the present, or 560 b.c. When calibrated, the two-sigma range of this date would be 790–500 BC.

Two chunks of pine charcoal from Feature 19 were also

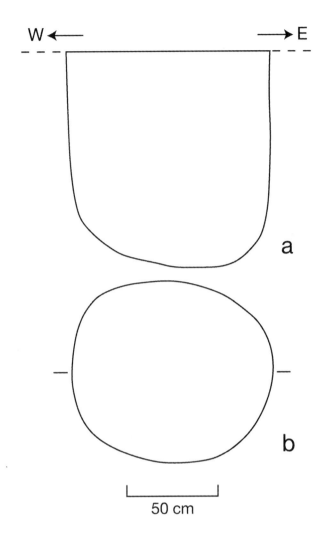

W ⟵   ⟶ E

a

b

⊢——————⊣
50 cm

Figure 9.15. Feature 17, a Rosario phase pit in the corridor between Structures 14 and 19. *a*, cross-section. *b*, plan view. The contents of the pit were earth, ash, a dog vertebra, a cottontail rabbit pelvis, and sherds of late Guadalupe phase and early Rosario phase pottery.

submitted, becoming samples Beta-175897 and Beta-175898. The conventional date for Beta-175897 came out 2680 ± 40 years before the present, or 730 b.c.; when calibrated, the two-sigma range of this date would be 900–800 BC. The conventional date for Beta-175898 came out 2580 ± 40 years before the present, or 630 b.c.; when calibrated, the two-sigma range of this date has two possibilities: either 820–760 BC or 620–590 BC.

In our opinion, the somewhat different conventional dates for Features 18 and 19 reflect the difference between dating young tree branches (Feature 18) and dating prepared charcoal made by the felling and burning of mature pine trees (Feature 19). The dates of 560 b.c. and 630 b.c. are within 70 years of each other, and could indicate the presence of charcoal from young branches. The older date of 730 b.c. could indicate the presence of charcoal from the inner growth rings of a mature tree.

The Discovery of Monument 3

As we continued excavating below the A zone of the old land surface, we came upon a stamped earth floor at a depth of about 1.7 m. We swept this floor carefully, trying to discover its limits. On the west, it passed beneath the paving stones of the so-called *laja* porch or flagstone pavement. On the east we traced it as far as we could, but eventually it had been destroyed by the same intrusive pit that had truncated the two stucco floors found earlier. By now we had accumulated so many brazier and urn fragments from this huge pit that we decided it needed a feature number. It therefore became Feature 20 (see Chapter 13).

It began to rain just as we finished sweeping the stamped earth floor at a depth of 1.7 m. Since rain makes it nearly impossible to trace earthen floors, we suspended work on the corridor for

Feature 18

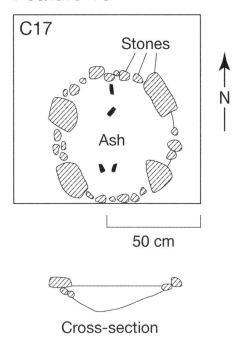

Above: Figure 9.16. Feature 18, a stone-lined hearth found in Square C17 of the corridor between Structures 14 and 19. The fill of the hearth was white ash and charcoal, and some of the stones were broken manos. Feature 18 yielded a radiocarbon date of 560 b.c. (uncalibrated).

Right: Figure 9.17. Feature 19, a stone-lined hearth found in Squares C23 and C24 of the corridor between Structures 14 and 19. The fill of the hearth was white ash, with fragments of what appeared to be prepared pine charcoal. Feature 19 had been dug into the dark, humic layer (or "A zone") of an old land surface that lay stratigraphically above Monument 3. Feature 19 yielded a radiocarbon date of 630 b.c. (uncalibrated).

Feature 19

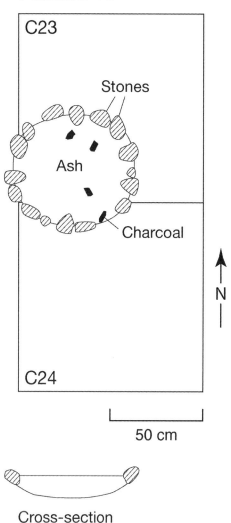

several days while it dried out. We covered the floor with plastic sheets to protect it while we worked elsewhere.

A few days later, we returned to the corridor and lifted the plastic sheets. Despite our best efforts to protect the earthen floor, a little rivulet of rainwater had run the length of the corridor and descended into the partially explored Feature 20 trash pit. In Square C23, the rivulet had exposed a large stone, placed level with the stamped earth floor at a depth of 1.72 m (Fig. 9.18). Workmen Germán Cruz and Leobardo Hernández were assigned to clean the mud from this stone, whose roughly trimmed eastern edge appeared in Squares C25 and C26. We began to suspect that the stone might have served as a threshold for the corridor.

Suddenly, as Germán and Leobardo cleaned the mud from the stone, they announced, "*Está grabada.*" The threshold for the corridor had turned out to be a carved stone, which we desig-

nated Monument 3 (Fig. 9.19). Further excavation showed that this stone not only filled the 2 m width of the corridor, but had also been carefully leveled by being set on a layer of flagstones (Fig. 9.20).

As Figure 9.21 shows, anyone entering the corridor from the east during the Rosario phase would have had to step on Monument 3. This act would have been a powerful metaphor, since the figure carved on the stone was that of a naked captive whose heart had been removed. Monument 3 would therefore seem to be our oldest example of what became a longstanding Mesoamerican tradition: metaphorically treading on the corpse of a defeated enemy. This tradition was later carried out on the Building L staircase at Monte Albán (Marcus and Flannery 1996: Fig. 174); on the prisoner staircases at Yaxchilán, Dos Pilas, Palenque, Dzibanché, and Naranjo in the Maya region (Marcus

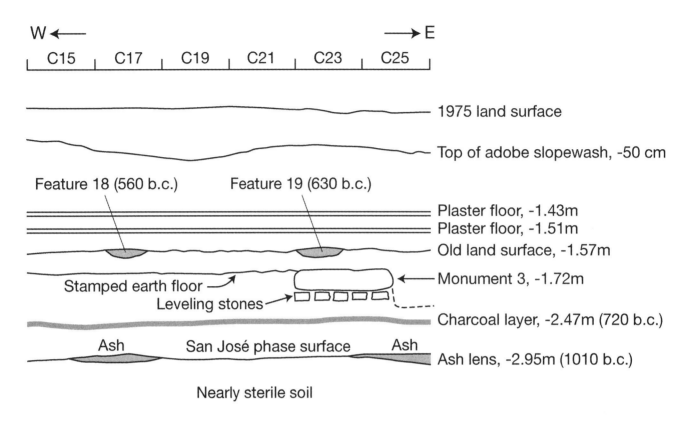

W ←——   ——→ E

| C15 | C17 | C19 | C21 | C23 | C25 |

——————————————————————————————————— 1975 land surface

——————————————————————————————————— Top of adobe slopewash, -50 cm

Feature 18 (560 b.c.)   Feature 19 (630 b.c.)

——————————————————————————————————— Plaster floor, -1.43m
——————————————————————————————————— Plaster floor, -1.51m
——————————————————————————————————— Old land surface, -1.57m

Stamped earth floor ——→   ←—— Monument 3, -1.72m
Leveling stones ——→

——————————————————————————————————— Charcoal layer, -2.47m (720 b.c.)

Ash   San José phase surface   Ash

——————————————————————————————————— Ash lens, -2.95m (1010 b.c.)

Nearly sterile soil

Figure 9.18. As shown in this diagram, Monument 3 was discovered at a depth of 1.72 m in Squares C23–C25 of the corridor between Structures 14 and 19. It was found stratigraphically above a charcoal layer with a radiocarbon date of 720 b.c., and stratigraphically *below* an old land surface with two hearths yielding dates of 630 b.c. and 560 b.c. At a later date (Monte Albán II), all those layers and features were sealed below two plaster floors.

Below left: Figure 9.19. Monument 3 at the moment of its discovery. The workman on the left has just washed its surface with water.
Below right: Figure 9.20. A view of Monument 3 from the east, showing the layer of flagstones used to level it.

Figure 9.21. Artist's reconstruction of Monument 3 as it would have looked during the late Rosario phase. This view is from the east. The monument served as the threshold for the corridor between Structure 19 (L.) and Structure 14 (R.). The floor of the corridor was stamped earth. (Drawing by John Klausmeyer)

Figure 9.22. The top surface (*right*) and eastern edge (*left*) of Monument 3. (Drawing by Mark Orsen).

1974, 1992); and on a prisoner step at Cacaxtla in Tlaxcala (Stuart and Ferorelli 1992:130–131).

The Iconography of Monument 3

Figure 9.22 shows both the top surface and the eastern edge of Monument 3. The figure is that of a man stripped of his clothing and ornaments and sprawled awkwardly on the ground. His eyes are closed and his mouth slightly open. On his chest is a large trilobed scroll, indicating that his heart has been removed. A surgeon to whom we have shown this drawing suggests that what is being depicted are the cross-sections of the severed blood vessels one would see in a victim's chest following the removal of his heart. A ribbon of blood extends from the victim's chest to the eastern edge of the monument, where it runs down in the form of two drops. Each drop is depicted as a circle and triangle, an artistic convention for blood drops that goes back as far as the Guadalupe phase (see Drennan 1976: Fig. 78*d*). That same symbol can also be found on a stairway riser at Temple T of Monte Negro in the Mixteca during the later Formative (Flannery 2003: Fig. 4.10*b*).

One of the most exciting features of Monument 3 is that it contains our earliest example of a date in the Zapotec 260-day calendar. Between the feet of the sprawled figure is a dot for the number one, and the Zapotec glyph for motion or earthquake (Caso's Glyph L). This caption to the scene almost certainly represents the calendric name of the sacrificed captive. The fact that the victim's calendric name is given strongly suggests that he was an important prisoner, perhaps a hereditary noble from a rival community.

This depiction of an elite victim reminds us of a comment on Maori warfare made by Sir Peter Buck (1949:400). "No matter how great the casualty list after an engagement," says Buck, "if there were no chiefs killed, there was nothing much to talk about. If there was no chiefly name to connect the engagement with a tribal genealogy, the battle was without a name."

Buck's description of Maori warfare allows us to suggest a reason why hieroglyphic writing might have appeared at this moment in the Formative. Chiefly individuals in rank societies are extremely interested in political competition, self-aggrandizement, and the defeat and humiliation of their rivals. One of the strongest stimuli for writing may have been the desire to name, for all time, vanquished chiefly rivals such as the one shown on Monument 3.

Dating Monument 3 with Ceramics

Once we had cleaned Monument 3, we were faced with the task of dating it as precisely as we could. To be sure, we knew that any radiocarbon dates we obtained from Features 18 and 19 would provide us with a *terminus ante quem* for the carved stone. At that time, however, we had not yet submitted the charcoal from either hearth for dating.

We knew that between the old land surface at a depth of 1.57

m and the stamped earth floor at a depth of 1.72 m (Fig. 9.18), we had found no sherds later in age than the Rosario phase. We also knew, however, that finding the sherds trapped beneath Monument 3 would be crucial to its dating. The logistical problem facing us, therefore, was this: How could we excavate below the carved stone while still leaving it in situ, preventing it from falling or rolling over on its side?

Figure 9.23 illustrates the method we chose. First, we created a temporary cement apron to prevent rainwater from undercutting the exposed monument. We added a temporary stone-lined drain to divert rain runoff in the corridor away from the stone. That having been done, we decided to explore the area beneath the monument by tunneling in from both sides. To prevent the heavy stone from collapsing, we decided to do this tunneling in three stages. First we would remove the southern third of the underlying earth, as shown in Figure 9.23. We would then backfill and allow the fill to firm up for a year. In a later season, we would remove the next third of the underlying earth. This process would continue into a third field season. Finally, as a result of this slow, laborious process, we managed both to get a ceramic sample from beneath the stone and to continue our corridor excavation to sterile soil.

Let us deal first with the stratigraphy. At a depth of 2.47 m, or 75 cm below the stamped earth floor, we encountered an extensive charcoal layer with Guadalupe phase sherds (Fig. 9.18). Charcoal from this layer became radiocarbon sample Beta-179879. The conventional date of this sample is 2670 ± 40 years before the present, or 720 b.c. When this date is dendrocalibrated, its two-sigma range is 900–790 BC. We consider this to be a late Guadalupe phase date.

Stratigraphically, this Guadalupe phase charcoal layer antedated the building of both Structures 14 and 19. In the most general terms, we consider it to be contemporaneous with Burial 65, a Guadalupe phase secondary burial intrusive into Zone F below Structure 28 (see Chapter 6).

As we continued downward from the charcoal layer, we came upon an old land surface at a depth of 2.95 m (Fig. 9.18), which produced San José phase sherds and occasional ash lenses. One of those ash lenses contained enough charcoal to provide radiocarbon sample Beta-176907. The conventional age of this sample was 2960 ± 40 years before the present, or 1010 b.c. When calibrated, the two-sigma range for this sample is 1300–1030 BC. We consider this San José phase land surface to be broadly contemporaneous with House 13, a wattle-and-daub house whose northern half later came to be buried beneath Structure 14 (Flannery and Marcus 2005:396–408). That San José phase residence had been built on sterile soil, and the soil appeared virtually sterile beneath the old San José phase land surface at the bottom of our corridor excavation as well.

As for our attempt to recover ceramics immediately below Monument 3, it was a successful (if slow and painstaking) endeavor. Over the course of three field seasons we managed to recover 122 diagnostic sherds, many of which can be seen in Figures 9.24–9.28. Those diagnostics were as follows:

Figure 9.23. Tunneling below Monument 3 to reveal the sequence of underlying strata. (In order to prevent the heavy stone from falling, only one third of the earth below it could be removed during any one field season.) *a* is the monument itself. *b* is a temporary drain, designed to divert rain runoff. *c* is a temporary cement apron, designed to prevent rain from undercutting the exposed monument.

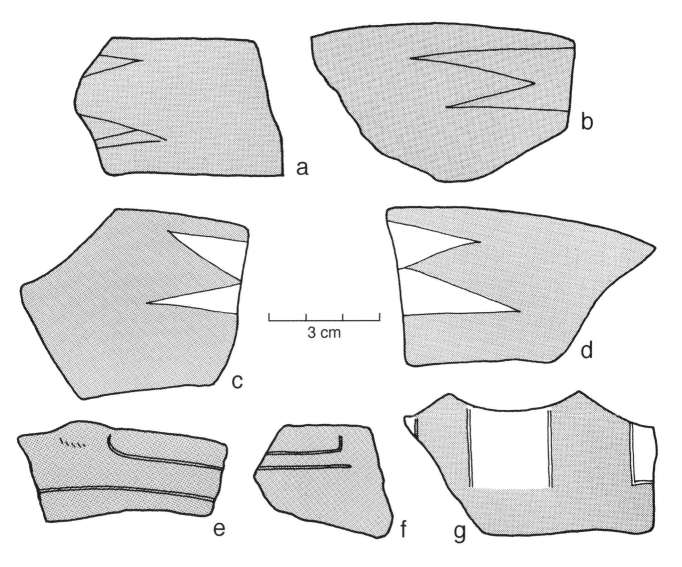

Figure 9.24. Socorro Fine Gray decorated bowl sherds from below Monument 3. *a, b,* rims with incised pennant motif (*a* is Rim Form 3, *b* is Rim Form 5). *c–d,* rims of Rim Form 2 with pennant motif in zoned toning (matte areas are shown as white). *e,* rim with Eccentricity 3 and Motif g. *f,* Rim Form 2 with Motif g. *g,* rim of Rim Form 5, Eccentricity 1, with zoned toning and apparent line-break motif (matte areas are shown as white).

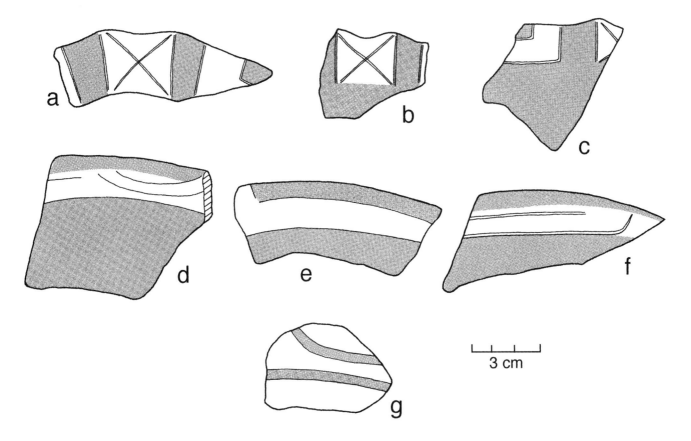

Figure 9.25. Socorro Fine Gray decorated bowl sherds from below Monument 3. *a–c*, rims of bowls with Rim Form 5, Eccentricity 7(?), featuring incised lines with bowtie motif and zoned toning (matte areas are shown as white). *d–e*, rims of Rim Form 5 with zoned toning (matte areas are shown as white). The incising on *d* is Drennan's Type a scallop, while *e* is a double-line-break. *f*, Rim Form 4 with zoned toning and incising. *g*, Rim Form 5 with wideline incising and Motif g.

SOCORRO FINE GRAY
    composite silhouette bowls with sharp carinations
        plain rims: 2
        rims with negative white above carination: 3
        rim with negative white and pattern burnishing: 1
    composite silhouette bowls with pattern burnishing or zoned
        toning
        rims: 2
    composite silhouette bowls, incised on exterior
        rims: 3
    composite silhouette bowl with exterior incising and nega-
        tive white
        rim: 1
    body sherds of composite silhouette bowls
        with pattern burnishing: 2
        with negative white: 1
        with incising and negative white: 1
    miniature composite silhouette bowl
        body sherd: 1
    outleaned/outcurved-wall bowls
        rims: 38 (see below)

JOSEFINA FINE GRAY
    composite silhouette bowls
        rims with incising and negative white: 2
    beakers
        plain rim: 1
        incised rim: 1
    outleaned/outcurved-wall bowl
        sherd: 1

GUADALUPE BURNISHED BROWN
    outleaned/outcurved-wall bowls
        rims: 5

COATEPEC WHITE
    composite silhouette bowls
        rim sherd with exterior incising: 1
        body sherd with exterior incising: 1
        body sherd, plain: 1

FIDENCIO COARSE
    jars with flaring necks
        rims: 11
    jar or *tecomate* with zoned slashes/jabs
        body sherd: 1

LUPITA HEAVY PLAIN
    outleaned-wall bowl
        rim: 1
    tecomate with zoned sloppy jabs
        body sherd: 1
    Suchilquitongo tripod dishes, undecorated
        rims: 2
        foot: 1

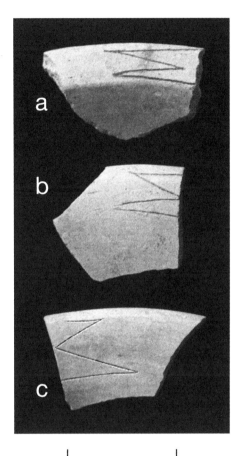

5 cm

Figure 9.26. Socorro Fine Gray bowl rims from below Monument 3. All specimens display the incised pennant motif. *a* displays Drennan's Rim Form 5; *b* and *c* have Rim Form 2.

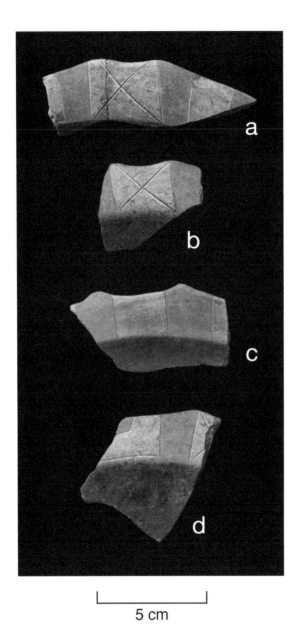

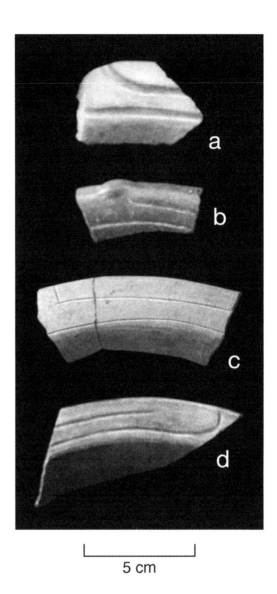

Figure 9.27. Socorro Fine Gray bowl rims from below Monument 3. All specimens shown have Drennan's Rim Form 5 with incised "line-break" motifs featuring zoned toning. *a*, *b*, and *d* also have Drennan's Eccentricity 7 and the bowtie motif. *c* has Drennan's Eccentricity 1 and lacks the bowtie motif.

Figure 9.28. Socorro Fine Gray bowl rims from below Monument 3. All specimens have some version of the double-line-break motif. In *a*, the motif is executed in wide lines. *a* and *c* have Drennan's Rim Form 5; *d* has Rim Form 4. *b* displays Drennan's Eccentricity 3.

ATOYAC YELLOW-WHITE
    outleaned/outcurved-wall bowls
        plain rim: 1
        rims, two incised parallel lines: 4
        rims, three incised parallel lines: 2
        rim with Motif 35 of Plog (2009): 1
    cylinders
        plain rims: 2
        rims with three incised parallel lines: 2
        rim with Motif 4 of Plog (2009): 1
        rim with fineline hachure: 1
    oval bowl with pinched-in sides
        plain rim: 1
    jar with tall vertical neck
        rim, incised with two parallel lines: 1
    tecomate, zoned, perforated for suspension
        rim: 1

LEANDRO GRAY
    cylinder
        plain rim: 1
    bowl, incised on exterior
        base: 1

SAN JOSÉ RED-ON-WHITE
    bowl with bolstered rim, interior slipped white with red band
        at rim, exterior incised but unslipped
        rim sherd: 1

AVELINA RED-ON-BUFF
    hemispherical bowls
        rim sherds with red band on interior and exterior: 3

TIERRAS LARGAS BURNISHED PLAIN
    hemispherical bowls
        rim sherds: 5
    jar: 1 rim

MATADAMAS ORANGE
    jars: 2 rims

FIGURINE FRAGMENTS
    Guadalupe phase figurine: 1 head
    San José phase figurines: 2 heads
    figurine bodies: 3

In addition to counting all the diagnostics, we coded all 38 rims of Socorro Fine Gray outleaned/outcurved-wall bowls in the system created by Drennan (Chapter 7). The results were as follows:

Rim Form 1, no decoration: 1
Rim Form 2, no decoration: 3
Rim Form 2, negative white, crescent motif: 1

Rim Form 2, wide incised lines, Motif g: 3
Rim Form 2, single wide incised line: 1
Rim Form 2, fineline incising and zoned toning, pennant motif: 3
Rim Form 3, no decoration: 1
Rim Form 3, negative white, crescent motif: 1
Rim Form 3, negative white, crescent-and-blob motif: 1
Rim Form 3, two fine incised parallel lines: 1
Rim Form 3, fineline incising, pennant motif: 1
Rim Form 4, zoned toning, fineline incising: 1
Rim Form 4, zoned toning, Motif g: 1
Rim Form 5, no decoration: 1
Rim Form 5, zoned toning, band at rim: 4
Rim Form 5, zoned toning, two incised lines: 1
Rim Form 5, zoned toning, incised Motif a (scallop): 1
Rim Form 5, zoned toning, incised double-line-break: 1
Rim Form 5, two fine incised parallel lines: 1
Rim Form 5, wide incised lines, Motif g: 1
Rim Form 5, fineline incising, pennant motif: 1
Rim Form 5, Eccentricity 1, zoned toning, fineline incising, double-line-break: 1
Rim Form 5, Eccentricity 7?, zoned toning, incised bowtie motif and double-line-break: 3
Rim Form ?, fineline incising, Motif h: 2
Rim Form ?, zoned toning, incised Motif b (scallop): 1
Rim Form ?, Eccentricity 3, fineline incising, Motif g: 1

Our evaluation of the ceramics found just beneath Monument 3 is that they consist mainly of well-known Rosario phase types (Socorro Fine Gray, Josefina Fine Gray, Guadalupe Burnished Brown, Fidencio Coarse, and Lupita Heavy Plain), along with redeposited sherds of the Guadalupe, San José, and Tierras Largas phases. When we look in detail at the 38 rims of Socorro Fine Gray outleaned/outcurved-wall bowls, we see two rim eccentricities (Numbers 3 and 7) that do not continue into Monte Albán Ia (Drennan 1976:56). We also see abundant evidence for decorative attributes (zoned toning, negative white, and pennant incising) that do not continue into Monte Albán Ia. We see undecorated Suchilquitongo tripod dishes, which are characteristic of the Rosario phase, but no red-rimmed Suchilquitongo dishes like those of Monte Albán Ia. Just as significant is the complete absence of Caso's Types G15, G16, G17, and C4, all of which are diagnostic of Period Ia.

We should not be surprised to learn that Monument 3 dates to the Rosario phase. It was, after all, found stratigraphically below two hearths with radiocarbon dates of 560 b.c. and 630 b.c., and not far above a charcoal layer with a radiocarbon date of 720 b.c.

The Chronology of the Corridor

Finally, with our radiocarbon dates run and all the ceramics analyzed, we can reconstruct the chronology of the corridor between Structures 14 and 19. Our story begins in the San José phase.

1. We know of at least two buildings constructed on the summit of Mound 1 during the San José phase. One was House 13, a wattle-and-daub residence built near the spot later chosen for Structure 14 (Flannery and Marcus 2005:396–408). The other was a likely men's house (see Chapter 4), built just above sterile soil on the spot later chosen for Structure 19B. At that time, the corridor did not yet exist.

2. During the Guadalupe phase there was a bit of activity on Mound 1. A building of some kind might have been involved, but we cannot be sure. Late Guadalupe phase and early Rosario phase secondary burials were placed in the area later chosen for Structure 19B (see Chapter 6). A charcoal layer was laid down on the spot that later became the corridor between Structures 14 and 19.

3. The building of Structure 19B began early in the Rosario phase. This building was subsequently enlarged twice, resulting in Structures 19A and 19. The second and third stages had a different orientation and were, at least in part, attempts to keep Structure 19B from collapsing by surrounding it with tons of fill.

4. An adobe temple, Structure 28, was placed atop the masonry platform during Stage 19B. It was eventually burned in a raid (see Chapter 8).

5. Once Structure 28 had been burned, the leaders of San José Mogote built a plus-sign-shaped stone masonry platform, Structure 14, only a few meters north of Structure 19. They then placed a new adobe temple, Structure 37, atop Structure 14.

6. By building Structure 14 right beside Structure 19, the Rosario phase architects created a corridor between the two platforms. They then hauled in a big, heavy metamorphic rock to serve as the eastern threshold for this corridor. This stone was carved with the figure of an elite prisoner whose heart had been removed. Anyone who traversed the corridor would wind up stepping on the sacrificed enemy, communicating a powerful message about victory and defeat.

7. Eventually the temples on Structures 14 and 19 fell into disuse, and layers of slopewash accumulated in the corridor. This probably happened after the bulk of San José Mogote's population left to participate in the founding of Monte Albán.

8. Eventually, a land surface with an organic A zone formed in the corridor. At some point, someone excavated two stone-lined hearths (Features 18 and 19) into the A zone of this old land surface. Both hearths yielded Rosario phase radiocarbon dates.

9. After a considerable hiatus—including all or most of the Monte Albán I period—San José Mogote enjoyed a kind of renaissance (see Chapter 13). During Monte Albán II, brand new temples were built above the ruins of Structures 28 and 37. At roughly the same time, Monte Albán II masons paved over the corridor with white stucco.

10. At a still later time—possibly corresponding to the use of the Monte Albán II temple we have designated Structure 13—someone created a huge trash pit off the southeast corner of Structure 14. This pit, Feature 20, was so deep that it passed through both Monte Albán II stucco floors, the old Rosario land surface, and the Guadalupe phase charcoal layer (Chapter 13).

The Removal of Monument 3

At the time we excavated Monument 3, we wondered whether it would be better to leave it in situ or move it to a safer location, but for us the question was moot, since we did not have the equipment to move such a heavy stone. Leaving it could expose it to vandalism; on the other hand, attempting to move it could expose it to damage. We compromised by leaving Monument 3 in situ and protected by a metal cover that could be padlocked.

During the 1990s, archaeologist Enrique Fernández Dávila (1997) of the Oaxaca Regional Center (INAH) was supplied with the proper equipment to move Monument 3 to a newly created San José Mogote museum. Fernández Dávila skillfully moved the carved stone out of the corridor, down the side of Mound 1, and into the museum where it can be viewed today. In the process of removing the monument, he recovered additional ceramics just below it; none, according to him, were later than Rosario phase in date (Fernández Dávila, personal communication, 1997).

Fernández Dávila also resolved a question that had intrigued us for years. Recall that we excavated below Monument 3 for three field seasons, backfilling at the end of each season and allowing the fill to become firm. Because of the reduced space in which we were working, this backfilling was done with hundreds of individual bucketloads of earth. What—we wondered—would an area backfilled this way look like, if re-excavated years later?

Fernández Dávila gave us the answer. The stratigraphic profile of the backfilled corridor, after being re-excavated by him, consisted of hundreds of small lenses of earth of slightly different colors. Each lens represented the contents of one bucket of fill dirt. To be sure, Fernández also recovered the modern soft drink bottles we always added to our backfill to let future archaeologists know that they were not in a primary deposit.

In sum, we can now add hieroglyphic writing to the skilled activities of Rosario society. The stratigraphic position of Monument 3 should be clear from Figure 9.18, which lists multiple radiocarbon dates. Two independent excavations—ours and Fernández's—found the stone to be in association with Rosario phase sherds. Those sherds satisfy all the ceramic criteria for the Rosario phase: not only those originally established by Flannery at the type site (Barrio del Rosario Huitzo), but also those recorded by Drennan (1976) at Fábrica San José and Winter (1976) at Tierras Largas.

It now seems likely that Zapotec writing arose in the context of chiefly competition, eventually becoming one more strategy of that competition. In the case of Monument 3, the intent was to provide the calendric name of an elite victim of heart sacrifice. To paraphrase Sir Peter Buck, this would have tied an important battle to a chiefly genealogy, thereby making it live on in oral history.

Structure 31: A Rosario Phase "Performance Platform"

When their Structure 28 temple was burned, the leaders of San José Mogote chose not to replace it on that same spot. Instead, they built their next temple (Structure 37) a few meters to the north and gave it an even more sturdy masonry platform (Structure 14).

Eventually, however, the ruins of Structure 28 were leveled, and that area was chosen for a pair of new buildings. One of those buildings, Structure 27, was an adobe-walled residence. The other, Structure 31, was an unusual public building with a circular plan. The collapse of these two buildings created Stratigraphic Zone C of the overburden above Structure 19 (see Figs. 8.5–8.7). Structure 27 dated to the late Rosario phase and has already been described by Flannery and Marcus (2005:411–417). We now describe Structure 31, which also dated to the late Rosario phase.

Structure 31

Structure 27 lay in the southern half of Stratigraphic Zone C. It had been badly eroded because Zone C sloped downward toward the south; its average depth was 1.4 m to 1.7 m below the geodesic benchmark we had used as our datum. The northern half of Zone C, on the other hand, lay at an average depth of only 1.0 to 1.35 m below the benchmark. We began our excavation of that area expecting to find better preserved residences. Instead, we encountered the remains of Structure 31, a circular adobe platform unlike any building we had ever excavated.

Unfortunately, only the northern half of this platform had been preserved. As can be seen in Figure 9.29, the southern half of the platform had been destroyed when the occupants of a later stratigraphic level (Zone B) went on to excavate space for both a subterranean tomb (Tomb 10) and a semi-subterranean storage room (Room 1 of Structure 26; see Flannery and Marcus 2005:417–443).

As a result of this later digging and remodeling, numerous adobe bricks from Structure 31 had been brought to a higher level and redeposited in Stratigraphic Zone B; we began finding them at depths of 75–80 cm below datum (Fig. 9.30). We were later able to identify those rectangular adobes as having come from Structure 31 because they displayed the same dimensions (40 × 20 × 10 cm) and the same color as the adobes remaining in the platform.

The surviving foundations of Structure 31 were largely confined to Squares S4E8–S5E10 (Figs. 9.29, 9.31). We estimate that the platform originally had a diameter of more than 5.5 m and a height of 50–60 cm. Owing to its eventual collapse, however, its height had slumped to 35 cm in most places and its walls had bulged outward. This increased the building's diameter to more than 6.0 m in places, making it difficult to measure the platform accurately.

Structure 31 had been constructed as follows. First, the builders created a circle by laying out dozens of adobes with their long axes facing in toward the center. Then—at intervals of roughly 3.3 m along the periphery of the circle—they created a series of adobe walls that ran from the center of the circle to the periphery, like the spokes of a wheel (Fig. 9.32). Successive layers of adobes were then added both to the spokes and to the periphery until the desired height was reached. Next, the triangular spaces left open between the spokes were filled with hard yellow pottery clay, almost certainly mined from the lower piedmont of the Etla subvalley. Finally, the top and sides of the platform were given several coats of this same hard clay and carefully smoothed. Figure 9.33 gives the reader an idea of the platform's size and shape.

Comparisons with Other Regions

Circular structures were rare in the Valley of Oaxaca, and Structure 31 is so far unique for the Rosario phase. Similar Middle Formative platforms, however, are known from the Upper Belize River Valley in the lowland Maya region. For example, four circular platforms have so far been excavated at the site of Cahal Pech (Aimers, Powis, and Awe 2000). Figure 9.34 shows one of these platforms: Structure 14.

Aimers, Powis, and Awe describe Structure 14 as having no evidence of a superstructure, and suggest that it may have been an exposed platform for ritual performances such as oratory or dancing. Structure 14 was somewhat larger and more elegant than Structure 31, having nine courses of cut stone on its periphery and a thick layer of white lime plaster. All four circular platforms at Cahal Pech date to 650–300 b.c., a time span that overlaps with the Rosario phase.

We agree with the interpretation offered by Aimers, Powis, and Awe, and believe that the circular ground plan of these platforms is singularly appropriate for dancing. For rapid motion on an elevated surface, the last thing participants would want to encounter is straight sides and sharp corners. The use of hard pottery clay for the fill in Structure 31 would also be appropriate for a platform subjected to the repeated pounding of dancers' feet.

Dating Structure 31 with Ceramics

No ceramics were included in the adobe walls of Structure 31, but we recovered a sample from the fill between the spoke-like walls. The diagnostic sherds were as follows:

SOCORRO FINE GRAY
bowls with outleaned/outcurved walls, rims: 9 (Fig. 9.35)
composite silhouette bowl with negative white alone: 1 (Fig. 9.36*b*)
composite silhouette, incised, with negative white: 1 (Fig. 9.36*a*)
cylinders, plain rims: 2

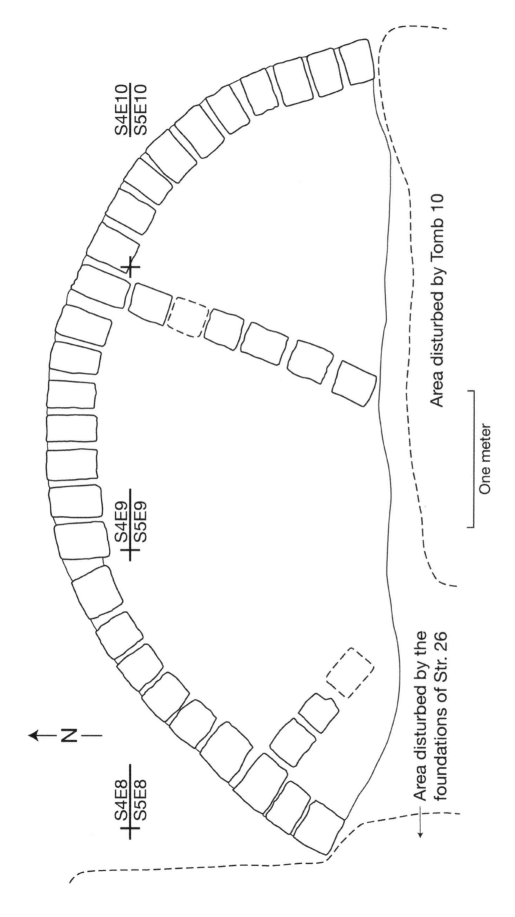

S4E10
S5E10

S4E9
S5E9

S4E8
S5E8

—N—

Area disturbed by Tomb 10

One meter

Area disturbed by the
foundations of Str. 26

Figure 9.29. Only the northern half of Structure 31, a circular platform, had survived later disturbance. This drawing shows the basal level of the structure, which consisted of adobe retaining walls enclosing earthen fill.

Figure 9.30. Loose (and broken) adobe bricks from Structure 31 began to appear at a depth of 75 to 80 cm below datum. (The white arrow points north, and the total length of the scale is 30 cm.)

Figure 9.31. The foundations of Structure 31 were encountered at a depth of 1.0 to 1.35 m below datum. This view is from the northwest.

Figure 9.32. In this view of Structure 31, a workman cleans one of the adobe retaining walls that strengthened the earthen fill. These retaining walls radiated out from the center of the platform like the spokes of a wheel.

Figure 9.33. Structure 31 was roughly 5.5–6.0 m in diameter and originally stood 50–60 cm high. After partial razing by the architects of the Zone B Residence, this was all that remained of the platform's foundation.

Figure 9.34. The Middle Formative occupation at Cahal Pech in Belize has produced a number of circular earthen platforms; the one shown here is Structure 14. (Photo courtesy of Jaime Awe)

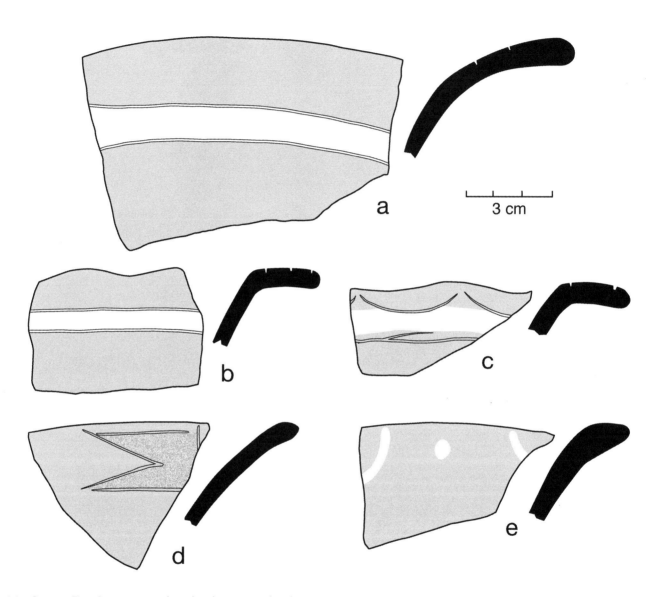

Figure 9.35. Socorro Fine Gray outcurved-rim bowls associated with Structure 31. *a* has Drennan's Rim Form 3 with incising and negative white; *b* and *c* have Rim Form 5 with Eccentricity 1, incising and negative white; *d* has Rim Form 2, pennant incising and zoned toning; *e* has Rim Form 2 with negative white (crescent and dot motif).

JOSEFINA FINE GRAY
  bowl with outleaned wall, incised rim: 1
  composite silhouette bowl, rim: 1
  composite silhouette bowl, body sherd: 1
  multicompartment vessel: 1

GUADALUPE BURNISHED BROWN
  bowls with outleaned walls, rims: 4 (Fig. 9.37*a, b*)

FIDENCIO COARSE
  jar rims: 3 (Fig. 9.37*c*)

LUPITA HEAVY PLAIN
  bowl with outleaned wall, rim: 1
  tecomate: 1 (Fig. 9.37*d*)
  charcoal braziers, rims: 4

ATOYAC YELLOW-WHITE
  bowl with outleaned wall, plain rim: 1
  bowl with outleaned wall, beveled rim: 1
  bowls with outleaned wall, bolstered rims: 2
  cylinder, plain rim: 1

LEANDRO GRAY
  bowl with outleaned wall, rim: 1
  hemispherical bowl, rim: 1

DELIA WHITE
  beaker, rim: 1

FIGURINES
  fragment of typical Guadalupe phase figurine with pendant
    and necklace: 1

We coded all 9 rims of Socorro Fine Gray outleaned/
outcurved-wall bowls in Drennan's system. The attributes were
as follows:
  Rim Form 2, fineline incised pennant and zoned toning: 1
  Rim Form 2, crescents in negative white: 1
  Rim Form 3, fine horizontal incised lines with negative
    white: 2
  Rim Form 5, no decoration: 1
  Rim Form 5, wideline incised scallop and negative white: 2
  Rim Form 5, horizontal lines in negative white: 1
  Rim Form 5, Eccentricity 1, wideline incised scallop and
    negative white: 1

In sum, our sherd sample from Structure 31 places it in the
Rosario phase. Since we earlier concluded that Structure 27
belonged to the Rosario phase (Flannery and Marcus 2005:411–
417), the ceramics from Structure 31 simply confirm our date
for Zone C.

We wish that San José Mogote had produced more examples
of circular platforms, for which the Belize River Valley has a

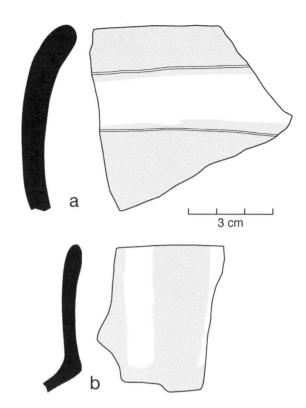

Figure 9.36. Sherds from Socorro Fine Gray composite silhouette
bowls associated with Structure 31. *a* has exterior incising and a
horizontal band of negative white. *b* has vertical stripes of negative
white.

much larger sample (Aimers, Powis, and Awe 2000: Table 1).
Until more cases are found, we are left wondering whether the
highland Oaxaca and lowland Maya platforms are independent
developments, or reflect a widespread pattern in southern Mesoamerica. To us, the creation of platforms for ritual performances
(such as dancing) seems so logical an activity for Middle Formative rank societies that we expect more examples to be found.

Mound 1 at the End of the Rosario Phase

Structures 27 and 31 were not the last Rosario phase buildings on that spot. An elite residence of the late Rosario phase
was eventually built above them, creating Stratigraphic Zone B
(Figs. 8.6–8.7). The Zone B Residence (consisting of Structures
25, 26, and 30 and Tombs 10 and 11) has already been published
by Flannery and Marcus (2005:417–443). It was clearly occupied
by a family of high rank.

Here, then, is how we picture the summit of Mound 1 as the
Rosario phase drew to a close. Structure 37, a temple whose roof
was supported by wooden columns set on volcanic tuff bases,
stood atop Structure 14, a stone masonry platform shaped like a
plus sign. The Zone B Residence, consisting of multiple rooms
around a central patio with a two-chambered tomb, stood atop

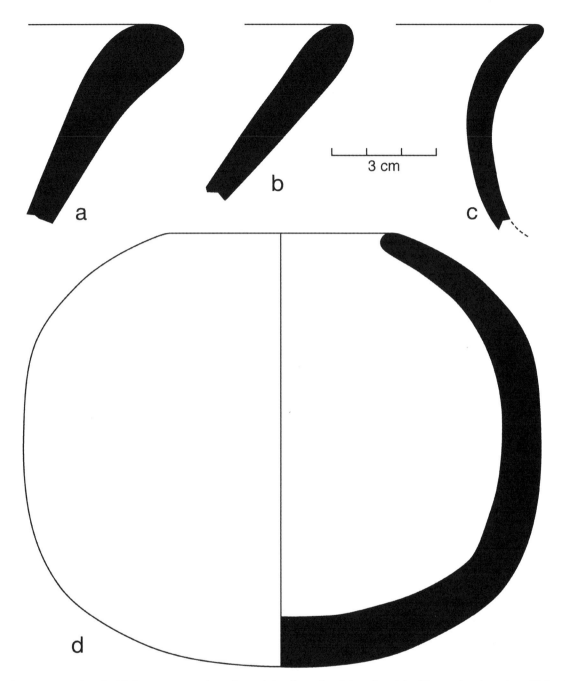

Figure 9.37. Ceramics associated with Structure 31. *a, b*, outleaned rims from Guadalupe Burnished Brown bowls. *c*, rim of Fidencio Coarse jar. *d*, reconstruction of Lupita Heavy Plain *tecomate*.

Structure 19. Between Structures 14 and 19 ran a corridor whose stone threshold was Monument 3, the carved image of a sacrificed captive whose hieroglyphic name was included.

The chiefly lineage of San José Mogote had used their architects, artisans, and labor crews in every way possible to communicate their political, religious, and military power to their neighbors. Their main temple and most elegant residence occupied an acropolis that could be seen for miles. They trod daily on the stony corpse of an elite enemy. Yet they knew that

their village was not in a particularly defensible location.

To the south, rising out of the buffer zone that separated them from their rivals, they saw an unoccupied 400 m mountain whose summit could be fortified. Perhaps that was where their next acropolis should be built.

10 | Monte Albán Ia: Synoikism and Social Memory

At the close of the Rosario phase, San José Mogote—the largest village in the Valley of Oaxaca—abruptly lost most of its population. Monumental construction on Mound 1 was suspended, not to resume for more than 400 years. Residential areas A, B, and C were abandoned. While clusters of ordinary residences could still be found in the piedmont around San José Mogote, the ceremonial and elite-residential core of the village now lay empty.

To understand what happened to San José Mogote, we must step back and take a look at the valley-wide pattern of sociopolitical change. San José was, in fact, not the only village in the Etla subvalley to lose population at this time; most of its satellite communities, including Tierras Largas and Fábrica San José, suffered the same fate. When we look at the valley as a whole, we discover that half the Rosario phase villages whose occupation did not last into Monte Albán Ia can be found in the southern half of the Etla subvalley (Kowalewski et al. 1989).

This abandonment of villages in the Etla region occurred simultaneously with the founding of Monte Albán. At least 2000 people had moved to the summit of that previously unoccupied mountain, located in what had once been a buffer zone in the central Valley of Oaxaca. We believe that 1000 of these colonists came from San José Mogote and another 1000 from its satellite villages. During the next 200 years, from 500 to 300 b.c., Monte Albán's population would grow to 5000.

We have previously compared this demographic shift to the process the ancient Greeks called *synoikism*, or deliberate urban relocation (Marcus and Flannery 1996:139–146). The motivation behind a Greek synoikism was power building (Demand 1990), often an attempt to create a community so large as to be invulnerable. There is abundant evidence that this was a major goal of the founders of Monte Albán, since they soon began building a 3 km defensive wall along the mountain's more easily climbed western slopes (Blanton 1978).

Recall that during the Rosario phase, the Valley of Oaxaca was divided among (at least) three rank societies—a polity of 2000 people in the Etla subvalley, with its chiefly center at San José Mogote; a polity of 700–1000 persons in the Tlacolula subvalley, with its chiefly center at Yegüih; and a polity of 700–1000 persons in the Zimatlán subvalley, with its chiefly center at San Martín Tilcajete. There is so far no evidence that Yegüih or Tilcajete participated in the founding of Monte Albán. There is, in fact, considerable evidence that Tilcajete was Monte Albán's main rival for control of the Valley of Oaxaca, and that Tilcajete engaged in its own power building, deliberately doubling its size and building its own defensive walls (Spencer and Redmond 2003, 2006).

Our explanation for the virtual abandonment of San José Mogote, therefore, lies in the intense political competition of the sixth century b.c. San José Mogote lay too close to the valley floor to be safe from raids. Despite its size, its most important Rosario phase temple had already been burned. The outraged community had responded by sacrificing an elite enemy, someone important enough to be commemorated on Monument 3. Now, in a move that probably caught their rivals by surprise, the leaders of San José Mogote had taken over the summit of a defensible, 400 m high mountain in the center of the former buffer zone. From this strongpoint they probably expected to be able to wage war on their rivals until they controlled the entire valley. As it turns out, their campaign took almost five centuries to complete.

Visits during the Early Monte Albán I Hiatus

Most archaeologists who spend time in the Valley of Oaxaca have observed the following pattern: at some point after an important site has been abandoned, a small group of people returns there to build an altar, conduct a ritual, and/or bury someone on the highest promontory at the site.

This happened to San José Mogote as well. After a hiatus of perhaps a century, someone returned and created two small ritual structures on the highest point of Mound 1, which happened to be the mounded ruins of the so-called Zone B Residence of the Rosario phase (Flannery and Marcus 2005:417–443).

By the time these new structures were built, the Zone B Residence itself had virtually eroded down to its foundations. The small structures built above its ruins created a new stratigraphic level, designated Zone A2 (see Figs. 8.6–8.7). This zone can be dated to the period referred to either as Early Monte Albán I or Monte Albán Ia (Bernal 1946).

The Internal Ceramic Chronology of Monte Albán I

Before proceeding to a description of the two new ritual buildings on Mound 1, let us look at the chronological markers that allow us to date Zone A2 to Monte Albán Ia. Recall that we were able to date the Zone B Residence on Mound 1 to the Rosario phase by using its associated ceramics—including the especially diagnostic Socorro Fine Gray outleaned/outcurved-wall bowls (Flannery and Marcus 2005:412–417, 422–425, 427, 431, 435). These bowls display all the attributes used by Drennan (1976) in his multidimensional scaling of Rosario ceramics. No hints of Monte Albán Ia pottery (such as Caso, Bernal, and Acosta's [CBA] Types G15, G16, G17 or C4) were found in Stratigraphic Zone B of the Structure 19 overburden.

Alfonso Caso's 1942–1944 stratigraphic excavations into Monte Albán's North Platform, at a place called "the patio south of Mound A" (hereafter PSA), allowed the Monte Albán I period to be divided into three phases, called Ia, Ib, and Ic. These excavations exposed a Late Monte Albán I public building with serpentine motifs modeled in stucco. Below this building were several more levels, which provided the stratigraphy necessary to divide Monte Albán I into three phases. Resting on bedrock

were the remains of a public building that dated to Early Monte Albán I, or Phase Ia. The two levels above this building were used to define Phases Ib and Ic. Ignacio Bernal presented the definitions of these phases (Bernal 1946), drawing on a sample of 47,000 sherds and 303 whole vessels.

In Table 10.1 we present the CBA pottery types Bernal used to define Monte Albán Ia, Ib, and Ic, based on the stratigraphy of the PSA. All pottery types are presented in the order in which they made their first appearance.

Both the Monte Albán urban settlement pattern project (Blanton 1978) and the valley-wide settlement pattern project (Kowalewski et al. 1989), as well as our own excavation project (Flannery and Marcus 2005), have found Bernal's subdivisions of Monte Albán I useful. Members of these projects, however, have found that Phase Ib is difficult to recognize in small pottery samples or surface collections. As a result, we have decided that Ib should probably just be considered the transition between Early Monte Albán I (Phase Ia) and Late Monte Albán I (Phase Ic), which have easy-to-recognize ceramic assemblages. While the settlement pattern project tends to prefer the terms Early I and Late I, our project has generally used Ia and Ic. That having been said, we consider the terms to be synonyms, and have no strong feelings either way. What we will not do is adopt still a third set of labels for periods that have served us well for more than 60 years.

Significantly, the abandonment of San José Mogote and the founding of Monte Albán did not change the ceramics of the valley dramatically. There were many continuities between the Rosario phase and Monte Albán Ia. Essentially, Socorro Fine Gray ware of the Rosario phase was ancestral to many Monte Albán I burnished grayware types, such as G3, G15, G16, and G17. Fidencio Coarse ware of the Rosario phase gradually turned into Type C2 of Monte Albán I. Guadalupe Burnished Brown of the Rosario phase is virtually indistinguishable from Types K3 and K8 of Monte Albán I—so much so that we doubt that isolated sherds of the former could be distinguished from the latter on surface survey.

As for Drennan's rim forms of Socorro Fine Gray outleaned/outcurved-wall bowls, it is only Forms 6, 7, 8, and 12 that failed to continue into Monte Albán Ia (Chapter 7). On the other hand, all of Drennan's Rosario phase rim eccentricities, save for numbers 1 and 5, dropped out in Monte Albán Ia. Incised motifs such as the line break and scallop continued into Ia, while pennant and crescent motifs largely disappeared. Frog effigies (and frog faces modeled on bowl rims) continued from Rosario into Monte Albán Ia, but zoned areas of dashes and punctations disappeared (Drennan 1976:56–57). Most significantly, the highly diagnostic Rosario phase attributes of zoned toning and negative white decoration were unknown in Monte Albán Ia.

Appearing for the first time in Monte Albán Ia were CBA Types G15, G16, and G17. Zones of incised hachure, always rare in Rosario, became common in Ia. CBA Type C4, featuring a garnet red slip over a *crema* clay body, became a reliable diagnostic of Ia.

Table 10.1. Initial appearance of pottery types in basal stratigraphic levels of the patio south of Mound A, North Platform, Monte Albán.

Stratigraphic Level	Pottery Type
Already appearing in Level 1 (MA Ia)	G1, G3, G5, G15, G16, G17, G18, G24, G30
	C1, C2, C3, C4, C5, C6, C20
	K1, K3, K3a, K8
	A4, A6, A12, A17
Not appearing until Level 2 (MA Ib)	G2, G6, G10, G12, G13, G14, G19, G32, G33
	C7
	K2, K6, K13, K19
	A1, A10, A13, A18
Not appearing until Level 3 (MA Ic)	G7, G25, G26
	C13, C14
	K5
	A2, A5

Bernal 1946:29

Based on these and other diagnostics, we can say with confidence that the Zone B Residence on Mound 1 of San José Mogote was built during the Rosario phase (Flannery and Marcus 2005:417–443). We can also say that after Mound 1 had lain abandoned for perhaps a century, someone using Monte Albán Ia pottery came to San José Mogote, climbed to the top of Mound 1, and created two small ritual buildings: Structures 23 and 24.

Dating the Disconformity between Stratigraphic Zones B and A2

The Zone B/A2 contact constitutes a genuine stratigraphic disconformity in the Structure 19 overburden. It appears that a substantial period of time elapsed between the abandonment of Zone B and the deposition of Zone A2 (Figs. 8.6, 8.7).

In general, the sherds from Zone B/A2 contact were about 40 percent Rosario phase types, 20 percent redeposited Early Formative pottery, and 40 percent Monte Albán Ia types. Some examples of diagnostic sherds from the disconformity are given below.

Sherds from the Zone B/A2 Disconformity in Square S7E5

The 25 sherds in this collection included Socorro Fine Gray outleaned/outcurved-wall bowls with incised double-line-breaks; Socorro composite silhouette bowls with negative white; miniature Suchilquitongo tripod dishes in Lupita Heavy Plain; a few Monte Albán Ia sherds; and some redeposited San José phase sherds.

Sherds from the Zone B/A2 Disconformity in Square S6E6

The 10 sherds in this collection were about half Rosario phase and half Monte Albán Ia. Included was a Socorro Fine Gray outleaned/outcurved-wall bowl with Drennan's Rim Type 3, double-line-break incising, and negative white decoration.

Sherds from the Zone B/A2 Disconformity in Squares S8E7–S8E10

This collection included both Monte Albán Ia pottery (Suchilquitongo tripod dishes in CBA Type C4; several CBA Type G3 bowls) and Rosario phase pottery (Socorro Fine Gray

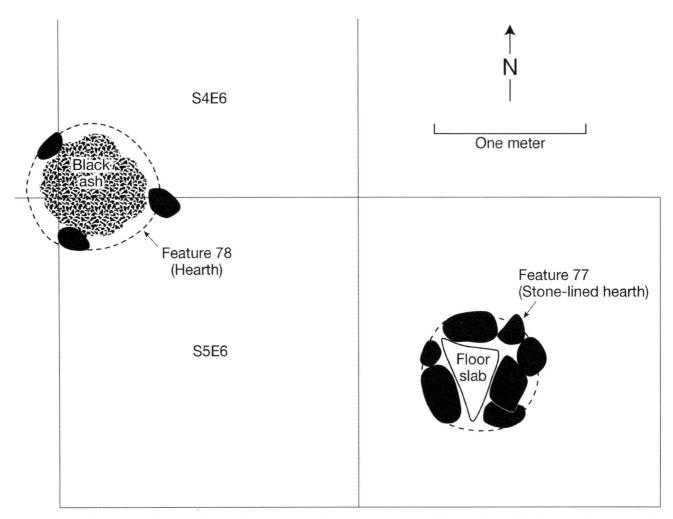

Figure 10.1. Two hearths (Features 77 and 78) were found within 2 m of each other at the interface of Stratigraphic Zones B and A2.

composite silhouette bowls; Coatepec White bowls). There was also a mix of brown wares, including both our Guadalupe Burnished Brown and CBA Types K1 and K3.

Sherds from the Zone B/A2 Disconformity in Squares S6E8–S7E8

The most significant sherds in this collection came from a jar of CBA Type C4; a bowl of CBA Type C1; and a cylinder of CBA Type G16, with fineline incising separating zones of fine crosshatching. These were clearly Monte Albán Ia types.

Feature 77

Two hearths—Features 77 and 78—were found at the inter-face of Stratigraphic Zones B and A2 (Fig. 10.1). These hearths

lay within 2 m of each other, and both had been created by scoop-ing out shallow basins in the top of Zone B. Stratigraphically, they postdated the Zone B Residence and predated the building of Structures 23 and 24.

Feature 77 lay in the center of Square S5E7 (Fig. 10.2). It was roughly 84 cm in diameter and 15 cm deep. The floor of the basin was covered by a flat, triangular stone slab, and seven other large stones had been arranged around its periphery. All the stones had been reddened by heat. Charcoal from Feature 77 yielded a conventional radiocarbon date of 490 b.c. ± 40 years (Beta-179880), placing it right near the end of the Rosario phase and the start of Monte Albán Ia. The dendrocalibrated age range would be 770–400 BC.

The small pottery collection from Feature 77 included six worn sherds that could be interpreted either as Fidencio Coarse or CBA Type C2. There were also a few sherds of CBA Types C5 and G24; some redeposited Atoyac Yellow-white sherds; and two

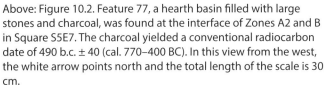

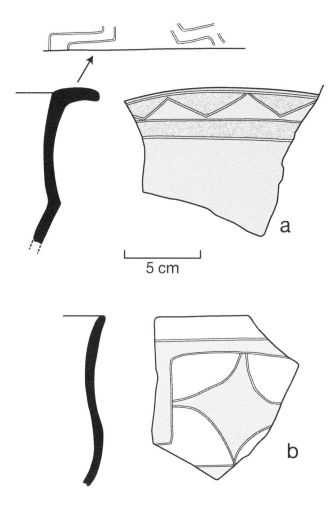

Above: Figure 10.2. Feature 77, a hearth basin filled with large stones and charcoal, was found at the interface of Zones A2 and B in Square S5E7. The charcoal yielded a conventional radiocarbon date of 490 b.c. ± 40 (cal. 770–400 BC). In this view from the west, the white arrow points north and the total length of the scale is 30 cm.

Right: Figure 10.3. Socorro Fine Gray rim sherds found at the interface of Zones A2 and B. *a*, sharply carinated bowl with wide everted rim (incised as shown); zoned toning on exterior. *b*, composite silhouette bowl with negative white in zones.

rims from Socorro Fine Gray outleaned/outcurved-wall bowls. One of the latter bowls had Drennan's Rim Form 2, undecorated. The other had Drennan's Rim Form 2, with a crescent incised on Rim Eccentricity 4.

Feature 78

Feature 78 was the second hearth we found at the interface between Zones B and A2; it lay mostly in the southwest corner of Square S4E6 and the northwest corner of S5E6 (Fig. 10.1). This hearth was roughly 90 cm in diameter and 15 cm deep. When discovered, it was filled with black ash and had three stones placed at intervals along its periphery.

We found two Socorro Fine Gray sherds near Features 77 and 78 (Fig. 10.3). Both were Rosario phase diagnostics. One was from a sharply carinated bowl with a wide everted rim,

decorated with incising and zoned toning. The other was from a composite silhouette bowl with negative white decoration confined to incised zones.

It appears that the disconformity between Zone B and Zone A2 fell near the end of the Rosario phase and the beginning of Monte Albán Ia. Whatever the purpose for which the Feature 77 and Feature 78 hearths had been made, they seem to have been dug into the collapsed remains of the Zone B Residence sometime after its abandonment, at a time when there were still Rosario phase sherds lying around.

The Ritual Buildings of Zone A2

The matrix of Stratigraphic Zone A2 consisted in part of the breakdown products of two small ritual buildings, Structures 23 and 24. The building of these structures seems to be one of our

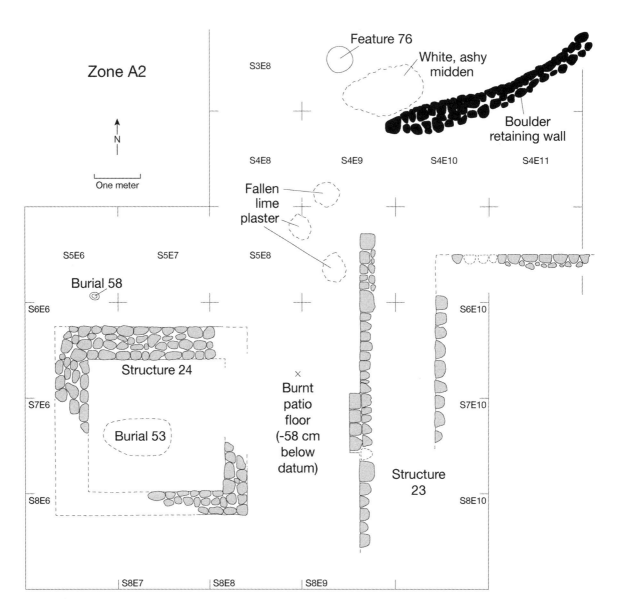

Figure 10.4. Plan of Stratigraphic Zone A2, showing Structures 23 and 24, Burials 53 and 58, Feature 76, and the boulder retaining wall on the northeast.

Figure 10.5. Workmen exposing the boulder retaining wall in Squares S3E9–S3E11 of Zone A2.

first examples of what was to become a familiar pattern in the Valley of Oaxaca:

1. An important community is abandoned.
2. Some period of time elapses without any major building activity.
3. Eventually the abandoned community is revisited, not with the aim of recolonizing it but simply to conduct a ritual on the highest point of the site.
4. In the course of that visit, a ritual structure or structures—possibly including an altar and/or an offering box—may be built.
5. After the ritual is concluded, the visitors return to the place from which they came, and the site remains abandoned.

We cannot usually specify the details of the ritual visit, nor guess from which place the visitors came. However, everything we know about traditional Zapotec religion leads us to suspect that the participants believed that some of their ancestors once lived at the now-abandoned community, and that the ritual was designed to honor them. Sometimes, as in the case of Zone A2 of the Structure 19 overburden, burials were included in the ritual. Such burials could be those of individuals seen as having ancestral ties to the site, or they could be victims sacrificed to honor the ancestors. Burials 53 and 58, which we found in Zone A2, could represent either or both alternatives.

In Figure 10.4, we present a plan of Stratigraphic Zone A2 that shows all relevant buildings and features. In addition to Structures 23 and 24, Zone A2 had a boulder retaining wall placed near its northeastern limits (Fig. 10.5). The likely purpose of this retaining wall was to protect Structure 23 from erosion, given how steep the slopes around it were.

As Figure 10.4 shows, we found two informative features in Square S3E9, just outside the boulder retaining wall. One of these was Feature 76, a circular pit filled with white ash and 134 fragments from five or six Monte Albán Ia incense burners. All the incense burners had been made of *café* clay like that used for CBA Type K3 ceramics. The ashy matrix in which they had been discarded was almost certainly the remains of the fuel used to heat the incense.

It appeared that the incense burners had been deliberately smashed after use. Of the 34 rim sherds, 19 had simple, direct rims; 9 had slightly flaring rims; and 6 had rounded rims that curved slightly inward. There were also at least 15 sherds from incense burner floors. All or most of the vessels had annular bases, and at least one had a fenestrated base—a tall support perforated by small openings (see Drennan 1976: Fig. 17 for examples).

Very near Feature 76 lay a midden composed almost entirely of the same kind of white ash found in the pit. It seemed likely to us that this midden (which was not given a feature number) was simply another place where consumed fuel from the *incensarios* had been dumped.

Figure 10.6. Two views of Structure 23. On the left, Armando Jiménez exposes the masonry foundations on the west side. On the right, Francisco Gómez perches on the northwest corner. .

The evidence from Square S3E9 strongly suggested that the burning of incense was part of the ritual(s) carried out in Zone A2. As for where the incense burners had been placed when in use, we suspect that it was in Squares S6E8–9 and S7E8–9, midway between Structures 23 and 24. In those squares, we found evidence that the informal earthen floor between the two structures had been repeatedly burned, with many burned areas exhibiting a circular shape like the base of an *incensario*. Evidently this simple earthen floor had served as a kind of patio between Structures 23 and 24.

A small number of sherds were recovered from the area of overlapping, circular burn marks. Included were the annular base of a Monte Albán Ia grayware bowl; 1 fragment of a bowl of CBA Type K3; the rim of a bowl of Type C2; 1 body sherd of Type C6; the base of an outleaned-wall bowl of Socorro Fine Gray; 3 other sherds of Socorro Fine Gray; and a dozen redeposited San José phase sherds.

Structure 23

Owing to erosion, the full dimensions of Structure 23 will never be known. Our best estimate is that its maximum north-south dimension might once have been 7.8 m.

What remained of Structure 23 suggested that it had once

been a low rectangular platform of stone masonry and earthen fill (Fig. 10.6). Its west wall stood 21 cm high, and its most prominent feature was a single stone masonry step 1.2 m wide. This wall delimited the lower tier of the platform. About 1.6 m east of the west wall, we found a 15 cm step-up to a second tier of the platform, also composed of stone masonry and earthen fill. This higher tier (which may once have measured 6.8 m from north to south) was flat on top and showed no evidence of having ever supported a building. Based on the surviving architectural remains, we interpret Structure 23 as a simple, flat-topped altar or shrine, not unlike the later *adoratorios* built in the Zapotec region. It is likely that the altar had once been plastered white, since we found at least three areas of fallen plaster in Squares S4E9 and S5E9 (Fig. 10.4).

The diagnostic sherds from the earthen fill of Structure 23 represented a mixture of Monte Albán Ia types, Rosario phase types, and redeposited Guadalupe and San José phase types. The diagnostics were as follows:

GRIS SHERDS OF MONTE ALBÁN IA (FIG. 10.7)
   bowls with outleaned/outcurved walls, Type G15: 3
   bowls with outleaned/outcurved walls, Type G16: 3
   bowl with outleaned/outcurved wall, Type G17: 1
   bowl with outleaned/outcurved wall, incised rim, Type G24
      pattern burnishing on base: 1

bowl with everted rim, fineline incised volutes: 1
rim of globular jar, Type G3: 1
rim of bottle, Type G3: 1
saucer rim, Type G3: 1
body sherd of bottle, Type G24 pattern burnishing: 1
potstand base, Type G15 incising: 1
rims from hemispherical bowls, incised: 2
rim from hemispherical bowl, plain, Type G3: 1

CREMA SHERDS OF MONTE ALBÁN IA (FIG. 10.8)
foot from Suchilquitongo tripod dish, Type C1: 1
rims from jars, Type C2: 6
shoulders from jars, Type C2: 2
rims from outleaned-wall bowls, Type C2: 2
rims from outleaned-wall bowls with Type C4 garnet slip: 3
beveled rim from outleaned-wall bowl, incised, Type C4 slip: 1
rim from hemispherical bowl, Type C4 slip: 1
flaring rims from jars, Type C4 slip: 2
rims from Suchilquitongo tripod dishes, Type C4 slip: 2
rims from outleaned-wall bowls, Type C5: 2
rim, oval bowl with pinched-in sides, Type C5: 1
hollow vessel support, Type C5: 1
rim from bowl with wide everted rim, smudged, Type C5: 1
incurved rim from bowl, incised and smudged, Type C5: 1

CAFÉ SHERDS OF MONTE ALBÁN IA (FIG. 10.8)
rims from outleaned-wall bowls, Type K3: 6
bases from outleaned-wall bowls, Type K3: 2
rims from hemispherical bowls, Type K3: 2
rims, Suchilquitongo tripod dishes, Type K8: 2

SOCORRO FINE GRAY VESSELS (ROSARIO PHASE)
rims of outleaned/outcurved-wall bowls: 26
composite silhouette bowl with incising and zoned toning: 1
composite silhouette bowl, eroded: 1
rim of hemispherical bowl, incised with double-line-break: 1
body sherd of bottle, zoned toning: 1
body sherd of bottle, negative white: 1

JOSEFINA FINE GRAY VESSEL (ROSARIO PHASE)
hemispherical bowl, incised: 1

OTHER
redeposited sherds of miscellaneous Rosario, Guadalupe, and San José phase types: ca. 40

We coded all 26 rims of Socorro Fine Gray outleaned/outcurved-wall bowls in Drennan's system. The attributes were as follows:
Rim Form 2, no decoration: 1
Rim Form 3, Eccentricity 3, wide horizontal incised lines: 1
Rim Form 3, Eccentricity 3, wideline incised crescents: 1

Rim Form 3, Eccentricity 4, negative paint, motif unclear: 1
Rim Form 5, fine horizontal incised lines: 1
Rim Form 5, wide horizontal incised lines: 2
Rim Form 5, Eccentricity 6, wide horizontal incised lines: 3
Rim Form 5, Eccentricity 6, wideline incised crescents: 1
Rim Form 5, Eccentricity 6, wideline incising, motif unclear: 1
Rim Form 6, wideline incised scallops and negative white: 1
Rim Form 9, no decoration: 1
Rim Form 9, fine horizontal incised lines: 1
Rim Form 9, wide horizontal incised lines: 1
Rim Form 10, no decoration: 1
Rim Form 10, wide horizontal incised lines: 1
Rim Form 10, Eccentricity 5, wideline incised crescents: 1
Rim Form 11, wideline incised crescents: 2
Rim Form 11, wideline incised Motif i: 1
Rim Form 11, Eccentricity 5, wideline incised wavy lines: 2
Rim Form 11, Eccentricity 5, wideline incised crescents: 1
Rim Form (?), Eccentricity (?), wide incised horizontal lines and negative white: 1

In addition to the ceramics described above, we recovered a small sherd sample from the stone masonry step on the west face of Structure 23. Included were fragments of CBA Type G3 jars, Type G24 pattern-burnished jars, and a Type C4 bowl with incising and a garnet slip (all from Monte Albán Ia); Socorro Fine Gray bowls with zoned toning or incised pennant motifs on the rim (all from the Rosario phase); and several sherds of Fidencio Coarse and Guadalupe Burnished Brown from earlier periods, obviously redeposited.

Additional sherds had been trapped below the west wall of Structure 23 at the time it was built. Included in this collection were a palm-impressed bowl of CBA Type G33, which according to Bernal first appeared during Monte Albán Ib; 11 body sherds from Type G3 bottles; 4 fragments of an amphibian effigy vessel in Monte Albán Ia grayware; 1 fragment of a grayware annular base; 3 fragments of a Type C1 brazier; 15 other *crema* sherds; 3 sherds of Socorro Fine Gray bowls; and a dozen redeposited sherds of San José phase types.

Conspicuous by their absence were any examples of CBA Type G12 bowls with combed designs on the interior of the base. While these bowls made their appearance during Monte Albán Ib, they did not become common until Ic. Their absence suggests that Structure 23 was more likely built during Early Monte Albán I than Late I.

Structure 24

Structure 24 lay 2.4 m due west of Structure 23 and was aligned perfectly with the small step on the west wall of the latter building. This structure's plan was almost a perfect square, measuring 4.14 m north-south and 3.92 m east-west (Figs. 10.4, 10.9). What Structure 24 most looked like was a better built,

Figure 10.7. Monte Albán I grayware sherds from Structure 23.

"supersized" version of the offering boxes placed below the floors of later Zapotec temples. Its stone masonry walls varied between 50 and 70 cm thick, and rose no higher than the step on the west wall of Structure 23.

No doors or staircases were associated with Structure 24. It gave us the impression of a semi-subterranean room that had been entered from above, then filled with dirt once its period of use was over. Its only interesting internal feature was Burial 53, which was intrusive through the room's earthen floor at a point 20–40 cm below the top of the wall.

Burial 53

Burial 53 included the remains of a child, 5–8 years old. Despite the fact that its remaining bones had been laid out roughly in anatomical order (Fig. 10.10), this child was missing so many bones that it was almost certainly a secondary burial. It had no hands and no feet, lacked many arm bones, and presented only a few pieces of its cranium. Two volcanic tuff stones had been placed above the skeleton. The offerings included two garnet flasks of CBA Type C4 (Figs. 10.11, 10.12) and 11 miniature Suchilquitongo tripod dishes (Fig. 10.13*a, b*). Both C4 flasks had been ritually "killed" by having a small hole drilled through the vessel near the base. The miniature Suchilquitongo tripod dishes had been made of a lightly fired *café* clay, painted inside and out with the type of red wash usually seen on CBA Type C2. A large obsidian blade, found near the child's mandible, may have been an additional burial offering (Fig. 10.13*c*).

The pottery from Burial 53 clearly dates it to Monte Albán Ia.

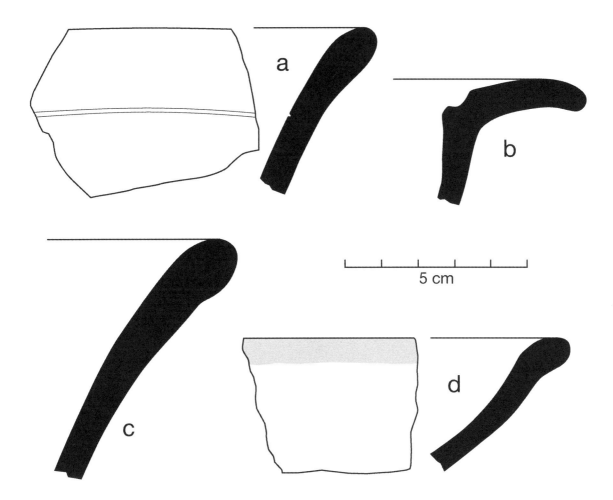

Figure 10.8. Sherds of other Monte Albán I types from Structure 23. *a*, outleaned-wall bowl of Type C4, with a single horizontal groove and garnet-colored slip. *b*, Type C5 bowl with wide-everted rim; white slip, smudged on interior. *c*, outleaned-wall bowl, Guadalupe Burnished Brown or CBA Type K3. *d*, possible rim of Suchilquitongo tripod dish with burnished brick red band at the rim, Type K8.

Dating Structure 24

The diagnostic sherds from the upper fill of Structure 24 were as follows:

MONTE ALBÁN IA DIAGNOSTICS
fragments of Type G3 bottles: 2
sherds from jars, Type C2: 2
bolstered rim from bowl, Type K3: 1

ROSARIO PHASE DIAGNOSTICS
Socorro Fine Gray bowl, Rim Form 2, plain: 1
Socorro Fine Gray bowl, Rim Form 3, plain: 1
Socorro Fine Gray bowl, Rim Form 2, negative white: 1
Socorro Fine Gray composite silhouette bowls: 2

Socorro Fine Gray incurved-rim bowl: 1
Suchilquitongo tripod dish, undecorated: 1

OTHER DIAGNOSTICS
Fidencio Coarse jar rims: 3
Guadalupe Burnished Brown bowl rims: 4
redeposited San José phase sherds: 5

We also found a small number of sherds in the earthen fill around Burial 53. Included were fragments of an incised bottle of CBA Type G3; a Suchilquitongo tripod dish of Type C2; 2 sherds of Type C2 jars; 2 sherds of Type C4 jars; 1 incurved rim bowl of Type K3; the mat-impressed base of a Type K8 bowl; and an everted-rim bowl of Type A4 (all dating to Monte Albán Ia). There were also rims from 3 Rosario phase Socorro Fine Gray

Figure 10.9. A view of Structure 24 from the southeast. The black-and-white ranging pole, resting against the building's north wall, measures 2.0 m. (The linear structure in the foreground is a subfloor drain, intrusive into Zone A2, from a building in Zone A1.)

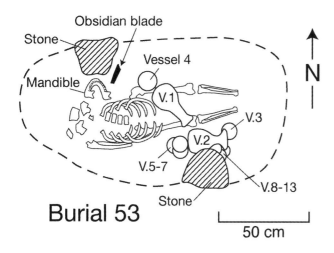

Figure 10.10. Burial 53 was found in Square S7E7 and was intrusive through the floor of Structure 24. It consisted of a child 5–8 years old and missing some bones. Rough volcanic stones had been placed over the burial. The skeleton was accompanied by 2 garnet (Type C4) flasks, 11 miniature tripod dishes, and an obsidian blade.

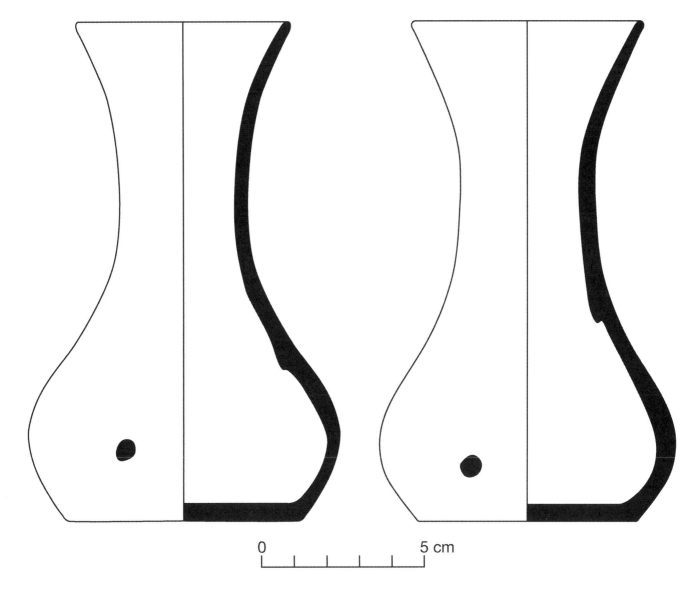

Figure 10.11. Vessels 1 (*left*) and 2 (*right*) from Burial 53. Both vessels are burnished, garnet-slipped flasks (CBA Type C4), typical of Monte Albán Ia. The black dot on each flask represents a deliberately drilled hole, made when the vessel was ritually "killed."

3 cm

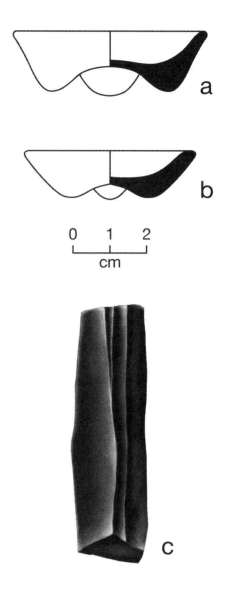

Above: Figure 10.12. Vessels 1 and 2 from Burial 53.

Right: Figure 10.13. Objects found with Burial 53. *a* and *b* are miniature Suchilquitongo tripod dishes, made of lightly fired brown (*café*) paste and painted inside and out with red pigment resembling CBA Type C2 wash. (*a* is Vessel 4; *b* is Vessel 13.) *c* is an obsidian blade found near the burial's mandible.

composite silhouette bowls (2 with negative white decoration) and several redeposited San José phase sherds.

Burial 58

Burial 58 was found in Square S5E6, some 60 cm north of Structure 24. This burial consisted of an isolated adult cranium, covered by an inverted outleaned-wall bowl of CBA Type K3 (Fig. 10.14).

Sherds from the General Fill of Zone A2

After the Monte Albán Ia rituals had ended and Structure 23 had been abandoned, all the buildings of Stratigraphic Zone A2 began to erode. Eventually, someone deliberately covered the whole area with earthen fill to provide a level surface for the buildings of Zone A1.

Our pottery samples from this layer of deliberate fill contained nothing later than Monte Albán Ia. We will let a few of these samples serve as examples.

The sherds from Square S5E9 of Zone A2 came from a tall cylinder of CBA Type G16; 2 Monte Albán Ia bottles; several

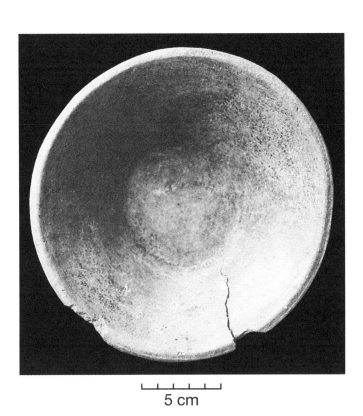

5 cm

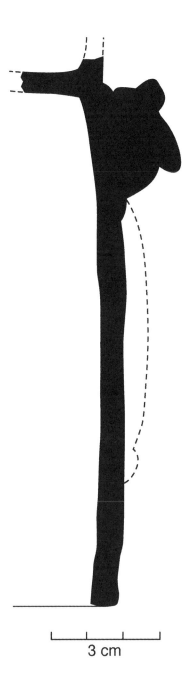

3 cm

Above: Figure 10.14. This outleaned-wall bowl (CBA Type K3) was inverted and used to cover the isolated adult cranium called Burial 58.

Right: Figure 10.15. Pedestal base from a grayware effigy incense burner, found in Square S1E7 of Zone A2. Though damaged, the appliqué motif appears to depict an owl.

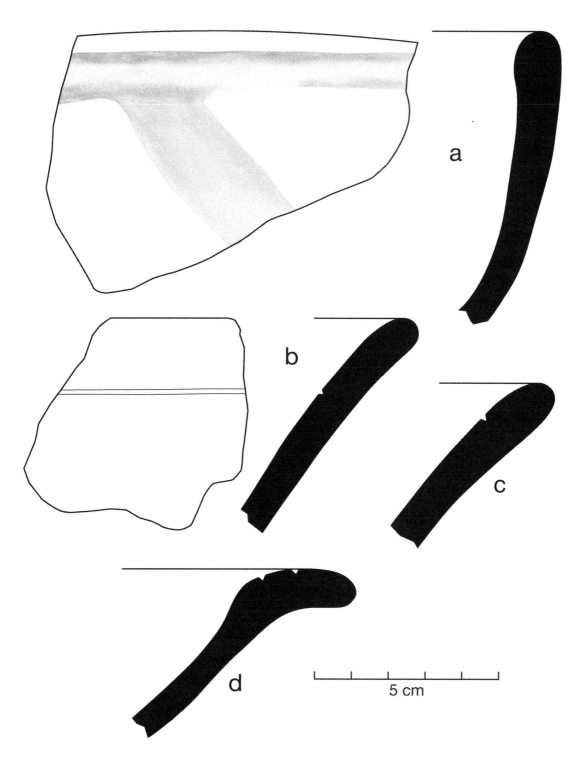

Figure 10.16. *Crema* ware sherds from Zone A2. *a*, hemispherical bowl with red wash, Type C2. *b*, *c*, outleaned-wall bowls with burnished garnet slip, Type C4. *d*, everted-rim bowl with white slip, smudged on the interior, Type C5.

Type C2 jar shoulders; 2 Guadalupe Burnished Brown bowls; 2 Socorro Fine Gray outleaned/outcurved-wall bowls; and a Josefina Fine Gray bowl.

The sherds from Square S1E7 came from a bowl of CBA Type G15; the pedestal base of a Monte Albán Ia owl-effigy incense burner (Fig. 10.15); a Suchilquitongo tripod dish with Type C4 garnet slip; incised Type C4 bowls (Fig. 10.16*b*, *c*); a Type C5 bowl (Fig. 10.16*d*); 4 Type K3 bowls; an incised Type A6 bowl with a slightly everted rim; a series of Socorro Fine Gray outleaned/outcurved-wall bowls, some with annular bases (Fig. 10.17); and 2 Socorro Fine Gray composite silhouette bowls with negative white decoration.

The sherds from Square S4E9 came from a Monte Albán Ia effigy vessel; bowls and jars of Types G15 and G16 (Fig. 10.18); a Type C4 bottle; vessels of CBA Types C2 (Fig. 10.16*a*), C5, and K3; and 2 Socorro Fine Gray outleaned/outcurved-wall bowls of the Rosario phase, 1 of which was incised with a double-line-break.

The Activities of Zone A2: A Reconstruction

By 500 b.c. or so, most of the occupants of San José Mogote had moved to the summit of Monte Albán. Without anyone around to repair it, the Zone B Residence on Mound 1 gradually collapsed. A mound of adobe debris accumulated over its wall stubs.

At some point, someone visited Mound 1 and constructed two stone-lined hearths—Features 77 and 78—by making shallow basins in the mound of debris that now covered the remains of the Zone B Residence. A radiocarbon date from Feature 77 places this event around 490 b.c., near the transition from the Rosario phase to Monte Albán Ia. Once the hearths had been used, activity on Mound 1 ceased for a time.

Then, sometime during Monte Albán Ia, a larger group of people visited the summit of Mound 1. Over the ruins of the Zone B Residence they constructed two small stone masonry buildings, separated by an earthen patio floor. One building, Structure 23, was a two-tiered, lime-plastered altar of some kind. The other building, Structure 24, was a simple semi-subterranean room or oversized offering box. The associated pottery was a mixture of Monte Albán Ia sherds, Rosario phase sherds, and redeposited earlier wares.

Part of the ritual carried out in Zone A2 included the burying of a child in Structure 24. Another part of the ritual consisted of burning incense on the patio floor between Structures 23 and 24. Five or six of the incense burners used in this ritual were then deliberately broken and discarded in Feature 76, a pit near the northern limits of Zone A2. The ash from the incense burners was dumped both in Feature 76 and on the ground nearby.

At some point, the skull of an adult individual was covered with an inverted bowl and buried near Structure 23. Then, once all rituals had been completed, the participants withdrew and Mound 1 once again lay abandoned—perhaps for as much as two or three hundred years.

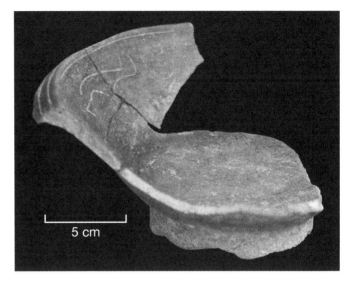

Figure 10.17. Fragment of a grayware bowl with everted rim and annular base, found in the debris of Stratigraphic Zone A2. It is incised with a motif resembling sine curves.

"Social Memory": The Cognitive Aspects of Ritual Visits to Abandoned Sites

What does it mean when a settlement is left abandoned for decades—even centuries—only to have a small group of people return and build an altar on its highest promontory? This kind of event happened so often in ancient Oaxaca that it can be considered a recurring process.

We suspect that Structures 23 and 24 are examples of a phenomenon that has become fashionable to call "social memory." We are not particularly fond of this term, since it too often serves as a shiny new package for what anthropologists previously called "tradition." Nor do we necessarily believe that the Zapotec of 400 b.c. remembered everything they had done at 700–500 b.c. By then, it is more likely that they had begun to revise their own history to accomplish new goals.

We do know, however, that many Mesoamerican societies memorialized past events in terms of legendary homelands and heroes. The Zapotec, in particular, referred to dynastic founders or "founder couples" to whom crucial past events were

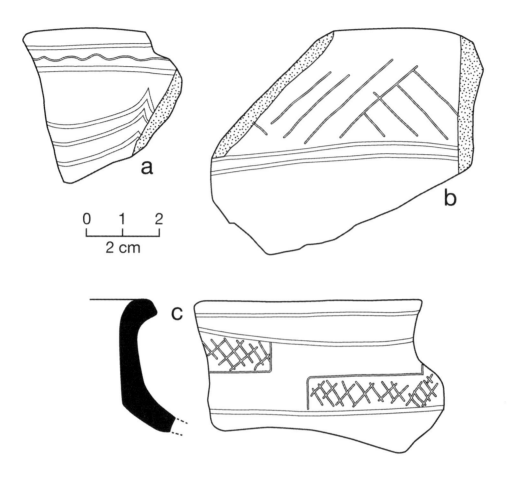

Figure 10.18. Incised grayware sherds from Zone A2. *a*, bowl rim, Type G15. *b*, bowl rim, Type G16. *c*, rim of small globular jar, Type G16.

attributed (Caso and Bernal 1952; Marcus 2006; Miller 1995). The legendary royal couple, Lord 1 Jaguar and Lady 2 Maize, memorialized on beakers at Monte Albán, constitute but one example (see Chapter 13).

It is possible that San José Mogote was remembered, at least in legend, as a place from which many of the founders of Monte Albán had come. In that case, it might be appropriate for the now-legendary hereditary leaders of San José Mogote to be memorialized as important (if remote) ancestors of Monte Albán's ruling lineage. At some point, perhaps during some perceived anniversary, it may have seemed appropriate to send ritual specialists and construction crews back to the highest point on the

"built environment" of San José Mogote. Whoever directed the building of Structures 23 and 24 may even have seen it as an act of religious piety and ancestor veneration that would put him in a favorable light. We will never know the details, but such an interpretation of Zone A2 on Mound 1 fits with everything we know of later Zapotec religion and politics.

11 | The Monte Albán Ic Hiatus (with Observations on the Lack of Fit between Survey and Excavation Results)

Monte Albán Ic (300–100 b.c.) was a tumultuous period in the Valley of Oaxaca. It was toward the end of this period that Monte Albán finally succeeded in crushing its main political rival, San Martín Tilcajete, thereby establishing itself as the undisputed capital of the valley (Spencer and Redmond 2003). The royal palace and the two-room temple, two institutions of the Zapotec state, came into being during Monte Albán Ic. Tilcajete's palace and main temple were burned between 30 b.c. and 20 b.c., after which Monte Albán established its own second-tier administrative center on a hill nearby (Elson 2007).

The abandonment of San José Mogote seems to have been even more extensive during Monte Albán Ic than it had been during Monte Albán Ia. During the course of our 15 years of excavation at the site, not one artifact that can be unequivocally linked to Late Monte Albán I ever came to light.

The Master Profile we produced in Area C was 93 m long and excavated to bedrock (Flannery and Marcus 2005:104). Not so much as a feature in that profile dated to Monte Albán Ic. The Master Profile of Area B was 99.5 m long and also excavated to bedrock (Flannery and Marcus 2005:302). Not so much as a feature in that profile dated to Ic. The same was true of Area A, where we removed thousands of cubic meters of soil during the exposure of Structures 1 and 2. No one seems to have visited the summit of Mound 1 to conduct a ritual during Late Monte

Albán I. No unequivocally Monte Albán Ic sherds showed up in the 92 surface collection circles we spread widely over the 42 ha "downtown" area of the site (Flannery 2009b: Fig. 3.4). Just as importantly, no Monte Albán Ic sherds were redeposited in the earthen fill of any of our Monte Albán II public buildings. Given how many basketloads of earth that entails—and how far they were probably carried—that fact has to be considered significant.

In light of our inability to find Monte Albán Ic occupation at San José Mogote, why did an independent surface survey (Kowalewski et al. 1989) record the site as possibly being occupied during that period? We believe that we understand why, and that the answer is inherent in the difference between surface pickup and excavation at large, multicomponent sites. This difference is coming to light in a number of world regions, including the Maya area (Johnson 2014), and has even been the subject of discussion by Gordon R. Willey, the scholar most often credited with having created settlement pattern archaeology in the first place.

The Limitations of Surface Survey

Settlement pattern archaeology is generally believed to date from Willey's monograph on the Virú Valley of Peru (Willey 1953). In that volume, Willey used surface collections from 315 sites to estimate the number and size of all occupied communities for every period of the prehistoric sequence in Virú. Among the sites surveyed in the middle Virú Valley were two called El Gallo and La Gallina, which Willey assigned to Peru's Middle Horizon (*sensu latu*).

Subsequent to the publication of Willey's monograph, Collier (1955) published the results of his post-survey excavations at a series of Virú sites, including Puerto Moorín near Guañape. By excavating to depths of 4 or 5 meters, Collier found preceramic occupations that had gone undetected during the Puerto Moorín surface survey. This was one of our first clues that surface collections, no matter how carefully made, may not tell us the whole story about a multicomponent site.

In the 1990s, Thomas Zoubek (1997) excavated the aforementioned sites of El Gallo and La Gallina. He did in fact find Middle Horizon materials in the upper strata, but at greater depths he found Initial Period (Peruvian Early Formative) deposits with impressive public architecture. There had simply been no evidence on the surface that El Gallo and La Gallina were important Initial Period communities.

In a retrospective paper on settlement pattern studies, Willey (1999:11) reflected on the implications of the new work at El Gallo and La Gallina. "There were no clues to these earlier occupations in the surface pottery collections we made at these two sites," he said, "nor did we have any evidence of earlier ceremonial structures. These were only revealed by Zoubek's deep digging. To me…it looks like settlement archaeology, like most field archaeology, will be heavily dependent upon excavation for fully accurate and complete results, at least in many situations."

These new excavations in the Virú Valley do not diminish the importance of settlement pattern survey, which remains an invaluable weapon in the archaeologist's arsenal. The new work shows that we cannot base our understanding of a large, complex, multicomponent site entirely on the sherds from the surface. It is simply not the case that those sherds are a straightforward reflection of what is under the ground.

At San José Mogote, a 60 to 65 ha site with at least nine phases of occupation, the limitations of surface survey cannot be ignored. Here are just a few of the problems for which we have empirical evidence:

1. Virtually every time the occupants of the village constructed a public building, they used basketloads of earthen fill that contained sherds from earlier periods. These earlier sherds then made their way to the surface through erosion and plowing.
2. In some cases, the earthen fill for public buildings was carried hundreds of meters from its point of origin, ending up on parts of the site where there are no primary deposits belonging to the earlier periods.
3. The present-day occupants of San José Mogote frequently make adobe bricks out of earth that contains prehistoric sherds, transporting those ceramics far from their original place of deposition.
4. Repeated plowing has moved sherds around and damaged

or destroyed ancient constructions.

5. The laying down of stucco floors for Monte Albán II public buildings and patios frequently sealed in earlier materials, preventing them from making their way to the surface.
6. Some of the pottery types most often used by survey crews for chronological purposes were not fully restricted to one archaeological phase. For example, Avelina Red-on-Buff—frequently used as a type fossil for the Tierras Largas phase—lasted into the early San José phase (Flannery and Marcus 1994). The CBA Type G12—frequently used as a type fossil for Monte Albán Ic—lasted into early Monte Albán II (see below). And as Drennan (1976) has shown, many forms of rim decoration on Socorro Fine Gray bowls of the Rosario phase lasted into Monte Albán Ia.
7. Because some pottery types span two periods, large multicomponent sites can present what Stephen Kowalewski (personal communication, 1989) calls "the shadow effect." For example, if a site has abundant late Rosario sherds and early Monte Albán II sherds on its surface, survey crews may conclude that the site was also occupied during Monte Albán I—simply because so many of the pottery types span the period Rosario/Monte Albán Ia or Monte Albán Ic/Monte Albán II.

Surface Sherds at San José Mogote

Our 1967 surface survey of San José Mogote involved scattering 92 collection circles, each 5 m in diameter, over 40–50 ha of the site. This procedure yielded more than 25,000 diagnostic sherds. We were struck at that time by how few Monte Albán I sherds we had recovered, especially in view of the fact that Monte Albán II sherds were abundant. Unfortunately, in 1967 we did not know as much as we do now about the attributes distinguishing Rosario and Monte Albán Ia. At that time, many sherds simply had to be recorded "Rosario or M.A. Ia."

The Valley of Oaxaca Settlement Pattern Project (Kowalewski et al. 1989:72) surface-collected San José Mogote in 1977, and in 1980 they came back again to "survey areas away from the site center." We now consider many of the latter areas to be separate archaeological sites or, at the very least, outlying residential wards placed on neighboring piedmont spurs. "We did not take as many collections" [in 1980], Kowalewski et al. (1989:72) report, "bringing back a total of 26 from all parts of the site."

Kowalewski et al. (1989:72) stress that "in the field it was much more difficult to separate the Rosario [sherds] from the general run of San José to Early I utility wares." We agree, especially in the case of sherds that have been on the surface long enough to be weathered. A student assigned to the San José Mogote surface pickup is quoted by Kowalewski et al. (1989:90) as saying: "San José, Guadalupe, Rosario, and I are impossible (or close to it) to distinguish on the basis of café/crema 'crudwares' (e.g. Fidencio Coarse and C-2s). Since that was basically what was distributed all over San José Mogote, site boundaries for San José/Guadalupe/Rosario and [Monte Albán] I will tend to be isomorphic."

Kowalewski et al. (1989:90) conclude as follows: "Plenty of diagnostic sherds were found from Rosario and M.A. II. The question is whether the apparent Early I is a real occupation or an after-image caused by the unusual situation of a site with large and intensive Rosario and M.A. II components…The thinness of the ceramic distribution, and the paucity of C-4s and highly decorated gray wares, suggests that San José [Mogote] was of far less importance during Early I. It undoubtedly retained an aura of sacred and secular power, permanently marked by major Rosario public buildings."

We agree with, and are happy to enlarge upon, this thoughtful comment by the leaders of the Valley of Oaxaca Settlement Pattern Project. Not only are the aforementioned "crudwares" difficult to assign to a specific period, it is only by excavating that one can really be sure whether primary deposits of Rosario or Monte Albán I were actually present on a particular area of the site.

Kowalewski et al. (1989: Table 5.3) found only 11 possible sherds that could be from Monte Albán Ia types G15, G16, or G17 in their surface collections (which, as mentioned, included "survey areas away from the site center"). They also found only three possible sherds from the diagnostic Monte Albán Ia Type C4. In our opinion, any of the alleged Type C2 sherds they found could, in reality, belong to the Rosario phase version of Fidencio Coarse, which utilized *crema* clay. Any of the survey project's alleged K3s and K8s could, in reality, be sherds of Guadalupe Burnished Brown. It is an inescapable fact that CBA Type C2 evolved from Fidencio Coarse, and that all the Monte Albán I *café* wares appear to have evolved from Guadalupe Burnished Brown of the Rosario phase.

We see the Settlement Pattern Project's observations as confirming our own conclusion (based on 15 years of excavation) that San José Mogote was virtually abandoned at the start of Monte Albán I, but revisited from time to time during Period Ia by small groups that conducted rituals above the ruins of the abandoned Rosario phase public buildings (Chapter 10).

Late Monte Albán I and the Problems of Caso, Bernal, and Acosta's Type G12

Just as there are difficulties distinguishing Rosario and Monte Albán Ia surface sherds, there are difficulties separating the surface sherds of Monte Albán Ic and early Monte Albán II. These problems are particularly evident at San José Mogote because it was reoccupied on such a large scale in early II.

One of the most frequently relied on horizon markers for Monte Albán Ic is CBA Type G12, an outcurved-wall bowl with (1) parallel incised lines encircling the inner rim and (2) complex incised designs on the interior of the base. The problem with the use of G12 as a type fossil is that while it *does* reach its maximum popularity during Monte Albán Ic, it also lasts into early Monte

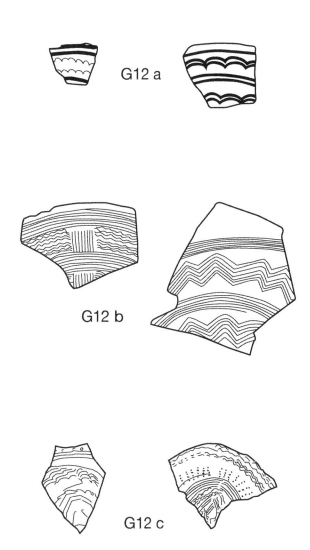

Figure 11.1. Incised bases from G12 bowls, showing the subtypes G12a, G12b, and G12c. For fuller descriptions and a wider range of illustrations, see Spencer, Redmond, and Elson (2008).

Albán II. What this means is that when a site has a heavy early II occupation, anyone involved in surface collection is likely to find enough G12 sherds to suggest a Ic occupation as well. San José Mogote is covered with G12 sherds, but 15 seasons of excavation have failed to produce so much as a feature dating to Monte Albán Ic.

Recently—based on their stratigraphic excavations at San Martín Tilcajete—Spencer, Redmond, and Elson (2008) have made discoveries that will help future surface survey crews. They have identified three subtypes of G12 basal incising that seem to have chronological significance. They refer to these three subtypes as G12a, G12b, and G12c (Fig. 11.1).

In the case of subtype G12a, the incised designs on the interior of the base seem to have been made with a thorn, rather than a multitoothed comb. The designs tend to feature alternating straight and wavy lines arranged in concentric patterns.

In the case of subtype G12b, the designs on the base seem to have been made with a fine, multitoothed comb, and are carried out with "minimal skipping or disjointed motifs" (Spencer, Redmond, and Elson 2008: Fig. 5).

In subtype G12c, the designs are "more sloppily executed" than is the case with G12b, and one finds more skipping, disjointed motifs, and breaks in lines (Spencer, Redmond, and Elson 2008: Fig. 6). There are also more likely to be lines of dots or punctations included in the design.

The chronological evidence is as follows. Subtype G12a (thorn-incised) bases appeared at the end of Monte Albán Ia, reached maximum popularity early, and disappeared by Monte Albán II. Subtype G12b (finely comb-incised) bases surged in popularity during Monte Albán Ic, and lasted into early Monte Albán II. Subtype G12c (sloppily comb-incised) bases appeared in low frequency during Ic and grew in popularity during early Monte Albán II.

Spencer, Redmond, and Elson (2008) stress that any chronology based on these variants of Type G12 depends on the relative frequency of subtypes, rather than their simple presence or absence. As a result, they will almost certainly be more useful in dating coherent excavated deposits than surface collections. This having been said, it is significant that none of the G12s we recovered in our excavations at San José Mogote belonged to the earliest subtype, G12a. All of our G12s were of subtypes G12b or G12c, and all were found in association with diagnostics of Monte Albán II.

This fact makes us very skeptical of any claim, based on surface sherds alone, that San José Mogote had any substantial Monte Albán Ic occupation. So large was the early Monte Albán II occupation at San José Mogote that one would fully expect to find lots of G12b bases on the surface.

Conclusions

We conclude that Monte Albán Ic was a period during which San José Mogote (especially the "downtown" area) lay virtually abandoned. We cannot rule out the possibility of Ic components on outlying piedmont spurs in the places Kowalewski et al. (1989) refer to as "survey areas away from the site center." Our suspicion, however, is that during Monte Albán Ic, Monte Albán was so busy subduing the Cuicatlán Cañada and battling Tilcajete that it had little or no time to concern itself with visiting Mound 1 at San José Mogote to conduct rituals. Not until early Monte Albán II—when it finally controlled the entire Valley of Oaxaca—did Monte Albán have time to turn its attention again to San José Mogote.

12 | The Monte Albán-Tilcajete Conflict and the Origins of the Two-Room Temple

As Chapters 10 and 11 have shown, San José Mogote's ritual and political importance declined as soon as the bulk of its population had moved to Monte Albán. No longer were the Valley of Oaxaca's largest and most significant religious structures being built in the Etla subvalley.

Monte Albán I was a key period in the history of the Valley of Oaxaca. It witnessed the transition from rank society to monarchy, and we need to know what the elite residences and temples of that period looked like. The obvious place to look, of course, would be at Monte Albán itself. The problem is that Monte Albán's Period I public buildings are deeply buried beneath the later structures of Periods II, IIIa, and IIIb–IV.

At a place called "the patio south of Mound A"—near the southeast corner of Monte Albán's North Platform—a deep sounding exposed part of an early public building with "serpentine motifs modeled in stucco" (Acosta 1965:816 and Fig. 4). Unfortunately, this Monte Albán Ic structure could not be fully investigated. Three stratigraphic levels below it lay the sloping wall of an even earlier public building, apparently dating to Monte Albán Ia. This structure, too, remains to be fully exposed.

In other words, we know that a number of important Monte Albán I ritual buildings lie buried beneath the North Platform. We simply cannot get at them without destroying later buildings, many of which have been consolidated for tourism.

Fortunately, this lacuna in our knowledge of Monte Albán I ritual buildings has now been greatly reduced by the site of San Martín Tilcajete in the Zimatlán subvalley. There, years of patient work by Elsa Redmond and Charles Spencer have uncovered not only a Monte Albán Ia temple, but an entire temple precinct from Monte Albán Ic (Redmond and Spencer 2008, 2013). These public buildings could be excavated in their entirety because they are not buried beneath tons of later overburden. They lie just below the surface because Tilcajete was burned by Monte Albán at 30–20 b.c. and subsequently abandoned.

Structure 1

Structure 1, a one-room temple built during Monte Albán Ia, stood atop Mound K in the El Mogote sector of San Martín Tilcajete. The architects first constructed a platform measuring 12.6 m by 7.6 m (Fig. 12.1). Atop this platform they placed a rectangular temple, 6.7 m long by 2.7 m wide. The construction was of adobe brick over a fieldstone foundation.

The entrance to Structure 1 was on the west side, facing a 2.2 ha ceremonial plaza. The temple's features included two fire

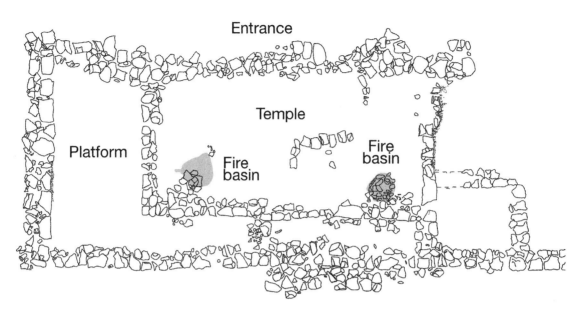

Figure 12.1. Structure 1 at San Martín Tilcajete, a one-room temple built during Monte Albán Ia. The temple was 6.7 m by 2.7 m and surrounded on three sides by a larger platform. Redrawn from Redmond and Spencer (2008: Figure 4).

basins, built into the floor in front of the rear wall. There also appears to have been a small storage room on the platform, just off the northeast corner of the temple.

Two radiocarbon dates place Structure 1 in Monte Albán Ia (Redmond and Spencer 2008:247). A charcoal sample from the northernmost fire basin dated to 500 b.c. ± 40 (the calibrated two-sigma range would be 780–400 BC). Charcoal from the floor dated to 550 b.c. ± 40 (the calibrated two-sigma range would be 790–420 BC).

Structure 1 of Tilcajete was burned at roughly 330 b.c., along with other buildings on the same plaza (Spencer and Redmond 2003). This attack, likely the work of Monte Albán, did not cause Tilcajete to capitulate; instead, its population doubled, moved upslope to the El Palenque sector, and built some defensive walls.

Structure 20

Structure 20 was built during Monte Albán Ic, atop Mound B in the El Palenque sector of Tilcajete. Its ground plan (Fig. 12.2) consisted of one very elongated room with symmetrical annexes at either end (Room 1), flanked by a series of smaller rooms (Rooms 2 and 3) and features. Once again, the construction was of adobes over a fieldstone foundation. The thick stucco floor had been heavily burned.

Room 1 was roughly 34 m long and 6.75 m wide. Its entrance lay on the west side, overlooking the 1.6 ha El Palenque ceremonial plaza. Entry seems to have been via a kind of narrow porch, flanked by four rectangular pillars whose surviving bases consisted of stony rubble. Recall that Structure 37 at San José Mogote, a late Rosario phase temple, appears to have had perishable columns set on stone bases (Chapter 9). The builders of Structure 20 at Tilcajete had taken the next step by creating rubble pillars. We note that a partially exposed building below Mound K of Monte Albán, believed to date to Monte Albán Ic, seems to have had cylindrical rubble columns (Flannery and Marcus 2003a: Fig. 4.3).

Rooms 2 and 3 of Structure 20 at Tilcajete might have been created for the storage of temple paraphernalia; Room 3 even had its own staircase. Next to Room 3 lay Feature 65, believed to be an adobe-lined cooking facility. On the floor of Room 1 were two shallow, irregular, unstandardized hearths. Scattered on the floor were an obsidian lancet and a number of obsidian blades that might have been used either for bloodletting or for the sacrifice of small animals such as quail.

A possible date for Structure 20 is provided by charcoal from the fill of Mound B. The date is 250 b.c. ± 50, not long after the start of Monte Albán Ic.

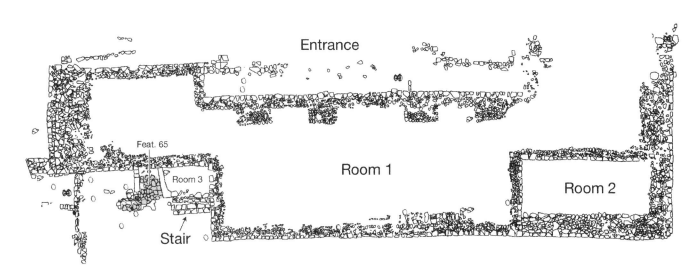

Figure 12.2. Structure 20 at San Martín Tilcajete, a temple built around 250 b.c. during Monte Albán Ic. Room 1 measured roughly 34 m by 6.75 m. Redrawn from Redmond and Spencer (2008: Figure 6).

Structure 16

Structure 16 of Tilcajete was built atop Mound G on the east side of the El Palenque ceremonial plaza. A radiocarbon sample from the fill of Mound G yielded a date of 100 b.c. ± 40, suggesting that Structure 16 was built late in Monte Albán Ic. This temple was eventually destroyed by fire at 30 b.c. ± 70, at the end of Period Ic or the start of Monte Albán II (the calibrated one-sigma range would be 165 BC–AD 155). This burning, presumably carried out by Monte Albán, ended the occupation at Tilcajete and left Monte Albán as the unchallenged capital of the Valley of Oaxaca.

Structure 16 is our oldest example of the Zapotec two-room temple. It signals to us that a second room had now been added to the temple so that the increasingly professional priests would have their own inner chamber, separate from that of ordinary worshipers. This change suggests that Zapotec society was now organized as a state, with the recognizable architecture of a state religious hierarchy.

Might there have been two-room Monte Albán Ic temples at Monte Albán as well? We strongly suspect that there were, but if so, they are now so deeply buried below other buildings that it would take great luck to find one.

Structure 16's entrance was on the west side, facing the plaza (Fig. 12.3). Its outer and less sacred room (Room 2) measured

12.8 m by 2.35 m, and was reached by a staircase of at least three steps. Its inner and more sacred room (Room 1) measured 9.8 m by 2.2 m, and was reached after a 10 cm step-up through a doorway reduced to 1.65 m wide. Two small cubicles (Rooms 3 and 4) flanked the main temple; these rooms could be seen (relative to Room 1) as more formal versions of the unwalled annexes seen in Structure 16's Room 1. Possibly Rooms 3 and 4 were used to store temple paraphernalia. Once again, the construction of the temple was adobe brick over fieldstone foundations.

The Significance of the Tilcajete Temples

Structures 1, 20, and 16 at Tilcajete greatly enhance our understanding of the evolution of the Zapotec temple. They show us that Monte Albán Ia temples were basically one-room structures like their Rosario phase antecedents, but with the addition of new features such as fire basins and storage spaces. Sometime after 300 b.c., during Monte Albán Ic, we see two significant innovations. A second room was added to the temple itself, probably to house the minor priests who maintained the building and carried out everyday rituals. At Tilcajete, two small residences (Structures 27 and 28) were built near Structure 16, presumably to house the higher-ranking priests who directed the work of the minor priests and organized the

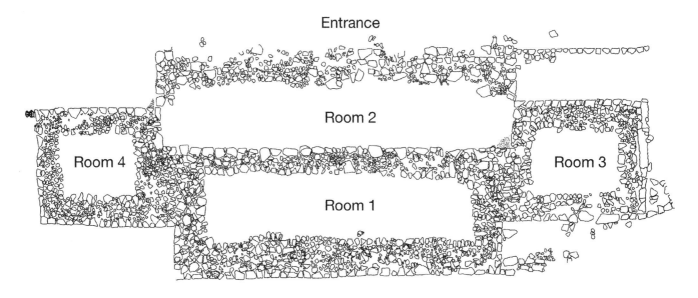

Figure 12.3. Structure 16 at San Martín Tilcajete, a temple that was burned around 30 b.c., either at the end of Monte Albán Ic or the start of Monte Albán II. This building has the look of a standard Zapotec state temple, with a less sacred outer room measuring 12.8 m by 2.35 m (Room 2) and a more sacred inner room measuring 9.8 m by 2.2 m (Room 1). Rooms 3 and 4 might have been used to store temple paraphernalia. Redrawn from Redmond and Spencer (2008: Figure 9).

major rituals. Pillars and modest cooking facilities were added to some temples at that time.

It would seem, therefore, that 300 b.c. (in conventional radiocarbon years) was a watershed moment, one after which there is increasing circumstantial evidence for state religious institutions and a priestly hierarchy. In light of this evidence for the coevolution of society and religion, Redmond and Spencer (2008) see analogies with the creation of the Hawai'ian state under King Kamehameha (AD 1790–1810). As part of his military campaign to bring all of the Hawai'ian archipelago under his control, Kamehameha systematically rededicated preexisting temples to Kū, a warlike deity, and created new ideologies to transform himself from an enemy conqueror to the legitimate ruler of each newly conquered district (Redmond and Spencer 2008:249).

It is likely that both Monte Albán and Tilcajete were engaged in creating state-like societies during Monte Albán Ic. Monte Albán certainly controlled the larger polity; owing to a lack of stratigraphic overburden, however, Tilcajete's royal and sacred buildings are far more accessible. Its buildings and plazas also tell us that one way Tilcajete communicated its resistance to Monte Albán's aggression was by maintaining a different astronomical orientation—25° east of north, in contrast to Monte Albán's true north orientation.

The data for Monte Albán Ic, therefore, allow us to see the changes in religion and ideology that accompanied the gradual creation of monarchy during the centuries-long competition between two powerful rank societies. Monte Albán and Tilcajete spoke the same language, were aware of each other's political strategies and architectural innovations, undoubtedly borrowed some ideas from each other, but took pains to defend their autonomy. That is, until the moment when Monte Albán finally burned Tilcajete to the ground, then built its own second-tier administrative center on nearby Cerro Tilcajete—a site that oriented all its buildings true north-south—and built a road that led toward Monte Albán (Elson 2007).

13 | The Monte Albán II Renaissance at San José Mogote

After the burning of Tilcajete's palace at 20 b.c., Monte Albán finally controlled the entire Valley of Oaxaca. On nearby Cerro Tilcajete, the Zapotec state built a second-tier administrative center, one that displayed Monte Albán's astronomical alignment rather than Tilcajete's (Elson 2007). Cerro Tilcajete likely went on to serve as the administrative center for a series of third-tier sites such as Coyotepec, Cerro San Nicolás, Roaló, and Santa Ana Zegache (Kowalewski et al. 1989; Marcus and Flannery 1996: Figs. 196, 197).

Cerro Tilcajete was, of course, not the only second-tier center in the administrative hierarchy below Monte Albán. It was simply one of six second-tier communities with estimated populations between 970 and 1950 persons, all located between 14 and 28 km of Monte Albán (Kowalewski et al. 1989; Marcus and Flannery 1996: Fig. 194).

The fourth largest of these second-tier administrative centers was San José Mogote. After languishing for centuries, San José Mogote enjoyed a kind of renaissance; it appears to have been chosen as an important administrative center for the Etla subvalley, and came to be reoccupied on a large scale. We estimate the Monte Albán II occupation of San José Mogote to have covered 60–70 ha, and the ceramics we found indicate that this occupation went back to the very beginnings of Monte Albán II. Among the likely third-tier centers in the hierarchy below San José Mogote

were Santo Domingo Tlaltinango, Magdalena Apasco, Reyes Etla, and San Lorenzo Cacaotepec (Marcus and Flannery 1996: Figs. 196, 197).

Figure 13.1 is our artist's reconstruction of San José Mogote at the peak of Monte Albán II (100 b.c. –AD 150). The extent to which the site was laid out in imitation of Monte Albán itself will be evident. San José Mogote was given a main plaza measuring 300 m north-south and 200 m east-west. At the south end of the plaza lay Mound 1, a smaller version of Monte Albán's South Platform. At the north end of the plaza lay Mound 8, a smaller version of Monte Albán's North Platform. Both Mound 8 and the North Platform supported governmental structures, reached in each case by climbing a wide stairway and passing through a colonnaded portico; Monte Albán's portico had a double row of six columns, while San José Mogote's had a single row of six. Monte Albán's North Platform had a sunken patio 50 m across and 4 m deep; Mound 8 at San José Mogote had a shallower sunken patio, only 20 m across.

As for Mound 1 at San José Mogote, its summit now featured a patio surrounded by four two-room temples, some of them placed atop the ruins of long-abandoned Rosario buildings. There were also temples on Monte Albán's South Platform, but exactly how many of them date to Monte Albán II is not yet clear.

To continue our comparison of Monte Albán and San José

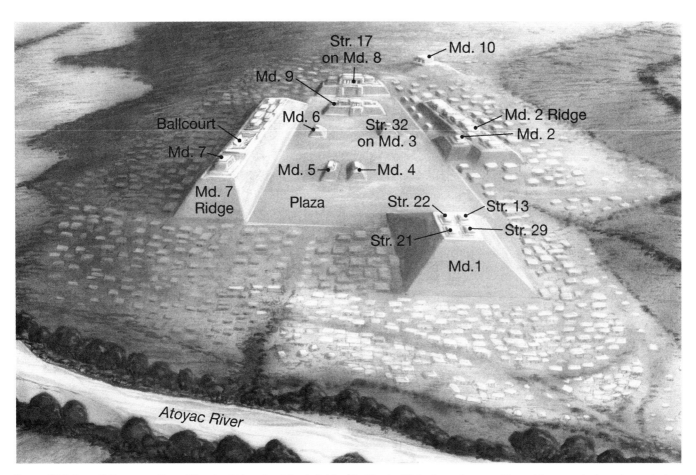

Figure 13.1. An artist's conception of San José Mogote at the height of its Monte Albán II renaissance. Mound 8 supported a colonnaded governmental palace; Mound 9 supported residences for the ruling elite. At least five pairs of temples faced each other: Mounds 3 & 6 and 4 & 5 in the plaza; Mounds 2 & 7 on their respective ridges; and Structures 13 & 22 and 21 & 29 atop Mound 1. Drawing by David West Reynolds.

Mogote, both sites had numerous two-room temples along the eastern and western borders of their respective main plazas, as well as on natural rises within the plaza. San José Mogote had at least ten such temples in Period II, while Monte Albán may have had twice that many. The vast majority of these temples faced east or west; in perhaps five cases at San José Mogote (and more than that at Monte Albán), a pair of temples faced each other. Thus, although we think of both plazas as having a north-south axis, at the level of the actual temple it was the east-west path of the sun that provided the most significant sacred orientation. No Monte Albán II temples so far found at San José Mogote had their doorways facing north or south.

The ten temples at San José Mogote were as follows. The Mound 7 temple (on the west side of the plaza) and the Mound 2 temple (on the east side) faced each other. Within the plaza itself, the Mound 6 and Mound 3 temples faced each other; the Mound 5 and Mound 4 temples also faced each other. (Because these temples had been placed on natural rises in the plaza, they had an irregular spacing, rather than occupying a central spine like Buildings G, H, and I at Monte Albán.) As for the four temples

on Mound 1, they consisted of two pairs of buildings facing each other; Structures 21 and 22 faced east, while Structures 13 and 29 faced west (Fig. 13.2).

Both Monte Albán and San José Mogote had ballcourts, shaped like Roman numeral ones, on one side of the main plaza. Monte Albán's ballcourt was on the east side of its plaza, while San José Mogote's was on the west. We will see in Chapter 19 that these ballcourts were virtually identical in size, suggesting not only a common layout but standard units of measurement as well.

In addition, San José Mogote seems to have had several types of palaces. One, which could be described as a governmental palace, featured a colonnaded portico and a sunken court (Chapter 17). Such a palace appears to have been a place of assembly for the community's power elite, but could turn out to have had royal residential apartments in the rear as well. The second type of palace appears more residential than administrative, but was still elevated above the plaza in such a way as to suggest that it housed important noble families.

Mound 9 at San José Mogote was an example of this second type of palace, whose partial excavation is described in Chapter 18.

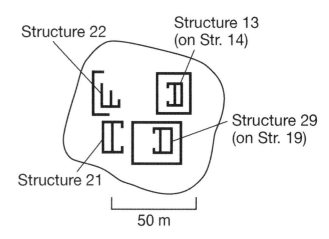

Figure 13.2. At the peak of the Monte Albán II renaissance, there were four two-room temples atop Mound 1 of San José Mogote. Structures 21 and 22 faced east; Structures 13 and 29 faced west. (The linear border shown is a contour line from the base of the mound, prior to excavation.)

Consisting of multiple patios surrounded by groups of three to four rooms, this building seems to have been modified continuously throughout its occupation. Many of those modifications involved the division of preexisting rooms and patios into smaller spaces, possibly in response to an increase in the number of occupants over time. The two types of palaces represented by Mounds 8 and 9 at San José Mogote suggest the presence of at least two levels of elites—major and minor nobles, for want of better terms.

Finally, there is Mound 10 at San José Mogote, an isolated mound that lies about 90 m northeast of the Mound 8 palace. We had neither the time nor the funds to investigate Mound 10, so we cannot claim to know either its age or its function. We cannot help but wonder, however, if it housed a temple whose use was restricted to the major nobles at San José Mogote, analogous to temples d, e, and g on Monte Albán's North Platform.

The Sequence of Monte Albán II Temples on Structure 14

As we explained in Chapter 8, Structure 14 was originally built during the Rosario phase to serve as a platform for Structure 37, a temple. During the Monte Albán II renaissance, Structure 14 was extensively modified to serve as a platform for Structure 36, the earliest of a series of Monte Albán II temples. These modifications included raising the height of the platform by almost a meter, building it a new north wall, and changing the location of its staircase.

Like the Middle Formative Recinto at Teopantecuanitlán, Guerrero (Martínez Donjuán 1985, 2010), the Rosario phase version of Structure 14 was shaped like a giant plus sign, measuring 21 m east-west and 19 m north-south. The plus sign shape was achieved by creating a 7 m wide jog in the north and south walls (Fig. 13.3). The original Rosario phase staircase was on the east side of Structure 14, facing Area A of San José Mogote (Fig. 9.2). Both the Rosario phase staircase and the plus sign version of the platform featured immense limestone blocks hauled across the Atoyac River from the Matadamas quarries, some of them weighing half a ton or more. The fill inside the Rosario stage of the platform was a combination of bowling ball-sized ignimbrite boulders and basketloads of the gritty black clay that forms above ignimbrite bedrock as it weathers.

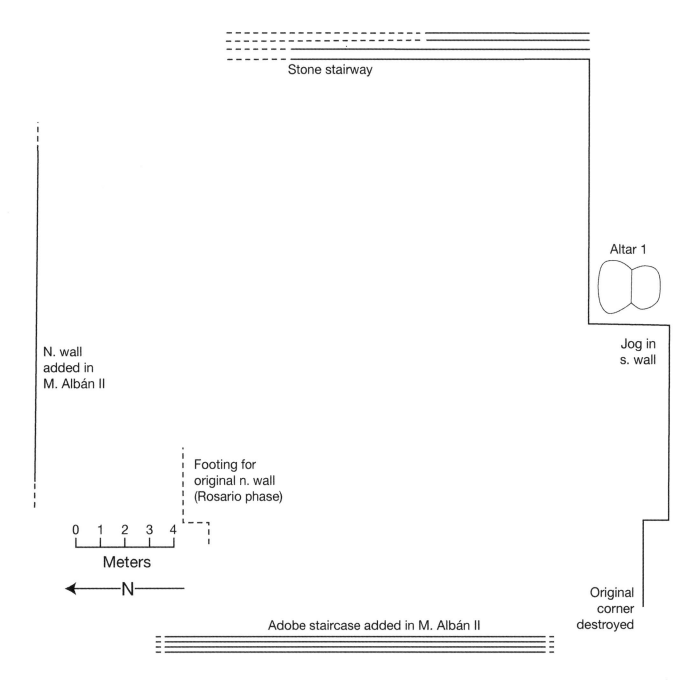

Figure 13.3. Plan view of the ruins of Structure 14, a platform that had suffered considerable prehispanic modification and hacienda-era stone robbing.

The Monte Albán II architects preserved parts of the Rosario phase platform and destroyed others. The parts they destroyed became a source of reusable building stone, leaving many areas of Structure 14 looking ragged.

The Monte Albán II architects evidently found Structure 14 too narrow to accommodate the temple they were preparing to build. They therefore widened it by creating a whole new north wall, 5.7 m north of the jog in the Rosario phase north wall. The Monte Albán II north wall had no jog in it, eliminating the old plus-sign shape.

The Monte Albán II architects also did not need a staircase on the east side of the platform, providing access from Area A. They intended to build a two-room temple with its doorway on the west, facing across a small patio toward Structure 22; they therefore needed a staircase on the west side of the platform. Unfortunately, the west side of the plus-sign-shaped Rosario platform was the rear side, and consisted of a blank wall made from limestone blocks. The Monte Albán II architects tore out virtually this entire wall, including the northwest and southwest corners (see Fig. 13.3). In its place, they built a staircase using rectangular adobe bricks. This adobe staircase contrasts architecturally with the stone masonry of the original Rosario building, and was one of our first clues that the building had been extensively modified. Stone masonry temples built during Monte Albán II (like Structures 21 and 22 on Mound 1) have stone masonry staircases, not adobe ones.

Since the old stone staircase on the east side of Structure 14 was no longer needed, the Monte Albán II architects saw it as a ready source of limestone blocks, which they borrowed extensively. This borrowing of staircase stones resumed in the Colonial era. We believe that many of the loose limestone blocks we found on the east slope of Mound 1 when we arrived had been pulled out of the Rosario phase staircase (see Appendix A).

Since the Monte Albán II architects intended to build Structure 36 over the ruins of Structure 37—an old Rosario phase temple—they also decided to raise the height of Structure 14, to keep up with the increasing height of the temples above it. One of the areas in which their new construction can be seen most clearly is the south wall, especially in the area of the jog. As shown in Figures 9.3 and 9.4, we excavated the jog to bedrock, noting not only the difference in construction between the Rosario walls and the Monte Albán II walls, but also the difference between the earlier and later fills. For one thing, the Rosario masons had used very large limestone blocks, while the Monte Albán II masons preferred smaller dressed stones. And whereas the Rosario builders had preferred large boulders and gritty black clay for their fill, the Monte Albán II builders preferred chunks of reused adobes, along with golf ball- and baseball-sized stones. In addition, there were no Monte Albán II sherds in the lower fill of the jog, only redeposited Early and Middle Formative ceramics.

It would have been nice if the Monte Albán II architects had left Structure 37—the old Rosario temple—intact beneath the new building they created. Unfortunately, they did not. They intended to build a much bigger temple, requiring a much larger and sturdier substructure. They therefore dismantled most of Structure 37, using many of its stones in the densely packed layer of fill they created to support the weight of Structure 36. In part, it was the thickness of this subfloor fill that necessitated raising the height of Structure 14.

Altar 1

Now we come to an enigmatic feature found near Structure 14. Two immense blocks of Matadamas limestone, with an estimated combined weight of 5.5 metric tons, had been set against the south wall of Structure 14 just east of the jog. These two blocks can be seen in Figure 13.4, and their location relative to the jog is given in Figure 13.3.

There can be no doubt that the placement of these two blocks was deliberate, since they had been carefully leveled in situ using smaller stones as wedges. Unfortunately, the date of their placement is unknown because we did not recover any diagnostic sherds that could be associated with them. To be sure, their size and weight make these stones similar to those used in the original Rosario phase version of Structure 14. Given the extensive Monte Albán II modifications of the building, however, that may not be significant. The Monte Albán II architects had clearly pulled out and reused some of the biggest Rosario phase stones.

Our use of the term "Altar 1" for these paired blocks is based on a hunch: they remind us of the stone altars on which many Mesoamerican societies sacrificed human captives. And as we shall see, at least one of the Monte Albán II temples on Structure 14 contained obsidian daggers of the type used by the Zapotec and Aztec for heart sacrifice.

A Possible Post-occupation Offering above the Ruins of Structure 37

In the course of creating a densely packed layer of subfloor fill for Structure 36, the Monte Albán II architects came upon—and broke—a possible Monte Albán I "frying pan" incense burner, deliberately buried in the post-occupation debris of Structure 37 (Fig. 13.5). We found this grayware incense burner face up in a level of adobe fragments from the collapsed walls of Structure 37. Significantly, we recovered no other vessels of Monte Albán I age in this area, which produced only Rosario phase (and earlier) sherds.

This incense burner appears to have been placed as an isolated offering in the mounded debris of Structure 37, centuries after its abandonment and collapse. It may have been used to burn incense in a ritual of some kind, after which it was buried. This ritual may have taken place about the time Structures 23 and 24 were built (Chapter 10).

Figure 13.4. Altar 1, set in an angle of the south wall of Structure 14. It has been estimated that these two limestone blocks weigh a combined 5.5 metric tons. Tomás Cruz serves as scale.

3 cm

Figure 13.5. Grayware "frying pan" incense burner in Monte Albán I style. This ritual vessel was left as an offering in the debris above Structure 37, long after the abandonment and collapse of that building.

Possible Rituals of Sanctification, Conducted before the Building of Structure 36

Once the densely packed layer of subfloor fill for Structure 36 had been created, the area set aside for the building of the temple became the scene of rituals involving human sacrifice and cannibalism. The likely first step in these rituals was the preparation of Feature 98, an earth oven measuring 1.1 m north-south, 65 cm east-west, and 53 cm deep (Figs. 13.6, 13.7). This earth oven, whose walls had been subjected to such intense heat that they were surrounded by layers of burned earth, contained the partial remains of a child 2–3 years old. This child (designated Burial 70) appears to have been cooked over heated rocks and partially eaten; its arms were completely missing.

Less than a meter north of Feature 98 we found Burial 69, the partial remains of an adult (Fig. 13.6). This individual (whose sex could not be determined) lay in a shallow oval pit and had been covered with a *laja*, or flat paving stone. We found several additional stones in the area.

There were no signs of burning in the pit with Burial 69. Its proximity to Feature 98 suggests that Burial 69 was part of the same ritual, but we are uncertain whether this adult was an additional sacrificial victim, or simply an individual whose exhumed remains were reburied during the ceremony.

Significantly, Feature 98 and Burial 69 lay just below the space set aside for the future outer room of Structure 36, and roughly half a meter west of the step-up to the inner room. Since Structure 36 was to be an important temple of the Monte Albán II period, we suspect that what took place on this spot was what Rappaport (1971, 1999) has called a "ritual of sanctification." This term refers to a ceremony whose purpose was to convert secular to sacred ground so that a religious building could be built.

To be sure, a late Rosario phase temple had once been built on an earlier stage of the same platform. However, more than 500 years had elapsed since that earlier temple was abandoned. Evidently, that span of time was too long (or "cultural memory" too short) for the place to be still considered a sacred venue. Thus it became necessary to hold a new ritual of sanctification before Structure 36 could be built.

In addition to Feature 98 and Burials 69 and 70, we made one more significant discovery in the subfloor fill below the outer room of Structure 36. A complete bowl of CBA Type G12—broken under the weight of Structure 36, but still restorable—had been left in the fill as well (Fig. 13.8). This grayware bowl bears on the interior of its base the kind of finely executed, multitoothed comb incising that Spencer, Redmond, and Elson (2008) have classified as subtype G12b (see Chapter 11). That subtype spans the period from Monte Albán Ic through early Monte Albán II. Since the sherds in the subfloor fill around the bowl included a number of Monte Albán II types (most notably, Types C11 and C12), this G12b vessel reinforces all our other lines of evidence that suggest an early Monte Albán II date for Structure 36.

We suspect that this bowl (most likely filled with some desirable food) was an additional offering left in the fill below

Structure 36. All that remained now was for the Monte Albán II architects to construct the temple.

Structure 36

Structure 36 was the first of a series of Monte Albán II temples built atop Structure 14. It resembled other temples of its period in having an inner (presumably more sacred) room and an outer (presumably less sacred) room. Its inner room was substantially larger than its outer room, giving it a T-shaped building plan.

We excavated Structure 36 using the grid of 2 × 2 m squares already established for the Mound 1/Area A step trench (Appendix A) and the Structure 14 overburden. Opening up 36 of these squares, from N2E4 in the northeast to S4W2 in the southwest, proved sufficient to uncover all of the temple's surviving floor (Fig. 13.9). Owing to postabandonment erosion, some of the edges of the floor had not been preserved. In most places, only the lowest course of adobe bricks in the temple's walls had remained in place, since the builders of a later temple (Structure 35) had dismantled the upper walls of Structure 36 and reused the adobes as fill. Our artist's reconstruction of Structure 36 can be seen in Figure 13.10.

The outer room of the temple measured roughly 10.9 m north-south and 4.1 m east-west, with its doorway on the west. This room turned out to have two superimposed stucco floors. Its original floor lay 2.69 m below the datum established for the step trench and Structure 14. When this early floor became worn, a second stucco floor was laid above it at a depth of 2.25–2.30 m below datum. This floor was no longer level, having been warped by the overburden of later buildings.

As was usual with Zapotec two-room temples, there was a step-up between the outer and inner room. At the time of the original floor of the outer room, this step-up would have been 44 cm; once the second floor had been laid, the step-up was reduced to 18–22 cm (Fig. 13.11).

The inner room of the temple measured roughly 9.85 m north-south and 7.30 m east-west, with its doorway on the west. A pair of north-south adobe walls served to narrow this doorway to 4.9 m (Fig. 13.12), and this space was further reduced to 2.6 m by a pair of columns. In other words, the architects communicated the more sacred character of the inner room by giving it a narrower doorway and raising its floor above that of the outer room. The inner room still retained its original floor, which (allowing for warping caused by the overburden) was discovered at depths varying from 2.07 m to 2.25 m below datum.

Unfortunately, the postabandonment razing of Structure 36 had left no interesting artifacts in situ on the floor of either room. The temple did, however, have a number of features worthy of note. One of its most unusual attributes was the fact that the columns flanking its doorways were made from the trunks of baldcypress trees (Figs. 13.13–13.15). This fact makes Structure 36 unique among the two-room temples we have excavated, virtually all of which had stone masonry columns of some kind.

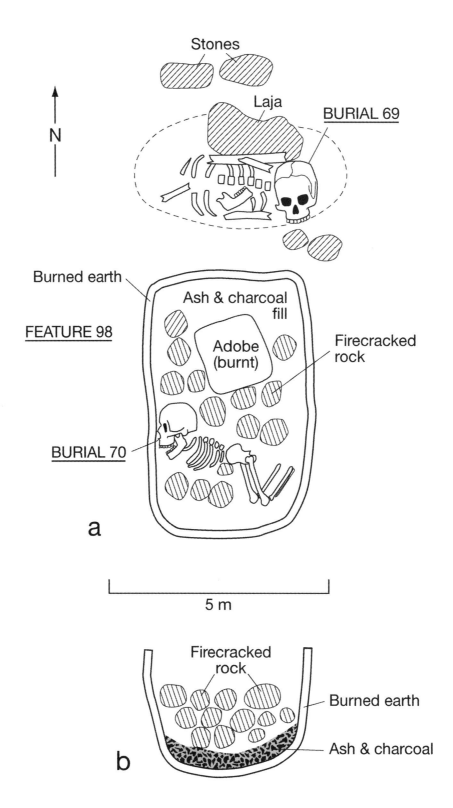

Figure 13.6. Feature 98 (an earth oven), Burial 69 (an adult), and Burial 70 (a child of 2–3 years), all found below the floor of the outer room, Structure 36. *a*, plan view. *b*, cross-section of Feature 98. All items resulted from an early Monte Albán II ritual that preceded the building of Structure 36.

Left: Figure 13.7. Feature 98 (an earth oven) and the partial remains of Burial 70 (a cooked child), seen from the south. The child may have been cooked over heated rocks and partially eaten during a ritual of sanctification that preceded the building of Structure 36 (early Monte Albán II).

Below: Figure 13.8. Grayware bowl with combed design on the interior, found in the fill below the floor of the outer room of Structure 36. The bowl belongs to the type Caso, Bernal, and Acosta called G12. A recent refinement of this type, based on careful stratigraphy by Spencer, Redmond, and Elson (2008), places this bowl in subtype G12b, whose temporal span runs from Monte Albán Ic through early Monte Albán II. Other sherds in the same fill include the Monte Albán II types C11 and C12.

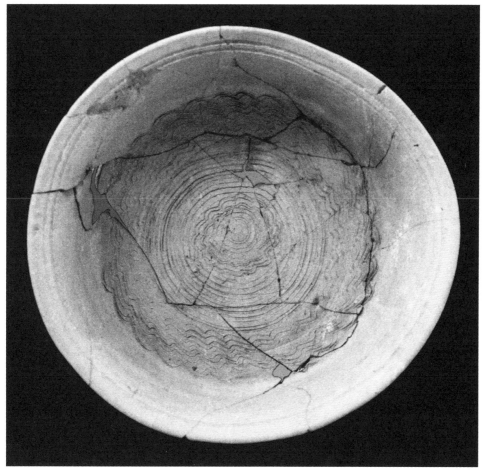

10 cm

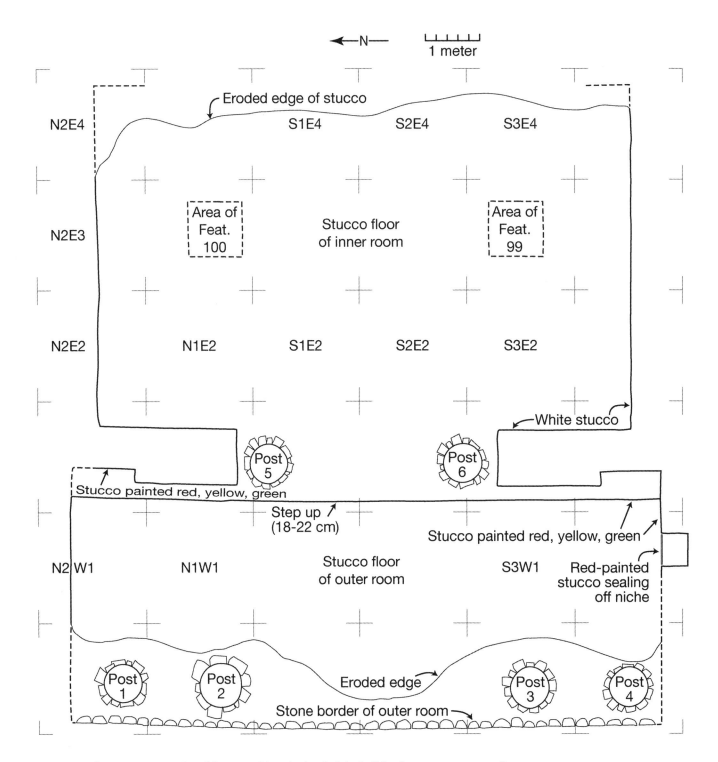

Figure 13.9. The surviving remains of Structure 36, at the level of the building's uppermost stucco floor.

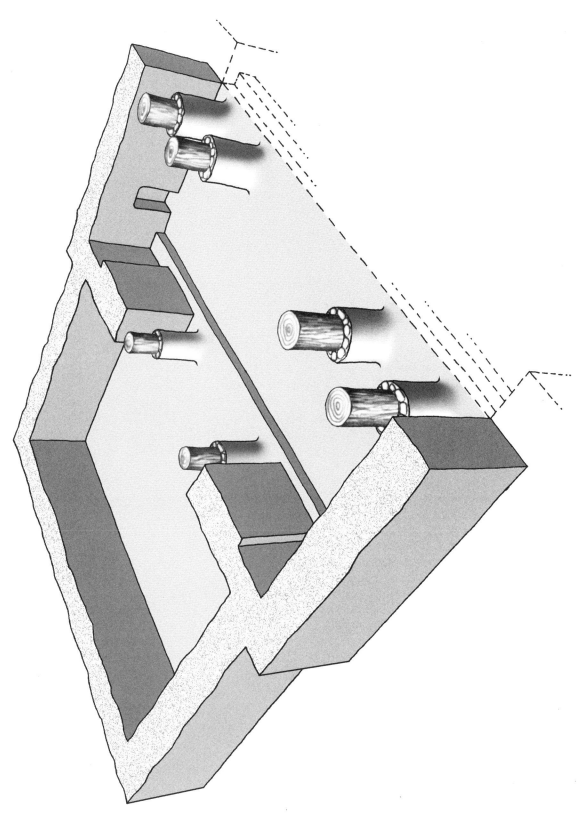

Figure 13.10. Artist's reconstruction of Structure 36. Original drawing by David West Reynolds, modified slightly by John Klausmeyer.

Figure 13.11. A view of Structure 36 from the south. The step-up from the outer room to the inner room, the subfloor cavities for Posts 5 and 6, and the stubs of the west wall of the inner room are all visible. In the lower left corner of the photo, one can see charcoal stains on the white stucco floor of the outer room. These dark areas seem to be made up of overlapping circular stains left by lit incense burners.

Figure 13.12. Two views of the adobe wall flanking the doorway to the inner room, Structure 36. *a*, a view down the length of the wall from south to north. *b*, the northern wall stub, seen from the northwest corner of the outer room. Traces of stucco can be seen on the face of the stub.

Figure 13.13. The stone masonry subfloor cavities for the baldcypress columns flanking the doorway to the inner room, Structure 36. *a,* the cavity for Post 5 (to N. of door). *b,* the cavity for Post 6 (to S. of door). The arrow points north and is marked in both inches and centimeters.

The baldcypress (*Taxodium mucrunatum*) was once a part of the mesophytic riverine forest of the ancient Valley of Oaxaca (Flannery and Marcus 2005: Figs. 2.4, 2.5). In 1970, octogenarians at San José Mogote recalled that in their youth, the Atoyac River that flows by the village had been lined with these trees, which they referred to as *ahuehuetes* or *tules*; most of those trees have long since succumbed to deforestation. The baldcypress is a tree that can live 1000 years or more and grow to be immense. Those used for the columns in Structure 36 were about 70–80 cm in diameter—mere youngsters when compared to the famous *Taxodium* at Santa María del Tule in the Tlacolula subvalley.

The broad doorway to the temple's outer room was flanked by four baldcypress trunks—Posts 1 and 2 on the north and 3 and 4 on the south (Fig. 13.9). The narrower door to the inner room was flanked only by two, Posts 5 and 6. Each tree trunk had been set 80 cm to a meter below floor level, in a cylindrical cavity lined with clay plaster (Fig. 13.15). Flat stone slabs supported the weight of the trunk, and stone masonry prevented the base of the post from moving.

Above the level of the floor, each trunk had been encased with small stones set in lime plaster and covered with a heavy layer of stucco, giving the outward appearance of a masonry column (Fig. 13.10). So resistant to decay is baldcypress that each subfloor post cavity contained up to 5 kg of wood, rotten

but still identifiable after 1800 years (Fig. 13.14*b*).

Structure 36 raised the immediate question of whether tree trunks had been forerunners of the rubble columns in Zapotec temples. When future excavators finally discover the oldest colonnaded temple below the North Platform at Monte Albán, what type of column will it have?

A second interesting feature of Structure 36 was the fact that the lime-plastered walls of its outer room had been extensively painted in red, black, yellow, and green. Sadly, the full decorative scheme of this room could not be reconstructed because of the razing mentioned above. Hundreds of adobe bricks from its walls, reused as fill to level the area before Structure 35 was built, bore traces of brightly painted stucco. Only in a few areas (indicated by arrows in Fig. 13.9) was the lower wall sufficiently undamaged to allow us to see that the designs had been geometric. Perhaps the best preserved area was a stretch of lower wall between the southeast corner of the outer room and a stucco-sealed niche in its south wall. Here we were able to record a green and vermilion "bulls-eye," bracketed by dark red and green panels (Fig. 13.16).

A third interesting feature of the outer room was the aforementioned niche, originally 51 cm north-south by 60 cm east-west, built into the south wall and stuccoed on its floor and sides (Figs. 13.9, 13.17). At some point, the niche was hidden from view as the result of having been plastered over and painted with

Figure 13.14. The doorway to the outer room of Structure 36 was flanked by four columns, made from the trunks of baldcypress trees. *a* shows the stone masonry subfloor cavities for Posts 1 (background) and 2 (foreground), seen from the south. *b* shows some of the baldcypress wood preserved in the subfloor cavity for Post 2.

the same colors as the rest of the south wall. We suspected that this niche might once have contained a sacred object of some kind, and we wondered if the north wall of the outer room had contained a similar niche. Unfortunately, the relevant part of the north wall had been destroyed just above the level of the floor.

A fourth feature of the outer room was the fact that its floor—although originally plastered white—revealed extensive areas of gray smudging when swept (see Fig. 13.11). Based on our previous experience with Monte Albán II temples, we knew that these gray smudges had resulted from the frequent use of incense burners. Such *incensarios* were typically placed on the temple floor and fueled with prepared pine charcoal. In the case of those incense burners with ring or pedestal bases, the charcoal was often placed directly on the floor beneath them. This left a dark, circular stain that smudged and spread around when swept.

In contrast to the brightly painted outer room, the more sacred inner room appears to have had only a white plaster surface. Its floor lacked the built-in basin seen in some Monte Albán II temples, but it did have two stone masonry offering boxes—Features 99 and 100—hidden beneath its floor (see Fig. 13.9 for their locations).

No offerings were found in either box, and both boxes appeared to have been damaged, perhaps because the offerings had been removed when the temple was abandoned. The stucco floor above the boxes showed signs of having been broken through and hastily replastered, which was our first clue that we might find something of interest below the floor (Figs. 13.18, 13.19).

As previously mentioned, the floor of the inner room ranged between 2.07 and 2.25 m below datum; the wall stones of Feature 100 began at 2.5 m below datum, and its floor of paving stones lay at 2.9–3.0 m below datum. Each offering box had been dug down into the layer of subfloor fill created to support the weight of Structure 36.

In addition to Features 99 and 100, three whole pottery vessels had been placed immediately below the floor of the inner room. One, a beaker, had been badly crushed by the overburden. A second beaker (Type G3) was found below the midpoint of the room (Fig. 13.20*a*). A Type G3 bowl with a recessed rim for a lid had been placed below the floor near Feature 100 (Fig. 13.20*b*). In each case we suspect that the vessel had once contained a ritual beverage, such as pulque or chocolate.

Dating Structure 36 with Ceramics

Archaeologists seek to place public buildings within a cultural sequence by studying the associated pottery. When several temples are built one above another, however, one cannot always be sure which sherds date the temple, which have been redeposited in the fill, and which entered the area when one temple was leveled to make way for another. Such was the case with Structure 36, which was razed to make way for Structure 35.

What we decided to do in the case of Structure 36 was to date only those sherds trapped between the upper and lower floors of the outer room. While this sherd sample could not be described

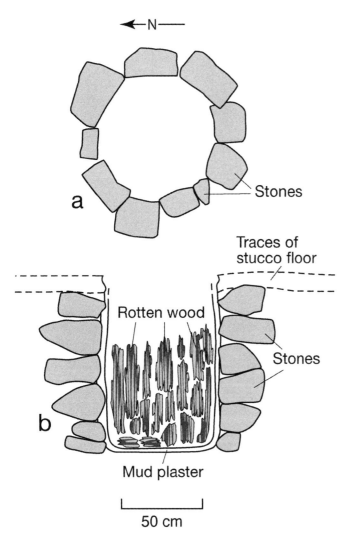

Figure 13.15. Plan and cross-section of the subfloor cavity for the base of Post 2, outer room, Structure 36. *a*, plan view. *b*, cross-section.

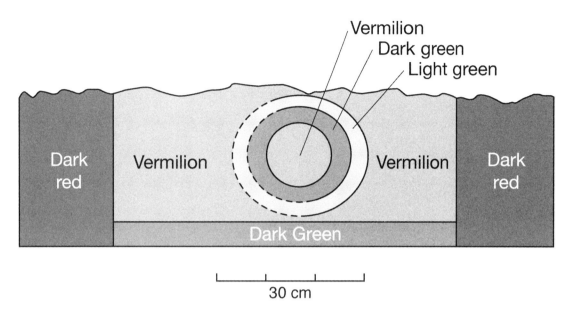

Figure 13.16. Artist's reconstruction of the polychrome design painted on the lowest part of the south wall of the outer room of Structure 36. This stretch of wall occurred between the southeast corner of the outer room and the stucco-sealed niche in the wall (see Fig. 13.9).

as a primary deposit, it could serve as a guide to the pottery types present during the lifetime of the temple—that is, those types that were in use between the laying of the first stucco floor and the laying of the second. While the sample was not large, it contained between 30 and 35 diagnostics of Monte Albán II and nothing from later periods. Those diagnostics were as follows:

CBA *GRIS* WARE DIAGNOSTICS
  rims of G21 bowls: 4
  cane-swirled base, G21 bowl: 1
  rims of likely G12 bowls: 6+
  sherds of G3 bowls: 4+
  rims with two broad, shallow grooves: 2

CBA *CREMA* WARE DIAGNOSTICS
  vertical wall of C20 bowl: 1
  C12 bowl with postfiring zigzags: 1 sherd
  C11 bowl with postfiring zigzags: 1 sherd
  vertical walls of C7 bowls: 2

CBA *CAFÉ* WARE DIAGNOSTICS
  rims of K3 bowls: 6+
  pichanchas (perforated, colander-like vessels): 2 sherds

CBA *AMARILLO* WARE DIAGNOSTICS
  effigy brazier fragment, showing collar or ruff with appliqué disk: 1

REDEPOSITED EARLIER CERAMICS
  sherds of the San José, Guadalupe, and Rosario phases: 20+

In sum, our small sample of ceramics from Structure 36—combined with the intact or restorable vessels left as offerings beneath it—indicated a date within Monte Albán II. To determine whether the building fell early or late within that period, however, we would need an actual radiocarbon date.

A Radiocarbon Date for Structure 36

Radiocarbon samples from temples that have been razed are problematic. One cannot assume that chunks of charcoal lying on the floor go with the building; they could have been introduced when it was leveled to make way for the next temple. Nor could we date the building by its baldcypress trunks, since the trees might have been 500 years old when cut down.

Fortunately, there was a solution. We had noted that the floor of the outer room was heavily smudged from the use of incense

Figure 13.17. Two views of the niche in the south wall of the outer room, Structure 36. *a*, Gil Matadamas sweeps the step-up to the inner room, near the southeast corner of the outer room. The letter "N" marks the patch of red-painted stucco sealing off the niche. *b*, the niche (marked "N") after its fill had been removed.

Figure 13.18. The remains of stone masonry offering boxes found below the inner room of Structure 36. *a*, Feature 99, seen from the west before excavation. *b*, Feature 100, seen from the west after excavation. Isaac Jiménez serves as scale.

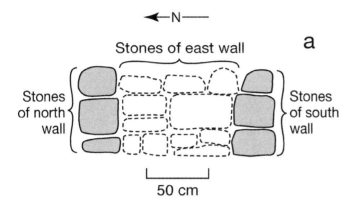

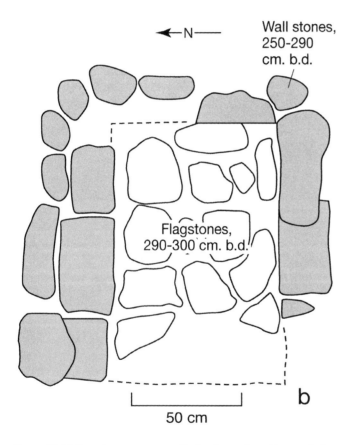

Figure 13.19. Two stone masonry offering boxes found beneath the floor of the inner room, Structure 36. *a*, cross-section of Feature 99. *b*, plan view of Feature 100.

burners, for which the typical fuel was pine charcoal. This was just as true of the earlier floor of the room as it was of the later floor above it, and any incense burner charcoal trapped between the earlier and later floors could be used to date the temple. We were fortunate enough to find a circular area of charcoal fragments left by an incense burner on the earlier floor, and this became sample Beta-190922. It produced a conventional date of 1990 ± 40 years before the present, or 40 b.c. When dendrocalibrated, this date has a two-sigma range between 60 BC and AD 90. Such a date seems reasonable for early Monte Albán II.

The Layer of Fill between Structures 36 and 35

To prepare for the building of Structure 35—the next temple in the sequence—the Monte Albán II architects removed all but the lowest row of adobes from most of the walls of Structure 36. These adobes were then combined with basketloads of earth to create a meter-thick layer of subfloor fill. Not only was this fill dense enough to support the weight of the new temple, it was also thick enough to accommodate a series of subfloor offering boxes. These stone masonry boxes had to be built and filled with dedicatory offerings before the floor of the new temple was laid.

While we were aware that this layer of fill did not constitute a primary deposit, we felt that its sherds could provide us with a look at the pottery types present when Structure 36 was razed and Structure 35 was built. We therefore decided to take a screened sample of sherds from the fill. We chose for this purpose an area of fill that was sealed beneath the stucco floor of Structure 35 and far removed from any offering box.

This screened sample of fill produced 620 diagnostic sherds of Monte Albán II pottery types, plus more than a thousand undiagnostic body sherds and redeposited Rosario, Guadalupe, and San José phase sherds. The Monte Albán II diagnostics were as follows:

CBA *GRIS* WARE DIAGNOSTICS
    Type G1 sherds: 37
    Type G3 cylinders with recessed rims for lids: 3 sherds
    Type G3 bridgespout sherds: 4
    Type G3, miscellaneous sherds: 126
    Type G11 vessel, stuccoed, painted green and white: 1 sherd
      (Fig. 13.21)
    Type G21 bowls: 65 rims, 33 bases (Fig. 13.22)
    Monte Albán II version of Type G35: 12 sherds

CBA *CREMA* WARE DIAGNOSTICS
    Type C1 sherds: 56
    Type C6 sherds: 21
    Type C7 bowl with basal flange: 1 sherd
    Type C7, miscellaneous sherds: 43
    Type C11 sherds with postfiring zigzags: 48 (Fig. 13.23)
    Type C12 sherds: 61 (Fig. 13.24)
    Type C20 sherds: 19

Figure 13.20. Offerings found below the floor of the inner room of Structure 36. *a*, G3 beaker found below the point estimated to be the center of the room. *b*, G3 bowl with recessed rim for lid, found below the floor near Feature 100.

CBA *CAFÉ* WARE DIAGNOSTICS
　Type K1 "frying pan" *incensario*: 1 sherd

CBA *AMARILLO* WARE DIAGNOSTICS
　Type A9 sherds: 13 (Fig. 13.25)

FRAGMENTS OF EFFIGY URNS AND INCENSE BURNERS (FIG. 13.26)
　petal from a flower headdress: 1
　sandaled foot: 1
　collar ruffs: 12 sherds
　miscellaneous fragments: 62

TOTAL DIAGNOSTIC SHERDS: 620

One feature of the Type G11 sherd shown in Figure 13.21 is worthy of mention. The vessel had been stuccoed on the exterior in typical G11 style, but on the interior it was unstuccoed and appears to have been fired white-rimmed black. The specimen resembles, in this regard, some of the Monte Albán II white-rimmed black vessels found by John Paddock (personal communication, 1980) in his excavations at Caballito Blanco, a Monte Albán II site in the Tlacolula subvalley.

Despite the inherent problems of a sample taken from subfloor fill, this collection of 620 diagnostic sherds tells us a number of things about the relatively brief period between the razing of Structure 36 and the building of Structure 35. For one thing, 249 of the 620 diagnostics—roughly 40 percent—are *crema* types. This high percentage of cream wares compares favorably with Monte Albán itself, reinforcing the close relationship between the Zapotec capital city and its second-tier administrative center at San José Mogote. In contrast, *crema* types such as C6, C7, and C20 were among the luxury pottery to which Tilcajete was denied access when it was at war with Monte Albán (Spencer and Redmond 2003:38–39).

Significantly, not one of the 620 sherds in our screened sample came from grayware bowls of subtype G12b or G12c. That means that Type G12 had now been largely replaced by Type G21 bowls with cane-swirled interior bases, suggesting that Structure 35 was more likely built in middle Monte Albán II than in early Monte Albán II.

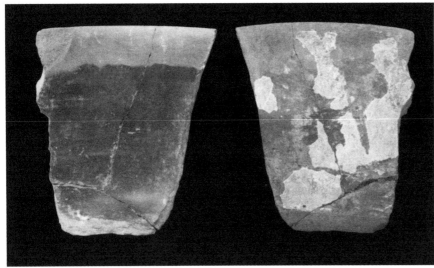

Left: Figure 13.21. Rim-to-base sherd from a bowl that was white-rimmed black on the interior (*left*) and covered with green-and-white painted stucco on the exterior, in the manner typical of Type G11 (*right*). Found in the fill between Structures 36 and 35.

Below: Figure 13.22. Sherds of Type G21 bowls from the fill between Structures 36 and 35.

Opposite top: Figure 13.23. Sherds from Type C11 bowls with zigzag postfiring incisions/excisions, found in the fill between Structures 36 and 35.

Opposite below: Figure 13.24. Sherds from Type C12 bowls with zigzag postfiring incisions/excisions, found in the fill between Structures 36 and 35.

5 cm

10 cm

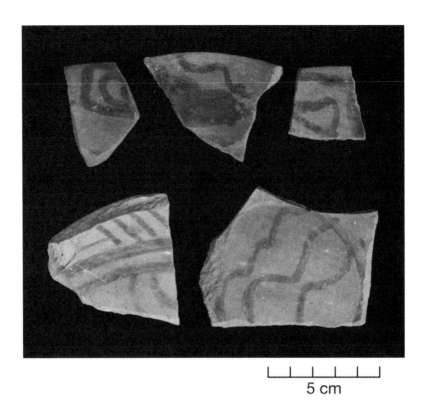

5 cm

Above: Figure 13.25. Sherds from A9 bowls found in the fill between Structures 36 and 35.

Opposite: Figure 13.26. Fragments of urns and incense burners found in the fill between Structures 36 and 35. These fragments are similar to those found in Feature 20 (see Figs. 13.66–13.91).

Structure 35

Structure 35 was the second in a sequence of Monte Albán II temples built atop the Structure 14 platform. It consisted of two rooms, with its doorway on the west. Its walls were composed of uniform adobe bricks (40 × 25 × 10 cm) over a foundation of roughly trimmed stones. In places (especially on the south side) we could see that the building had been flanked by a walkway more than a meter wide, composed of *lajas* or flagstones (Figs. 13.27, 13.28).

Structure 35 was somewhat T-shaped, with its inner room 3 m narrower than its outer room. By opening up some 48 2 × 2 m squares (from N2E3 in the northeast to S6W3 in the southwest), we were able to recover virtually all that remained of the building. Although its stucco floor was almost 20 cm thick in places, substantial areas had been lost to erosion. We found no evidence that the white stucco of Structure 35 had been painted in the manner of Structure 36.

The outer room of the temple measured 11.4 m north-south and 4.4 m east-west (Fig. 13.29). On its west side it had a doorway 10.4 m wide, but entry to the room was reduced to less than 6 m by a pair of columns. The actual diameter of these columns could not be determined with accuracy, owing to postabandonment destruction; we estimate their diameters at roughly 1 m. Traces of the exterior walls indicated that they had been 80–90 cm thick. The stucco floor of the outer room lay roughly 62 cm below our arbitrary datum point for the Structure 14 overburden.

On the west, the floor of the outer room ended in a series of flagstones that seemed to be all that remained of the top step of the temple's staircase. This was the last use of stone, since, as already explained, the staircase added to Structure 14 in Monte Albán II was of adobe (Fig. 13.30).

The step-up from the outer room to the inner room of the temple was roughly 24 cm. We reconstruct the inner room as measuring 8.8 m north-south and roughly 6 m east-west, based on surviving stones from the foundations of its rear wall (Fig. 13.31). A pair of

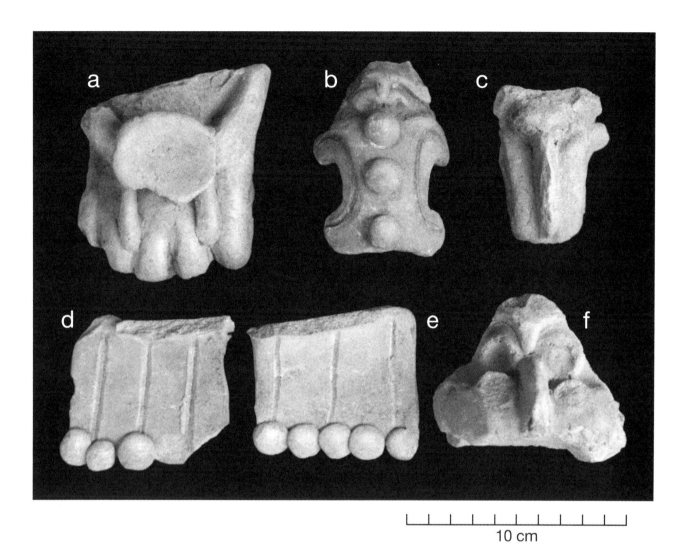

north-south adobe walls reduced the inner room's doorway to 5.6 m, and entry was further reduced to 3.5 m by a pair of columns 60 cm in diameter. These columns, now badly destroyed, were of stone masonry rather than tree trunks. The floor of the inner room varied from 38 to 57 cm below datum, having warped and buckled under the weight of the overburden.

How Structure 35 Was Built

Although the floor of Structure 35 had been considerably reduced in size by downslope erosion, enough of its substructure remained so that we could reconstruct the way it was built. The first step, of course, was to raze Structure 36 and use its adobes to create a meter-thick layer of fill. This dense layer of fill extended 1 to 2 m beyond the future limits of Structure 35 and was shored up on all four sides by boulder rubble. This rubble, in turn, was held in place by the upper walls of Structure 14, which had been deliberately raised for that purpose by the Monte Albán II architects.

The next move by the builders of Structure 35 was to lay out the exterior frame of the building, using flagstones two courses high. These flagstones were used not only as support for the stone masonry walls but also for the step-up to the inner room. The next move was to construct the five offering boxes that would be hidden below the temple floor. These boxes would be sunk roughly 60 cm into the layer of subfloor fill. In most cases, the architects laid down small areas of flagstones to support the masonry walls of the offering boxes; in the case of Feature 95, however, they simply used the old stucco floor of Structure 36 as the bottom of the box.

The builders next divided the future outer room of the temple into three sections, separated by adobe retaining walls. They then filled the areas between these retaining walls with a dense mixture of reused adobes, stony rubble, and hard-packed earthen fill. Over this fill went a stucco floor 15–20 cm thick. The substructure of the inner room was prepared in a similar way—dense fill between retaining walls—but less of this room had survived to be studied.

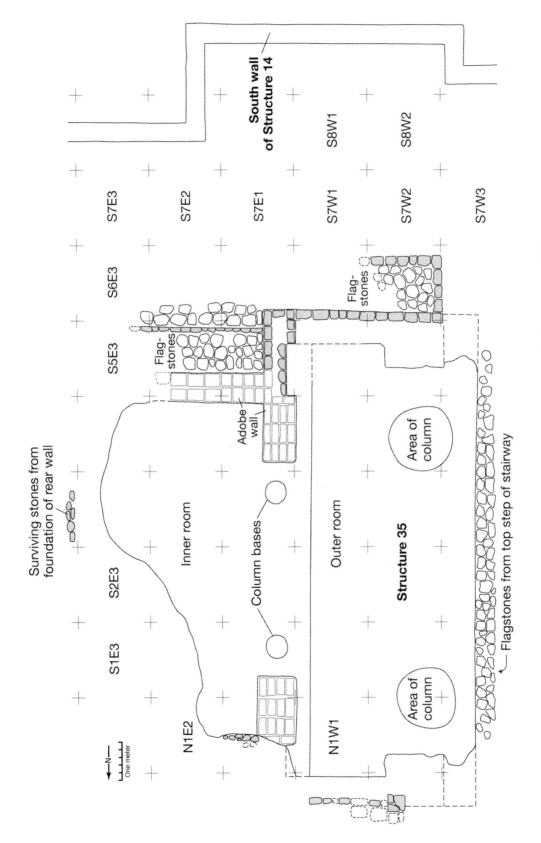

Figure 13.27. The surviving remains of Structure 35, showing that building's placement on the remodeled Structure 14 platform.

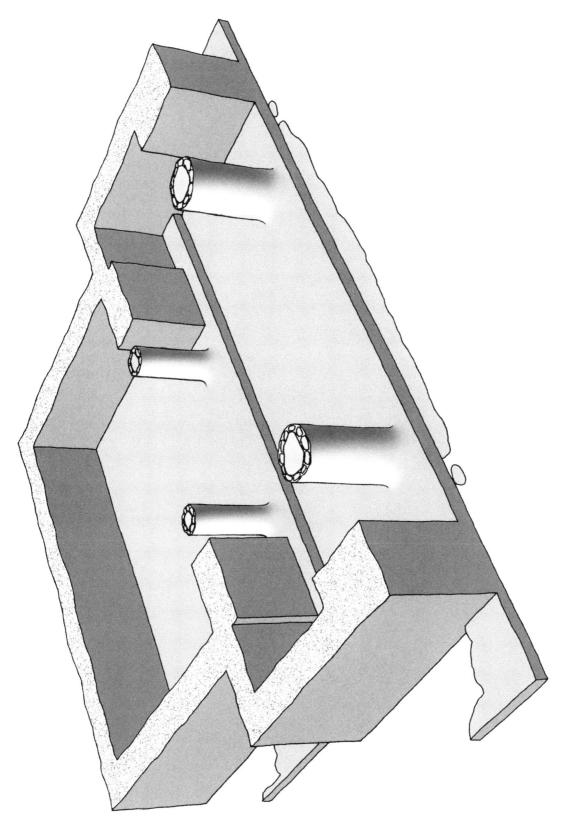

Figure 13.28. Artist's reconstruction of Structure 35. (Based on a drawing by David West Reynolds)

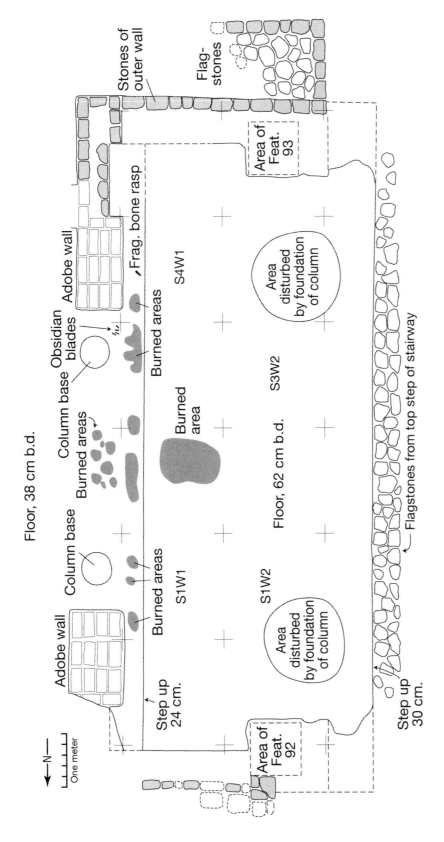

Figure 13.29. Plan of the outer room of Structure 35 and the step-up to the inner room, at the level of the stucco floor.

Figure 13.30. Two views of the stairway provided for Structure 35. *a*, view from the southwest, showing how the western stone wall of the earlier Rosario platform (Structure 14) had been removed so that Monte Albán II stairways could be built on that side. The three surviving steps of Structure 35 are visible. *b*, closeup of the three surviving steps (made of adobes covered with stucco) as seen from the south.

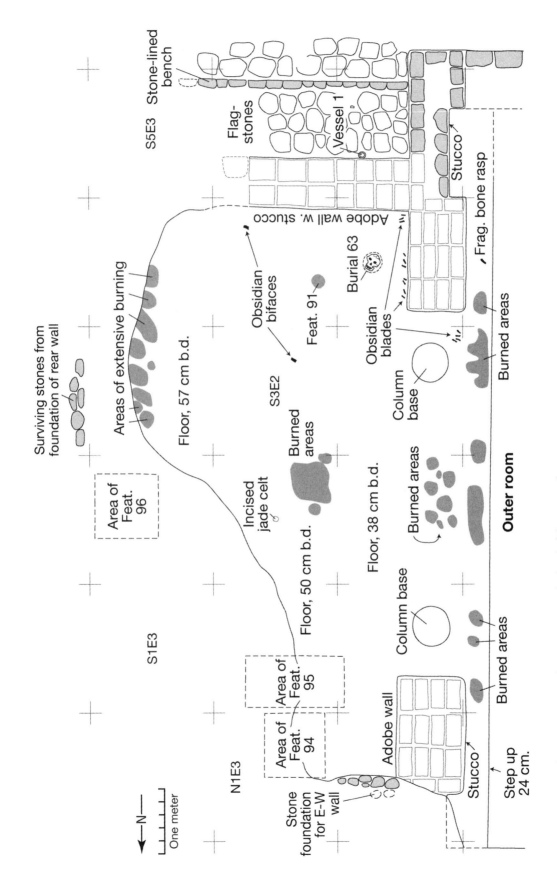

Figure 13.31. Plan of the inner room of Structure 35 at the level of the stucco floor.

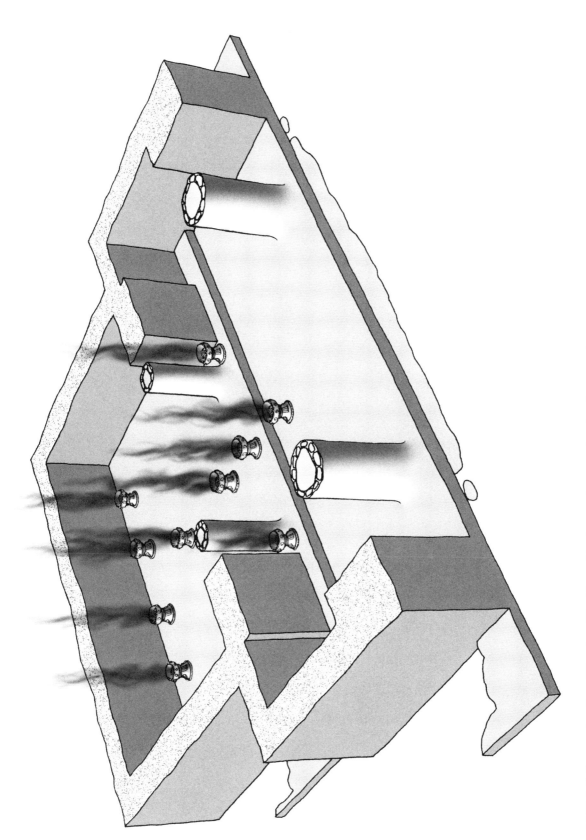

Figure 13.32. Artist's reconstruction of Structure 35, with smoking incense burners placed in the areas where they were most frequently used, based on burnt areas of stucco floor. (It is not assumed that this many *incensarios* would have been in simultaneous use.)

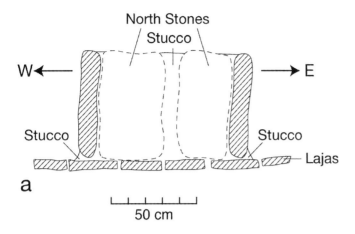

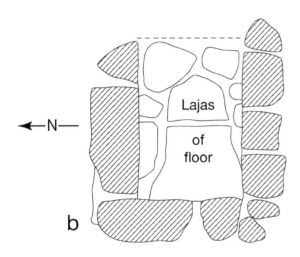

Figure 13.33. Features 92 and 93, two offering boxes found below the floor of the outer room, Structure 35. *a*, cross-section of Feature 92. *b*, plan view of Feature 93.

The Details of the Outer Room

The outer room of the temple had been swept frequently enough so that we found no significant artifacts in situ. We did, however, find a major area of burned floor in Square S2W2 (Fig. 13.29). This was one of four areas where repeated use of incense burners had created so many overlapping charcoal circles that a permanent dark stain existed. These stains let us determine the four places where incense burners were most often placed: (1) in the center of the outer room, just in front of the step-up to the inner room; (2) all along the top of the step-up; (3) in the center of the inner room; and (4) along the back wall of the inner room (see Fig. 13.32).

Significant discoveries made below the floor of the outer room were Features 92 and 93, a pair of offering boxes (Figs. 13.33–13.35). Both boxes extended to a depth of 60 cm below the floor, at which point we came upon a floor of flat paving stones. The interior space of each box measured roughly a meter on a side. Neither box contained any offerings, although Feature 93 produced two bones of the Montezuma quail (*Cyrtonyx montezumae*), a bird favored for sacrifice by the Zapotec. Given that the floor above both boxes had been damaged and repaired, we suspect that any imperishable offerings had been deliberately removed.

Details of the Inner Room

The inner room of the temple had not been swept as completely as the outer room, perhaps because it was less well lit than the latter; indeed, it may have been dark and smoky because it was left windowless to ensure privacy for the priests. The darkest part of the inner room would have been the southwest quadrant, especially the corner made by the western and southern walls (Fig. 13.31). In this area, where the shadows were deepest and the sweeping less thorough, we recovered the tip of a bifacial obsidian lancet, 5 obsidian flakes, and 42 prismatic obsidian blades of the type associated with ritual bloodletting (Fig. 13.36; see also Parry 1987: Chapter 8). Not far away, in Squares S3E2 and S4E2, we found 2 broken bifacial obsidian daggers of the type used for heart sacrifice (Figs. 13.37, 13.38). This scatter of discarded ritual artifacts, evidently overlooked when the temple was swept for the last time, probably represents only a fraction of those used during the lifetime of the temple.

Another possible ritual artifact overlooked during the final

Figure 13.34. Two views of Feature 92, a stone masonry offering box found below the floor of the outer room, Structure 35. *Left*, view from the south before the interior was excavated. Irán ("El Chato") Matadamas and Francisco ("El Toro") Gómez serve as scale. *Right*, view from the east after excavation (east wall removed to show the paved floor). Armando Jiménez serves as scale.

sweeping of the temple was the broken bone rasp shown in Figure 13.39. This fragment of a musical instrument was found on the step-up to the inner room, not far from its southern limit.

An unexpected find in Structure 35 was the incised celt of jadeite or serpentinite found on the floor of the inner room in Square S2E2 (Fig. 13.40). This apple green celt was biconically drilled for suspension and has a human face incised on its obverse side. Vermilion powder had been rubbed into the incisions to highlight the features.

A similarly incised apple green celt had been found by Caso (1938:Fig. 84c) in Mound M at Monte Albán. Caso described the incising of the human face as "geometric" in character, with the eyes and mouth formed by circles and the nose formed by parallel lines "as in certain representations of the Maya day sign *ahau*." Both Caso's Mound M celt and our Structure 35 celt may depict trophy heads, like the human head pendants suspended from the necks of some figures on Zapotec urns and incense burners.

Further evidence that the final sweeping of the inner room may have been only perfunctory came to light in Square S4E2. Here we discovered Feature 91, the broken-off pedestal base of an incense burner, still sitting on the floor in a circular deposit of pine charcoal. The floor below the charcoal fragments had been

burned, and no one had removed the last pieces of the *incensario*. The charcoal from this feature became radiocarbon sample Beta-189254 (see below).

Finally, our plan of the inner room and its adjacent flagstone walkway (Fig. 13.31) shows a human skull (Burial 63) and a grayware beaker (Vessel 1). Since these items appeared to postdate the temple's use, they are discussed in a later section.

Features 94 and 95

Beneath the floor of the inner room we found 3 offering boxes: 2 made of stone masonry and 1 of adobe brick. Features 94 and 95 had been placed under the northwest corner of the room; Structure 96 had been placed below the midline of the room, near the back wall (Fig. 13.31). The most remarkable objects found in Structure 35 came from these offering boxes.

Features 94 and 95 were of stone masonry and lay side by side, sharing a wall and displaying the plan of a capital T (Figs. 13.41, 13.42). The builders of Feature 95 had taken advantage of the stucco floor of Structure 36—the previous temple—by using it as the floor of the offering box. Feature 94 was not as deep; its floor was a layer of clay above the old Structure 36 floor.

Above: Figure 13.35. View (from the east) of Feature 93, a stone masonry offering box found below the floor of the outer room, Structure 35. Miguel ("El Siete Perros") Gómez serves as scale.

Below left: Figure 13.36. Broken obsidian blades found on the floor of the inner room, Structure 35 (Square S4E1).

Below right: Figure 13.37. Obsidian tools for sacrificial rites, found on the floor of the inner room, Structure 35. *Left*, broken dagger for heart sacrifice, Square S4E2. *Center*, broken dagger for heart sacrifice, Square S3E2. *Right*, broken tip of lancet for bloodletting, Square S4E1.

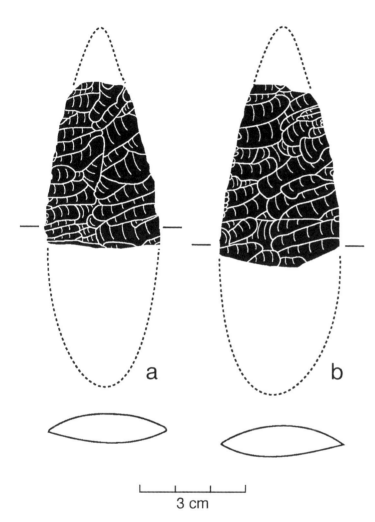

Left: Figure 13.38. Artist's reconstruction of two broken obsidian daggers, found on the floor of the inner room, Structure 35. *a* is from Square S3E2; *b* is from Square S4E2.

Above: Figure 13.39. Fragment of bone rasp, found on the step-up from the outer room to the inner room, Structure 35 (Square S4W1).

Below: Figure 13.40. Highly polished apple green celt, drilled for suspension. A face has been incised on the obverse side, with vermilion powder rubbed into the incisions. This celt, which appears to be jadeite or serpentinite, was found in the fill above the final floor of Structure 35 (Square S2E2). A similarly incised apple green celt was found by Caso (1938: Figure 84c) in Mound M at Monte Albán. Both celts may represent trophy heads, like those shown suspended from the necks of some personages depicted on urns and incense burners.

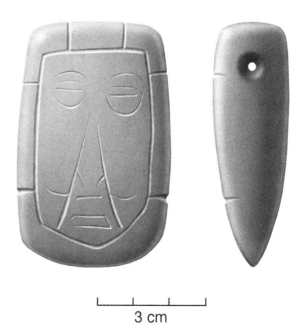

Figure 13.41. Two views of Features 94 and 95, offering boxes found side by side below the floor of the inner room, Structure 35. *a*, a view of both offering boxes (from the west) after they had been emptied. *b*, a closeup of Feature 95, showing how the stucco floor of Structure 36, an earlier temple, was used as the floor of the offering box. The black arrow points north.

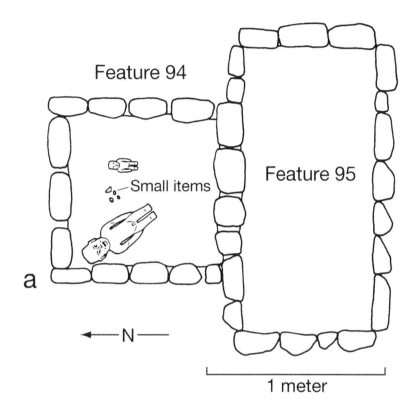

Feature 94

Small items

Feature 95

a

←—N—→

1 meter

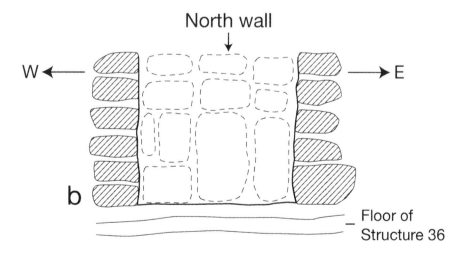

North wall

W ←   → E

b

Floor of
Structure 36

Figure 13.42. Features 94 and 95, two offering boxes found below the floor of the inner room, Structure 35. *a*, plan view of both features. *b*, cross-section of Feature 94, showing how close it came to the floor of the previous temple, Structure 36.

Figure 13.43. Two views of the jadeite figures from Feature 94, Structure 35. *Left*, the two figures lying in situ on the floor of the offering box. *Right*, a very pleased Francisco Gómez cradles the large jadeite statue.

We found Feature 95 empty. Feature 94, however, contained a jadeite statue, a jadeite figurine, and several small pieces of jadeite that looked like material left over from the making of the statue (Figs. 13.42*a*, 13.43).

The jadeite statue from Feature 94 is shown in Figure 13.44. It is 49 cm tall and 19 cm wide at the shoulders; its thickness is 10 cm at the nose and 6.5 cm at the feet. The figure is that of a nude man, standing stiffly erect with his hands touching his hips. His almond-shaped eyes are indicated by incisions, while his nose is well developed in high relief. His mouth is open and his upper lip curled up at the sides, while the middle part of the lip meets his upper teeth. His slab-shaped ears are typical of Monte Albán II, and the lobes have been pierced to receive ornaments. His fingers are indicated by incisions, as are his nails, and the thumbnails can be seen clearly in frontal view. His ankle bones are shown as small bumps, and his feet have flat soles with no delineation of the toes.

Viewed from the side, the statue's skull appears to have been artificially deformed. On the crown of his head he has a cavity 3.2 cm in diameter and 2 cm deep, possibly created to receive the base of a headdress. When the figure was discovered, however, this cavity was filled only with vermilion pigment; indeed, traces of this pigment were found on various parts of the statue.

While we cannot rule out the possibility that this statue was once dressed in perishable clothing, the fact that his male organs

are clearly delineated suggests that he was meant to be seen as naked—perhaps, in fact, as a victim of sacrifice, stripped of his clothing and ear ornaments, but with his deformed skull and perforated ear lobes indicating his high rank. The statue appears to have been carved from a type of mottled jadeite native to Guatemala's Motagua Valley. Such use of semiprecious stone would make the figure into a sacrificial victim whose corpse would never decay.

The smaller jadeite figurine is shown in Figure 13.45. He, too, stands stiffly erect with his hands at his sides. His height is 15 cm, his width 6 cm at the shoulders, and his thickness 4.5 cm at the nose. His eyes are simple horizontal slots, while his mouth is delimited by drill holes at both corners. Two circular holes indicate his nostrils, and two more small holes have been made in his earlobes. Incisions have been used to indicate a long lock of hair on the right side of his head and a short bun on the left side. There is a bump (possibly representing a forelock) on his forehead, below which a vertical incision descends to a point between his eyebrows. Other incisions, possibly representing age lines, run from the inner corner of each eye to near the corner of his mouth. His hands have only their fingers delineated, not the thumb, and he is without sex organs of any kind.

An impressive hole has been drilled for suspension from one side of the figure's neck to the other. This suspension hole, coupled with the fact that virtually no anatomical details are

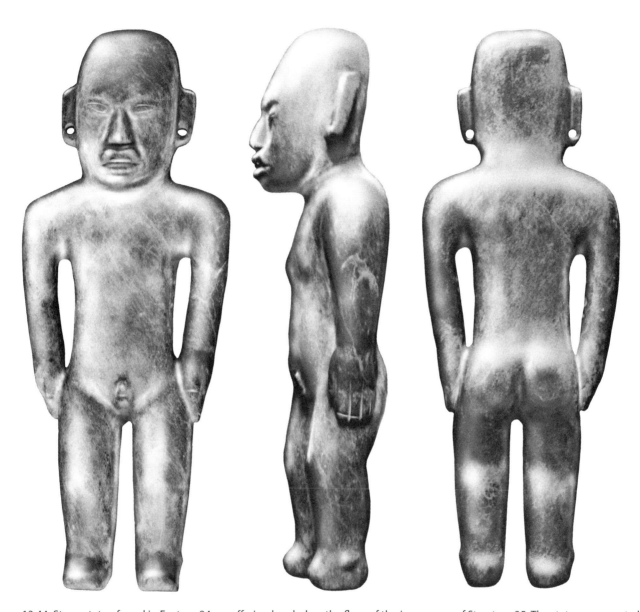

Figure 13.44. Stone statue found in Feature 94, an offering box below the floor of the inner room of Structure 35. The statue appears to be made of jadeite from the Motagua Valley source in Guatemala. (Height, 49 cm)

Left: Figure 13.45. Stone figurine from Feature 94, an offering box below the floor of the inner room of Structure 35. The figure appears to be of jadeite or serpentinite. (Height, 15 cm)

Opposite, above: Figure 13.46. Overhead view of Feature 96, an adobe offering box found below the floor of the inner room, Structure 35 (Square S2E3). Vessels 6 and 7 were below the large white *laja* and therefore not visible in this view.

Opposite, below: Figure 13.47. Excavating Feature 96. *a*, workmen gently brush Vessel 5, the "flying figure," as it lies atop the large white *laja* (flat stone slab), which served as the roof for a miniature tomb. To the left of the paint brushes, one can see one of the adobes in the north wall of the offering box. *b*, the *laja* has been lifted, exposing the miniature tomb. Vessel 6, an *acompañante* urn, has toppled over inside Vessel 7, an open bowl that broke under the weight of the overburden.

shown on the reverse side of the figurine, suggests that it was designed to be worn on someone's chest. When found, the figure was covered with red pigment.

This jadeite figurine can be compared and contrasted with Offering 1, number 1, discovered by Caso (1965a:900, Fig. 5) in Mound X at Monte Albán. While there are similarities, the Mound X figurine has its arms crossed on its chest, seems to have clothing indicated, and was less skillfully executed than the one from our Feature 94.

The "small items" shown in Figure 13.42*a* include 2 circular jadeite beads and 3 irregularly shaped pieces that (as already mentioned) might be manufacturing waste. One bead was 1.5 cm in diameter, the other 9 mm. The possible pieces of jadeite manufacturing waste were all in the 2.2–3.2 cm size range and had been polished into roughly geometric shapes.

Features 94 and 95 left us with a number of questions. Why—when so many offering boxes appear to have been opened and their offerings removed—would anyone leave such a spectacular jadeite statue beneath the floor of an abandoned temple? And what other offerings might once have been in Features 94 and 95? We note that Feature 95, which measured 1.6 m by 72 cm, was large enough to have once contained actual human sacrificial victims, yet it was empty when we found it. Were all its contents perishable, or had they simply been removed?

Feature 96

Nothing we had found so far prepared us for Feature 96, an adobe brick offering box hidden beneath an area of the inner room where the floor was almost black from incense burning. This box

filled virtually all of Square S2E3 (Fig. 13.46).

As we began to remove the fill, the first object that came to light was Vessel 5, the pottery sculpture of a "flying figure" wearing a cape. Our workmen immediately christened this figure "El Kalimán," after a caped comic book superhero of that era. As can be seen in Figure 13.47, the flying figure was recumbent upon a large, flat limestone slab; when lifted, this slab turned out to be the roof of a miniature tomb. Inside this tomb, whose walls were made from adobes set on edge, we found Vessels 6 and 7. Vessel 6 was a ceramic effigy of the type Caso and Bernal (1952) refer to as an *acompañante* or "companion figure": an item often found in Zapotec royal tombs. This *acompañante* sat inside Vessel 7, a grayware Monte Albán II *cajete* (flat-based, outleaned-wall bowl). Beside the *cajete* lay the complete skeleton of a bobwhite quail (*Colinus virginianus*), one of the Zapotecs' most popular birds for sacrifice. Just outside the miniature tomb lay a pair of white-tailed deer antlers and a broken flute made from the limb bone of an unidentified large bird. Since antlers were used by the Zapotec as drumsticks for turtleshell drums, we consider both the flute and antlers to be musical instruments left as offerings.

Finally, as we moved east from the flying figure and the miniature tomb, we came upon Vessels 1–4, a set of effigy urns depicting women in grotesque masks. These four women appeared to have been arranged as spectators to the scene created by Vessels 5–7. Our artist's reconstruction of the contents of Feature 96 can be seen in Figure 13.48.

Vessel 5, the flying figure, measures 33 cm in length. The sculpture depicts a male individual lying on his stomach, with his elbows bent and his head erect, making his height 22 cm (Fig. 13.49). A full-length cape covers the figure from his headdress to

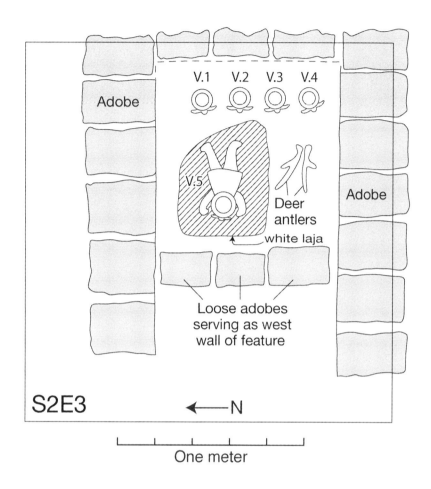

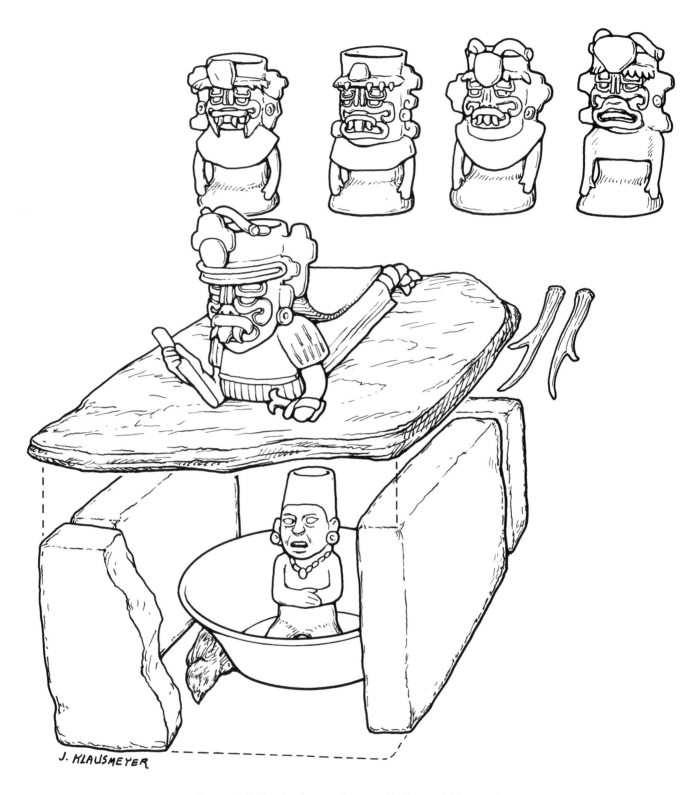

Figure 13.48. The ritual scene discovered in Feature 96 (see text).

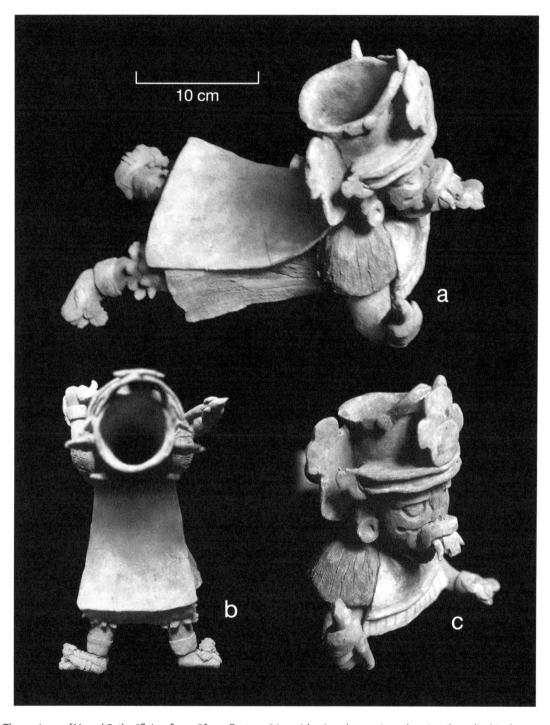

Figure 13.49. Three views of Vessel 5, the "flying figure" from Feature 96. *a*, side view. *b*, top view, showing the cylindrical receptacle on the figure's head. *c*, three-quarter frontal view, showing the items carried in the hands.

Above: Figure 13.50. Zapotec nobles often pictured their "cloud ancestors" as flying figures, or even flying turtles, perhaps because cumulonimbus clouds reminded them of turtle carapaces. This flying figure was modeled in stucco on a tomb at Zaachila (Caso 1966: Fig. 20).

Below: Figure 13.51. Vessels 6 and 7 from Feature 96. *a, b*, front and side views of Vessel 6, an *acompañante. c*, Vessel 7, a grayware bowl with streaky, quartz pebble burnishing.

his lower legs. The sculpture is executed in grayware, but orange paint was used to highlight certain areas.

The figure wears a grotesque *Cociyo* (Lightning) mask with protruding fangs and has eyes with U-shaped elements for eyebrows. The centerpiece of his headdress is a cylindrical receptacle 9 cm deep, possibly for incense. He wears a disk and a cloverleaf-shaped element on his forehead and a bib around his neck. Under his cape he wears what looks like a feather robe. There is orange paint on the tips of his slab ears, on his disk and cloverleaf element, on his arms, and on his spiked leggings. His feet have sandals.

In his left hand, Vessel 5 carries the bifid tongue of a serpent; in his right, he holds a stick of some kind. Since the Zapotec words for "serpent" and "young maize" are homonyms (*zee* or *ziy*), we suspect that what we see in the figure's hands are an agricultural dibble stick and a metaphor for newly sprouted maize.

What might this flying figure represent? We know that Zapotec nobles often pictured their "cloud ancestors" as flying figures, or even as flying turtles, perhaps because cumulonimbus clouds reminded them of turtle carapaces (see Fig. 13.50). The flying figure in Feature 96, therefore, might represent a deceased noble who is undergoing the metamorphosis necessary to become a cloud ancestor—a semidivine being with the power to make maize sprout.

Let us turn now to Vessel 6, the "companion figure" from the miniature tomb (Fig. 13.51). This ceramic sculpture is 20 cm high and a maximum of 9 cm in width; some 18 cm of its height is made up by the hollow cylindrical receptacle that forms its back. Whether this receptacle was for incense, or for a ritual beverage, is unclear.

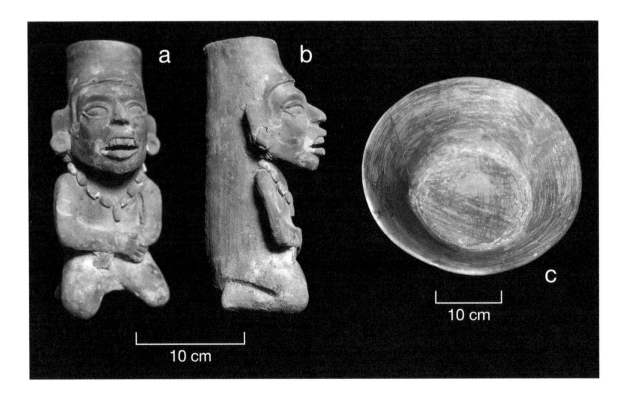

The figure on the front of the sculpture depicts an individual, presumably male, kneeling in a position of obeisance with his arms folded across his chest. He wears a necklace consisting of eight spherical beads, four to either side of an elongated central pendant; there are earspools in the lobes of his slab ears. Assuming that jadeite ornaments are what was being depicted, he probably represents a member of the lesser nobility whose role was to attend someone of even higher status.

The figure's eyes and mouth are open, exposing his maxillary teeth. His face, ears, teeth, neck, and arms are covered not with orange paint but with the type of red ocher usually applied to burials. This ocher—combined with the fact that the figure was found in a miniature tomb—makes it likely that he was considered part of a burial. The vessel in which he was placed is a grayware bowl with streaky, quartz pebble burnishing. It appears that Vessel 6 was originally set upright, but slumped under the weight of the earthen fill above it.

Now let us turn to the four effigy urns of female spectators. Vessels 1–4 all depict women wearing a *huipil* (or overblouse) and a skirt; all are seated crosslegged with their hands on their knees. They wear grotesque Lightning masks with protruding teeth and U-shaped elements for eyebrows. Each also has a cylindrical receptacle behind her head, like the one seen on the flying figure (Fig. 13.52).

Vessel 1 is a grayware urn 21 cm high and 13 cm wide. She has slab ears shaped like parentheses, and orange paint has been applied to the elements at the top of each ear. Her headdress bears an ovoid plaque and a line of fringe.

Vessel 2 is a grayware urn 20 cm high and generally similar to Vessel 1; however, it has no orange paint. Her masked face appears to have been mold-made, with some elements of the mouth added later. Her ear slabs, although parenthesis-shaped, are different from those of Vessel 1.

Vessel 3 resembles Vessels 1 and 2, with a mold-made masked face to which additional elements have been added; however, her headdress bears a square plaque and two filaments resembling antennae. At 19 cm she is the shortest of the four female urns, and she bears no orange paint. Her slab ears appear unfinished.

Vessel 4 stands 21 cm high and has orange paint applied to her nose, her neck, the sides of her head, her torso below the *huipil*, her arms, and her back (extending to the cylindrical receptacle). Her slab ears are less ornate than those of Vessels 2 and 3, and her three protruding teeth seem to have been broken off. The plaque on her headdress is triangular, and she has antennae-like filaments similar to those of Vessel 3. Parts of her *huipil* are missing, possibly broken.

Our overall impression is that Vessels 1–4 were made by different craftsmen, but according to one general plan, and using identical molds for the grotesque Lightning mask. The damage suffered by some of these vessels suggests that they may have been in use for a time before being placed in Feature 96.

We cannot read the minds of the ritual specialists who arranged Vessels 1–7 in the offering box. Let us attempt, however, to interpret the scene, based on what we know of later Zapotec ethnohistory (Córdova 1886[1578], 1942[1578]; del Paso y Troncoso 1905). The sixteenth-century Zapotec believed that after death, their rulers would metamorphose into "cloud people" and ascend to the heavens. There they would live close to *Cociyo*, or Lightning, and his four companions—Clouds, Rain, Wind, and Hail. Indeed, some prehispanic sculptures of *Cociyo* show him carrying four receptacles on his back for his aforementioned companions (Marcus and Flannery 1996: Fig. 10).

We suspect that the scene in Feature 96 represents the metamorphosis of a deceased Zapotec lord into a cloud person. Below the limestone slab lies the tomb in which he had been buried, still furnished with a ceramic vessel, a sacrificed quail, and an ocher-covered *acompañante*. Beside the tomb were musical instruments left as offerings after the funerary ceremony. Atop the limestone slab lies the tomb's former occupant, caught in the process of metamorphosis into a semidivine cloud ancestor. Observing his metamorphosis are Clouds, Rain, Wind, and Hail, portrayed as female consorts of *Cociyo*.

The remarkable scene in Feature 96—like the jadeite statue from Feature 94—raises the question of why certain offerings were left below the floor of Structure 35 while others were evidently removed. It is a question we may never be able to answer.

Diagnostic Sherds from the Floor of Structure 35

We found hundreds of sherds while excavating Structure 35, but none came from contexts that we considered primary. Nor did we come upon a substantial collection sealed below an intact floor, like our screened sample from Structure 36. About 60–70 sherds were lying in direct contact with the floor in poorly swept areas, and we list them below for what they are worth.

CBA *GRIS* WARE DIAGNOSTICS
   Type G3 globular jar sherds: 3
   Type G3 bridgespout sherd: 1
   Type G3 incense burner sherds: 5
   Type G12 rim sherds: 3
   Type G21 sherds: 7
   Monte Albán II version of Type G35: 4 sherds

CBA *CREMA* WARE DIAGNOSTICS
   Type C2 jar rims: 5
   Type C4 bottle rims: 2
   Type C6 bowl rims: 2
   Type C6, miscellaneous fragment: 1
   Type C7 jar rim: 1
   Type C20 bowl rims: 5

REDEPOSITED SHERDS FROM EARLIER PERIODS
   sherds of the Rosario, Guadalupe, and San José phases: 25–30

Our evaluation of this collection is that it is a mixture of Monte Albán II sherds and redeposited ceramics from earlier

Figure 13.52. Vessels 1–4 of Feature 96, a set of small urns depicting women masked as the four companions of *Cociyo. Above,* all four urns in roughly the positions in which they were found. *Below,* closeups of Vessels 3 and 4.

periods. About all we can say is that none of the diagnostics are later than Monte Albán II.

A Radiocarbon Date for Structure 35

We decided that our most promising radiocarbon sample from Structure 35 was probably the charcoal from Feature 91, the remains of an incense burner pedestal resting on the floor of the inner room (Fig. 13.31). This charcoal became sample Beta-189254; it yielded a conventional date of 1930 ± 40 years before the present, or AD 20. When dendrocalibrated, this sample has a two-sigma range of 10 BC–AD 140. We see this as a plausible date for middle Monte Albán II.

The Layer of Fill between Structures 35 and 13

When use of the Structure 35 temple had ended, the Monte Albán II architects followed the same strategy they had shown when Structure 36 was abandoned. They knocked down the adobe walls of Structure 35 and created a layer of fill to support Structure 13, the next temple in the sequence. The layer of fill created below Structure 13, however, was only 47 cm thick—less than half the thickness of the fill between Structures 36 and 35.

One of the consequences of dealing with such a relatively thin layer of fill is that it is not always clear whether the objects placed in the fill should be considered (1) postabandonment offerings for the old temple or (2) pre-construction offerings for the new temple. This was certainly the case with Vessel 1, the *crema* vase shown in Figures 13.31 and 13.53. This Type C1 vase lay just below the original floor of Structure 13's inner room; however, it also rested virtually on the flagstones of the walkway flanking Structure 35. We could, in other words, consider it to be associated with either temple.

The same ambiguity surrounds the isolated skull we have designated Burial 63 (Fig. 13.54). This skull, identified by Hodges (1989:87) as possibly that of an adult woman, was found in the fill between Structures 35 and 13. Its atlas vertebra was still attached to the occipital condyles, making it unlikely that it was simply a loose skull retrieved from an exhumed burial. Might this be the head of a woman decapitated as a sacrificial offering? We suspect that such an offering would be more likely to have accompanied the dedication of Structure 13 than the postabandonment honoring of Structure 35, but we do not know which was the case.

Structure 13

Structure 13 was the third Monte Albán II temple in the sequence that had begun with the building of Structure 36. It was also the most eroded of the three temples, perched as it was atop the others and with steep gradients on all sides (Fig. 13.55). The degree of erosion made it difficult to get an accurate estimate of the temple's dimensions. We calculate that the intact building

5 cm

Above: Figure 13.53. Vessel 1, a Type C1 *crema* vase found below the floor of the inner room of Structure 13. We are not sure whether this vase was left as a postabandonment offering for Structure 35, or a pre-construction offering for Structure 13.

Below: Figure 13.54. Burial 63, the isolated skull of an adult, possibly female, placed in the layer of fill between Structure 35 and Structure 13. The atlas vertebra was still attached to the occipital condyles, suggesting that this individual may have been decapitated as a sacrificial offering.

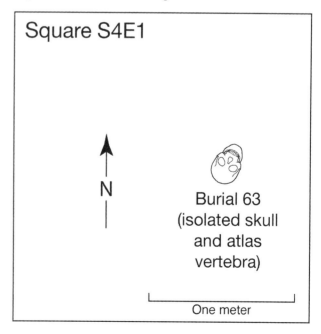

Square S4E1

N

Burial 63 (isolated skull and atlas vertebra)

One meter

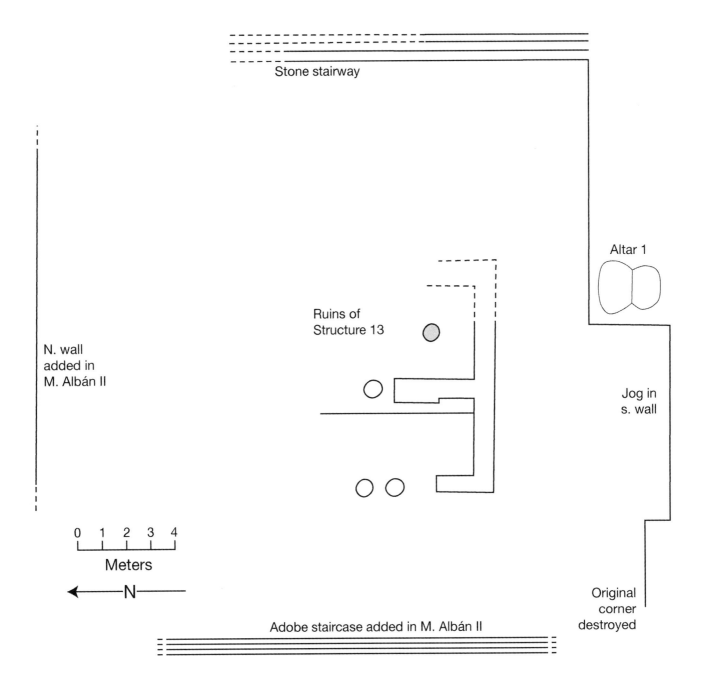

Stone stairway

Altar 1

Ruins of
Structure 13

N. wall
added in
M. Albán II

Jog in
s. wall

0 1 2 3 4
Meters

← —N—→

Original
corner
destroyed

Adobe staircase added in M. Albán II

Figure 13.55. The ruins of the Structure 13 temple, perched on the Monte Albán II version of the Structure 14 platform.

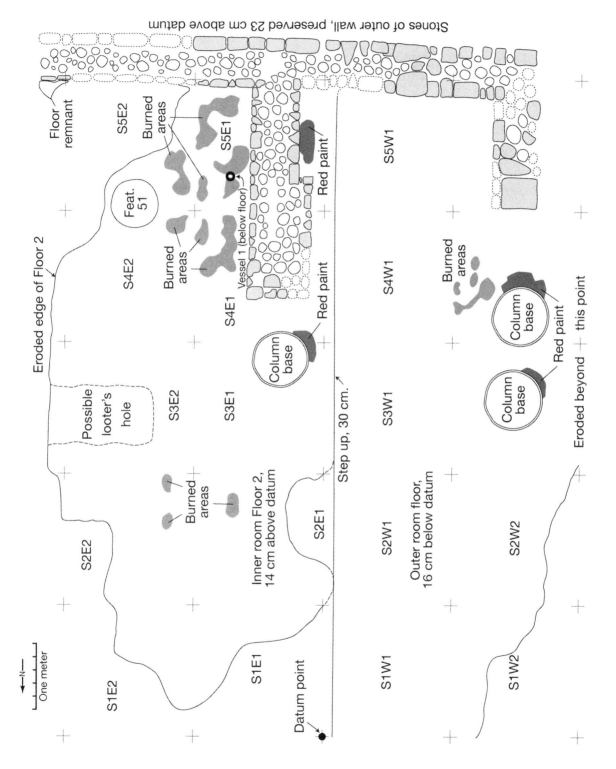

Figure 13.56. Plan of the surviving portion of Structure 13, at the level of its final stucco floor.

Figure 13.57. Beginning work on Structure 13. Squares S1E1–S4E1 have been excavated down to the stucco floor of the inner room, and a circular column base has come to light in Square S3E1. Fallen adobes can be seen in the lower right corner of the photo; in the background can be seen the site's recently plowed main plaza. (Black arrow points north.)

might have covered a rectangular area 15 m by 8 m, with its long axis running north-south.

Structure 13 had two superimposed stucco floors. The older of these, we now know, was Floor 3 of our 1974 Mound 1/Area A step trench (see Appendix A); the younger was Floor 2 of that same trench. The plan of Structure 13 seen in Figure 13.56 was drawn at the level of Floor 2.

The south wall of Structure 13 consisted of adobe bricks laid over a stone foundation 80 cm wide. Extending out from that south wall were the north-south wall stubs that established the western limits of the temple's two rooms. The outer room measured 2.42 m east-west and more than 10 m north-south. We estimate the inner room to have measured at least 3.3 m east-west and more than 10 m north-south.

Judging by the north-south wall stubs, the doorway to the outer

room was about 2.7 m wider than the doorway to the inner room. Entry into both rooms would have taken place between columns, two to either side of the outer doorway and one to either side of the inner doorway. All columns were composed of a core of stone slabs stacked one upon another, surrounded by stony rubble in a matrix of cement-hard mortar (Fig. 13.57). The column bases of the outer room were 90 cm in diameter; those of the inner room measured 80 cm.

Structure 13's older and younger floors were separated by 20–25 cm of fill. In the case of Floor 2 (the younger), the step-up from the outer room to the inner room was 30–32 cm (Fig. 13.58). The internal structure of the step-up was a layer of adobe bricks and small stones, its stucco covering strengthened by the addition of gravel to the lime plaster.

As one can see in Figure 13.56, the datum point established for

Figure 13.58. Excavation of the outer room, Structure 13. In the foreground, two circular column bases are coming to light in Squares S3W2 and S4W2. Behind Armando Jiménez, the workman on the right, one can see the 30 cm step-up to the inner room. (View from the west-southwest.)

our 1974 step trench (and used for the excavation of Structures 36, 35, and 13) lay in the northwest corner of Square S1E1. Almost all of the surviving portion of Structure 13 could be exposed by opening up 24 2 × 2 m squares, from S1E2 in the northeast to S5W2 in the southwest; a few areas of the inner room required the excavation of Squares S3E3–S5E3. The younger floor of the inner room lay 10–15 cm above our datum point, while the outer room lay 13–16 cm below datum; both floors had warped and buckled after the abandonment of the temple. An artist's reconstruction of the building can be seen in Figure 13.59.

The floor of Structure 13 had been swept clean to the point where no significant artifacts were found in situ. We did, however, find evidence that the floor of both rooms had once been painted red. In addition, the floor had been burned or smudged in places by the fuel from incense burners. The most frequent areas of burning are indicated in Figure 13.56.

Feature 51

In Squares S4E2 and S5E2 of the inner room we found Feature 51, a circular *tlecuil* or fire basin (Figs. 13.60–13.62). This basin had been built into the younger of the two floors and plastered with stucco at the same time the floor was laid down. Its diameter was 75 cm and its greatest depth 22 cm, meaning that its bottom nearly touched the older of the two room floors. Feature 51 showed signs of repeated exposure to fire, presumably from the burning of offerings by the priests occupying the inner room. The number of items that might have been burned in this way is extensive. We know, for example, that sixteenth-century

278 *San José Mogote 2*

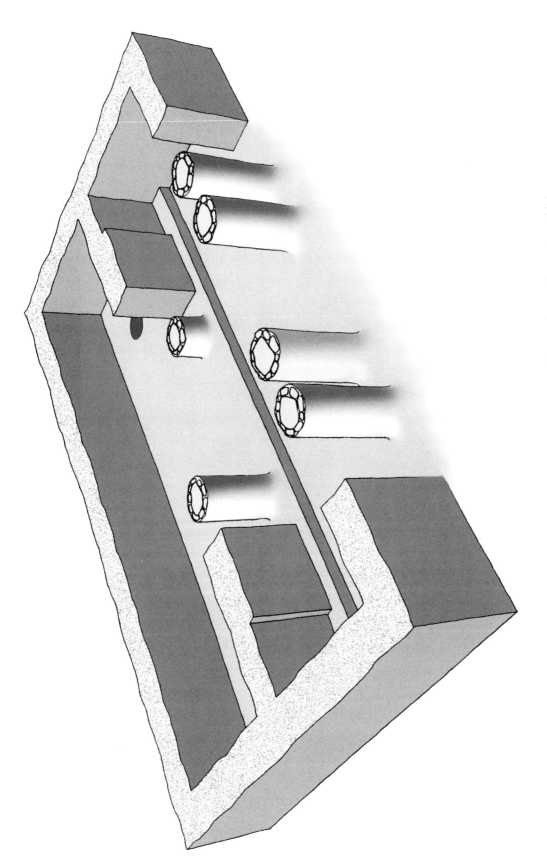

Figure 13.59. Artist's reconstruction of Structure 13. (Based on a drawing by David West Reynolds.)

Figure 13.60. Excavation of the inner room, Structure 13. In the foreground we see Feature 51, a circular basin built into the stucco floor. In the background, workmen investigate a possible looter's hole in Square S3E2. The object in the lower right corner of the photo is the root system of a modern mesquite tree.

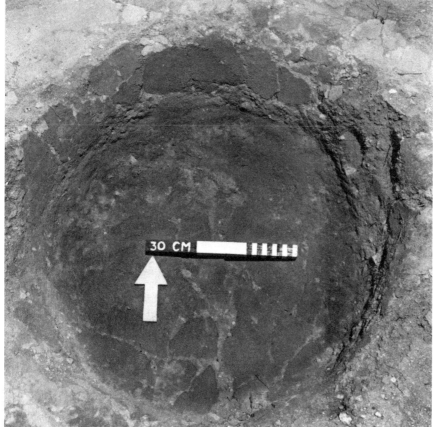

Figure 13.61. Feature 51, a basin built into the stucco floor of the inner room of Structure 13. Total length of scale, 30 cm (arrow points north).

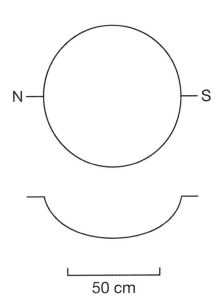

Figure 13.62. Plan and cross-section of Feature 51, a basin incorporated into the stucco floor of the inner room, Structure 13.

Zapotec priests performed autosacrifice, letting their blood drip onto strips of bark paper, then burning the paper so that the smoke would carry the offering to the heavens.

Dating Structure 13 with Ceramics

When it came time to date Structure 13 by its associated ceramics, we decided to use the sherds trapped between the temple's first and second floors. We knew that this did not constitute a primary deposit, but we felt that it should at least give us an indication of the pottery types prevalent in the area when the second floor was laid down. The diagnostic sherds were as follows:

CBA *GRIS* WARE DIAGNOSTICS
Type G1 bowl sherds: 1
Type G3 globular jar sherds: 2
Type G3 body sherds: 10
Type G12 incised rims: 2
Type G21 rims: 6
Type G21 cane-swirled base: 1
Monte Albán II version of Type G35: 2–3 sherds
incense burner fragments: 3

CBA *CREMA* WARE DIAGNOSTICS
Type C1 sherds: 3
Type C6 bowl sherds: 2 (one with postfiring zigzags)

CBA *CAFÉ* WARE DIAGNOSTICS
Type K1 sherds: 3

CBA *AMARILLO* WARE DIAGNOSTICS
incense burner fragment: 1

REDEPOSITED EARLIER CERAMICS
sherds of the San José, Guadalupe, and Rosario phases: 12+

While this sherd sample suggested that Structure 13 was built during Monte Albán II, it was too small to allow assignation of the temple to middle or late Period II. For that we would need a radiocarbon date.

A Radiocarbon Date for Structure 13

Fortunately, the earlier of Structure 13's two stucco floors provided us with charcoal left by an incense burner with a ring or pedestal base. The fact that this charcoal was sealed below a later stucco floor made it our best chance for dating, and it became sample Beta-190921. The conventional date was 1900 ± 40 years BP, or AD 50. When dendrocalibrated, this date has a two-sigma range of AD 30–AD 220. We consider this a plausible late Monte Albán II date.

Temple Renovation and the 52-Year Calendar Round

Structures 36, 35, and 13 provide us with a sequence of three temples, built one above another on the same spot and featuring similar (though not identical) ground plans. Figure 13.63 presents our artist's view of the three temples in stratigraphic order. Having such a sequence forced us to give some thought to the frequency with which Zapotec temples might have been renovated or rebuilt.

By Monte Albán II, two-room temples were standard features at the Zapotec capital and its second- and third-tier administrative centers (Marcus and Flannery 1996:178–188). Hieroglyphic texts indicate that both the 260-day ritual calendar and the 365-day secular calendar were in use even before Monte Albán II (Marcus 1976, 1992). Over much of ancient Mesoamerica, these two calendars were combined to produce a 52-year cycle called the Calendar Round. This cycle was of great importance to the Aztec, for example, who believed that their world would cease at the end of a 52-year cycle unless old fires were extinguished and new ones lit (Durán 1964:239). New archaeological evidence from the Great Temple of the Aztecs in ancient Tenochtitlán confirms that that building was renovated and rededicated every 52 years (Elson and Smith 2001).

The Zapotec also recognized a 52-year cycle (Marcus 1992:95–142; Caso 1965b:932), and they had a history of building new temples directly above the old. This raises the question of whether such renovations took place at 52-year intervals. Our radiocarbon dates from Structures 36, 35, and 13 allow us to examine this possibility.

We must turn to the dendrocalibrated versions of our dates,

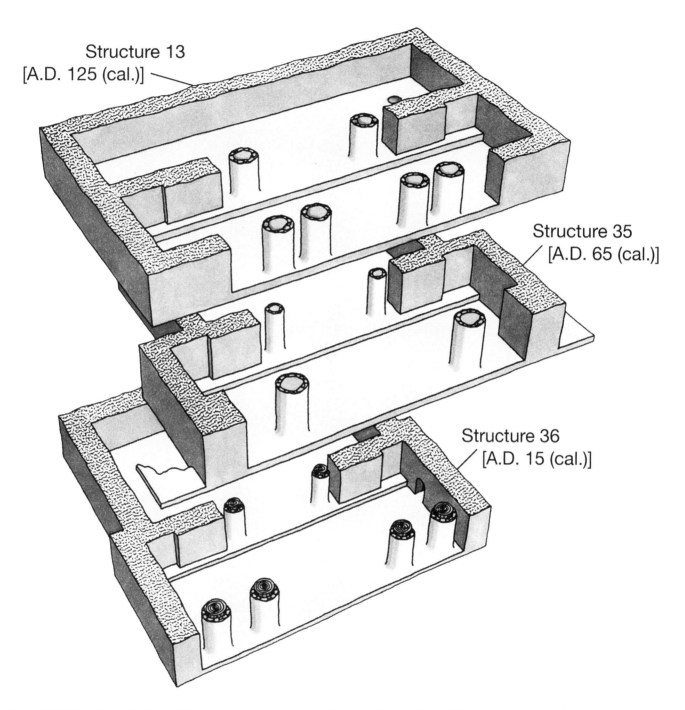

Figure 13.63. Structures 13, 35, and 36, superimposed in stratigraphic order. Their calibrated ^{14}C dates raise the possibility that old temples were razed and new ones built at the end of each 52-year Calendar Round.

L___I___I___I___I___I
5 cm

Figure 13.64. Carved grayware drinking vessel with the hieroglyphic name of Lord 1 Jaguar, left as an offering in the fill between Structure 13 and Floor 1. Height, 10.5 cm. 13.65.

Figure 13.65. Carved grayware drinking vessel with the hieroglyphic name of Lord 1 Jaguar, found at Monte Albán. (Photo courtesy of James B. Griffin.)

since the Calendar Round operated in "real time" rather than radiocarbon years. The midpoints for each two-sigma range are AD 15 for Structure 36; AD 65 for Structure 35; and AD 125 for Structure 13. These midpoints suggest an interval of ± 50 years between Structures 36 and 35 and another of ± 60 years between Structures 35 and 13. Although not conclusive, such intervals make it hard to rule out the possibility that San José Mogote commissioned a new temple on the Structure 14 platform every 52 years.

An Offering in the Fill between Structure 13 and Floor 1

Once Structure 13 had been abandoned, its adobe walls were dismantled and used to create a 30 cm thick layer of fill. Included in this fill were heavy stones, smaller stony rubble, and basketloads of earth. The density of the fill was sufficient to make it appropriate for the support of a new temple, and sure enough, we found a stucco floor lying atop it. Unfortunately, the building associated with this layer of stucco—Floor 1 of our original

1974 step trench (Appendix A)—had long since eroded away.

Sitting upright in the layer of fill between Structure 13 and Floor 1 was the carved grayware drinking vessel shown in Figure 13.64. The carving on the vessel, which stands 10.5 cm tall, depicts a calendric name that would be given in Zapotec as 1 Peeche (One Jaguar).

We recognized this calendric name as belonging to the male member of a legendary Zapotec "founder couple," Lord 1 Jaguar and Lady 2 Maize, whose calendric names repeatedly show up on carved beakers at Monte Albán and elsewhere (Marcus and Flannery 1996:224, Figs. 269–270). Lord 1 Jaguar and Lady 2 Maize are likely to have been the legendary founders of one of Monte Albán's royal dynasties, making them the Zapotec equivalent of the legendary Mixtec royal couple, Lord 1 Deer and Lady 1 Deer (Furst 1978: Fig. 16). A second example of a vessel dedicated to 1 Jaguar—this one from Monte Albán—is shown in Figure 13.65.

Our 1 Jaguar vessel presents us with the same dilemma mentioned earlier for Vessel 1, found in the fill between Structures 35 and 13. Was it a postabandonment offering left in the ruins

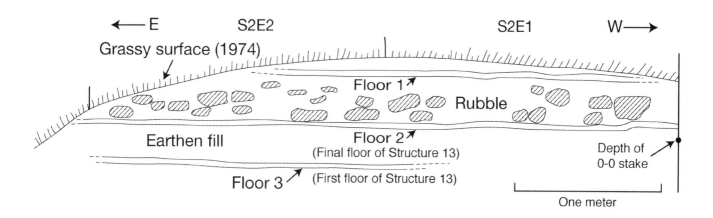

Figure 13.66. The south profile of Squares S2E1 and S2E2, the beginning of the 1974 step trench from Mound 1 to Area A (Appendix A).

of Structure 13, or a pre-construction offering left below Floor 1? Whatever the case, we would assign the 1 Jaguar vessel to a period later than that of Structure 13. Most 1 Jaguar/2 Maize beakers have been found in Monte Albán IIIa contexts; at the earliest, they might go back to the period Caso, Bernal, and Acosta (1967) called Transición II–IIIa.

Did Floor 1 Belong to a Temple?

Floor 1 first appeared in the south profile of our 1974 Mound 1/Area A step trench (Fig. 13.66; see also Appendix A). It lay 46 cm above the datum point established for the step trench, and occupied most of the squares between S2E1–S2E2 and S4E1–S4E2. Near the border between Squares S4E1 and S4E2, we came upon the remnants of a stone masonry wall foundation, presumably part of the building associated with Floor 1 (Fig. 13.67). Thanks to the erosion of Mound 1, these bits of architecture were all that remained of the building itself, which may have been a fourth temple in the sequence that began with Structure 36.

We decided that there was so little of the building left that it did not need a structure number. We were, nevertheless, interested in establishing a date for Floor 1. Fortunately there were sherds trapped in the construction fill between Structure 13 and Floor 1, allowing us to obtain a screened sample for analysis. The diagnostic sherds were as follows:

CBA *GRIS* WARE DIAGNOSTICS
    Type G1 sherds: 7
    Type G3 jar rims: 7
    Type G3 bowl rims: 26
    Type G3 cylinder with rim recessed for lid: 1
    Type G3 body sherds: 12
    Type G12 rims: 2
    Subtype G12b bases: 6
    Type G21 cane-swirled base: 1
    Monte Albán II version of Type G35: 4

CBA *CREMA* WARE DIAGNOSTICS
    Type C1 bowl rims: 3

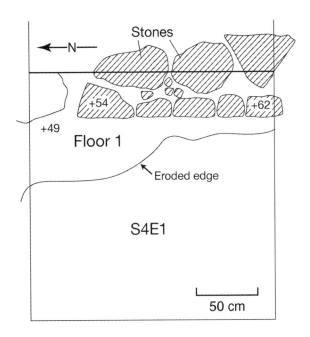

Figure 13.67. A remnant of the stone foundation of the building associated with Floor 1, which had survived at the border between Squares S4E1 and S4E2. Depths given are in centimeters above the 0-0 datum point.

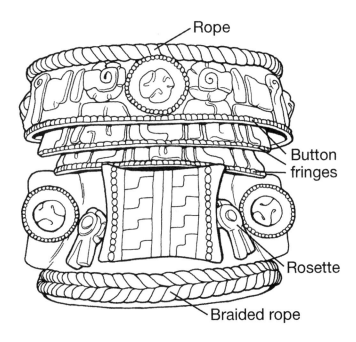

Figure 13.68. Elements of a non-effigy incense burner dating to Monte Albán II or IIIa (drawing by John Klausmeyer).

Type C7 sherds: 12
Type C12 sherds with postfiring zigzags: 5
fragment of Suchilquitongo tripod dish: 1

CBA *CAFÉ* WARE DIAGNOSTICS
   Type K1 charcoal brazier with fillet band: 1
   Type K1 *comal* sherds: 3
   Type K3 sherd, mat-impressed: 1

CBA *AMARILLO* WARE DIAGNOSTICS
   Type A6 rim sherd: 1
   Type A11 cylinder, incised and excised, rim recessed for lid: 1
   carved sherds resembling Transición II–IIIa examples in Caso, Bernal, and Acosta (1967): 4

REDEPOSITED EARLIER SHERDS
   sherds of Tierras Largas, San José, Guadalupe, and Rosario phase types: 100+
   Early Formative figurine fragments: 6

In evaluating this mixture of pottery types, our attention is called to the Transición-style *amarillo* sherds with incising and carving. When these sherds are combined with the carved 1 Jaguar vessel left below Floor 1, one could perhaps assign Floor 1 to the transition from Monte Albán II to Monte Albán IIIa.

If there was indeed a "Floor 1 temple," it is possible that it may have been built 52 years after Structure 13, or about AD 175. Unfortunately, Floor 1 produced no charcoal for radiocarbon dating.

Feature 20

Our account of the temple sequence on the Structure 14 platform would not be complete without a discussion of Feature 20, an immense trash pit filled with broken urns and incense burners. This pit began just east of the jog in the south wall of Structure 14, and extended so many meters to the east that its limits had

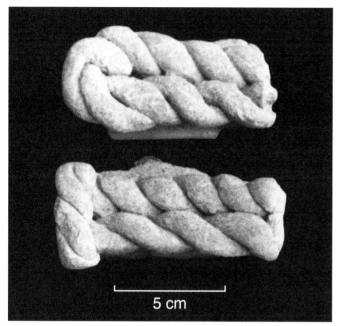

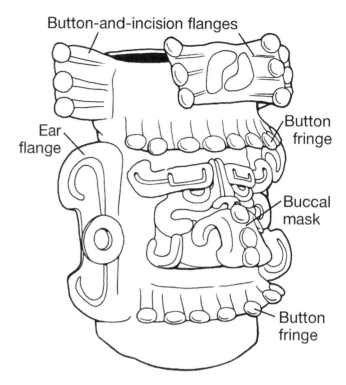

Left above: Figure 13.69. Braided rope from incense burners, Feature 20.

Left below: Figure 13.70. Fragment of incense burner from Feature 20, with crosshatching and serrated border.

Above: Figure 13.71. Elements of a Monte Albán II effigy incense burner (drawing by John Klausmeyer).

been lost to erosion. The pit's original depth had been greater than 3 m and when it became full to overflowing, the temple staff continued to dump broken vessels until an additional meter of debris had accumulated. There were no easily discernible stratigraphic breaks within Feature 20, but the material near the bottom seemed to belong to Monte Albán II, while the overflow material at the top included fragments from the Period II–IIIa transition.

We were not surprised to find such a feature, given that the practice of dumping ceremonial debris behind (or at the base of) temples was widespread in Mesoamerica. In the Maya region, for example, large ceremonial dumps have been found at Lagartero (Ekholm 1990) and Tikal (Ferree 1972). Included in the material discarded were hundreds of the incense burners used in temple rituals.

Our workmen at San José Mogote, noting the abundance of highly decorated ceramic pieces in Feature 20, proclaimed it a deposit of *puros fantásticos*. Highest in frequency were fragments of incense burners, some bearing effigies of deities or ancestors. Less frequent were the fragments of urns. Vessels with stirrup

handles, spiked bridgespout jars, and "frying pan" *sahumadores* occurred in the overflow at the top of the pit. Let us consider some of the major categories of material.

Non-Effigy Incense Burners

One class of incense burner used during Monte Albán II and IIIa did not feature the visage of a deity or culture hero. Such "non-effigy" incense burners, nevertheless, were elaborately decorated with elements such as braided rope, rosettes, and button fringes (Fig. 13.68). Fragments of braided rope were common elements in Feature 20 (Fig. 13.69). So, too, were button fringes, although serrated borders sometimes provided an alternative (Fig. 13.70).

Effigy Incense Burners

Many Monte Albán II incense burners bore images of *Cociyo* himself, wearing a buccal mask; his decoration included ear

Figure 13.72. Two broken Monte Albán II effigy incense burners, recovered in the plow zone (Zone A) of Area C, Squares S14P and S14Q. Both vessels share diagnostic elements with the incense burner fragments recovered from Feature 20.

The Monte Albán II Renaissance at San José Mogote

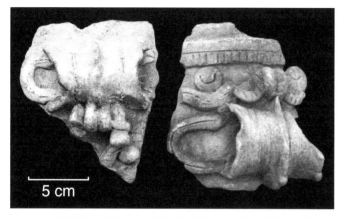

Feather headdress

Ear flanges

Buccal mask

Step-incised border

Trophy skull pendant

Top left: Figure 13.73. Fragments of effigy incense burners, Feature 20.

Above left: Figure 13.74. Fragments of flanges with button-and-incision decoration on their edges. From incense burners, Feature 20.

Above right: Figure 13.75. Elements of an effigy incense burner of Monte Albán II or IIIa (drawing by John Klausmeyer).

flanges, button-and-incision flanges, and button fringes (Fig. 13.71). Broken examples of such incense burners, in fact, can be found eroding from the plow zone at San José Mogote, often in areas far removed from Mound 1 (Fig. 13.72). In Feature 20, however, we recovered a high density of buccal masks (Fig. 13.73) and button-and-incision flanges (Fig. 13.74).

Still other effigy incense burners featured what appear to be royal ancestors wearing quetzal feather headdresses, *Cociyo* masks, trophy skull pendants, and ear flanges with "ring and dot" decoration (Fig. 13.75). Fragments of both headdresses (Fig. 13.76) and ear flanges with "ring and dot" elements (Fig. 13.77) were abundant in Feature 20.

Effigy Urns

A number of the ceramic fragments in Feature 20 came from typical Monte Albán II urns; the overflow pile at the top of the pit included pieces that could date to the Period II–IIIa transition. Figure 13.78 shows some of the decorative elements of these urns, which included earspools, button fringes, side flanges, rosettes, and plaques carved with variants of the hieroglyph called Glyph C by Caso (Caso 1928). To be sure, fragments of Monte Albán II urns were present in the plow zone all over the site of San José Mogote (Fig. 13.79); nowhere, however, were they as abundant as in Feature 20.

It appears that many urns depicted noble ancestors sitting

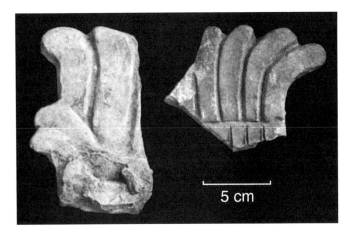

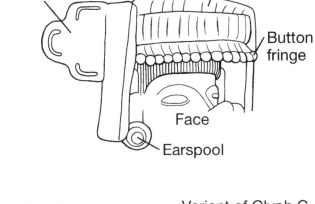

Above: Figure 13.76. Feathers from headdresses on effigy incense burners, Feature 20.

Below: Figure 13.77. Fragments of large "ear flanges" from effigy incense burners, Feature 20. Each bears a different version of the "ring and dot" decoration.

Right: Figure 13.78. Elements found on the face and headdress of Monte Albán II and IIIa urns (drawings by John Klausmeyer).

Below right: Figure 13.79. Two fragments of a Monte Albán II urn, recovered in the plow zone (Zone A) of Area C, Square S19R. This vessel shares elements with many urn fragments recovered from Feature 20.

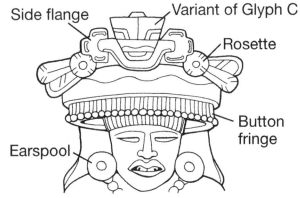

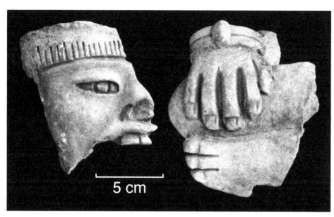

Figure 13.80. Urn fragments from Feature 20. *Left*, face. *Right*, hand resting on knee.

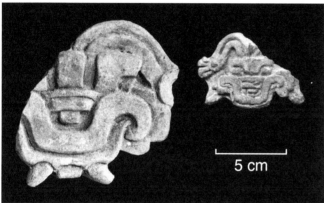

Figure 13.81. Examples of Caso's Glyph C from Feature 20. These glyphs were often incorporated into the headdresses of human figures on effigy urns.

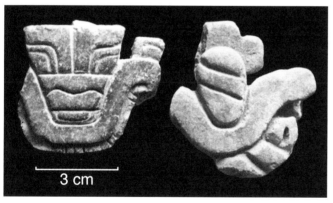

Figure 13.82. Two hieroglyphs broken off urns, found on the surface of Mound 1 not far from Feature 20. *Left*, variant of Caso's Glyph C (see Boos 1966:263, Figure 241). *Right*, Caso's Glyph J ("Maize").

Figure 13.83. Common elements found in the headdresses of anthropomorphic urns, Feature 20. *Left*, side flange. *Right*, mask (or head) of *Cociyo*.

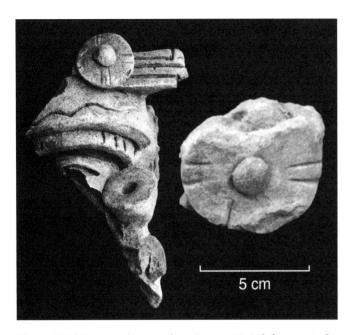

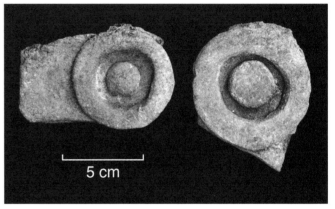

Figure 13.84. Rosette elements from Feature 20. *Left*, fragment of small anthropomorphic urn showing the rosette in the headdress above the eye and earplug of a human figure. *Right*, larger rosette element.

Figure 13.85. Fragments of probable earspools from human figures on effigy urns, Feature 20.

crosslegged with their hands on their knees (Fig. 13.80). Variants of Caso's Glyph C—some of which appeared mold-made—were also common (Figs. 13.81, 13.82). Headdress components such as side flanges, *Cociyo* masks (Fig. 13.83), and rosettes (Fig. 13.84) were frequent. So, too, were broken-off earspools (Fig. 13.85).

Some effigy urns show the attributes of animals, or humans in animal costumes (Fig. 13.86). There were also fragments of what may be garments (Figs. 13.87, 13.88). Some human effigy figures were shown holding small bowls in their hands, and those bowls frequently broke off (Fig. 13.89).

Pottery Vessels

Caso, Bernal, and Acosta (1967) illustrate unusual box-shaped vessels with stirrup-shaped handles: several of these appeared near the top of the Feature 20 deposit (Fig. 13.90). This overflow

area also produced grayware bridgespout jars with decorative spikes (Fig. 13.91). *Sahumadores*, or "frying pan" incense burners in coarse *café* ware also appeared in the overflow from the pit (Fig. 13.92). The boxes, stirrup handles, spiked bridgespouts, and frying-pan incense burners were all found high enough in the deposit to be Transición II–IIIa in age.

Figurines

Other items that we consider late enough to be Transición II–IIIa in age are the small solid grayware figurines shown in Figure 13.93. These figurines—widely believed to represent dogs—reached their peak in Monte Albán IIIa. Their presence in the Feature 20 overflow not only makes it likely that Floor 1 belonged to a temple, but also suggests that it may indeed have been built during Transición, 52 years later than Structure 13.

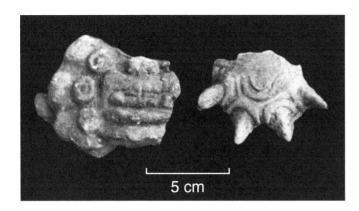

Figure 13.86. Fragments of animal effigies, Feature 20. Without seeing the whole figure, it is sometimes difficult to decide whether these fragments represent pumas/jaguars or bats.

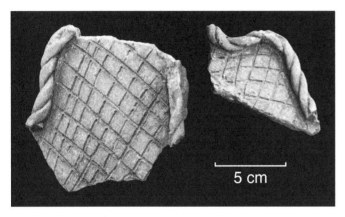

Figure 13.87. Two examples of crosshatched, braid-bordered elements that sometimes depict the garments worn by human figures on effigy urns. Found in Feature 20.

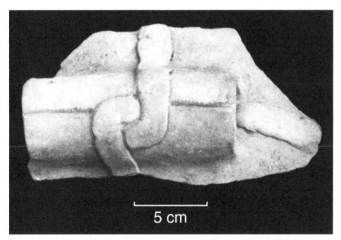

Figure 13.88. Tied element from belt of individual depicted on urn or incense burner, Feature 20.

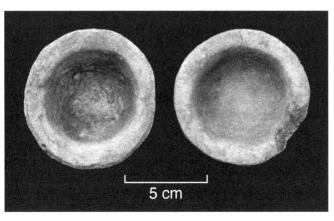

Figure 13.89. Some figures on anthropomorphic urns are shown holding small bowls like these in their hands. Found in Feature 20.

Above: Figure 13.90. Fragments of box-shaped pottery vessels with stirrup-shaped handles, Feature 20. *Left*, handle. *Right*, fragment of boxlike vessel body.

Below: Figure 13.91. Fragments of grayware bridgespout jars with decorative spikes, Feature 20.

Above right: Figure 13.92. Fragments of *sahumadores* ("frying-pan" incense burners) from Feature 20.

Below right: Figure 13.93. Fragments of grayware dog figurines from Feature 20. *Upper row*, heads. *Lower row*, bodies.

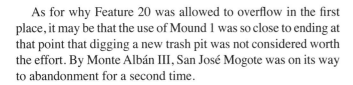

As for why Feature 20 was allowed to overflow in the first place, it may be that the use of Mound 1 was so close to ending at that point that digging a new trash pit was not considered worth the effort. By Monte Albán III, San José Mogote was on its way to abandonment for a second time.

Other Trash Pits

It should be noted that we found traces of other pits dedicated to temple trash, both within the jog in the south wall of Struc-

ture 14 and in the upper fill of the corridor to the south. Owing to post-occupational erosion we were unable to determine the dimensions of these pits, and therefore decided not to assign them feature numbers. None had overflowed like Feature 20, and none yielded the diversity of urn and incense burner fragments.

In the end, we decided that Feature 20 and the smaller trash pits nearby could not be linked to any one specific temple in the Monte Albán II–IIIa sequence. Rather, it looked as if the dumping of temple trash had gone on for centuries, with the overflow dating to the period of Structure 13 and/or the temple associated with Floor 1.

14 | The Remaining Temples on the Monte Albán II Acropolis

The sequence of temples built on the remodeled Structure 14 platform—Structure 36, Structure 35, Structure 13, and Floor 1—was one of our most informative windows into state-level ritual at a second-tier administrative center. Each of the Monte Albán II buildings on Structure 14, however, was simply the northeasternmost of a group of four temples flanking a small patio (see Fig. 13.2). The other three temples on that patio were Structures 21, 22, and 29.

Structure 29

Structure 29 came to light the moment we began excavating the overburden above Structure 19. It belonged to Stratigraphic Zone A1 of that overburden, having been built directly over the ruins of the small ritual buildings of Zone A2 (see Fig. 8.6).

All that remained of Structure 29 were patches of its stucco floor; its walls had long since eroded down the slopes of Mound 1. We found only one fragment of the step-up between the inner and outer rooms, but that was enough to tell us that the temple had faced west.

In Figure 14.1, one can see the largest piece of floor, an 8 m² patch of stucco that occupied parts of Squares S5E8, S5E9, S6E8, and S6E9. This patch, stained by the charcoal from countless incense burners, was part of the floor of the inner room of the temple. We encountered it just 12 cm below the datum point established for Structure 19 and its overburden.

Structure 29 had been protected from summer rains by the drain shown in Figure 14.1. This drain—whose walls, roof, and floor consisted of small stone slabs (Fig. 14.2)—was intact below the floor of the inner room and ran toward the southeast, gradually descending to a point where its floor lay 48 cm below datum. At that point the drain had become intrusive into Stratigraphic Zone A2, as can be seen in Figure 10.9. We do not know where the rainwater ended up, since the terminus of the drain had eroded away.

Feature 75

Buried beneath a floor patch of Structure 29 we found Feature 75, a stone masonry offering box measuring 80 by 85 cm (Fig. 14.3). In Squares S6E8 and S7E8, the stucco floor of the temple was still intact above the north wall of the box; farther to the

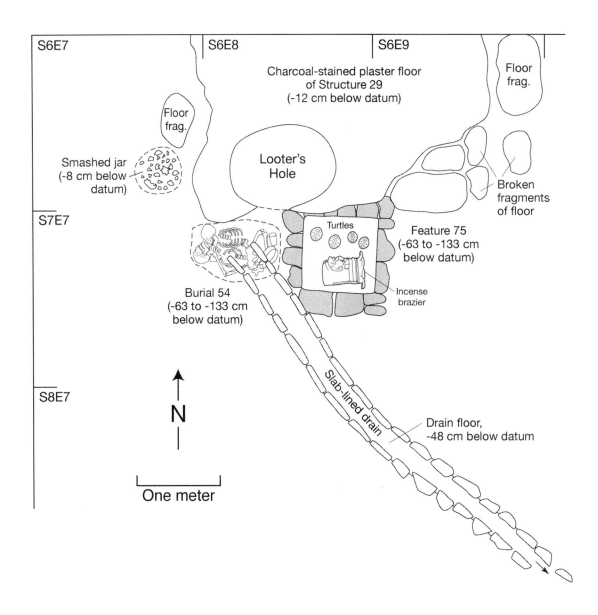

Figure 14.1. Plan view of Stratigraphic Zone A1, showing a patch of floor from Structure 29; a subfloor drain; Feature 75 (a subfloor offering box); and Burial 54.

Above: Figure 14.2. Two views of the slab-lined drain running southeast from Structure 29. At *a*, we see Sergio Cruz cleaning the dirt from the drain (the white arrow points north). At *b*, we see a cross-section of the drain.

Below: Figure 14.3. East-west cross-section through Feature 75.

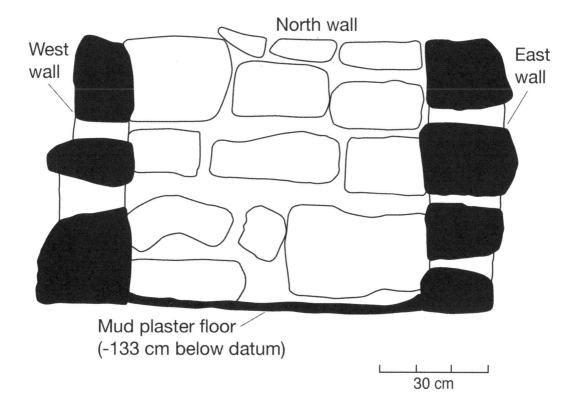

Figure 14.4. Two stages in the excavation of Feature 75. On the left we see the large incense brazier, broken by the weight of the overburden, being freed from the earthen fill of the offering box. On the right, excavation of the box has been completed. North is at the top in both photos.

south, the floor had eroded away. The depth of the offering box below our datum point was 63 cm to 1.33 m.

Lying on its side in Feature 75—broken by the weight of the overburden, but readily restorable—was a remarkable effigy incense brazier whose burnished cream slip was almost invisible below a heavy coating of dry vermilion pigment (Figs. 14.4–14.6). When restored, this brazier stood 55 cm tall. Its pedestal base bears the visage of a man wearing earspools and displaying a spherical ornament in the septum of his nose. His open mouth reveals his tongue and two canine teeth, but no incisors; the missing teeth—combined with four facial incisions that may depict wrinkles—suggest that the sculptor intended to portray him as elderly. His headdress (which served as the receptacle for the incense) bears a ring of large flower petals.

Given the figure's angry expression and fiery red color, our workmen immediately dubbed him *el Diablo Enchilado*. Adding to his devilish appearance was the fact that his eyes and mouth were perforated in such a way that smoke would have issued from them when the fuel for the brazier was lit.

Sharing the offering box with the "devil in chile sauce" were four complete mud turtles (*Kinosternon integrum*), also crushed by the overburden (Fig. 14.7). We are not sure what this offering of four turtles represents; our first thought was that they might be turtleshell rattles, but this seems unlikely in light of the fact that all of their limb bones were present. One possibility is that the contents of Feature 75 refer symbolically to cloud ancestors, either as wrinkled elders or as "flying turtles" like the one shown in Figure 13.50.

A second possibility is that each of the turtles stands for one of the four world quadrants. Among the Maya, for example, the turtle served as an important representation of Earth (Taube 1988); accordingly, a turtleshell was worn by each of the four Bacabs who stood at the corners of the earth while holding up the sky. It is significant that at the Postclassic Maya site of Mayapan, stone turtles were associated with incense burners in the shrines and altars of ceremonial structures (Winters 1955; Proskouriakoff

Figure 14.5. Front and side views of the *Diablo Enchilado*.

1962). The association of turtles with an incense brazier in our Feature 75 might be analogous.

Burial 54

Immediately to the west of Feature 75, and at exactly the same depth below datum, we discovered Burial 54. This was not an elegant grave, but a cramped pit in which two individuals had been awkwardly accommodated (Fig. 14.8). Individual 1, a woman more than 55 years of age (Hodges 1989:87), lay on her back with her knees drawn up and her head twisted to one side. At her feet was Vessel 1, a Type C20 bowl with a burnished black wash (Fig. 14.9a); this vessel can be compared to Figure 174b in Caso, Bernal, and Acosta (1967). Not far away lay Vessel 2, a Type G1 *vaso* (Fig. 14.9b); this vessel can be compared to Figure 215c in Caso, Bernal, and Acosta (1967). In the mouth of Individual 1 we discovered 26 stone beads, some of which are illustrated in Figure 14.10.

Individual 2 of Burial 54 was a child between 8 and 9 years old (Hodges 1989:87). It lay on its right side, facing and partially below Individual 1. At the child's feet we found 18 mother-of-pearl "buttons" that may once have been sewn to a garment (Fig. 14.11). Beside Individual 2 lay a bone needle, complete except for a broken tip (Fig. 14.12). Against the north wall of the burial pit (and therefore closer to Individual 2 than to Individual 1) were the remains of a juvenile mud turtle.

We suspect that both Feature 75 and Burial 54 may have resulted from rituals of sanctification, carried out before the floor of the Structure 29 temple was laid. The incense brazier may have been used in such a ritual, then sealed up in the offering box. The fact that Individuals 1 and 2 had been placed so awkwardly in the Burial 54 pit suggests that they were more likely sacrificial victims than honored dead. Whether the objects found with them were their possessions, or simply additional offerings left below the temple, we do not know.

Figure 14.6. Artist's rendering of the *Diablo Enchilado*, the effigy incense brazier found in Feature 75. The brazier is cream-slipped and heavily coated with dry vermilion pigment. Smoke from the burning charcoal used as fuel would have issued from the eyes and mouth.

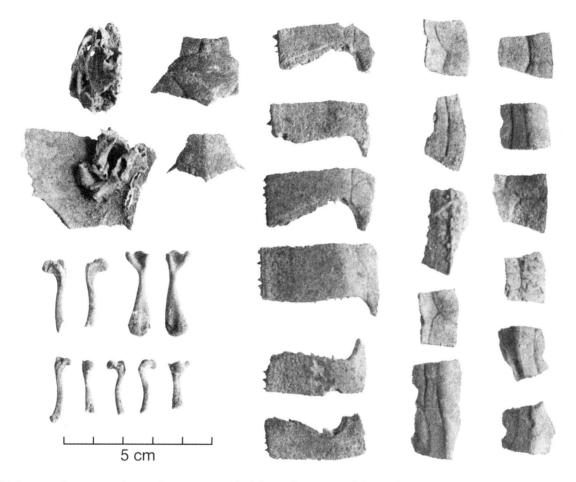

Figure 14.7. Carapace fragments, plastron fragments, and limb bones from some of the mud turtles found in Feature 75.

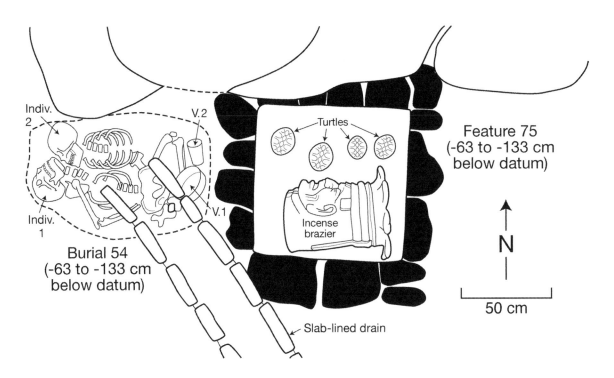

Figure 14.8. Plan view of Feature 75 and Burial 54, found below the disintegrating floor of Structure 29.

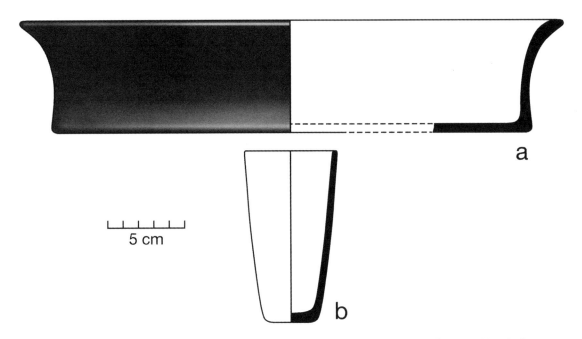

Figure 14.9. Pottery vessels found with Burial 54 below Structure 29. *a*, Vessel 1, an outcurved-wall, flat-based bowl of Caso, Bernal, and Acosta's Type C20. *b*, Vessel 2, a *vaso* or tall drinking vessel of Caso, Bernal, and Acosta's Type G1. Both vessels were found with Individual 1.

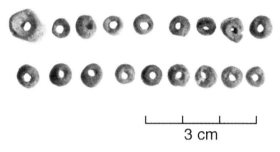

Figure 14.10. Eighteen of the 26 stone beads found in the mouth of Individual 1, Burial 54. (The beads not illustrated were small, like those in the lower row.)

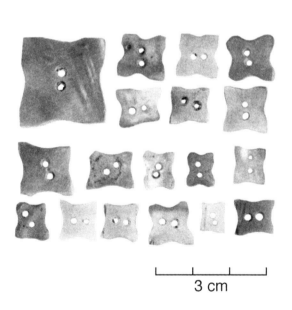

Figure 14.11. Mother-of-pearl "buttons" (1 large, 17 small) found near the feet of Individual 2, Burial 54. These ornaments may have been sewn to a garment that had disintegrated.

Figure 14.12. Bone needle, complete except for a broken tip, found beside Individual 2 of Burial 54.

Dating Structure 29 with Ceramics

Roughly 80 sherds were found lying on the surviving patches of Structure 29's stucco floor. The diagnostics were as follows:

CBA *GRIS* WARE DIAGNOSTICS
rims of G3 bowls: 5
sherds of subtype G12b: 2

CBA *CREMA* WARE DIAGNOSTICS
rims of C1 bowls: 2
rims of C2 bowls: 3
sherd of Type C4: 1
rim of C7 bowl: 1
brazier fragments: 2

CBA *CAFÉ* WARE DIAGNOSTICS
rims of K3 bowls: 6
rim of K4 bowl: 1

CBA *AMARILLO* WARE DIAGNOSTICS
sherd from a frog effigy vessel: 1

REDEPOSITED EARLIER CERAMICS
sherds of the San José, Guadalupe, Rosario, and Monte Albán
    Ia phases

In addition to the sherds we recovered from the floor of Structure 29, we found 25–30 sherds in the upper fill of Feature 75. The diagnostics were as follows:

CBA *GRIS* WARE DIAGNOSTICS
sherd of Type G21: 1

CBA *CREMA* WARE DIAGNOSTICS
rims of C1 bowls: 8
slightly flaring rim, C7 bowl: 1
beveled rim, C7 bowl: 1
C7 bowl with postfiring zigzags: 1 sherd
C11 bowl with postfiring zigzags: 1 sherd
C12 bowl with postfiring zigzags: 1 sherd

REDEPOSITED EARLIER CERAMICS
sherds of the San José, Guadalupe, and Rosario phases: 12+

While the ceramic samples from Structure 29 and Feature 75 were made up largely of redeposited sherds from earlier periods, they did contain a number of G21, C7, C11, and C12 diagnostics from Monte Albán II. In addition, no diagnostics of Monte Albán IIIa (or later periods) were present. When these sherds are combined with the complete Type C20 bowl found with Burial 54, it seems clear that Structure 29 dated to Monte Albán II.

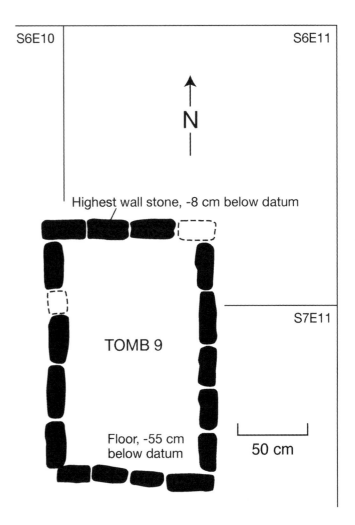

Figure 14.13. Plan view of Tomb 9, which lay mostly within Squares S6E11 and S7E11.

Figure 14.14. Armando and Isaac Jiménez provide scale for Tomb 9 (the black arrow points north).

Tomb 9

One other discovery made in Stratigraphic Zone A1 is worthy of mention. This was Tomb 9, a drylaid stone masonry sepulcher that lay mostly within excavation Squares S6E11 and S7E11 (Fig. 14.13). Figure 14.14 shows how close to the grassy surface of the Structure 19 overburden this tomb appeared; its highest surviving wall stone was only 8 cm below datum, while its earthen floor lay at a depth of 55 cm below datum (intrusive into Zone A2).

Tomb 9 measured 1.91 m north-south and 1.05 m east-west. We do not know who had been buried in the tomb, because his or her remains had been almost entirely removed. All that remained were a few fragments of cranium and ribs. We suspect that this tomb, like the other constructions originating in Zone A1, dated to Monte Albán II, but we cannot prove it.

Modifications to Structure 19 Made during Monte Albán II

Structure 29, as mentioned earlier, was found in Stratigraphic Zone A1 of the overburden above Structure 19. By the time Structure 29 was built, this overburden had risen more than 3.5 m above Structure 19 (and that figure does not include the full height of Structure 29 when it was an intact temple).

Structure 19 had never been designed to support all this additional weight, and its walls eventually began to lean outward. The Monte Albán II architects took a number of steps to prevent the collapse of Structure 19, since it now supported a Period II temple. Against the leaning north wall of the old Rosario phase building, they built a thick pavement of flagstones that we nicknamed "the *laja* porch" (Fig. 14.15). This pavement averaged 2.7 m wide and ran for at least 16.5 m along the north wall of Structure 19. While it was sufficiently well made to resemble an actual porch, we soon realized that its real purpose was to keep the north wall of Structure 19 from leaning further.

The stones used in the *laja* porch came from a variety of sources. Some had been quarried from bedrock; some appeared to have been robbed from earlier buildings, such as Structure 14; and a few were the circular volcanic tuff bases for roof-support columns. It seemed likely that the latter had been taken from the ruins of Structure 37, a late Rosario phase temple, which had contained such column bases before it was dismantled by the Monte Albán II architects (see Figs. 9.10, 9.11).

Still other measures were used to keep the west wall of Structure 19 from collapsing outward. In this case, the Monte Albán II architects built a thick masonry pavement all the way from Structure 19 to Structure 21 (a Monte Albán II temple to be discussed below). This pavement was designed to be level

Figure 14.15. The "*laja* porch," a pavement of flagstones laid down during Monte Albán II in order to keep the north wall of Structure 19 from collapsing outward under the weight of its later overburden. Among the flagstones were volcanic tuff bases for roof-support columns, robbed from Structure 37 (see Figs. 9.10 and 9.11).

with the lowest step of Structure 21's staircase (Fig. 14.16). Since we found the staircase to be complete and intact behind the pavement, the slumping of Structure 19's west wall may have occurred only after Structure 21 had been in use for some time.

While this pavement kept Structure 19 from collapsing, it evidently blocked the flow of rain runoff in front of Structure 21. As a result, the pavement had a built-in stone-lined drain that kept water from ponding up in the small patio between the four Monte Albán II temples.

It should be noted that the Monte Albán II architects also piled boulders against the south and east walls of Structure 19 to keep them upright. These boulder piles, of course, were not as attractive as the pavements built to the west and north of Structure 19. That probably did not matter, since the south and east sides of the building were almost certainly viewed less frequently by visitors during Monte Albán II.

Structures 21 and 22

Structures 21 and 22 were the two remaining Monte Albán II temples on the summit of Mound 1. Structure 22 had its staircase on the east, facing Structure 36 (or 35 or 13, depending on which was in use at the time). Structure 21 also had its staircase on the east, facing Structure 29. The alignments of these pairs of temples were not perfect, since Structures 36 and 29 had been built atop old Rosario phase platforms, while Structures 21 and 22 were built directly on the surface of the hill.

Figure 14.17 shows the location of Structures 21 and 22, relative to the northwest corner of Structure 19. Neither temple was well preserved; most of the western, or rear, wall of Structure 21 had eroded down the slopes of Mound 1. Structure 22 was even more badly destroyed, since the late-nineteenth-century owner of the hacienda to which Mound 1 belonged had sent workmen to quarry it for its dressed stones. One of our older workmen had lived on the hacienda at that time, and he remembered the stone robbing.

Drain

Figure 14.16. At some point, the west wall of Structure 19 began to lean outward under the weight of its overburden (far right). The Monte Albán II architects braced it by building a thick masonry pavement between it and Structure 21. The workmen who removed the pavement to expose the façade of Structure 21 discovered a drain to divert rain runoff. (In this photo, the eastern portion of the pavement has already been removed.)

We estimate that Structure 21 may originally have measured 11.7 m east-west and 12.5 m north-south. Its north-south dimension includes two exterior walkways that we called the north apron and the south apron (Fig. 14.17). These aprons would have allowed priests to leave Structure 21 without descending the broad staircase on its east side (Fig. 14.18); they could simply exit the outer room, turn a corner, and walk west along one of the aprons. Each apron had a step attached to it; one stepped down to the west from the north apron, and down to the south from the south apron (Fig. 14.19).

We immediately guessed that these walkways were designed to allow priests to enter the temple by a route not available to ordinary worshipers. We only grasped the full significance of this route, however, after we discovered that there were two secret staircases on the west side of Mound 1 (see Chapter 15). These two roofed staircases would have allowed priests to ascend the mound without being seen, appearing mysteriously on the summit.

The outer room of Structure 21 measured roughly 8 by 3 m, while the poorly preserved inner room was 8 m by more than 4.5 m. The step-up between rooms was 30–35 cm (Fig. 14.20). We found faint traces of rubble columns to either side of the doorway to the outer room, but no traces had been preserved in the inner room. For that reason, our artist has omitted inner room columns in his reconstruction drawing of Structure 21 (Fig. 14.21). The inner room did have a built-in basin in the floor, designated Feature 74; its location can be seen in Figures 14.19 and 14.20.

While the stone foundation for the north wall of Structure 21 was preserved to a height of 1 m (Fig. 14.22), the adobe walls themselves had eroded away. We established an arbitrary datum point near a surviving patch of floor in the inner room, and from there all depths were taken. No offering boxes were discovered below the building, and all we found in Feature 74 was a pecked stone ball 4 cm in diameter, an artifact that could date to any period (Fig. 14.23*b*).

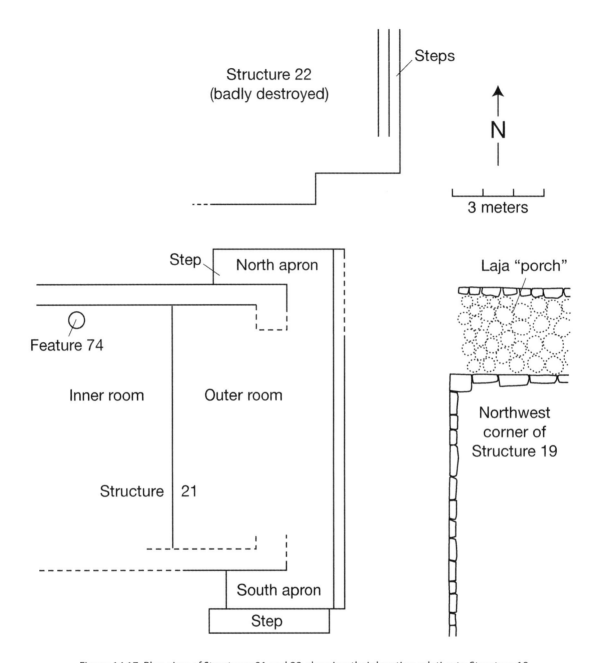

Figure 14.17. Plan view of Structures 21 and 22, showing their location relative to Structure 19.

Figure 14.18. The relationship of Structures 21 and 22. In this photo (taken from the south) the workman at left sweeps the outer room of Structure 21, which extends into the foreground. The low mound in the background covers what is left of Structure 22. Note that the stairway for Structure 21 runs the entire length of the temple's east side.

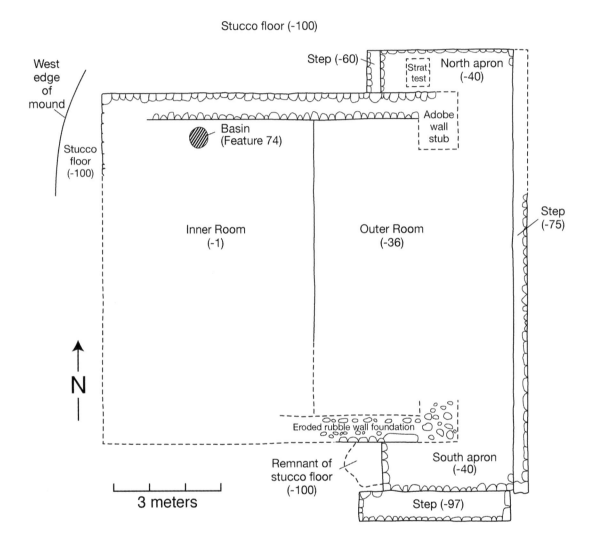

Stucco floor (-100)

West edge of mound

Step (-60)

Strat test

North apron (-40)

Stucco floor (-100)

Basin (Feature 74)

Adobe wall stub

Inner Room (-1)

Outer Room (-36)

Step (-75)

N

Eroded rubble wall foundation

3 meters

Remnant of stucco floor (-100)

South apron (-40)

Step (-97)

Figure 14.19. Plan view of Structure 21. The depths shown are in centimeters below the arbitrary datum established in the inner room.

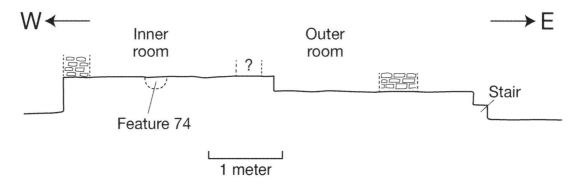

Figure 14.20. West-to-east cross-section of Structure 21.

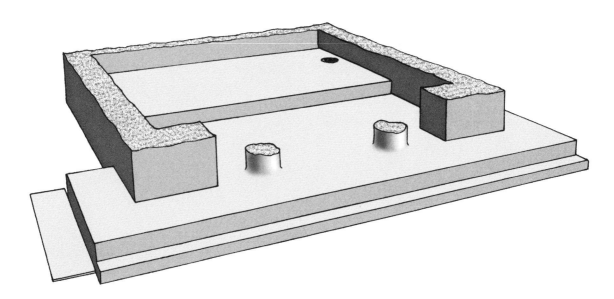

Figure 14.21. Artist's conception of Structure 21 as it might have looked not long after abandonment. (Based on a drawing by David West Reynolds.)

Figure 14.22. Two views of Structure 21. *Left*, a mason consolidates the north wall, while excavators expose the outer room (*L*) and the inner room (*R*). *Right*, the northwest corner of the outer room, showing the 30 cm step-up to the inner room.

Dating Structure 21 with Ceramics

To date Structure 21, we turned to the only part of the temple that seemed to have an unbroken plaster floor. This was the north apron, and we placed a stratigraphic test pit there to recover a sherd sample from the fill sealed below the stucco floor (Fig. 14.24).

The fill of the apron was 70 cm deep and featured a layer of fallen stucco at a depth of 45 cm. The diagnostic sherds in the upper 45 cm were as follows:

CBA *GRIS* WARE DIAGNOSTICS
rims of G3 bowls: 10
sherd of G21 bowl: 1

CBA *CREMA* WARE DIAGNOSTICS
sherds of C7 bowls: 5

REDEPOSITED EARLIER CERAMICS
sherds of the San José, Guadalupe, and Rosario phases: 20

There were fewer ceramics in the fill below the layer of fallen stucco. The diagnostic sherds at a depth of 45–70 cm were as follows:

CBA *GRIS* WARE DIAGNOSTICS
rims of G3 bowls: 6

CBA *CREMA* WARE DIAGNOSTICS
sherd of C7 bowl: 1

REDEPOSITED EARLIER CERAMICS
sherds of the Guadalupe and Rosario phases: 10

As mentioned earlier, no offering boxes were found below the badly destroyed floor of Structure 21. Our search for such boxes did, however, produce an additional collection of ceramics from the subfloor fill of the building. The diagnostic sherds from this collection were as follows:

CBA *GRIS* WARE DIAGNOSTICS
rims of G3 bowls: 3
sherd of subtype G12b: 1
sherd of G21 bowl: 1
sherds of Monte Albán II version of G35: 5

CBA *CREMA* WARE DIAGNOSTICS
fragment of effigy vessel, showing face of grotesque appliqué
    figure: 1 (Fig. 14.25)

In sum, while most ceramics from the fill of Structure 21 were redeposited sherds from earlier periods, the fill also had its share of Monte Albán II diagnostics.

Figure 14.23. Feature 74 was a plastered basin set in the floor of the inner room, Structure 21. *a*, masons consolidate the fragile rim of the basin. *b*, a pecked stone ball found in Feature 74.

Figure 14.24. The aprons flanking Structure 21. *Left*, workmen expose the step running next to the south apron. *Right*, the north apron and the step descending from it. The rectangular pit near the north arrow is a stratigraphic test excavated in the earthen fill below the undisturbed plaster floor.

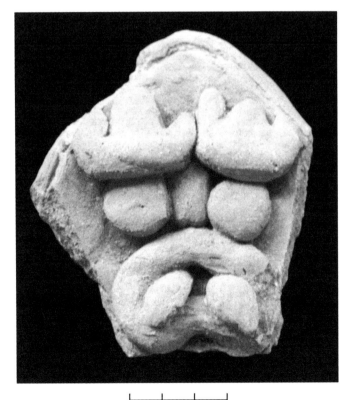

3 cm

Figure 14.25. Sherd from the fill of Structure 21, bearing a *Cociyo-*like face modeled in appliqué.

Figure 14.26. Structure 22, seen from the southeast. This corner of the temple was the least destroyed by stone-robbing.

Structure 22

As for Structure 22, it lay less than a meter and a half north of Structure 21 and seems to have been a larger temple. Unfortunately, as mentioned earlier, the work crews sent by the hacienda owner had left it virtually shapeless. We were able to map the southeast corner (Fig. 14.26), but the interior of the building had been ransacked for dressed stone. We were able to determine that the staircase had been on the east side and consisted of four well-made flagstone steps (Fig. 14.27).

The destruction of Structure 22 is unfortunate, because this building may once have been one of the largest and most important of the temples on Mound 1. None of the others had as labor-intensive a masonry staircase as this one. In addition to being a notable architectural feature in its own right, the Structure 22 staircase reinforces our conclusion that the adobe staircase built for Structure 36 was an anomaly resulting from the Monte Albán II remodeling of Structure 14.

Dating Structure 22 with Ceramics

While we were eager to date Structure 22, we feared that the destruction wrought by the *hacendado* might make that impossible. Despite our misgivings, we decided to make a 2 × 2 m stratigraphic test near the center of the building. The loose stones covering the surface yielded about 100 sherds, including such Monte Albán II diagnostics as Types G3, G12b, C7, C12, and C20. The bulk of the sherds, however, were redeposited diagnostics of the San José, Guadalupe, and Rosario phases.

Eventually we cleared the last of the rubble and came down on a firmer, stonier layer that seemed to represent actual building fill. The uppermost 20 cm of this fill contained 2 G1 sherds, 6 G3s, a C7 bowl rim, and 1 K3 sherd.

At a depth of 20 to 40 cm, the stony fill produced several G3s, a G12b base, a G21 rim, a misfired C12 with postfiring zigzags, and a number of redeposited Formative sherds. At a depth of 40–60 cm, the fill changed to densely packed earth with fewer

Figure 14.27. The staircase on the east side of Structure 22.

stones. This earth produced a G1 brazier fragment, many G3s, a G21 rim, and a mix of sherds from earlier phases.

Finally, at a depth of 87 cm, we encountered a stucco floor that might date to an early construction stage of Structure 22. The sherds from this floor included fragments of G1 and G3 braziers; a G12 rim of unknown subtype; 8 fragments of Type G21; 4 C7 bowl sherds; 2 C11 bowl sherds; and close to 100 undecorated body sherds, about a third of them displaying *café* paste. We suspended our excavation at that time because the damage to the temple appeared too great to justify our continuing, and we saw no reason to doubt that Structure 22 was another Monte Albán II temple.

15 | Solving the Mystery of don Leandro's Tunnel

The Monte Albán II architects did more than build a group of four temples on Mound 1 at San José Mogote. They also dressed up that natural hill to resemble an artificial pyramid.

San José's architects, of course, shared this strategy of dressing up natural hills with the builders of Monte Albán. Another shared strategy was to modify only as much of the hill as necessary; the south and east slopes of Mound 1 were not nearly as dressed up as the north and west slopes (Fig. 15.1).

On the important north side of Mound 1, which faced the site's main plaza, the Monte Albán II architects created a wide stone masonry staircase (Fig. 15.2). Our University of Michigan project detected this staircase during our work in the 1970s, but we had neither the time nor the budget to expose it. Fortunately, in 1996, Enrique Fernández Dávila of the Instituto Nacional de Antropología e Historia both excavated and consolidated the surviving north staircase (Fernández Dávila 1997).

Fernández's work leaves little doubt that the Monte Albán II architects considered Mound 1 at San José Mogote to be a counterpart to the South Platform at Monte Albán. It was on the plaza side of the mound that they created the broad, public-access staircase by means of which worshippers could ascend to the four temples on its summit. The east side of Mound 1 was given no comparable enhancement. We know this from the fact that in 1974 we made a step trench down the northeastern slope of Mound 1 and encountered no traces of a façade (see Appendix A).

It was on the west side of Mound 1 that the most interesting architectural enhancements were found. These were Stairways 1 and 2, whose locations are shown in Figure 15.1.

As mentioned in the previous chapter, the nineteenth-century owner of the Hacienda del Cacique had been active in robbing dressed stone from the buildings on Mound 1. One of our oldest workmen, don Leandro Méndez, had been a young boy on the hacienda during that era, and remembered watching the *hacendado*'s laborers removing the stones. What he remembered most vividly was that the workmen discovered a "tunnel" of some kind on the west side of the mound. One of the workmen entered the dark tunnel holding a candle, and when a wind gust blew it out, he changed his mind and retreated.

Amused by the story, our younger workmen soon began to refer jokingly to "don Leandro's tunnel." During most of the 1970s, when no tunnel had as yet come to light, the story began to take on the status of a myth. "Hey, tío Leandro," asked one of his many nephews, "how much mezcal had you had when you saw the tunnel?"

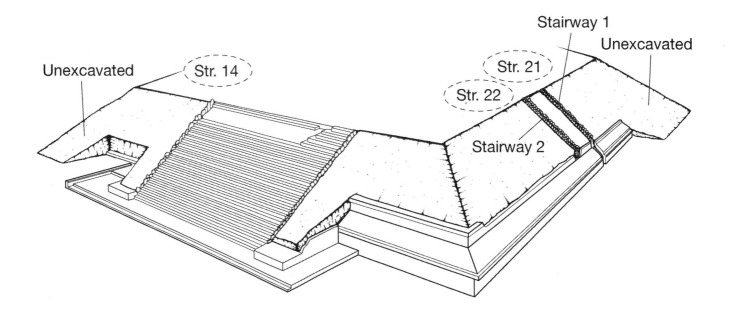

Figure 15.1. The Monte Albán II architects dressed Mound 1 up to resemble a giant pyramidal platform by adding stone masonry walls to the north and west sides. A wide staircase ascended the north side, which faced the main plaza; two narrow, roofed stairways (hidden on the west side) allowed priests to reach Structures 21 and 22. This drawing is based on the work of Enrique Fernández Dávila (1997:21).

And then, in 1980, while attempting to find the rear wall of Structure 21, we stumbled onto what we now believe was don Leandro's tunnel. It was a secret stairway on the west side of Mound 1, the kind of well-hidden access route that the excavators of Monte Negro in the Mixteca referred to as a *pasillo techado* (Acosta and Romero 1992).

Stairway 1 is shown in Figures 15.3–15.5. It was a narrow, single-file staircase that began at the base of the mound and ascended to the summit near the rear of Structure 21. Its walls were of strong limestone masonry, and it had originally been completely roofed with stones, allowing it to be covered with earth and effectively hidden from view. Unfortunately, the hacienda owner's workmen had removed all of the roof stones save for one, a specimen that may have been too heavy for them to lift. The surviving roof stone was 35 cm thick and 1.3 m wide, easily

spanning the stairway. This roof stone, which was located in the vicinity of Steps 5–7 (counting up from the bottom), would have rested at a height of 1.5–2.0 m, depending on where one stood on the steps below. In other words, a Zapotec man of average height could have remained fully upright on the stairs while ascending or descending.

Stairway 1 was clearly designed to allow a priest to enter a stone-lined, meter-wide doorway at ground level and vanish into darkness. He would travel 2.6 m through that darkness before he reached the first step up, probably giving the impression that he had disappeared into the interior of the mound. From that point on, he would ascend a staircase from which 20 steps still survive.

Those steps were limestone slabs, averaging 60–70 cm long from front to back and 33–38 cm thick. They overlapped in such a way that only half of each slab was exposed as a step, the rest

Figure 15.2. Remains of the wide Monte Albán II staircase ascending the north face of Mound 1. (Excavation and consolidation by Enrique Fernández Dávila 1997.)

Figure 15.3. Stairway 1, a roofed staircase on the west side of Mound 1, found by the University of Michigan in 1980. Only one of the roof stones of this staircase remained in situ, the others having been removed as construction material for the late nineteenth-century hacienda.

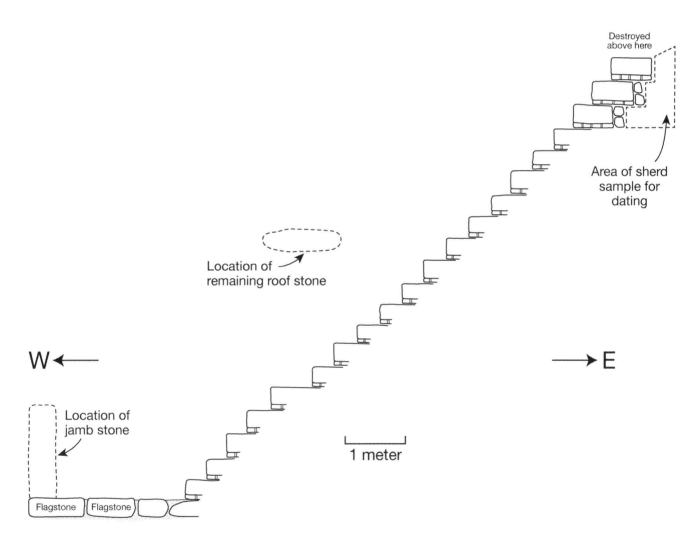

Destroyed
above here

Area of sherd
sample for
dating

Location of
remaining roof stone

W ←

→ E

1 meter

Location of
jamb stone

Flagstone   Flagstone

Figure 15.4. West-to-east cross-section of Stairway 1, showing the relationship of the 20 surviving steps to the northern jamb stone and the lone remaining roof stone. A sample of sherds from the area enclosed by dashed lines showed the staircase to be a Monte Albán II construction.

Figure 15.5. Stairway 1 on the west side of Mound 1 was exposed (and later backfilled) by the University of Michigan in 1980. Enrique Fernández Dávila (1997) later re-excavated the staircase and exposed the associated walls added to Mound 1 during Monte Albán II.

being buried under the slab above. As a result, the actual tread of each step measured 30–35 cm from front to back. Each step was leveled by being set on smaller *lajas*, or paving stones.

Not only had the *hacendado*'s workmen removed all but one of the stairway's roof stones, they had also destroyed everything above the twentieth step. The fill behind the eighteenth, nineteenth, and twentieth steps, however, appeared to be intact, so we screened it for ceramics. The diagnostics from this sherd sample were as follows:

CBA *GRIS* WARE DIAGNOSTICS
    rims of G1 bowls: 5–6
    rims of G3 bowls: 3
    cane-swirled base of G21 bowl: 1

rims from Monte Albán II version of G35: 3
fragment of brazier: 1

CBA *CREMA* WARE DIAGNOSTICS
    sherd of C6 bowl, postfiring zigzags: 1
    rim of C7 vertical-walled bowl: 1

CBA *CAFÉ* WARE DIAGNOSTICS
    sherds from K3 bowls: 3

REDEPOSITED DIAGNOSTICS FROM EARLIER PERIODS
    sherds of the San José, Guadalupe, Rosario, and Monte Albán
      Ia phases: 24

Figure 15.6. Excavations by Enrique Fernández Dávila (1997) exposed Stairway 2, a second single-file staircase on the west side of Mound 1.

In addition, while consolidating the remaining stairway, our masons found an eroded Type A11 sherd lodged between two limestone slabs. All in all, our sherd sample from Stairway 1 confirmed our expectation that this secret access route had been built during Monte Albán II, just like Structure 21. Hidden stairs, subplaza tunnels, and *pasillos techados* were not uncommon features of Monte Albán I and II, and suggest that the priests of that era carried out a great deal of ritual hocus-pocus.

In 1980, we were asked by the Instituto Nacional de Antropología e Historia to backfill Stairway 1, which they felt posed a danger to the small children who played around Mound 1. We agreed that a fall from the top of the stairway could be dangerous, and covered the feature with dirt. In 1996, however, Enrique Fernández Dávila reopened Stairway 1 and exposed the horizontal walls that had been added to either side of it by the Monte Albán II architects (Fig. 15.5). Fernández then went on to excavate and consolidate Stairway 2, a second, nearly identical secret stairway to the north (Fig. 15.6).

No roof stones were found in place on Stairway 2, which seems to have led to Structure 22. Either Stairway 2 was unroofed, or (more likely) the roof stones had all been removed by the *hacendado*'s workmen. Our eyewitness informant, don Leandro Méndez, always maintained that any "tunnel" or "tunnels" on the west side of the mound were roofed (and hence dark and scary) when originally discovered.

We are indebted to Fernández Dávila for his work on the façade of Mound 1. His excavations reinforce the fact that during the millennium from 500 BC to AD 500, religious buildings in Oaxaca—whether at Monte Negro, Monte Albán, or San José Mogote—sometimes had separate entrances for the worshipers and the priestly staff, and that the entrances for the priestly staff might be hidden from view. This fact underscores the growing divide between the commoner worshiper and the official priests of the Zapotec state, who possessed esoteric knowledge not shared with everyone.

16 | The Temples of Mound 3
by Ronald Spores

Mound 3 is a low promontory in the eastern half of the main plaza at San José Mogote (Fig. 13.1). Along with Mounds 4, 5, and 6, it is one of a group of four mounds in the plaza that likely supported temples in the past. Because the spacing of these four mounds is neither equidistant nor symmetrical, it seems possible that their placement was designed so as to take advantage of natural rises in the terrain.

In July of 1979, finding myself in a momentary pause between two stages of my research in the Mixteca, I was invited by the University of Michigan to undertake a stratigraphic investigation of Mound 3. Among the questions to be answered were: (1) Did the mound, indeed, house a temple? (2) Did that temple date to Monte Albán II, the period to which so many of the buildings on the main plaza dated? And (3) had any such temple been built on a natural rise, or was it placed atop a building from an earlier period?

Figure 16.1 provides a view of Mound 3 from the south at the beginning of work. Our first task was to clear the mesquite and acacia trees from the surface of the mound so that we could lay out a 2 × 2 m grid oriented magnetic north-south (Fig. 16.2). In the course of sweeping the mound surface in preparation for the grid, we recovered the following sherds:

1 waxy orange bowl base of the CBA Type C7
1 sherd of a Type C11 vessel with postfiring zigzags
2 sherds of a Type C20 vessel with a waxy black slip over *crema* paste
1 outleaned-wall bowl of Type G1
1 gray bowl rim with two parallel incised lines, reminiscent of Type G12b
1 brazier fragment with 2 appliqué disks

The mound surface also yielded a small jadeite bead of the type often placed in the mouths of San José phase burials (Fig. 16.3). To be sure, we knew that finding this bead did not necessarily mean that we would encounter in situ San José phase material; the bead might have come from a tertiary context, such as basketloads of building fill.

Structure 32

Less than 10 cm below the surface of the mound, in Square N7E8 of our grid, we encountered a patch of stucco floor. This patch of floor lay 0–5 cm above the arbitrary datum established

Figure 16.1. Mound 3 at the start of excavation, 1979.

for our excavation. It soon became clear that the floor belonged to the inner room of a two-room temple.

Not far to the west, in Squares N8E6–N6E6, we found the stucco floor of the outer room (Figs. 16.4, 16.5). This floor lay 29 to 32 cm below our arbitrary datum, reflecting the usual step-up between the outer and inner rooms of the temple.

The following diagnostic sherds lay stratigraphically above the surviving floor remnants of Structure 32:

4 sherds of CBA Type C7, including the flaring rim of a bowl
1 flaring rim from a Type C6 bowl
1 everted rim from a Type C11 bowl
1 sherd from a bowl of Type C20
1 jar rim of Type C2
1 fragment of mammiform support in *crema* ware
1 outleaned wall from a subtype G12b bowl
several rims of Type G3 bowls
several rims of Type G1 bowls
several redeposited sherds of the Rosario and San José phases

After drawing and photographing what remained of Structure 32, we proceeded downward to see if any earlier buildings lay below it. In the process, we carefully collected all the diagnostic sherds sealed beneath the surviving patches of stucco floor. That subfloor collection was as follows:

at least 2 rims of Type C2 jars
4 sherds of Type C7 bowls (Fig. 16.6a)
2 sherds of Type C11
1 slightly everted rim from a *crema* bowl
1 fragment from a Type C1 brazier
1 rim sherd of Type G12
9 sherds from Type G21 bowl bases, with swirling decoration done with a slat of cane
several rims of gray cylinders with ledges to support lids
1 perforated support from a Type G3 (?) bowl (Fig. 16.6b)
several sherds from Type G3 jars
1 sherd from the handle of a gray incense burner
1 sherd from a gray annular base

Figure 16.2. Workmen clearing the mesquite and acacia trees from Mound 3 prior to laying out the 2 × 2 m grid used during excavation.

several sherds with *café* paste
redeposited sherds of the Rosario and San José phases

Based on the ceramics found above and below the Structure 32 floor, we can assign the building to the Monte Albán II period.

Structure 33

Some 40 cm below Structure 32, we began finding traces of an earlier two-room temple, which we designated Structure 33. We reached the floor of the inner room at an average depth of 46 cm below datum. The floor of the outer room lay about 72 cm below datum, meaning that the step-up between the two rooms was roughly 26 cm.

Owing to erosion, Structure 33 was represented only by patches of stucco floor. Those patches, however, provided more information than we had recovered from Structure 32. This temple had also faced west, and the door to the inner room was flanked by two rubble columns spaced roughly 5 m apart (Fig. 16.7). Some

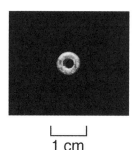

1 cm

Figure 16.3. Small jadeite bead from the surface of Mound 3. This bead resembles many of those placed in the mouths of San José phase burials.

Figure 16.4. In this view from the north, a workman sweeps what is left of the stucco floor of Structure 32. He kneels in the outer room; to the left of his whisk broom is the step-up to the inner room..

40 cm beyond the base of each column, as can be seen in the drawing, the stucco floor curled upward as if meeting the base of an adobe wall, since destroyed.

Enough remained of the northern column to suggest that it had consisted of a vertical stack of flat stone slabs, surrounded by smaller stony rubble set in mortar (Figs. 16.8, 16.9*b*). The southern column had been so completely destroyed that only a circular hole remained to indicate its location (Fig. 16.9*a*).

One of the most significant features of the inner room was a 12 m² intrusive pit through the stucco floor, placed between the two columns (Fig. 16.7). The pit had ragged edges but was generally rectangular, occupying parts of squares N8E8, N8E9, N7E8, and N7E9. This pit (which continued down to at least 2 m below datum) was clearly prehispanic, since it had been dug before Structure 32 was built.

While we do not know the purpose for the intrusive pit, we can offer a suggestion, based on the Monte Albán II temples found on Mound 1 of San José Mogote (Chapter 13). Many of those temples had dedicatory offerings below their floors, and at least some of those offerings appear to have been removed at the time that the temple was abandoned. It is possible, therefore, that an offering was removed from below the inner room of Structure 33 before that temple was abandoned.

We recovered additional data on Structure 33 from its outer room. A remnant of that room's stucco floor, 12 m long north-south and up to 4 m wide east-west, had been preserved. In places it exhibited dark areas of burnt floor, almost certainly locations where the glowing charcoal from incense burners had scorched the lime plaster.

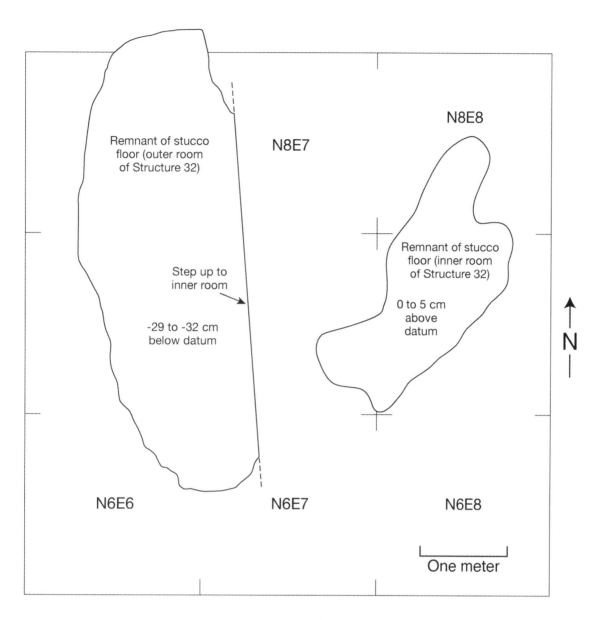

Above: Figure 16.5. Surviving remnants of Structure 32, the final Monte Albán II temple built on Mound 3. This temple would have faced true west (the arrow indicates magnetic north).

Left: Figure 16.6. Sherds found below Structure 32 and above Structure 33. *a*, rim of outleaned-wall bowl in CBA Type C7 (waxy orange on interior, waxy red on exterior). *b*, perforated support from tripod bowl, CBA Type G3 (?).

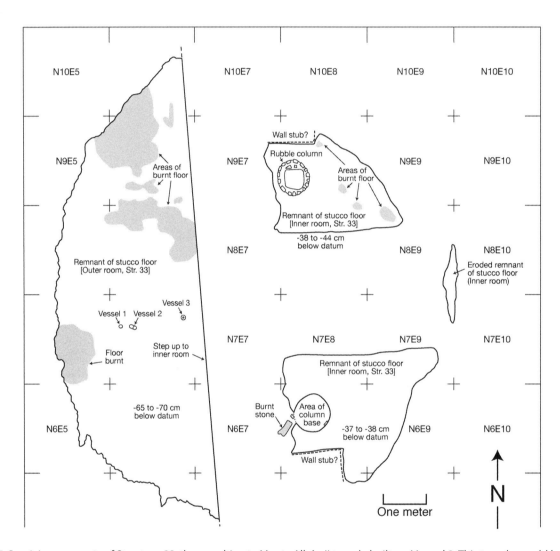

Figure 16.7. Surviving remnants of Structure 33, the penultimate Monte Albán II temple built on Mound 3. This temple would have faced true west (the arrow indicates magnetic north). In the southern half of Squares N8E8 and N8E9 and the northern half of N7E8 and N7E9, the floor of the inner room had been removed by an intrusive pit. This pit may have been made to retrieve a subfloor offering before Structure 33 was razed.

Left: Figure 16.8. The excavation of Structure 33. The workman in the foreground is sweeping the outer room of the temple; immediately behind his whisk broom lies the eroded step-up to the inner room. Two meters farther away, we see a circle of stones marking the base of a rubble column on the stucco floor of the inner room. (View from the west.)

Right: Figure 16.9. Surviving traces of the rubble columns from the inner room of Structure 33. In *a*, only a break in the stucco floor indicates where the southern column stood. In *b*, a stone slab from the core of the northern column remains.

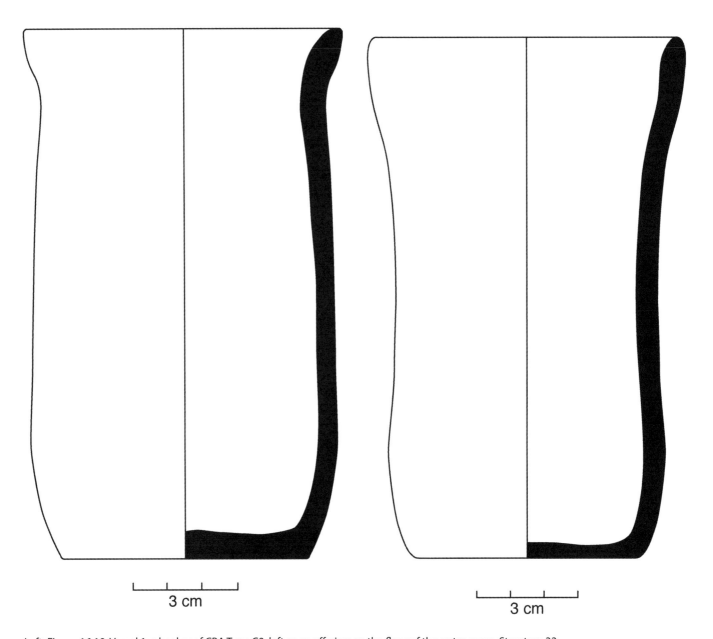

Left: Figure 16.10. Vessel 1, a beaker of CBA Type G3, left as an offering on the floor of the outer room, Structure 33.

Right: Figure 16.11. Vessel 2, a beaker of CBA Type G3, left as an offering on the floor of the outer room, Structure 33.

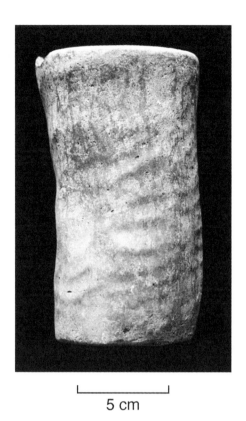

5 cm

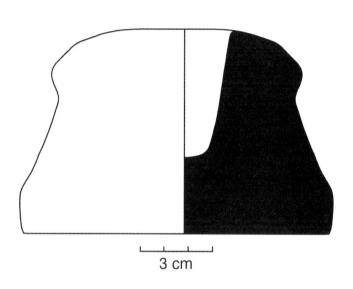

3 cm

Left: Figure 16.12. Vessel 2, showing the rippled surface left by streaky and unstandardized burnishing.

Right: Figure 16.13. Vessel 3, an object of unfired clay left on the floor of the outer room, Structure 33. We are not sure whether this object represents an unfinished ceramic vessel, or the mold around which other vessels would be formed. The clay body is of the *crema* type common at Atzompa and Cacaotepec.

Three complete vessels had been left behind on the floor of the outer room, presumably offerings made at the time of abandonment. These vessels, all found in Square N7E6, reminded us of the gray beakers left behind with Structures 13 and 35 of Mound 1 (Chapter 13). Vessel 1, the westernmost, was a beaker of CBA Type G3 (Fig. 16.10). Vessel 2 was also a Type G3 beaker, but with a slightly different rim form (Figs. 16.11, 16.12). Vessel 3, the easternmost, was an unusual object of unfired clay (Fig. 16.13). We are not sure whether this object was an unfinished vessel, or the clay mold from which additional vessels could be formed. Its clay body was of the same type used for *crema* ware.

After Structure 33 had been drawn and photographed, we removed some of the intact patches of stucco floor to obtain sealed-in sherd samples. The sherds trapped below the floor of the inner room came as close to being a pure Monte Albán II sample as any we recovered. Included were 6 fragments of Type G21 bowls with cane-swirled interior bases (Fig. 16.14*b*, *c*) and 2 large pieces of a Type K3 bowl.

Trapped below the floor of the outer room of Structure 33 were the following additional sherds:

2 incised bases of Type G12 bowls, all of the subtype called G12b by Spencer, Redmond, and Elson (2008) (Fig. 16.14*a*)
1 rim of a bridgespout vessel in Type G3 (?) (Fig. 16.15*a*).
several rims from composite silhouette bowls of Type C6 (Fig. 16.15*b*)
several fragments of G21 bowls
several redeposited sherds of the San José and Rosario phases (e.g., Fig. 16.15*c*)

Based on the ceramics trapped beneath the stucco floor, as well as the whole vessels found on the floor of the outer room, we concluded that Structure 33 dated to Monte Albán II.

The Intrusive Pit through the Floor of Structure 33

Before proceeding downward to see what earlier buildings might have preceded Structure 33, we turned our attention to the intrusive pit in Squares N8E8–9 and N7E8–9. As previously

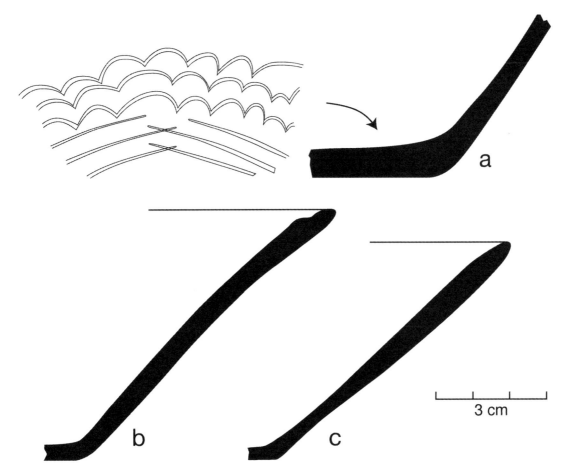

Figure 16.14. Sherds found stratigraphically below the floor of Structure 33. *a*, incised base of a Type G12b (accidentally oxidized). *b* and *c* are bowls of CBA Type G21, with swirls made on the interior of the base with a cane slat.

mentioned, we suspected that this pit had been dug in an effort to retrieve an important offering (or offerings) from below the inner room of Structure 33. Our suspicions were only strengthened by the fact that the fill of the pit contained objects of rock crystal, mother-of-pearl, and coral, found nowhere else in our excavation. This raised the possibility that in the process of retrieving any major offerings, the creators of the pit had left behind (and sometimes damaged) a range of smaller items.

Some of the objects recovered from the fill of the pit are shown in Figure 16.16. Items *a–d* are all of rock crystal. Figure 16.16*a* is a perforated disk that may have been part of an earspool. It is 34 mm in diameter and 3 mm thick; the central hole is 3 mm in diameter, flat on one side and beveled on the other. Figures 16.16*b* and *c* are tubular beads. Figure 16.16*b* is 25 mm long and 10 mm in diameter, and its wall less than a millimeter thick; Figure 16.16*c* is 27 mm long, 10 mm in diameter, and equally

thin-walled. Figure 16.16*d* is a circular bead 12 mm in diameter and 7 mm thick; it had been biconically drilled, with its opening 4 mm wide at the surface and 1 mm wide in the center.

Object Figure 16.16*e* is a circular greenstone bead, 13 mm in diameter and 8 mm thick, with a hole 2 mm in diameter (uniform rather than biconical).

The 5 items shown in Fig. 16.16*f* are all broken ornaments, cut from valves of the pearl oyster *Pinctada mazatlanica* and perforated for suspension. They were found together in Square N8E8 at a depth of 1.8 m below datum. The ornament at upper left may once have been rectangular and 25–30 mm on a side; the ornament at upper right was similar in shape but smaller. The items at center and lower left may once have been rectangular plaques, each estimated to have measured 30 cm by 14 cm. The ornament at lower right is too broken to reconstruct.

These 5 ornaments were accompanied by 8 leftover fragments

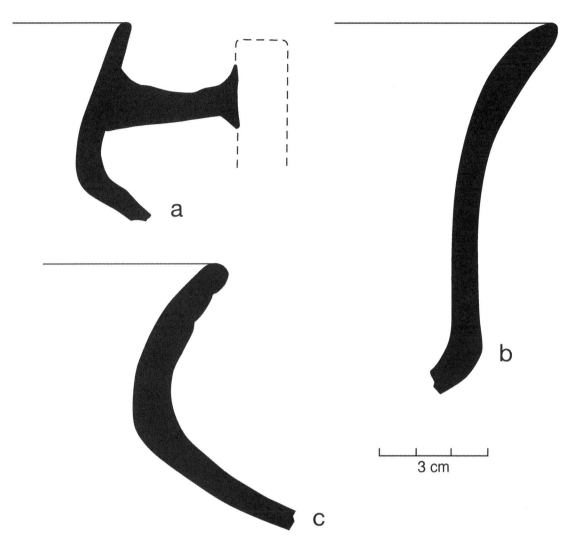

Figure 16.15. Sherds found stratigraphically below the floor of Structure 33. *a*, rim of bridgespout jar, Type G3 (?). *b*, composite silhouette bowl of Type C6 (streaky-burnished light brown slip over *crema* clay body). *c*, rim of Fidencio Coarse jar with weak red wash (redeposited Middle Formative sherd).

of pearl oyster valve, including the hinge section from one shell. It is possible, in other words, that all 5 ornaments were made from a single large oyster, with the leftover parts included by the artisan when the ornaments were delivered. This was a not uncommon practice at San José Mogote.

We found additional mother-of-pearl items in the fill of the pit. At a depth of 1.7 m in Square N8E8 there were 2 more broken ornaments. One was a rectangular plaque, roughly 30 mm by 14 mm, resembling the item at lower left in Figure 16.16*f*. The other item, too shattered to reconstruct, might once have measured 23 mm on a side. Both items had broken at or near the perforations, which is a weak point in most mother-of-pearl ornaments.

At a depth of 1.0 m in N8E8, we recovered 3 more shattered mother-of-pearl ornaments with perforations. Their original dimensions might have been (1) 25 × 15 mm, (2) 27 × 19 mm, and (3) 28 × 24 mm.

Finally, in Figure 16.16*g* we see a piece of branching, creamy white coral from a depth of 1.45 m in Square N8E8. This piece of coral was 10 cm long, 4.5 cm wide, and 3 cm high. Coral was extremely rare at San José Mogote, making it all the more likely that this item was once part of an offering.

A few other items in the fill of the pit are worthy of mention. At a depth of 1.7 m in Square N8E8, we found a small deposit of dry red pigment, strongly resembling that used to coat the jade offerings found with Structure 35 on Mound 1 (Chapter 13). At a depth of 1.35 m in the same square we found a blade of translucent gray obsidian, similar to the blades left behind on the floor of Structure 35.

The most numerous items found in the fill of the pit, to be sure, were pot sherds. The types present reinforce our conclusion that the pit cannot be later than Monte Albán II in date.

The grayware diagnostics in the pit fill included a dozen

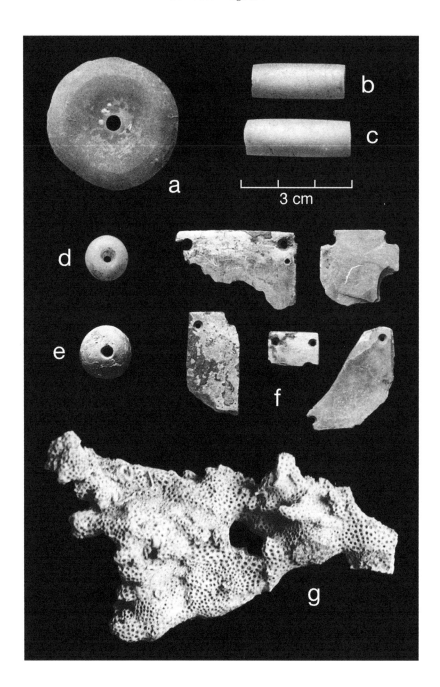

sherds of CBA Type G3; 2 comb-incised bowl bases of Spencer, Redmond, and Elson's subtype G12b; half a dozen bowl rims with the incised parallel lines typical of Type G12b; 9 or 10 clear examples of Type G21 cane-swirled bowl bases; several rim-to-base sections of the Monte Albán II version of the Type G35 bowl; 1 fragment from a bridgespout vessel; and 1 fragment of the pedestal base from an incense brazier.

Crema sherds from the fill of the pit included more than a dozen CBA Type C2 jar rims; 6 hollow supports from Type C7 bowls, 1 of them mammiform; and several waxy orange sherds from C7 bowls.

Café fragments from the fill consisted almost entirely of CBA Type K3 bowl sherds. *Amarillo* diagnostics, on the other hand,

were more varied. Included were 1 flaring wall bowl; the spout from a bridgespout vessel; and 2 fragments of Type A9 incense braziers. Most numerous of the *amarillos*, however, were sherds of Type A11. Included were 1 small hemispherical bowl with an incised design, and 2 or 3 fragments of tall, Type A11 cylinders with ledge rims that could have supported lids.

Structure 34

Once we had cleaned out the pit that intruded through the floor of Structure 33, we continued downward to see if any earlier buildings could be found. The fill below Structure 33 consisted

Opposite: Figure 16.16. Items recovered from the fill of an ancient pit, intrusive through the floor of Structure 33 and into Structure 34. *a*, rock crystal component from an earspool. *b, c*, tubular rock crystal beads. *d*, circular rock crystal bead. *e*, greenstone bead. *f*, five ornaments made from pearl oyster. *g*, section of branching coral.

Below: Figure 16.17. Sherds recovered below Structure 33 and above Structure 34. *a–c* are CBA Type G12 bowls of subtype G12b. *d* and *e* are bowls of CBA Type G21.

of brown earth with construction stones, fragments of charcoal and plaster, and loose adobes averaging 41 × 20 × 8 cm in size. Sherds were abundant in the fill and included many of the same Monte Albán II types we had encountered in the upper levels of the excavation. Figure 16.17 shows some of the Type G12 and G21 bowl sherds we recovered. All G12 comb-incised bases were of the subtypes G12b or G12c.

At depths varying from 1.04 to 1.16 m below datum, we came upon the eroded remains of an earlier stucco floor, which we designated Structure 34 (Fig. 16.18). We did not find the limits of this floor, which looked, in every way, like the floor of another Monte Albán II temple. Unfortunately, it had been damaged by the deep intrusive pit coming down from Structure 33.

On the floor of Structure 34, near the southern limits of Square N7E8, we found a hearthlike feature that may reflect ritual activity. A number of large incense brazier fragments lay directly on a patch of burned floor, covered by a heavy deposit of ash and charcoal. The fuel consisted of wood chunks, twigs, and reeds.

Figure 16.19 shows two of the brazier fragments from this deposit. The one on the left appears to be an animal effigy head, while the one on the right is a platelike flange bearing a red-painted design. Additional fragments of incense braziers appeared in the fill above the Structure 34 floor, reinforcing our evidence for the burning of incense. In Figure 16.20 we see two such fragments. The larger piece is one of the "ear flanges" that are often attached to the sides of braziers; it bears the "ring and

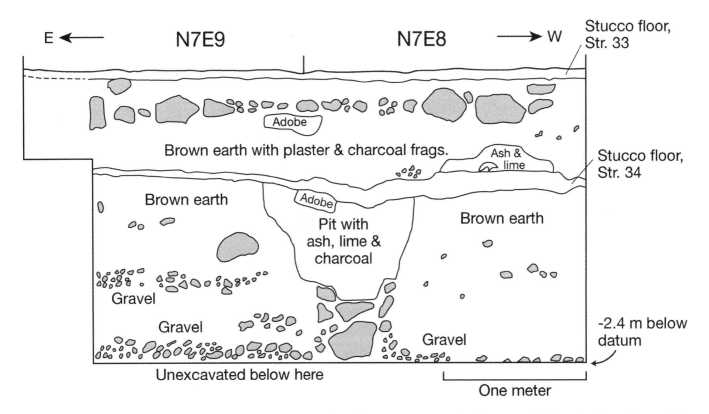

Figure 16.18. South profile of a stratigraphic pit below the stucco floor of Structure 33, Mound 3. This pit, made below the floor of the temple's inner room, revealed an earlier temple (Structure 34). Work was suspended after no further traces of architecture appeared in the next 1.2 m.

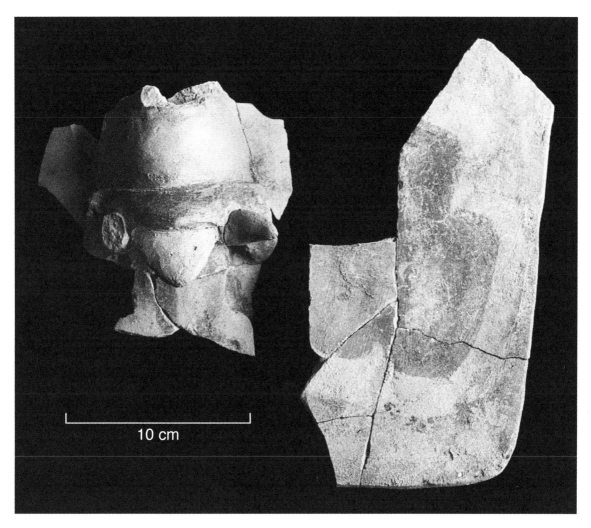

Figure 16.19. Incense brazier fragments recovered from a hearthlike area on the floor of Structure 34.

dot" motif, which is often interpreted as representing jadeite. The smaller piece may be part of a brazier fringe, and its motif suggests water droplets. None of the brazier fragments from Structure 34 would be out of place in Feature 20 of Mound 1, a huge deposit of temple trash (Chapter 13).

The Strata below Structure 34

After sweeping the floor of Structure 34, we removed it to search for earlier buildings. Sealed beneath the floor we found a small pit of unknown function, filled with ash, lime, and charcoal (Fig. 16.18).

The strata below Structure 34 consisted of brown earth with lenses of gravel. Sherds became increasingly less frequent as we proceeded downward, and we encountered no further traces of adobes, construction stone, plaster, or charcoal. By the time our excavation had reached a depth of 2.4 m below datum, we realized that we had seen no signs of an earlier building for the last 1.2 m.

After discussing the situation with Kent Flannery and Joyce Marcus, I decided to suspend work on Mound 3 at that point. Although we were still 3 m above the surface of the main plaza, all indications were that we were nearing sterile soil. This fact strongly suggested that part of Mound 3's height was indeed a low hill or natural rise. This use of natural rises was a common architectural strategy at San José Mogote.

While more of Mound 3 remains to be excavated—including any staircases on the west side, by means of which the temples would have been reached—our work had answered several questions. Structures 34, 33, and 32 very likely constituted a sequence of two-room temples, crowning a low natural hill in the main plaza. A possibility to be investigated in the future is that the Mound 3 temples were paired with a comparable sequence of east-facing temples atop Mound 6, some 50 m to the west.

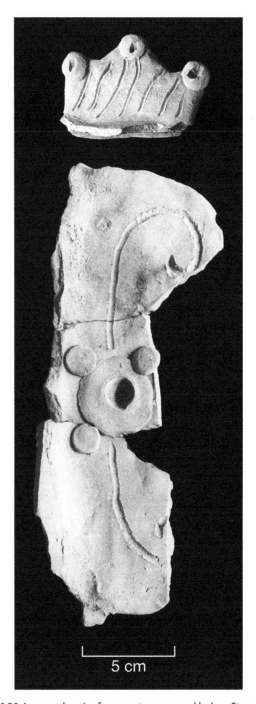

Figure 16.20. Incense brazier fragments recovered below Structure 33 and above Structure 34. The larger fragment is an "ear flange" with "ring and dot" decoration, similar to those from Feature 20 of Mound 1 (see Fig. 13.77).

17 | The Governmental Palace on Mound 8
by Kent V. Flannery and Dudley M. Varner

During the apogee of Monte Albán's role as their capital city, the Zapotec seem to have built at least two different kinds of palaces. The Patio Hundido on Monte Albán's North Platform was a likely place of assembly, one component of an administrative or governmental complex where affairs of state were conducted. That area of the North Platform may have served an important function, keeping the "palace of government" and the residence of the city's royal family in close proximity.

The Patio Hundido was elevated high above Monte Albán's main plaza, yet recessed deeply enough in the North Platform to hide its activities from the general public. Access to the patio required ascending a huge staircase, then passing through a portico with two echelons of heavy pilasters.

The Zapotec, however, also built palaces that were more private and residential. These residences consisted of 8–12 rooms arranged around an open interior court. The palaces associated with Tombs 104 and 105 are noteworthy examples. In both of the latter, an impressive royal tomb had been placed below the floor of the interior court. The heirs of the deceased lord evidently continued to live in his palace after his death, making offerings to him and sometimes adding deceased family members to the same tomb.

Early on, Kent Flannery and Joyce Marcus began to suspect that two mounds at the north end of San José Mogote's main plaza might house similar types of palaces. Mound 8, rising almost 8 m above the plaza, seemed to occupy a position analogous to the North Platform at Monte Albán (Fig. 17.1). On the other hand, Mound 9—directly south of Mound 8, and 6 m lower—looked like a good place for a residential palace.

Flannery and Marcus could not afford to investigate Mounds 8 and 9 in their entirety, but they felt that some sort of limited excavation might satisfy their curiosity about the role of these buildings. They eventually got their wish. In 1974, Judith and Robert Zeitlin agreed to test Mound 9, whose stratigraphy had been partially exposed by a bulldozer cut in the road between Guadalupe Etla and the Pan-American Highway (Chapter 18). In 1975, Dudley Varner joined Flannery in an effort to determine what kind of building had occupied the summit of Mound 8 (this chapter).

Mound 8

Mound 8 forms the northern border of the main plaza at San José Mogote. Two features led us to believe that a major public building might once have occupied its summit. First, the surface of the mound was extremely level, a condition we had come to associate with eroded adobe-walled palaces. Second, even before excavation began, we could see a series of huge limestone

Figure 17.1. The Monte Albán II nobles took over two elevated areas at San José Mogote. Mound 8, the higher, supported a likely governmental palace (Structure 17) and may also have been home to the site's most highly ranked noble family. Mound 9, the lower, had a residential complex for other noble families.

orthostats projecting above the surface. To reach their present position, these orthostats would have to have been dragged up the slopes of an 8 m high mound or natural hill.

In the summer of 1975, we began clearing brush from the summit of the mound with a crew of 13 experienced workmen. We next laid out a grid of 2 × 2 m squares, oriented magnetic north-south. We started our excavation in Square S5W6, just south of the line of orthostats, and almost immediately encountered a stucco-plastered step leading to the huge upright stones. It was soon clear that we were, in fact, dealing with a large building whose southern façade included the orthostats. Accordingly, we added 10 workmen to our crew and began excavating Squares S3W6 and S1W6.

Each square we excavated was taken down to the point where it reached a floor, a bench, or some other architectural feature. Within a week we had also opened up Squares S2W9, S3W8, and S3W10, giving us multiple stratigraphic profiles and architectural features. We could then begin to excavate the intervening squares with confidence. Soon we had exposed the entire row of orthostats and could see that they had been set upright on a raised masonry bench, just north of a stucco porch or portico (Fig. 17.2).

We soon decided to call the building with the orthostats Structure 17. We also formed two preliminary conclusions about the building. Our first conclusion was that we were probably dealing with a governmental palace, analogous to the one on Monte Albán's North Platform. Like the latter, Structure 17 had an impressive façade, a porch or portico whose roof had once been supported by large columns or pilasters, and an extensive sunken patio.

Our second conclusion was that the limestone orthostats had likely been robbed from Structure 14 on Mound 1 of San José Mogote. They strongly resembled the massive slabs used in the Rosario phase staircase on the east side of Structure 14. There was abundant evidence that many of those slabs had been pulled out of the original Rosario staircase during Monte Albán II (Chapter 13). Now we believed that we knew where many of those stones had been reused.

Figure 17.3 provides a plan view of the best-preserved part of Structure 17. Based on this portion of the building, we estimate Structure 17 to have once exceeded 30 m on a side. Its sunken patio, which may have been greater than 15 m west-to-east,

Figure 17.2. The façade of Structure 17 featured large limestone orthostats from the quarries at Rancho Matadamas. We suspect that many of these orthostats had been robbed from Structures 14 and 19 on Mound 1.

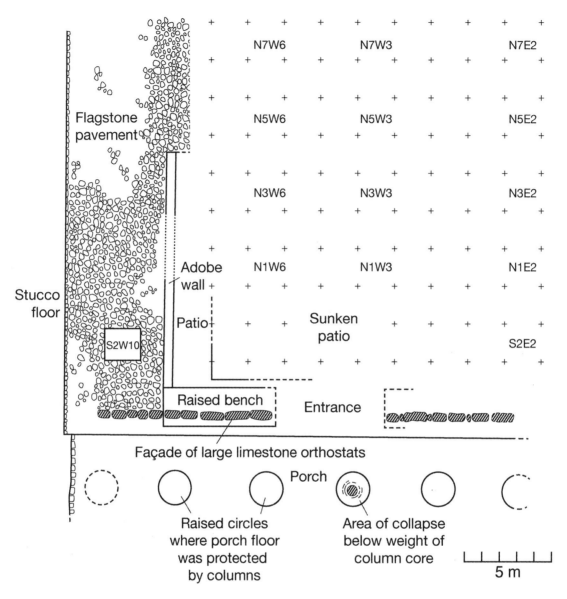

Figure 17.3. Plan view of Structure 17, a probable governmental palace on Mound 8. The entrance was on the south side, facing the main plaza. Square S2W10 was the site of a sounding that revealed an earlier building below Structure 17.

was recessed some 10–15 cm into a slightly larger patio (Figs. 17.4, 17.5).

This higher and larger patio was flanked on the west by a flagstone pavement, at least part of which had once supported an adobe wall (Fig. 17.6). All of the aforementioned architectural features rested on a stone masonry platform whose western wall rose 60–65 cm and consisted of three to four courses of stones (Fig. 17.7).

Access to Structure 17 had once been provided by a wide staircase that rose more than 8 m from the main plaza of San José Mogote. This staircase is now badly eroded, as is the stucco porch on the south that provided entry into the building.

Ironically, the best preserved patches of the porch floor were

those originally covered by circular columns. These columns, evidently more than a meter in diameter, seem to have protected the underlying stucco while the rest of the floor eroded away (Fig. 17.8). We found traces of at least six telltale circles of preserved stucco. One of these (Fig. 17.8b) provided us with a clue to the nature of the columns themselves. It included a circular area where the floor had collapsed under the weight of an upright object, perhaps a tree trunk or wooden post. If tree trunks had been used as the core of each column (as they were in the case of Structure 36 on Mound 1), it would explain why we found no evidence of stone slabs or rubble on the surviving column circles.

Once having passed the colonnaded porch or portico, a visitor to Structure 17 would have reached the entrance to the building.

Figure 17.4. The southwest corner of Structure 17's sunken patio, after cleaning and consolidation.

This entrance, perhaps 6 m wide, was flanked by heavy walls whose lower courses included the limestone orthostats shown in Figure 17.2. These orthostats were irregular in shape, and there was evidence that the gaps between them had been filled with smaller stones. Almost certainly the upper courses of the wall were of adobes, long since eroded away.

Once past the entrance, a visitor would have stepped down into the sunken patio, a place of assembly that could not be seen from the main plaza below. Nowhere in the interior of Structure 17 did we find evidence for the kinds of rooms one expects to find in a typical Zapotec residential palace. If any part of Structure 17 was residential, it would have to have been the rear portion, north of the N7 row of squares. That part of the building did provide

evidence of adobe construction, but much of it had eroded down the northern slope of Mound 8.

In sum, all the architectural evidence we encountered led us to believe that Structure 17 was a governmental or administrative palace, a smaller version of the one on Monte Albán's North Platform. Both buildings had a sunken patio reached by a wide staircase and entered via a colonnaded portico. In addition to its greater size, the portico at Monte Albán had its roof supported by rectangular pilasters rather than circular columns.

In Square S2W7, we found a collection of 23 sherds lying directly on the stucco floor of the sunken patio. Included were 1 mammiform support from a Type C6 bowl; 1 Type C7 body sherd; 3 bowl rims of Type G3; an outleaned-wall bowl rim, either

Figure 17.5. An interior view of Structure 17. In the background we see the orthostats of the façade, resting on their raised bench. In the foreground we see the flagstone pavement. In the middle ground we see the patio and the sunken patio.

Figure 17.6. On its west side, the patio of Structure 17 was separated from the flagstone pavement by a narrow adobe wall. In this photo, the north arrow rests on the patio floor. The white strip to the left of the arrow is the plastered surface on which the adobe wall rested.

Figure 17.7. The west wall and southwest corner of Structure 17. In places, the outer wall consisted of 3–4 courses of stone, 60–65 cm high.

of Caso's Type K3 or our type, Guadalupe Burnished Brown; a rim, either of Caso's Type C2 or our type, Fidencio Coarse; and a redeposited cylinder base of Atoyac Yellow-white. All the remaining sherds were unclassifiable.

The Stratigraphic Test in Square S2W10

As we exposed more and more of Structure 17, it became clear that we would have to be very selective when it came time to search for diagnostic sherds trapped beneath the building. In some places, the patio floor was virtually eroded away. In other places, the integrity of the building had been violated by intrusive Postclassic burials. As Flannery and Marcus (2003b:289) reported previously, the top of Mound 8 had eventually been

> … selected as the site for a small Monte Albán V hamlet or ranchería. Ash deposits, borrow pits filled with refuse, and storage jars buried flush with the old land surface have all survived; also discovered were the burials of more than a dozen adults… accompanied by fairly standardized lots of G3M gray bowls, jars, and pitchers.

We searched carefully for an area where Structure 17 had no intrusive features or post-occupation disturbance. We settled on Square S2W10, where the flagstone pavement of the building's west side was still intact (Fig. 17.3). Here we made our stratigraphic test. In Figure 17.9*a* we see three workmen removing the flagstones in S2W10. Below the flagstones we found 1.5 m of dense rubble fill, accompanied by sherds and tightly packed earth (Fig. 17.10). At a depth of 1.5 m below the flagstones (2.55 m below our arbitrary datum for Mound 8), we came upon the stucco floor (Fig. 17.9*b*) of an earlier building.

Since the fill below the flagstones in Square S2W10 was stony rubble, it could not be excavated by "natural" or "cultural" levels. We were forced to use arbitrary levels of 10–20 cm, depending on the size of the stones. All the sherds from each of these arbitrary levels were collected before we continued downward. This procedure resulted in six collections of diagnostic sherds, which were as follows.

Some 25 sherds were found in the first 20 cm below the flagstones. Included were a Type C12 bowl with postfiring zigzags scratched into it; 3 to 4 other possible Monte Albán II sherds; and redeposited sherds of the Tierras Largas, San José,

Figure 17.8. The porch in front of Structure 17 had once supported columns more than a meter in diameter. In some places (as in *a*), raised circles had been left where the column prevented erosion of the stucco floor. In other cases (as in *b*) the floor had collapsed under the weight of the column's core, which may have been a tree trunk or wooden post.

Figure 17.9. A stratigraphic test below Structure 17. In *a*, workmen remove the flagstone floor in Square S2W10 prior to excavation. In *b*, a workman squats on the stucco floor of an earlier building, 1.5 m below the flagstones seen in *a*.

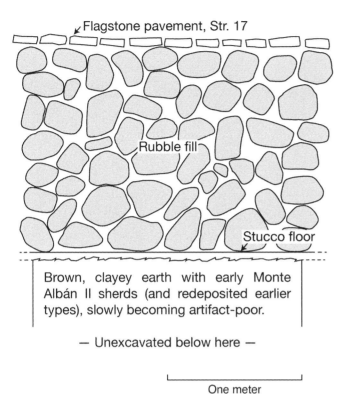

Figure 17.10. Stratigraphic profile of the east wall of Square S2W10, from the flagstone pavement of Structure 17 (1.05 m below datum) to the point where excavation was suspended (roughly 3.05 m below datum). This excavation revealed a building earlier than Structure 17.

and Rosario phases, including Avelina Red-on-buff, Fidencio Coarse, Atoyac Yellow-white, and Socorro Fine Gray.

Twenty-five more sherds appeared 20–30 cm below the flagstones. Included were a Type C6 bowl with postfiring zigzags; the comb-incised base of a Type G12 bowl, subtype G12b; a swollen vessel support in *gris* ware; an *amarillo* sherd; several other Monte Albán II fragments; and redeposited San José, Guadalupe, and Rosario sherds.

Twenty-six more sherds appeared 40–60 cm below the flagstones. Included were a Type C11 bowl with postfiring zigzags; several other Monte Albán II sherds; and redeposited material from the Tierras Largas, San José, and Rosario phases.

The sample found 60–80 cm below the flagstones consisted mainly of redeposited Tierras Largas, San José, and Rosario phase sherds, including an Atoyac Yellow-white bowl with a pennant-incised rim. There were, however, a few Monte Albán II sherds, such as a Type C6 bowl, a possible Type C5 bowl, and an *amarillo* sherd.

Only 15 sherds were found 80–100 cm below the flagstones. Most were redeposited Tierras Largas, San José, and Rosario specimens, but there was also one possible Type C20 bowl of the Monte Albán II period.

Twenty-eight sherds were recovered from dense rubble at a depth of 100–120 cm below the flagstones. Monte Albán II sherds dominated this sample. Included were at least 2 Type C12 bowls

with postfiring zigzags; 1 of these seems to have had a mammiform support. Also present were 2 Type C20 sherds. There were rims from Type G12 and G21 bowls, 1 Monte Albán II version of Type G35, and 3 Type G3 vessels. Rounding out the collection were 1 *café* sherd, 1 *amarillo* sherd, and several redeposited sherds of the Tierras Largas and San José phases. Included among the sherds was a small marine olive shell, drilled for suspension.

The Stucco Floor at 2.55 m below Datum

Once the stony rubble had been removed, we swept the stucco floor that lay 1.5 m below the flagstones (Figs. 17.9, 17.10). We were very curious to know whether this floor would antedate Monte Albán II. Riding on the outcome was the answer to one of our longstanding questions: Might the main plaza at San José Mogote have existed already in the Middle Formative, or was it a purely Monte Albán II innovation?

Additional excavation in Square S2W10 provided a partial answer. We removed a 2 × 2 m portion of the lower stucco floor and recovered a sample of 22 sherds trapped beneath it. Included were fragments of a Type C12 bowl; 2 Type G21 rims and 2 Type G21 cane-swirled bases; 1 Type A11 sherd; and some redeposited Socorro Fine Gray sherds. We now knew that this stucco floor, some 2.55 m below our arbitrary datum, belonged to another

Figure 17.11. Two bowls of Type G21 and the arm from a funerary urn, found in Feature 72. This feature was an intrusive pit, dug just outside the southwest corner of Structure 17 (Square S4W12).

Monte Albán II building—perhaps an earlier version of Structure 17. There was still no solid evidence, in other words, that San José Mogote had ever had a governmental palace or a main plaza before its Monte Albán II renaissance.

The earth below the lower stucco floor was brown and clayey, lacking the stony rubble found below Structure 17. This earth became increasingly artifact-poor as we proceeded downward; we found no loose adobes or other suggestions that there might be still earlier buildings below. Although our curiosity was not fully satisfied, we terminated the excavation of Square S2W10 at a depth of 3.05 m below datum.

Had the lower stucco floor turned out to be Rosario phase in date, we would have tried to expose the entire building. Given the goals of our project, however, we could not justify spending more time, money, and labor on what was probably just an earlier version of Structure 17.

Feature 72

In Square S4W12, near Structure 17 but just beyond its southwest corner, we discovered a large pit filled with Monte Albán II refuse. This pit, designated Feature 72, filled almost the entire 2 × 2 m square. We suspected that its contents consisted of trash swept from Structure 17. Diagnostic sherds recovered from Feature 72 were as follows:

6 rims from Type C6 hemispherical bowls or saucers
1 *pichancha* (or fenestrated vessel) in Type C6
4 sherds from funnel-necked jars, possibly Type C6
1 Type C12 bowl with postfiring zigzag incising
3 rims from Type G1 beakers
2 Type G3 bowls with outleaned walls
2 Type G3 hemispherical bowls
5 bridgespouts from Type G3 vessels
15 incised rims from Type G21 bowls
3 sherds from cane-swirled bases, Type G21 (Fig. 17.11)
1 Monte Albán II version of Type G35
4 rims of Type K1 outleaned-wall bowls
1 Type K1 bowl with a rim flange, incised
1 Type K1 bowl with appliqué spikes
2 Type K1 *pichanchas*
1 fragment of possible Type K1 charcoal brazier
3 other possible appliqué decorations from braziers
1 arm from a seated (?) figure on a grayware urn (Fig. 17.11)
3 figurine legs (2 gray, 1 cream)

Below: Figure 17.12. Carved sherd of the Monte Albán IIIa period, found on the surface of Mound 8.

Right: Figure 17.13. Fragments of funerary urns from Mound 8. *a*, human nose and mouth, recovered 1.5 m below the flagstone pavement of Structure 17 (Square S2W10). *b*, puma or jaguar nose and mouth, recovered 30 cm below the surface in Square S1W6 (above Structure 17).

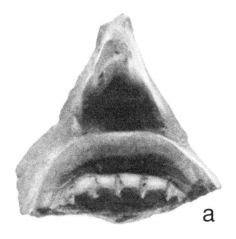

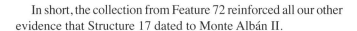

2 cm

In short, the collection from Feature 72 reinforced all our other evidence that Structure 17 dated to Monte Albán II.

Evidence of Monte Albán IIIa Occupation

The most impressive buildings created on Mound 8 dated to Monte Albán II, but it soon became clear that the occupation of the mound had continued into Monte Albán IIIa times. Our surface collection from the summit of the mound included numerous Monte Albán IIIa sherds, including the carved specimen shown in Figure 17.12. We also found a fragment from a possible Period IIIa funerary urn at a depth of only 30 cm in Square S1W6 (Fig. 17.13*b*). Based on its shallow depth, this urn postdated Structure 17.

In Square S5W8, we found an intrusive Monte Albán IIIa pit dug through the porch or portico floor of Structure 17 (Fig. 17.14). Designated Feature 68, this intrusive pit was 34 cm in diameter and 50 cm deep. Based on the way it tapered near the bottom, Feature 68 might have been the hole for a large wooden post that was later removed. Its contents included earthen fill and the following tiny sherds:

7 fragments of Type G23 carved cylindrical bowls, at least one of which had hollow slab feet
2 grayware sherds with traces of wide, shallow grooves
5 *crema* sherds, non-diagnostic

Structure 18

Finally, toward the end of our exploration of Mound 8, we found some architectural traces of an actual Monte Albán IIIa building. These remains were designated Structure 18, even though they were badly eroded and appeared to constitute little more than later additions to Structure 17.

Almost all that remained of Structure 18 was a three-step staircase that came to light in Squares S3E1 and SWE1 (Fig. 17.15). This staircase rose from west to east. On its south side it abutted the limestone orthostats of Structure 17, using them as a kind of rough-and-ready balustrade. On its north side, the staircase had been given a balustrade of rough boulders.

Lying on the steps of the staircase we discovered a brazier fragment in *café* ware. There were also sherds from a Type G23 cylindrical bowl with deep Monte Albán IIIa carving. Two

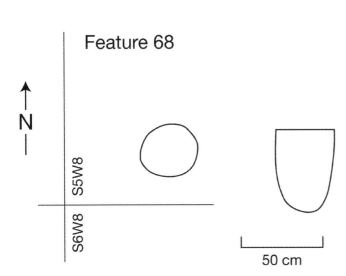

Figure 17.14. Plan (*left*) and cross-section (*right*) of Feature 68, an intrusive Monte Albán IIIa pit dug through the floor of Structure 17 (Square S5W8).

Figure 17.15. The modification of Structure 17 during Monte Albán IIIa included building a three-step staircase in Squares S3E1 and S4E1. On its south side, this staircase abutted the row of limestone orthostats; on its north side, a boulder wall served as a balustrade. This Period IIIa construction was designated Structure 18.

redeposited San José phase sherds lay on the steps, as well as pieces of a white-rimmed black bowl in Monte Albán grayware.

The top step of the staircase led to a white stucco floor, most of which had eroded away. Trapped below an intact remnant of this floor were 2 Type G3 sherds, 2 *café* sherds, and fragments of a type of animal figurine that occurs commonly in Monte Albán IIIa deposits (see Caso, Bernal, and Acosta 1967: Fig. 298). All indications were that Structure 18 dated to the Early Classic period, a time when many of Monte Albán's Type G23 vessels resembled Teotihuacán's cylindrical tripods with hollow slab feet (Marcus and Flannery 1996: Fig. 285).

Conclusions

Our discoveries on Mound 8 suggest the following scenario. Early in the Monte Albán II renaissance at San José Mogote, community leaders laid out the main plaza and selected a natural rise in the terrain—Mound 8—to become the site of a governmental palace.

Several versions of this palace were built over time. The oldest version, buried 2.55 m below our arbitrary datum point for Mound 8, remains largely unexplored. A later version, called Structure 17, measured more than 30 m on a side. It was smaller than its counterpart on the North Platform at Monte Albán, but was almost certainly modeled after the latter.

Structure 17 had a sunken central patio greater than 15 m from west to east. It was entered from a colonnaded porch or portico and had an impressive façade whose lower course of stones included massive limestone orthostats. Many of these limestone slabs were likely robbed from earlier (Rosario phase) buildings.

There were signs that Structure 17 had been repaired, replastered, or modified at least twice during Monte Albán II. Its final modification, however, took place during Monte Albán IIIa, when a stairway and some additional rooms were added on the east. This final modification, called Structure 18, was too eroded to provide us with a decent ground plan.

Our impression is that by the time Structure 18 was built, fewer people were in residence on Mound 8, and the building was less well maintained than it had been during Monte Albán II. All signs indicate that the renaissance at San José Mogote came to an end during Monte Albán IIIa, accompanied by a major loss of population.

18 | The Palatial Residence on Mound 9
by Judith Francis Zeitlin and Robert N. Zeitlin

Mound 9 of San José Mogote is the largest visible construction within the main plaza of the site. It lies just 75 m south of Mound 8, the counterpart to Monte Albán's North Platform (Chapter 17). Mound 9 is long and cigar-shaped, measuring 120 m east-west and 35 m north-south; its maximum elevation is about 3 m.

In 1974, Mound 9 itself was not farmed, although plowed fields extended right up to its base. Mesquite and cactus were dominant in the thick brush covering the mound. While erosion was perhaps the principal cause of deterioration of its architectural details, any destruction had been aggravated by recent bulldozer widening of the dirt road between Guadalupe Etla and the Panamerican Highway.

The road graders clipped off the southeast corner of the mound and bulldozed away more than 10 m of its length (Fig. 18.1). In the course of destroying important cultural features, this road widening exposed a long cross-section, providing us with details of the building's construction (Figs. 18.2–18.4). Of special interest were an east-west wall composed of megalithic stones and a thick plaster floor that extended for virtually the entirety of the mound. Neatly stacked rows of adobe bricks were visible atop this floor. These bricks were of at least three different colors and clay sources, suggesting that multiple work gangs had been involved.

The Objectives of Our 1974 Excavations

The cross-section created by the bulldozer provided us with an opportunity to find out what kind of building Mound 9 supported. We set ourselves the following objectives:

1. Investigate the structure and function of the building(s) associated with the thick plaster floor and the megalithic wall. We hoped to accomplish this by uncovering architectural features and floor plans suitable for comparison to those of contemporary structures at San José Mogote and other sites in the Valley of Oaxaca. An understanding of the nature of Mound 9 would help to clarify the layout of the main plaza itself.
2. Date the structure(s) associated with the plaster floor and the megalithic wall. We hoped that this would provide us with a *terminus ad quem* for the construction of the main plaza, since Mound 9 was obviously situated very carefully with respect to other structures in and around the plaza.
3. Look for constructions that antedated the megalithic building. There promised to be earlier phases of occupation in this sector of the site, which previously had been dated by surface collections alone.

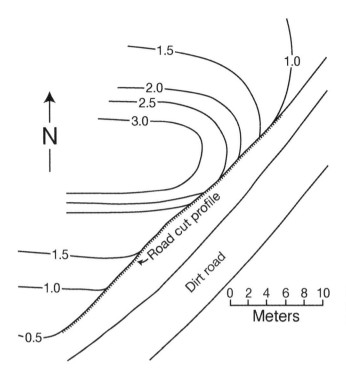

Figure 18.1. Contour map of Mound 9-east, showing the road cut profile and the 1974 dirt road between Guadalupe Etla and the Panamerican Highway. (Contour interval=0.5 m)

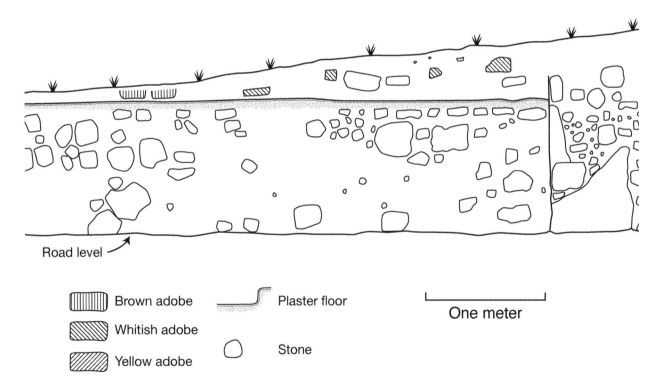

Figure 18.2. The southwesternmost 5.3 m of the road cut profile.

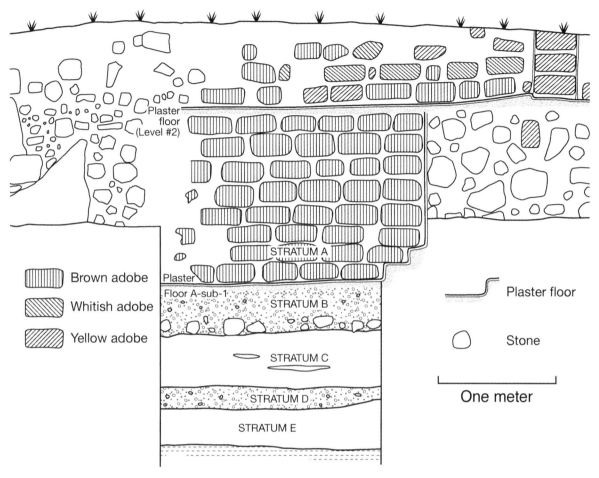

Figure 18.3. The central 5 m of the road cut profile. This section of the profile includes a deep sounding (Test Pit A) that revealed Strata B through E.

Excavation Strategy

Because of the limited time available, we concentrated our excavation on the east side of the mound (Mound 9-east), where the road-cut profile could be used as a stratigraphic guide. Our approach was to clear off the obvious later fill down to the level of the heavy plaster floor, whose walls and other construction features could then be dated by their associated ceramics. We hoped to determine the function of rooms within the building through an examination of their layout and the assemblages of artifacts within them. We hoped that any underlying constructions could also be investigated, including the building with its east-west megalithic wall. We would then make exploratory test pits to seek evidence of still earlier occupation phases, possibly even predating the construction of major public buildings in this area of the site.

We laid out a 2 × 2 m grid system along magnetic north-south lines, providing us with horizontal spatial control (Fig. 18.5). We then began our excavation near the high point on the mound's east

side. Here, we hoped, traces might be found of the most recent building on the mound, the height of which had been raised by superimposing nearly 2 m of adobe fill on top of the plaster floor of a previous building.

We removed the adobe fill to the level of the underlying plaster floor, grid unit by grid unit, using the profiles exposed by the excavation of one unit as a guide for the excavation of adjacent units. It soon became apparent, however, that the walls we were finding dated to several building stages. Apparently, over time, new rooms had been created by subdividing preexisting spaces.

We saved all sherds and artifacts by individual grid units (or by features in some cases) to see what distinctive distributions might occur. Finally, we placed two small stratigraphic tests (Test Pits A and B) in the road cut itself, straddling the megalithic wall. Cultural deposits extended well below the road surface.

While the stratigraphy exposed by the road cut was complex, we eventually came to realize that what we were seeing were successive architectural stages in the history of a Zapotec palatial

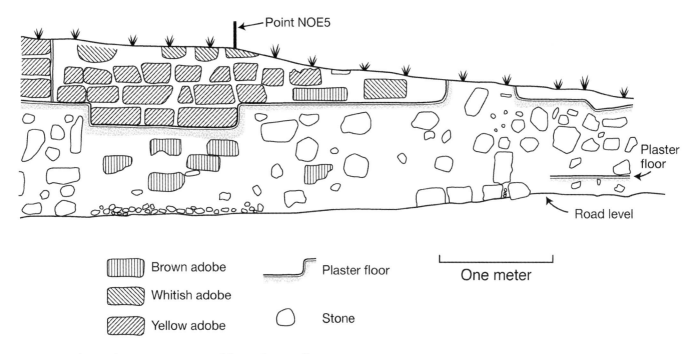

Figure 18.4. The northeasternmost 5.7 m of the road cut profile.

residence. This elite compound had originally been built during Monte Albán II, and during that period it was remodeled several times. The trend during this period was from a building having fewer and larger rooms to one having smaller and more numerous rooms, possibly because an increased number of residents had to be accommodated over time. The final modification of the building appears to have taken place at the start of Monte Albán IIIa. After that, most of San José Mogote was abandoned.

Construction Stages

By carefully taking apart the various superimposed adobe walls and stucco floors, we managed to define at least four major construction stages of the building. These stages do not, of course, document the full sequence of changes. Our season ended before we could expose enough of the building's earliest floor to produce a ground plan. Nor could we produce a complete plan of the final remodeling, since it had largely eroded away. In the discussion that follows, "Stage 1" simply refers to the earliest construction stage for which we could produce a ground plan.

Stage 1 (Fig. 18.6)

At this stage the megalithic wall was already present, and a thick plaster floor had been laid down over some adobe fill that covered an earlier construction. This floor was marked by

several changes in level, formed by abrupt steps about 5–10 cm in height. A sunken patio (nearly obliterated by the widening of the road) descended to a point 17 cm lower than the floor of the large room bounded by walls A, B, E, T, and M.

The building of Stage 1 had stone-footed adobe or rubble-and-earth walls and featured step-downs of 5–9 cm from one floor to the next. This is typical of many Zapotec palaces, which tend to have no two room floors on the same level.

Stage 2 (Fig. 18.7)

In the early part of this stage (Stage 2a), a small stepped platform (or higher room) of unknown function was constructed in the area of Squares N3E2–N3E4. This platform stepped down into other rooms on its north and west sides. To the south of the platform, a large pre-existing room was further enclosed by extending Wall A to the west. New walls, N and Q, were also added to the west of the platform. The floor was replastered after all these new features had been constructed.

Apparently not long after the platform or higher room was built, it was modified (Stage 2b). A new wall of stones (Wall O) was added on the west side, extending a wider ledge farther out from earlier Ledge U. Additional modifications in this area included Ledges R and S. These ledges widened and added a second step to Wall Q. (Wall Q may originally have been a ledge-type construction rather than an actual wall.) Again, the floor was replastered after these modifications.

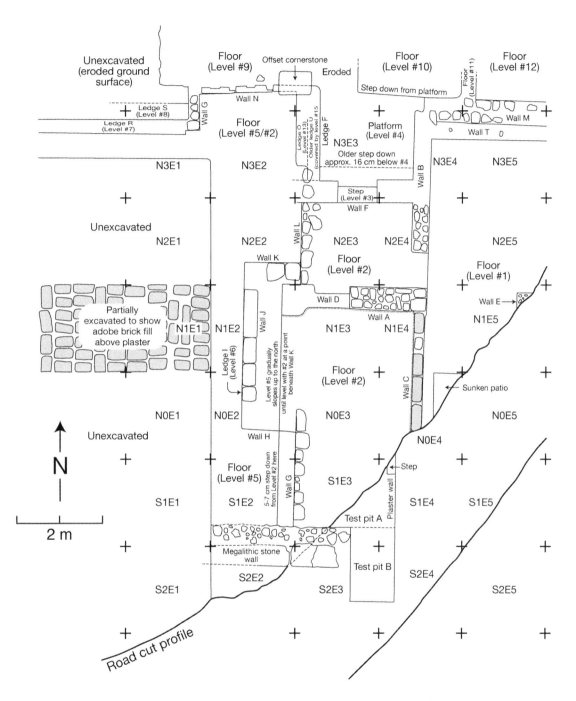

Figure 18.5. Plan view of Mound 9-east, showing the grid of 2 x 2 m squares. In this plan, all walls (from every construction stage) are shown.

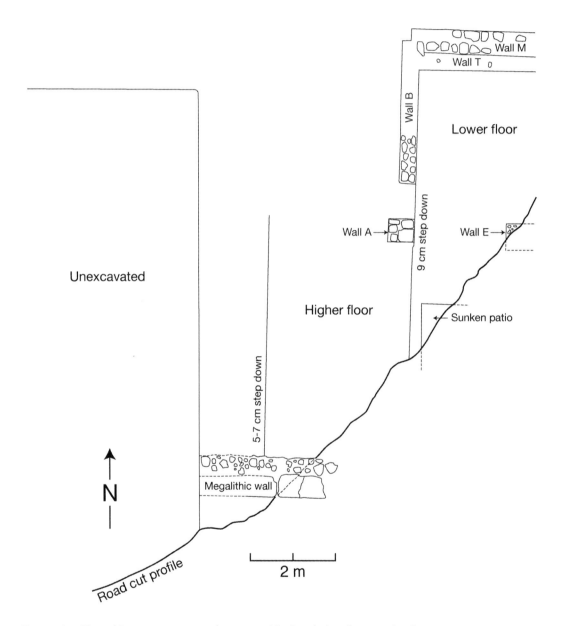

Figure 18.6. Mound 9-east: reconstructed room partitioning during Construction Stage 1.

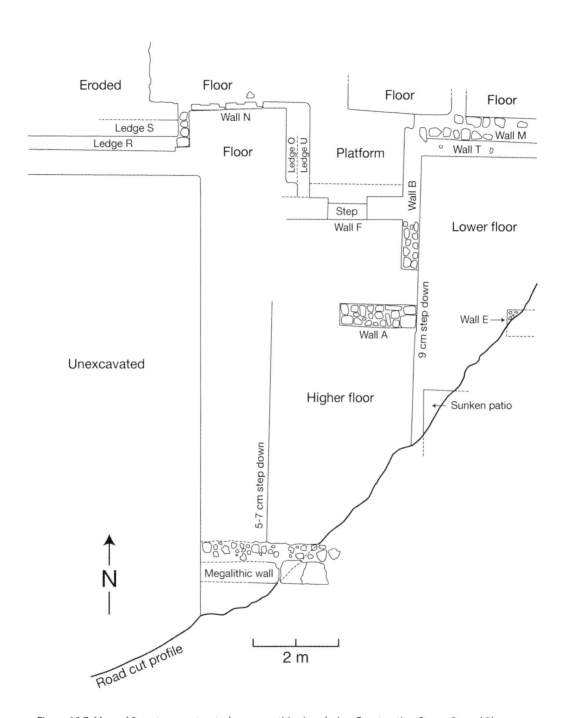

Figure 18.7. Mound 9-east: reconstructed room partitioning during Construction Stages 2a and 2b.

Modifications during this stage entailed more drastic changes in the use of space than did Stage 2b. Two new walls, C and D, were added to Wall A in the area of Squares N1E2–N1E4. These walls were of adobe and served to partition an area that had once been open. The new room created by these walls was then plastered, and its floor and walls were painted red.

Stage 4 (Figs. 18.9, 18.10)

The new walls built during this fourth phase of construction converted the whole area from Square N3E3 to Square S1E3 into a north-south row of fully enclosed rooms. The new walls were of two types: smooth-faced limestone blocks, neatly arranged to form another ledge construction (H, I, J, K), and more irregularly shaped stones that probably served as the foundation for adobe walls (G and L). The walls themselves were plastered, but the stucco floor was not replastered during this stage.

Owing to the nature of the soil, we found it nearly impossible to separate the east faces of these new walls from the reused adobes later stacked on the room floor as fill. It is even possible that the entire area east of the E2 column of squares was at that time filled with adobe bricks, and hence not used.

Activity in the building during this fourth stage may have been limited to whatever took place in the large, plaster-floored area west of the new walls. The ledge-type walls created during Stage 4 may have been specialized structures facilitating this activity.

To be sure, excavations farther to the west might turn up another block of open rooms beyond the brick fill—in other words, a second Stage 4 residential unit. It is notable that a dense concentration of carbonized wood, burned earth, and collapsed and burned limestone blocks was found close to the floor beyond the westernmost Stage 4 walls.

We believe that this fire was related to the abandonment of the Stage 4 residence. Early Monte Albán IIIa crews later covered the Stage 4 building with reused adobes and rubble.

Dating the Building with Diagnostic Ceramics

As often happens, many stucco floors of the residence had been swept so clean that few in situ ceramics remained. Only in the areas of burning, west of the Stage 4 walls, did we suspect that we were dealing with sherds that were covered up with debris before they could be swept out of the building. To date each construction stage, therefore, we relied mainly on the sherds trapped beneath each adobe wall or stucco floor.

The situation was different in Test Pits A and B, whose location is given in Figure 18.5. Both of these pits revealed four stratigraphic levels (Strata B, C, D, and E) below Plaster Floor A-sub-1, the oldest identifiable floor found in Test Pit A. We begin our discussion of dating, therefore, with Test Pit A, whose profile can be seen in Figure 18.11.

Stratum E. This was the oldest level yielding cultural remains. It consisted of hard-packed dark brown soil and rested upon a layer of sterile *tepetate* or hardpan. The diagnostic ceramics included 2 undecorated bases of Atoyac Yellow-white cylindrical bowls; 1 rim from an Atoyac Yellow-white bowl; 2 rims from Leandro Gray cylindrical bowls; 1 rim from a Leandro Gray outleaned-wall bowl; 1 or 2 body sherds of San José Red-on-White; 1 jar sherd of Matadamas Orange; 1 rim of a Matadamas Orange hemispherical bowl; 1 rim of a Clementina Fine Red-on-Buff hemispherical bowl; 1 rim of a Tierras Largas Burnished Plain hemispherical bowl; and 5 or 6 other Tierras Largas Burnished Plain sherds. The nondiagnostic ceramics included 22 miscellaneous body sherds, all from what appeared to be San José phase types. Our assessment of Stratum E is that it dates to the San José phase.

Surface collections had previously suggested that this part of the site might once have been the northernmost residential ward of the San José phase village. Stratum E only served to strengthen that possibility. Although we did not find evidence of a San José phase house, we did find typical household refuse: 1 piece of chipped stone, 1 trimmed-off valve of a pearl oyster shell, and the ulna of a white-tailed deer.

Stratum D. This was a sandy, yellowish brown layer with numerous pebbles. Its diagnostic ceramics included 1 basal sherd from a Socorro Fine Gray bowl; 1 sherd of Guadalupe Burnished Brown; 1 body sherd from a Fidencio Coarse jar; and 1 badly eroded red-on-white or red-on-buff sherd, probably redeposited. Our initial assessment of this stratum was that it was Middle Formative in date; the larger ceramic sample from Test Pit B convinced us that Stratum B belonged to the Rosario phase.

Stratum C. This was a layer of hard-packed dark brown soil with sand lenses, lacking the subdivisions we later observed in Test Pit B (see below). The most recent ceramics in this stratum belonged to Monte Albán II. Included were 1 sherd from a cylindrical vessel of Caso, Bernal, and Acosta's Type C6; 1 rim from bowls of Types C7 and C11; and 1 rim and 1 base from Type G21 bowls. Stratum C also produced about 25 sherds of redeposited Rosario phase and San José phase types. Included among the latter were sherds of Socorro Fine Gray composite silhouette bowls; a Fidencio Coarse jar rim; and a typical bolstered-rim bowl sherd, too eroded to be identified to type. Stratum C seemed, in other words, to reflect the first Monte Albán II occupation of the Mound 9 area.

Stratum B. This level consisted of dark brown earth, rock, and pebble fill between two plaster floors. It lay below Floor A-sub-1 of Test Pit A (Fig. 18.3) and above Floor B-sub-3 of Test Pit B (Fig. 18.11). Stratum B therefore lies between two of the earliest construction features of the Mound 9 residence.

The most recent ceramics in Stratum B belonged to Monte Albán II types. Included were 4 bowl sherds of Type G3; a cane-swirled bowl base of Type G21; and 1 other fragment of *gris* ware. We also found 1 sherd from a Type C1 jar; 1 base from a

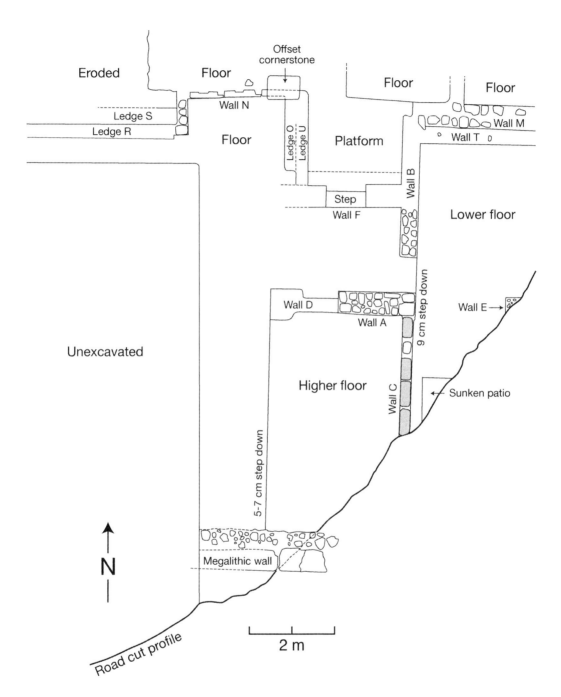

Figure 18.8. Mound 9-east: reconstructed room partitioning during Construction Stage 3.

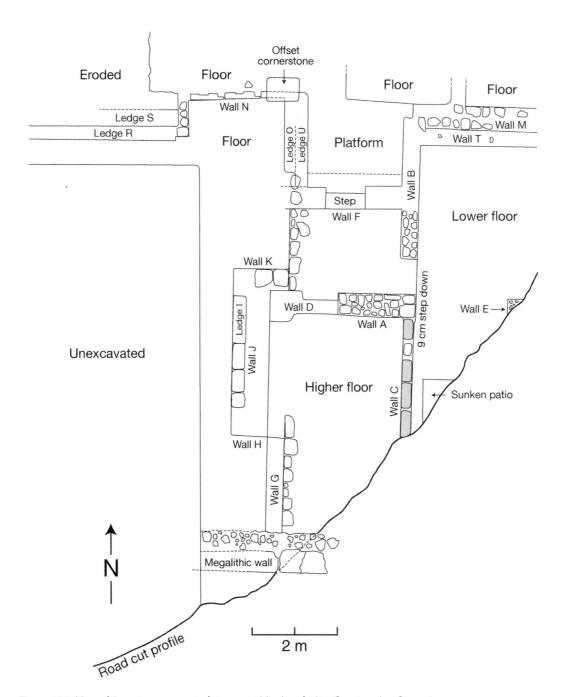

Figure 18.9. Mound 9-east: reconstructed room partitioning during Construction Stage 4.

Type C6 bowl; the sidewall of a Type C12 bowl; 3 sherds from Type C20 bowls; and 1 fragment of a figurine in *crema* ware. One sherd, from a hemispherical bowl, featured *amarillo* paste. There were also, to be sure, redeposited sherds from earlier periods.

Stratum A. In Test Pit A, Stratum A consisted largely of very regular adobe fill. The adobes, stacked eight rows high, had been placed atop Plaster Floor A-sub-1 (Fig. 18.3), presumably to level the area for new construction. The new construction included the Level #2 plaster floor spanning the large room shown in Squares N1E3–S1E3 of Figure 18.5. That floor existed already during Construction Stage 1 of the residence (Fig. 18.6), as did the adjacent megalithic wall. Obviously, therefore, we were curious to know the date of Stratum A.

The most recent ceramics from Stratum A belonged to Monte Albán II. Included among the *crema* wares were 1 sherd from a Type C6 bowl with post-firing incisions; the base of a Type C7 bowl with a hollow support; and 1 sherd from a cylindrical bowl of Type C20. The graywares included 5 rims of Type G3 bowls; the incised rim of a Type G12 bowl; and 1 fragment of Type G21 bowl. Also present were the rim of a Type K1 jar and the rim of a Type A11 outleaned-wall bowl. Among the redeposited sherds of earlier periods were the mat-impressed base of a Guadalupe Burnished Brown brazier or pot stand; a burnished brown bowl sherd; and the tall neck from a Socorro Fine Gray jar.

Above the Level #2 Floor. As Figure 18.3 makes clear, the eight layers of reused adobes seen in Stratum A were eventually capped by the Level #2 plaster floor. Diagnostic sherds found with the walls and ledges above this floor are not considered to fall within Test Pit A; they will be described in a later section.

Test Pit B

Stratum E. Just as in Test Pit A, Stratum E was a layer of hard-packed dark brown earth above sterile hardpan. Its diagnostic sherds, which are listed below, left no doubt that Stratum E dated to the San José phase.

AVELINA RED-ON-BUFF
Rims of hemispherical bowls: 3

LEANDRO GRAY
Rim of cylindrical bowl: 1
Base of outleaned-wall bowl: 1
Tecomate, rocker-stamped: 1

ATOYAC YELLOW-WHITE
Rims of cylindrical bowls: 2
Base of cylindrical bowl: 1
Rims of outleaned-wall bowls: 2
Bases of outleaned-wall bowls: 3
Rim of hemispherical bowl: 1
Rim from tall-necked jar: 1

FIDENCIO COARSE
Jar shoulder with herringbone (?) slashes: 1

LUPITA HEAVY PLAIN
Rim of charcoal brazier: 1
Annular base (?): 1

SAN JOSÉ RED-ON-BUFF
Rim of outleaned-wall bowl: 1

BODY SHERDS (all were San José phase types): 53

Stratum D. This was a continuation of the same sandy yellowish-brown layer seen in Test Pit A. It yielded only 6 eroded body sherds, definitely including Atoyac Yellow-white and Tierras Largas Burnished Plain. All 6 sherds were worn and looked redeposited.

Stratum C. This was the same layer of hard-packed, dark brown earth with sandy lenses seen in Test Pit A. In Test Pit B, however, one of the sandy lenses was so thick that we could divide Stratum C into Substrata C, C1, and C2 (Fig. 18.11).

Substratum C was the upper half of Stratum C. The bulk of the sherds from this substratum—25 in all—were redeposited Rosario phase and San José phase types. A handful of cane-swirled Type G21 bowls, however, showed us that Substratum C dated to Monte Albán II.

Substratum C1, a thick lens of light brown sand, also contained redeposited sherds of the Rosario phase. Among the Socorro Fine Gray sherds in Substratum C1 were 2 bases from outleaned-wall bowls; 1 everted bowl rim with pennant incising; 1 undecorated everted bowl rim; 1 fragment of composite silhouette bowl; and 1 body sherd with a stripe of negative white decoration. The remaining ceramics in this sand lens were Fidencio Coarse, and included 2 jar rims, a jar shoulder, and 18 body sherds.

Substratum C2, which contained more clay than sand, yielded 14 badly eroded sherds of what appear to be redeposited Rosario phase and San José phase types. In other words, although Stratum C dated to Monte Albán II, some individual lenses in its fill contained redeposited sherds of earlier periods.

Stratum B. As one can see in Figure 18.11, Stratum B in Test Pit B was more complicated than the equivalent level in Test Pit A. In both test pits, Stratum B was overlain by thick plaster floors (Floor A-sub-1 in Test Pit A, and Floor B-sub-1 in Test Pit B). In Test Pit A, Floor A-sub-1 was the oldest architectural feature. In Test Pit B, however, we found two even older floors, which we called B-sub-2 and B-sub-3. Floor B-sub-3, which lay at the very bottom of Stratum B, turned out to be the oldest architectural feature in all of Mound 9-east.

We recovered 2 ceramic samples from Stratum B. One sample consisted of the sherds trapped below Floor B-sub-2; this sample was virtually pure Monte Albán II. Included were 1 base of a Type G3 bowl; 1 rim of a Type G3 bowl; 2 sherds of Type G21 bowls; 1 base of a Type C6 bowl; 1 rim of a Type C7 bowl; and 1 base of a Type C20 bowl.

Figure 18.10. Work in progress on Mound 9-east. In this view from the northwest, we see Walls A, C, D, G, J, K, and L of Construction Stage 4. At this stage, several originally large rooms had been divided up into multiple smaller rooms.

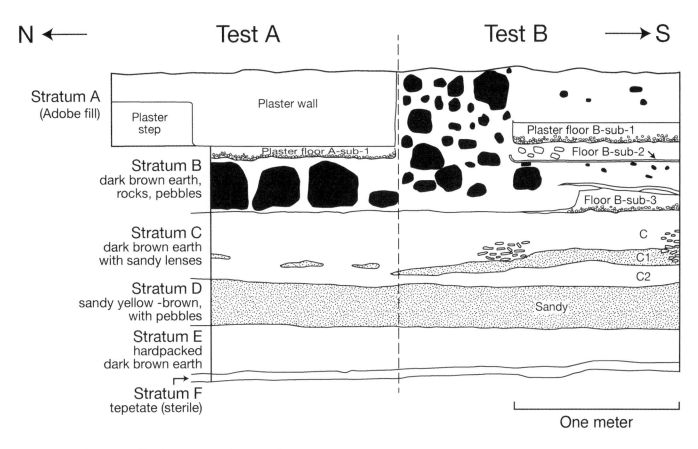

Figure 18.11. The east profile of Test Pits A and B, Mound 9-east.

Our second ceramic sample consisted of the sherds trapped just below Floor B-sub-3; they, too, dated to Monte Albán II. Included were 2 rims and 1 basal sherd from Type G21 bowls; 1 possible sherd from a Type C1 bowl; 1 body sherd of Type C6; and 2 body sherds of Type C7.

Stratum A. In Test Pit B, Stratum A consisted of rock and earth fill with occasional adobe bricks. Associated with Floor B-sub-1 we found 1 bowl sherd from the Monte Albán II version of Type G35; a hemispherical bowl sherd of grayware, not identifiable to type; a small *tecomate* sherd of Type C20; and a hemispherical bowl sherd in *café* ware.

Test Pit B lay too far out into the dirt road to reveal remnants of the Level #2 floor. The ceramics found in Stratum A, however, confirmed what we had learned from the same stratum in Test Pit A: the earliest stage of the Mound 9 residence dated no earlier than Monte Albán II. It was, in other words, one more product of the so-called Monte Albán II renaissance at San José Mogote, and did not go back to an earlier period.

The Dating of Specific Walls and Floors in Mound 9-east

Although Test Pits A and B were useful for establishing the presence of earlier periods in the Mound 9 area, they did not help us to date Stages 2–4 of the elite residence. For that task, we relied on small ceramic samples trapped below individual walls and floors. Here are a few of the most significant.

Possible Stage 1 Sherd

A jar neck of Type G1, bearing two decorative slashes, was found in Square N2E5, in the deliberate adobe fill laid on the Level #1 floor (see Fig. 18.12). This could be a Stage 1 sherd that got covered up with adobe fill, rather than being swept out of the building.

Stage 2

A wall made up of Ledges R and S was built during Construction Stage 2 (Fig. 18.7). A talus of fallen plaster fragments rested

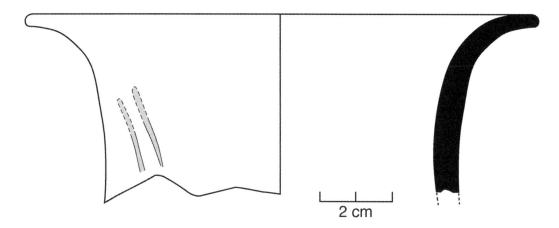

Figure 18.12. A jar neck of Type G1, with two decorative slashes on one side. This jar sherd was found in Square N2E5 in adobe fill deliberately laid in on a plaster floor of Level #1. This was one of the oldest floors discovered; it was present already in Construction Stage 1.

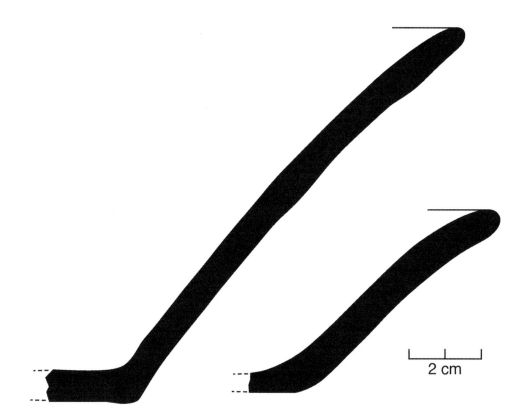

Figure 18.13. Two rim-to-base sections of bowls belonging to the Monte Albán II version of Type G35. These sherds were found in Square N0E3, in adobe fill that was deliberately laid over a plaster floor of Level #2 prior to the renovations of Construction Stage 4.

against the south side of this wall. Many of the plaster fragments were painted red, indicating that the lower half of this wall had likely been decorated with a red dado.

Covered up by this talus of fallen plaster were a number of Monte Albán II sherds. Included were 1 sherd from a Type G3 globular jar; 1 bowl rim of Type G12; 2 bowl rims of Type G21; a gray bridgespout; 1 rim and 1 body sherd of Type C7; 1 hollow support from a Type C7 vessel; 1 sherd of a Type C12 bowl; 2 sherds from outleaned-wall bowls of Type K1; 1 hemispherical bowl rim of Type K1; and 1 fragment of a *café* brazier with braided rope decoration and a layer of dry red pigment.

Possible Stage 3 Sherds

Two rim-to-base sections of bowls belonging to the Monte Albán II version of Type G35 were found in Square N0E3 (Fig. 18.13). They were trapped by deliberate adobe fill atop the Level #2 plaster floor, presumably laid there to level the area prior to Construction Stage 4.

Stage 4

Wall J and Ledge I were built during Construction Stage 4 (Fig. 18.9). In Square N0E3, just to the east of Wall J—trapped between the Stage 4 plaster and the later adobe fill above it—we found several Monte Albán II variants of Type G35; gray sherds with cane-swirled designs; and a bowl sherd of Type C7.

We found additional Monte Albán II sherds in another likely Stage 4 context, this time in Square N0E1. In this case, the sherds were trapped below a Stage 4 floor that had been severely burned and later was deliberately covered with adobes. Included were 1 rim of a *comal* in *crema* ware (possibly Type C2); 1 body sherd of Type C6; 1 sherd from a Type C20 bowl whose rim had been recessed to accommodate a lid; 1 rim of a G3 bowl; and 1 sherd of Type G21.

Sherds from Post-Stage 4 Adobe Fill

As mentioned earlier, the Stage 4 residence seems to have been abandoned after a conflagration of some kind. Reused adobes were later laid in over the ruins of Stage 4. Scattered among the adobes of this very late fill were a number of Monte Albán IIIa sherds. Included were the Type G23 bowl shown in Figure 18.14; bowl sherds of Type G4, which features black slip over *gris* paste; and Type A3 hemispherical bowls with ring bases, the Monte Albán equivalent of Teotihuacán's Thin Orange vessels. Such sherds were not numerous, but there were enough of them to suggest that the final modification of the Mound 9 residence took place during Monte Albán IIIa.

The Artifacts

As mentioned earlier, many floors of the Mound 9 residence

had been swept relatively clean. The result is that artifacts were not abundant. In this section, we list those artifacts we recovered; their locations can be checked by reference to Figure 18.5.

Griddles: Fragments of *comales* or tortilla griddles of dark brown pottery (Type K19) were found near Walls R & S; Wall F; Wall A; Wall T; Wall G; and Wall C. None of these griddles were necessarily in situ, but the sheer number of specimens suggested that food preparation was a common activity in the residence.

Chipped sherd disks: Three chipped sherd disks were found in Squares N2E4–N2E5, above the Level #1 floor.

Obsidian blades: Obsidian blades were found in Square N2E3 above the Level #2 floor, and in Square N2E4, also above the Level #2 floor.

Fragments of mica: Pieces of worked mica were found in Strata B and C of Test Pit A, and Stratum A of Test Pit B.

Pearl oyster: One worked valve of *Pinctada mazatlanica* was recovered from Stratum E of Test Pit A, a San José phase level.

Faunal Remains

Fragments of animal bone were scattered through the fill of the Mound 9 residence. None appeared to have been left in primary context. We list the species here simply to give an idea of the animals eaten during the occupation of Mound 9-east.

White-tailed deer (*Odocoileus virginianus*)
Domestic dog (*Canis familiaris*)
Domestic turkey (*Meleagris gallopavo*)

Occasional specimens of a carrion-eating land snail, *Euglandina* sp., were also present in the fill.

Conclusions

Let us now look at the extent to which we were able to reach our stated research goals.

1. The building of Stages 1–4 was clearly an elite residence of some kind. The area of Mound 9-east we exposed did not have the plan of a Classic (Monte Albán III) Zapotec palace, such as the one associated with Tomb 105 at Monte Albán. It did not, for example, consist of 8–14 rooms around a single large interior courtyard. (To be sure, a large courtyard might have come to light had we been able to excavate Mound 9 in its entirety.)

Even the limited area we were able to expose, however, suggested a noble residence: well-made adobe walls with plastered surfaces and an occasional red-painted dado, thick stucco floors, and differences in elevation between adjoining rooms. An interesting feature of the residence was that new rooms were continually being created by the

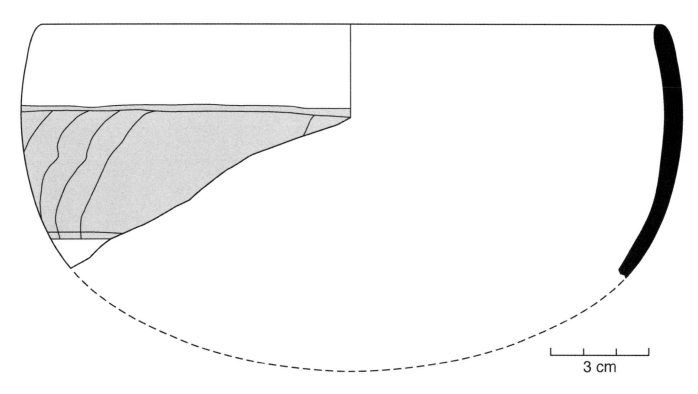

Figure 18.14. Hemispherical bowl of Type G23. The decoration consists of a roughened, incised band encircling the vessel. Sherds of this bowl, which dates to Monte Albán IIIa, were found in Square N3E5 at a point higher than the plaster floor of Level #3. Their presence suggests that the final remodeling of the Mound 9 residence dates to the Early Classic period.

erection of new walls, as if the number of occupants had increased over time.

In this regard, the Mound 9-east building reminds us of the noble residence on the Estacionamiento-A terrace at Monte Albán, excavated by Ernesto González Licón in 1991 (González Licón 2003). This multiroom residence was built during Monte Albán II and modified slightly during IIIa. It is believed to have housed an extended family that was "noble," but not necessarily "royal." Like the Mound 9 elite residence, the Estacionamiento-A building saw its room layout change over time.

2. Our stratigraphic excavations show that the entire span of time that began with Stratum C of Test Pit A and ended with Stage 4 of our main excavation belonged to the Monte Albán II period. We can therefore assign the Mound 9 residence to that period, while noting that the building underwent a bit of Period IIIa modification after the Stage 4 fire.

Unfortunately, our 1974 excavations were not extensive enough to specify the exact point at which the megalithic stone wall was built. We know that it already existed during Construction Stage 1, so it was presumably built early in the building's history. We can even suggest that

it influenced the laying out of the rooms, since both the megalithic wall and the interior walls of the residence were oriented roughly 3° east of magnetic north (11°–12° east of true north).

We can tentatively reconstruct the Mound 9 residence as sitting on a stone-faced platform whose southern façade (the side facing the central plaza) was the megalithic stone wall. Since the plaster floors in Stratum B of Test Pit B lay south of the megalithic wall, they must have been exterior plaster surfaces, leading up to the elite residence from the area of the main plaza.

3. The building of the Mound 9 residence was preceded by San José phase and Rosario phase occupations. Neither of these earlier occupations, however, was accompanied by evidence of monumental construction. It seems likely, therefore, that the Mound 9 residence was essentially a product of the Monte Albán II renaissance at San José Mogote.

While acknowledging that further excavation of Mound 9 would be useful, we are pleased that our 1974 work provided useful data on all three of our research questions.

19 | The Ballcourt on Mound 7
by Chris L. Moser

One of the most prominent artificial mounds at San José Mogote is Mound 7, which constituted the western border of the main plaza during Monte Albán II (Fig. 13.1). This mound has since been bisected by the main road to Guadalupe Etla; accordingly, we have designated its two halves Mound 7-north and Mound 7-south.

From the moment of our first arrival at San José Mogote in the late 1960s, it was clear to us that Mound 7-south contained an I-shaped ballcourt. Since Colonial times, unfortunately, the depression created by the central field of the ballcourt had become a popular place to dump domestic trash, and when we surveyed the area we found it filled with glass bottles, tin cans, dead dogs, worn-out sandals, and discarded plastic shoes. Despite this un-inviting collection of Colonial and modern trash, we knew that we needed to excavate enough of the ballcourt to determine its date and layout.

I began my excavation armed with a generic model for the layout of the standard I-shaped ballcourt, based on Linton Sat-terthwaite's (1944) work in the Maya region and Charles Wicke's (1957) work on the ballcourt at Yagul (Fig. 19.1). I also relied on Ignacio Marquina's (1951) analysis of the ballcourt on the main plaza at Monte Albán.

My first task was to clear the ballcourt of vegetation and trash (Fig. 19.2). I then laid out an east-west trench that would cross the central field of the ballcourt near its midpoint. This trench was 2 m wide and composed of 2 × 2 m squares that would eventually become part of a grid for the entire excavation. The three central squares of the trench became N1W1, N1, and N1E1.

Since we could not predict in advance the exact orientation of the still-unexcavated ballcourt, I simply laid out the trench (and eventual grid) magnetic east-west. As it turned out, the ballcourt was oriented true north, which at the time of my excavation was about 8° 45' east of magnetic north (Fig. 19.3).

We soon realized that we could learn most of what we needed to know by exposing two-thirds of the ballcourt. I wound up excavating the entire north end-field, half of the central field, and enough of the southern half of the ballcourt to see where the south end-field began. Assuming that the south end-field was a mirror image of the one on the north, the total length of the court would have been about 41 m. The central field (between its flanking *taludes*) was about 27 m long, and the maximum width of the north end-field was about 24 m.

These dimensions are almost identical to those of the consolidated (and partially reconstructed) ballcourt on the northeast corner of the main plaza at Monte Albán—close enough to suggest that either (1) there were standard dimensions for the ballcourts of that era, or (2) the ballcourt at San José was closely modeled after its counterpart at the Zapotec capital.

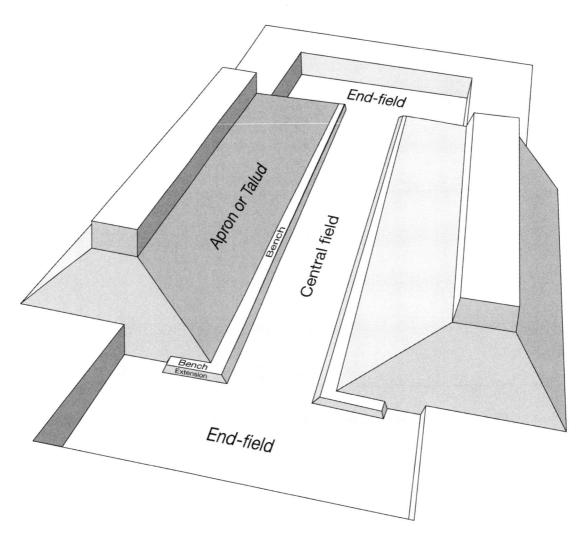

Figure 19.1. The generic layout of an I-shaped ballcourt, based on work by Satterthwaite (1944) and Wicke (1957).

The East-West Trench

The stratigraphy of the east-west trench is shown in Fig. 19.4. The first 2 × 2 m square (N1W1) was excavated by arbitrary 10 cm levels. We encountered lightly compacted tan to light brown soil, yielding few sherds, to a depth of 40 cm below the original grassy surface. At this depth we came upon a badly fragmented pavement, composed of cobbles and lime stucco. Several large pieces of red-painted fallen stucco were lying on this pavement. As our excavation moved east through Squares N1 and N1E1, this cobble and stucco pavement continued until it reached the stone and clay mortar wall that I have designated the east bench wall (Fig. 19.4, east half). The cobble and stucco pavement curled up against the east bench wall, suggesting that the wall had existed before the pavement was laid down. This bench wall represented the eastern limit of the central field, and corresponds to the architectural feature labeled "Bench" in Figure 19.1.

At this point, I extended my trench west until we encountered the corresponding west bench wall on the opposite side of the central field. Once again, the cobble and stucco pavement curled up to meet the bench wall (Fig. 19.4, west half). In this area, the stucco surface of the pavement was well preserved enough to show that it had been painted red.

The west bench wall was thick enough so that we could examine the fill of its interior. In the fill we found worn Monte Albán II (and earlier) sherds. The bench wall was sufficiently intact to allow us to estimate that it had once risen 60–65 cm above the pavement of the central field.

To either side of the bench walls, as can be seen in Fig. 19.4, we encountered the slanting aprons or *taludes* typical of an I-shaped ballcourt. Those aprons had once risen more than 4 m above the pavement of the central field, but they had slumped with the passage of time. The aprons were constructed of adobe and stone and coated with lime stucco. As the profile drawing

Figure 19.2. The ballcourt on Mound 7-south at San José Mogote. In this view from the south, one can see almost the full length of the central field.

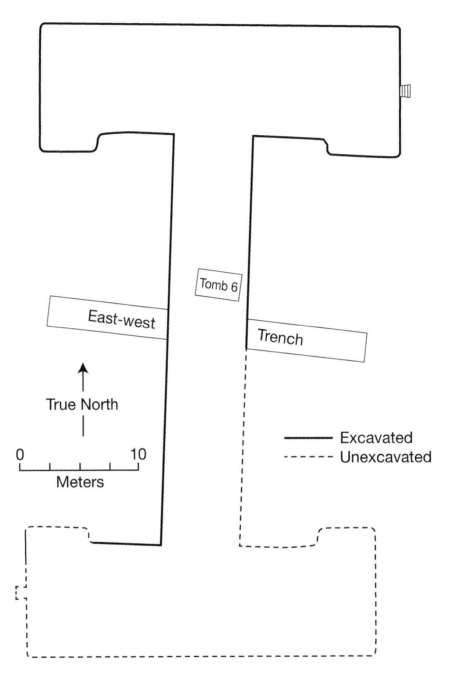

Figure 19.3. Plan view of the ballcourt, showing the areas excavated. (Although the orientation of the court turned out to be true north-south, the east-west stratigraphic trench was laid out magnetic east-west.) Assuming the south end-field to be identical to the one on the north, the total length of the ballcourt would have been about 41 m.

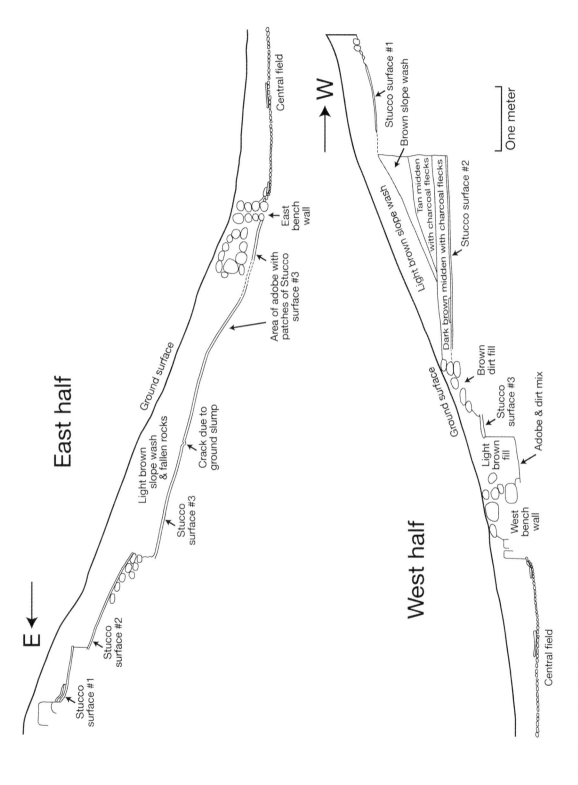

Figure 19.4. The south profile of the east-west trench through the central field of the ballcourt. The maximum height of the surviving structure was 3.4 m.

Figure 19.5. Work in progress on the ballcourt. At this stage the east-west trench has been completed, and one crew member is excavating the north end-field.

indicates, the aprons rose in a series of stages; I have labeled the stucco surfaces of these stages Stucco Surface #1, Stucco Surface #2, and Stucco Surface #3, with #3 being the lowest in elevation.

Excavation of the eastern apron, which was better preserved than its western counterpart, suggested that the ballcourt had undergone at least two major modifications following its original construction. Each time the aprons were modified, their slope became steeper. It appears that the second or final modification created a slope so steep that the bench walls were added for reinforcement. The relatively late construction date of the bench walls was confirmed by our excavation behind them, which revealed that Stucco Surface #3 had existed even before the bench walls were added.

Test excavations below Stucco Surfaces #1 and #2 showed that no stepped stone reinforcements had been placed beneath them, as was done with the ballcourts on Monte Albán's main plaza and at the site of Yagul. We did, however, find evidence that some parts of Stucco Surface #1 had been painted red. Interestingly enough, we found no evidence that Stucco Surface #2 had ever been painted; where well preserved, its surface was smooth and burnished and its color ranged from off-white to faded, yellowish cream.

We were able to recover fragments of pottery between Stucco Surfaces #1 and #2; included were Monte Albán II and eroded Middle Formative sherds. The sherds found between Stucco Surfaces #2 and #3 were similar. No Monte Albán IIIa sherds whatsoever were found beneath the original stucco surfaces. This is significant, for reasons that will become apparent later.

As can be seen in Figure 19.3, my excavation crew succeeded in finding the southern limits of the west bench wall. At this point it turned the corner into the south end-field, becoming what Satterthwaite (1944) calls a "bench extension" (Fig. 19.1). The overburden in the south end-field, which had clearly washed down from a nearby pyramidal mound, reached a depth of 2 m and was very hard digging. It soon became apparent that exposing the south end-field completely would put us over budget for the ballcourt excavation, and since it seemed likely that both end-fields would be identical in layout, we settled for making only a 1.5 m wide exploratory trench along the northwest wall of the south end-field.

The north end-field proved much easier to excavate. Its overburden was only 75 cm to 1.5 m in depth and comparatively soft digging, so we elected to expose the entire end-field. We began by tracing the east and west bench walls north until they both

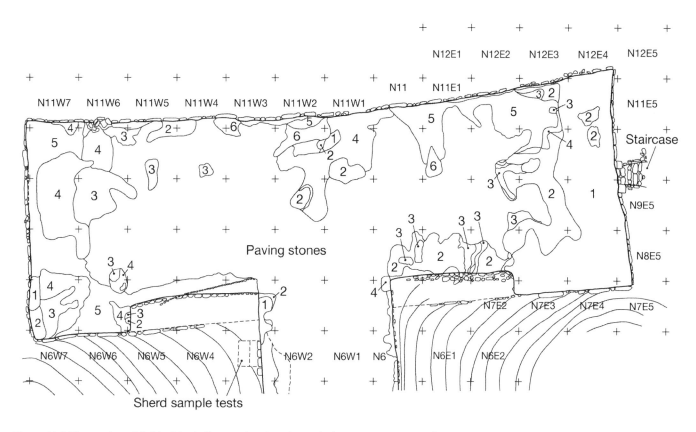

Figure 19.6. The north end-field of the ballcourt, showing the grid of 2 × 2 m squares used to excavate it. In some places, the end-field had been eroded down to its lowest stone paving. In other places, patches of up to six stucco floor surfaces (numbered from the top down) were discovered.

turned a corner and became bench extensions. We then used our grid of 2 × 2 m squares to expose the entire north end-field (Figs. 19.5, 19.6).

The North End-field

The north end-field (Fig. 19.7) was enclosed by stone masonry walls that may once have reached a height of 1.2 to 1.5 m. The stones used for the wall were not actually cut or trimmed, although the architects selected naturally rectangular stones as often as they could. They seem to have used large slabs for the base of the wall, with smaller stones used to fill the spaces among them. The mortar applied was a mixture of clay and sand. The entire surface of the wall had been covered with red-painted stucco (Fig. 19.8), hiding the fact that many stones were irregular in shape.

Each bench extension, whether on the east or on the west, was 1.2 m wide and a little over 5 m long (Fig. 19.6). Each extension's maximum height above the original floor of the end-field was 40–45 cm. In each case, the bench extension had been faced with stone slabs and plastered over with red-painted stucco.

Because the actual playing surface of the court was more eroded in some places than others, we could see that it had been plastered and replastered many times. Near the corners of the north end-field, where the preservation was better, we could detect as many as six superimposed plaster floors. We numbered these floors from the top down, with 1 being the youngest and 6 the oldest (see Figs. 19.6, 19.9).

It is logical to suppose that it was the wear and tear of repeated ballgames that had necessitated so many resurfacings. In the center of the north end-field, the floor had been worn down to its underlying paving stones, which consisted of a layer of relatively hard cobbles and pebbles. These cobbles and pebbles were 2–6 cm thick on average and ranged in length from 4 to 12 cm. They had once been covered with fine river sand to level the surface on which the first stucco floor had been laid.

The complete sequence of stucco floors was preserved only along the north wall of the end-field, and was as follows:

Floor 6 (the oldest) was 6–10 cm thick and painted red.
Floor 5 was a 1 cm thick resurfacing, painted red.
Floor 4 was 2–3 cm thick and had a smooth, red-painted surface.

Figure 19.7. The floor of the ballcourt had been plastered six times. Here we see workmen in the north end-field, isolating patches of stucco floor from various stages. Such patches were best preserved along the walls; in its center, the floor was often eroded down to an underlying pebble layer.

Floor 3 was a thin (0.5 cm) resurfacing, painted red.

Floor 2 was 2 cm thick and painted red.

Floor 1 (the most recent) was a thin (0.5 cm) resurfacing, painted red.

Finally, we should note that the ballcourt floor was not level, but sloped downward gently from the walls toward the center. Presumably this was done to direct rainwater to a drain somewhere, one whose opening we never found.

The North End-field Staircase

While cleaning the east wall of the north end-field, we discovered a small staircase hidden behind a group of loose stones from the final construction stage of the wall (Fig. 19.10). This staircase was evidently part of the original construction of the ballcourt, but had been filled in with stones and plastered over during a later period of architectural modification.

The staircase (Fig. 19.11) consisted of five relatively steep steps that would have allowed players or officials to enter and leave the north end-field. From the floor of the court to the top of the highest step was roughly 1.2 m. The staircase varied from 80 cm wide at the top to 70 cm wide at the base. Each step was composed of a series of naturally squarish stones and had an average rise of 23.2 cm (range was 14–30 cm). The average tread was 19 cm (range was 9–24 cm). The steps had been stuccoed over at least twice and showed signs of wear when discovered. The older layer of stucco was 1 cm thick and painted red; the younger layer was a thin (0.3–0.4 cm) resurfacing, also painted

Figure 19.8. A large patch of wall plaster was preserved in the extreme southwest corner of the north end-field. Here we see two views of that corner.

Figure 19.9. Along the north wall of the north end-field, one could find patches of four superimposed stucco floors. In this photo, the sequence of floors is indicated by black numbers on small white cards. Floor 1 is the uppermost (latest); Floor 4 is the lowest (earliest).

Figure 19.10. The east wall of the north end-field. In *a*, we see the final stage of the wall, with its small staircase hidden by stone fill. In *b*, the stone fill has been removed to reveal the staircase that went with the original Monte Albán II end-field.

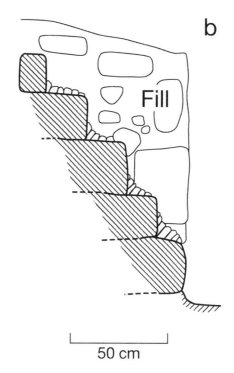

Figure 19.11. This small staircase in the original east wall of the north end-field presumably allowed ballplayers to enter and exit. *a*, the staircase as seen from the west. *b*, a cross-section of the staircase, showing the fill that later hid it from view.

red. Preparation for the first stucco floor included a mixture of clay and sand like that described for the cobble and pebble paving of the north end-field.

The N2W1 Stratigraphic Test

Once we had determined the size and layout of the ballcourt, cross-sectioned it through its sloping *taludes*, and fully exposed one of its end-fields, we turned our attention to the building's date and construction history. I chose Square N2W1 of the grid—very close to the midpoint of the central field—as the site of our main stratigraphic test. The west half of that square became a 1 × 2 m test pit, leaving us the option of expanding if we found interesting features.

Level A, 0–10 cm Depth

In Square N2W1, the original floor of the central field had eroded down to its underlying pavement of hard cobbles and pebbles. Below this pavement we found a fragment of *Spondylus* (spiny oyster) shell and the following sherds:

Subtype G12b bowl: 1 misfired rim
Type G21 bowl: 1 rim and 1 base
Eroded Monte Albán II (and earlier) sherds: 25

Level B, 10–25 cm Depth

Brown fill. About two dozen eroded sherds, none of which appears later than Monte Albán II.

Level C, 25–40 cm Depth

Brown fill.
Type G21 bowl: 1 rim
About a dozen eroded, redeposited Formative sherds such as Socorro Fine Gray, Guadalupe Burnished Brown, Coatepec White, and Avelina Red-on-Buff, mixed with typical Monte Albán II plainwares.

Interruption: One Corner of Tomb 6

At a depth of 56 cm—in the level we would later designate C2—we found human skeletal remains, and suspended our stratigraphic excavation while we cleaned and pedestalled the bones.

We soon realized that our test pit had caught the northwest corner of a tomb. Because most of the rough stone roof of the tomb had collapsed inward, some of the human remains were now at a higher level than the roof stones themselves. Only after we began to clean the skeletal remains did we finally discover the stone walls of the tomb.

Fearing that the tomb might be looted if we simply left it unexcavated, we opened up Square N3W1 to expose more of it. Designated Tomb 6, it dated to Monte Albán IIIa and yielded five individuals from several episodes of burial. Tomb 6 will be fully reported in *San José Mogote 3: The Mortuary Archaeology*.

This Early Classic Zapotec tomb did not have the same alignment as the central field (see Fig. 19.3), which suggested that it was intrusive through the original floor. It also seems to have been kept accessible long enough so that multiple individuals could be added over time, which is unlikely to have been done while the court was still being used for ballgames.

Tomb 6, however, had eventually been covered over again, albeit with cobbles and pebbles rather than an actual stucco floor.

Level C2, 45–65 cm Depth

Once we had dealt with Tomb 6, we were able to continue our stratigraphic excavation of Square N2W1. Level C2 yielded about 30 sherds, almost all of which were redeposited San José phase types. Included were Leandro Gray, Atoyac Yellow-white, Lupita Heavy Plain, and San José Black-and-White.

Rock Layer, 65–95 cm Depth

Between Levels C2 and D was a deposit with many rocks and boulders and few sherds.

Level D, 95–115 cm Depth

From this point downward, the earth in Square N2W1 was a homogeneous dark brown, hard-packed fill with scattered large rocks and boulders. It yielded 30 redeposited sherds of the Tierras Largas and San José phases, including Leandro Gray, Atoyac Yellow-white, Delia White, Avelina Red-on-Buff, and Matadamas Orange.

Level E, 115–125 cm Depth

Atoyac Yellow-white: 10 bowl sherds
Fidencio Coarse: 3 jar rims
Lupita Heavy Plain: 2 brazier sherds
Matadamas Orange: 6 sherds
Avelina Red-on-Buff: 6 sherds
Eroded body sherds: ca. 25

Level F, 125–150 cm Depth

About four dozen eroded sherds of Leandro Gray, Atoyac Yellow-white, Avelina Red-on-Buff, Matadamas Orange, and Tierras Largas Burnished Plain

Level G, 150–175 cm Depth

About four dozen eroded sherds of Leandro Gray, Atoyac

Yellow-white, Avelina Red-on-Buff, Matadamas Orange, and Tierras Largas Burnished Plain

Level H, 175–200 cm Depth

From this depth downward, the deposit had the look of mound fill from a Guadalupe or late San José phase public building.

Redeposited sherds of Tierras Largas and San José phase types: ca. 100

Level I, 200–230 cm Depth

About 40 eroded sherds of the same types seen in Level H

Level J, 230–250 cm Depth

About 25 eroded sherds of the same types seen in Levels H and I

At a depth of 2.5 m below the cobble and pebble paving stones of the central field, we decided to terminate our stratigraphic test in Square N2W1. For one thing, we had not seen a sherd more recent in age than the San José phase for about 2 m. For another, we had reached a level of boulders too large to remove or work around in such a reduced space. We now suspected that the ballcourt had been constructed above the ruins of an Early or Middle Formative public building of some kind. And while we would like to have explored that building, we could not do so without destroying the ballcourt.

Dating the Ballcourt with Ceramics

In addition to our stratigraphic pit in Square N2W1, we put a number of test pits into various parts of the ballcourt to date its construction. The fact that its playing surface had been stuccoed at least six times held out the possibility that it spanned several periods.

1. *Square N6W3*: Sherd sample from the fill of the lower *talud*, just behind the west bench wall (this pit is shown in Fig. 19.6).
   CBA types present included G3, G21, C7, C11, C20, and K3. We also found the mold-made effigy face from a bridge-spout vessel in *gris* ware.
   Date: Monte Albán II.

2. *Behind Stones of West Bench Wall, in East-West Trench*
   Several G1 sherds
   Several G3 bowl sherds
   Type G21 bowls: 2 rims, 1 base
   Type C6 bowl with postfiring zigzags: 1 sherd
   Type C7: several body sherds
   Type C12: 1 bowl rim
   Type K3: several brazier samples

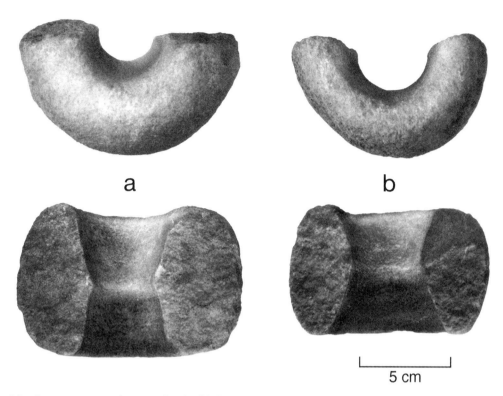

a   b

5 cm

Figure 19.12. Two of the three stone rings discovered in the fill above the ballcourt floor.

Type A9: bowl sherd with painted *xicalcoliuhqui* (step fret) motif
Type A11: 1 fragment of cylindrical bowl
Undecorated *gris* and *crema* body sherds: 40
Redeposited sherds of Guadalupe and San José phases: ± 50
Date: Monte Albán II.

3. *Sherds from Below Cobble and Pebble Pavement, Central Field*
Type C20: 1 sherd
Comal in *café* ware: 1 sherd
Redeposited sherds of Monte Albán II, Rosario, and San José phases: 30
Date: Monte Albán II.

4. *Sherds from Below Next-to-Last Plaster Surface, East Half of East-West Trench*
Type G3 jars: 2 rims
Type C11 bowl: 1 rim
Type C12 bowl: 1 rim
Redeposited San José phase sherds: 12
Date: Monte Albán II.

5. *Sherds Trapped Between Uppermost Stucco Surface and Next-to-Last Plaster Surface, East* Talud, *in East-West Trench*
Type G23 bowl: 2 sherds, showing Monte Albán IIIa-style carved cartouche
Type G3 bowls: several sherds
Type G21 bowl: 1 rim, 1 base

Type C7 bowl: 1 sherd
Body sherds, *gris* and *crema*: ± 30
Date: Most of these sherds are Monte Albán II, but the Type G23 bowl sherds suggest that the final plaster surface of the ballcourt dates to Monte Albán IIIa (as does Tomb 6).

Possible Ballgame-Related Artifacts

We found 3 unusual artifacts in the earthen fill above the floor of the ballcourt. Each was one-half of a broken stone ring, between 10.5 and 12.5 cm in diameter. Made from locally available ignimbrite (volcanic tuff), each had been carefully smoothed and biconically drilled in the center until it resembled a large doughnut.

In other parts of Mesoamerica, similar objects have been referred to as "loom weights" or "digging stick weights." If either of these terms applied in our case, however, we would expect such objects to have been more abundant in household areas. The fact is that none were found in the residential areas excavated at San José Mogote, nor were they common on the surface of the site. The 3 found above the floor of the ballcourt are the only ones for which we have a provenience. We must therefore consider the possibility that these rings had something to do with the ballgame, although we cannot specify their role.

Two of the rings are illustrated in Figure 19.12. The dimensions of all 3 specimens are as follows:

1. Diameter 12.5 cm; thickness, 8 cm. Biconically drilled, leaving a hole that tapers from 5 cm on its margins to 3.3 cm in the center.

2. Diameter, 12 cm; thickness, 7.3 cm. Biconically drilled, leaving a hole that tapers from 6.5 cm on its margins to 4.5 cm in the center.

3. Diameter, 10.5 cm; thickness, 6 cm. Biconically drilled, leaving a hole that tapers from 5 cm on its margins to 3.7 cm in the center.

Conclusions

Based on my excavation, it appears that the ballcourt on Mound 7-south was originally built during Monte Albán II. It was therefore one more component of the Monte Albán II renaissance at San José Mogote. There is some evidence to suggest that it may have been built on an artificial rise created by a public building of the San José or Guadalupe phase. We found no evidence, however, for Rosario phase or Monte Albán I construction on Mound 7-south.

The ballcourt underwent several architectural modifications during its period of use, and we found at least six superimposed plaster floors in places. The final modification of the court may have occurred in Monte Albán IIIa, about the time that the final modifications to the Mound 8 governmental palace were made (Chapter 18). At some point during Monte Albán IIIa—presumably after the ballgames on the court had ceased—Tomb 6 was excavated into the floor of the central field and kept accessible for a while so that later burials could be added alongside the original occupants. Finally, the tomb was hidden by being covered over with the same kinds of cobbles and pebbles used for the subfloor stone pavement of the playing surface.

The Mound 7 ballcourt was almost identical in its size and layout to the ballcourt on the main plaza at Monte Albán. It differs in a few architectural details, including the addition of a single-file staircase in the east wall of the north end-field. This staircase was later filled in and stuccoed over.

One of the surprises of our ballcourt excavation was the extent to which the court's stucco surfaces had been painted red. To be sure, this paint had faded with erosion and the passage of time, but it could still be detected. While Stucco Surface #2 of the sloping *talud* had apparently been left white, red would have been the dominant color of the original ballcourt. This makes us wonder, in turn, to what extent the various ballcourts at Monte Albán might once have been painted red.

20 | The Evolution of Zapotec State Religion

Spanish *conquistadores* reached the Valley of Oaxaca in 1529. One of their goals was to convert the Zapotec to Christianity. It is fortunate for all of us interested in the region, however, that some Spaniards undertook to describe Zapotec religion for Philip II.

These sixteenth-century descriptions are vital to our understanding of Zapotec religion. That is not to say, of course, that every Spanish priest or administrator really understood Zapotec cosmology, religion, and ideology. For example, some authors produced long lists of the "gods" worshiped by specific communities. All too often, once we begin to translate the names of those "gods," we discover that most of them were actually deceased rulers invoked by the community. Sometimes the title *coqui*, or hereditary lord, was even included in the name.

At Tlalixtac de Cabrera, for example, the Spaniards reported villagers sacrificing adults and children, quail and parrot feathers, and dogs to Coqui Huani. Macuilxochitl venerated a deceased ruler named Coqui Bila; Tlacolula prayed to Coqui Cehuiyo (Marcus 1992:287). These deceased rulers were revered as semidivine beings and received frequent sacrifices since they had the power to intercede with the supernatural on behalf of their living subjects.

To be sure, a few priests spent sufficient time among the Zapotec to develop great insight into the culture. This happened to fray Juan de Córdova (1942 [1578]) at Tlacochahuaya. In describing the use of color terms, Córdova wrote that the Zapotec "do not ask, as we would, what color is it?" For the Zapotec, each color was more an entity than an adjective; a particular flower, for example, might "partake of red" the way an event might "partake of justice."

The sixteenth-century Zapotec religion described by the Spaniards was clearly a state religion. Church and government were not separate. The most highly ranked priests were of noble birth, and the king himself underwent religious training before taking office. The head of the Zapotec church was known as the *uija-tao* or "great seer," a man the Spaniards described as "like our pope" (Canseco 1905 [1580]). He lived in an elegant residence decorated with stone mosaics, located in the rear of a colonnaded temple at Mitla in the Tlacolula subvalley (Marcus and Flannery 1996:14–16). Every year the Zapotec ruler (who lived at Zaachila in the Zimatlán subvalley) sent laborers to Mitla to cultivate the fields that supported the great seer.

We know more about sixteenth-century Zapotec religion than that of any other period. Unfortunately, we cannot simply use it as a template for the religion of earlier periods. One of the biggest myths in archaeology is that religion is so conservative, and changes so slowly, that it can readily be projected into the past. Sixteenth-century Zapotec religion was appropriate for a stratified society with royals, major nobles, minor nobles, commoners, and slaves. It thus does not work for the Formative period, much less the Archaic. But how about Monte Albán II? Might our sixteenth-century descriptions work for that state-level society, with its palaces and two-room temples?

What we propose for this final chapter is as follows. We will begin our discussion with the Archaic period, for which we have limited empirical evidence of cosmology, ritual, ideology, and iconography. We will then proceed slowly forward through time. Our expectation is that during each successive archaeological phase, we will see a few more recognizable aspects of Zapotec religion come into focus. Bit by bit, with the patience of a time-lapse photographer, we hope to document the gradual evolution of a religion that is recognizable as Zapotec (Table 20.1).

To be sure, that religion will not correspond exactly to the one described by the sixteenth-century Spaniards. A great deal of that religion consisted of sacred propositions that leave no archaeological trace. Our window into the cognitive past, as always, is ritual. We can get only as close to ancient Zapotec religion as the empirical evidence for ritual will permit.

The Era of Nomadic Foraging and Early Horticulture

For the Archaic period (8000–2000 b.c.), ritual data are so hard to come by that we must look at both Oaxaca and Tehuacán. The foragers of the Archaic spent part of the year dispersed in family-sized units and part of the year coalesced in camps of 25–50 people. It appears that much of their ritual was deferred until times when the largest number of families were living together.

At Gheo-Shih in the Valley of Oaxaca, space was set aside for *ad hoc* rituals in the center of a 1.5 ha camp. This ritual space was bounded by parallel lines of boulders, with the area between the lines kept free of refuse. We expect that dances, initiations, or even games might have been carried out there.

At Coxcatlán Cave in the Tehuacán Valley, a living floor dated by its plant remains to the harvest season became the scene of infant sacrifice and ritual cannibalism. It is significant that this type of sacrifice was carried out in the southern Mexican highlands thousands of years before village life began.

Ritual in the Era of Egalitarian Villages

During the Tierras Largas phase (1500–1150 b.c.) the establishment of permanent villages meant that groups even larger than 25–50 would be present year round. We suspect—but cannot yet prove—that many ceremonies could now be held on prearranged dates, changing the status of ritual from *ad hoc* to calendric. This might have provided impetus for the 260-day calendar.

One interesting aspect of early village life was the separation of venues for men's and women's rituals. In both cases we have reason to suspect that ancestor ritual was involved. The house and its dooryard were the province of women's ritual. There the women arranged scenes of small handmade figurines, tangible objects that provided the spirits of the ancestors with places to visit. While the women cajoled, propitiated, and sought advice from their immediate ancestors, the men of San José Mogote built white-plastered ritual houses with an orientation 8° north of east. In these small men's houses, whose use was probably restricted to full initiates, the men communed with more remote ancestors, such as lineage founders. We infer that men's ritual included a mixture of powdered tobacco and lime, along with the possible use of other narcotic plants. *Datura* and morning glory, for example, are part of the vegetation at San José Mogote.

Ritual paraphernalia of the Tierras Largas phase included ceramic masks, conch shell trumpets, and boxlike metates that we believe were for grinding tobacco. In at least two cases, necklaces of imported sea shells were left as offerings in the ruins of abandoned men's houses.

Finally, middle-aged men who may have been respected leaders were sometimes buried near the men's house in a seated, tightly bundled position.

The Escalation of Ritual and Social Inequality

During the San José phase (1150–850 b.c.), we see our first signs of hereditary social inequality. Among the sumptuary goods used by the emerging elite were jadeite ornaments, iron ore mirrors, mother-of-pearl and *Spondylus* shells, geometric cutouts of mica, and pottery vessels imported from distant regions. Some elite children had their heads deformed as a sign of rank. Our first iconographic representations of Earth (Earthquake), Sky (Lightning), and the four world quadrants were carved on black, gray, or white pottery of the San José phase. Such carved vessels were sometimes buried with adult men, and sometimes with infants or children, but never with adult women. One elite woman buried at Tomaltepec, however, had an ornament of iron ore in the shape of a Lightning symbol (Whalen 1981).

Men of high rank were buried in the seated, bundled position, and sometimes had secondary burials added to theirs. We have no seated bundle burials of women, but some highly ranked women were buried with half a dozen jadeite ornaments. The figurines of the San José phase depicted both positions of authority and positions of obeisance. Mat motifs and miniature four-legged stools—both references to chiefly paraphernalia—appeared for the first time during this period.

At the start of the San José phase, initiates were still building men's houses; one contained the skull of a spider monkey, a lowland animal that later became a day-sign in the Zapotec ritual calendar. By the late San José phase, however, men's houses had been replaced by temples on masonry platforms. The diverse stones used in these platforms suggest that satellite communities up to 5–6 km away were contributing construction materials. Despite this evidence that San José Mogote's temples had significance for an entire region, the stairways on the temple platforms were narrow and single file, suggesting that many rituals were still restricted to a small audience.

Table 20.1. The order in which various aspects of Zapotec religion appear in the archaeological record.

Period (Conventional ^{14}C Dates)	Archaeological Evidence
Archaic (8000–2000 b.c.)	Boulder-lined space set aside for *ad hoc* ritual. Infant sacrifice, including cannibalism.
Tierras Largas phase (1500–1150 b.c.)	Separate venues for men's and women's ritual. Ancestor ritual with handmade figurines. Men's houses, with use of masks, conch shell trumpets, narcotic plants. Ritual orientation 8° north of east. Calendric ritual?
San José phase (1150–850 b.c.)	First representations of Sky (Lightning), Earth (Earthquake), 4 world quadrants. Iconography of hereditary rank. Temples with single-file staircases. Water divination. Bloodletting with stingray spines. Feasting on dog meat.
Guadalupe phase (850–700 b.c.)	One-room temples with wide stairways. Patios with temples on all 4 sides. Special beakers for ritual beverages. Circle-and-triangle motif for flowing blood.
Rosario phase (700–500 b.c.)	Acropolis with highly visible temples. Shift from 8° north of east to true east-west orientation. Crocodile's foot as reference to Earth. Sacrifice of quail in temples. Bloodletting with obsidian lancets, heart sacrifice, cannibalism. Effigy incense burners. Circular performance platforms. Hieroglyphic writing used in chiefly propaganda. 260-day ritual calendar.
Monte Albán Ia (500–300 b.c.)	Temples with fire basins, storage rooms, sloping platforms. Large prisoner displays. Use of both 365-day and 260-day calendars. Visits to sites of historic significance for memorial rituals.
Monte Albán Ic (300–100 b.c.)	Rival emerging states display different plaza orientations. First two-room temples and priests' residences. "Frying pan" incense burners.
Monte Albán II (100 b.c.–AD 200)	State religion, with concept of ruler's metamorphosis into cloud person who has close ties with Lightning. Two-room temples rebuilt at 52-year intervals. Urns, incensarios in temple trash. Grand plaza layout. Rituals of sanctification; postabandonment offerings. Obsidian daggers for heart sacrifice. Veneration of deceased rulers with calendric names. Anthropomorphized depictions of *Cociyo*, Clouds, Rain, Wind, Hail, jaguars, bats, and maize.

In an earlier work (Flannery and Marcus 2012), we found worldwide evidence that temples tend to replace men's houses once a society has developed hereditary inequality. One reason for this is that emerging elites tend to explain their privileged position as the result of a close relationship to (or even descent from) the deity for whom the temple is built. As a result, the remote ancestors of most men—once honored in the men's house—decline in importance.

Women of the San José phase continued to use handmade figurines and conduct their ancestor rituals in the household. In one household unit, we found evidence for *quela hueniy niça*, a form of Zapotec divination that employed water-filled basins (Flannery and Marcus 2005:261–273). Not only were there two such basins in the dooryard of this house, but the basins were also painted with two of the primary colors associated with the four quarters of the Zapotec cosmos.

Our first evidence of ritual bloodletting with imported sting- ray spines comes from House 17 of San José Mogote (Flannery and Marcus 2005: Fig. 18.4). Our first evidence for feasting on domestic dogs, on the other hand, comes from House 4, and may have involved as much as 50 kg of meat (Flannery and Marcus 2005:188–189).

In sum, the creation of hereditary inequality during the San José phase brought about an escalation of archaeological evidence for belief in a quadripartite cosmos, reverence for Earth and Lightning, and the iconographic communication of differences in rank.

Ritual in an Era of Chiefly Cycling

During the Guadalupe phase (850–700 b.c.), San José Mogote was forced to compete with emerging chiefly centers at Huitzo and San Martín Tilcajete. Our evidence suggests that San José's chiefly elite strengthened its ties with the leaders of its satellite communities by sending them highly ranked brides. The site of Tierras Largas produced the remains of a second feast at which 50 kg of dog meat were consumed, reinforcing the likelihood that ritual feasts were a vehicle for strengthening sociopolitical ties and establishing chiefly generosity.

The figurines of the Guadalupe phase communicate hereditary rank even more strongly than those of the San José phase. They show women of rank wearing jadeite spools in their ears, elaborate turbans on their heads, shell pectorals, necklaces, and sandals that prevented their feet from touching the soil. Ritual beverages of chocolate or pulque could now be served in elegant white beakers, made from nonlocal clay.

The Guadalupe phase saw the creation of small ceremonial patios, flanked on all four sides by one-room temples. Those temples still had wattle-and-daub walls, but they now rested on rectangular platforms built from thousands of circular, plano-convex adobe bricks. Those platforms retained the 8° north of east orientation of earlier times, but they had abandoned the narrow, single-file staircases of the San José phase. The staircases now featured steps 5–8 m wide, allowing much larger groups of spectators to witness ritual events. The old "initiates only" privacy of the men's house had been replaced by a program of public performance.

One of the unresolved questions of Guadalupe phase religion is the extent to which the four temples around a patio served different purposes. We understand that a quadripartite cosmos may have been involved, but what made the temples complementary rather than redundant? Were they dedicated to different supernatural beings, used on different days of the ritual calendar, or built by different segments of society? Whatever the case, it is significant that 10–15 percent of the Guadalupe phase occupation at both Huitzo and San José Mogote may have been set aside for such ceremonial architecture.

Ritual in a Powerful, Militaristic, Three-Tiered Chiefdom

During the Rosario phase (700–500 b.c.), the leaders of San José Mogote combined bold and attention-grabbing public architecture, new varieties of sumptuary goods, corvée labor, chiefly hypogamy, social networking, and military force to create the most powerful multilevel rank society in the Valley of Oaxaca. One of their most dramatic moves was to turn Mound 1 into an acropolis, one whose major temple would have been visible for many kilometers. That temple was built of rectangular adobe bricks and extra thick wattle and daub, and rested upon a platform featuring half-ton limestone blocks from the opposite side of the Atoyac River. Built early in the Rosario phase, this one-room temple was oriented 8° north of east. By the late Rosario phase, however, its supporting platform had been enlarged twice, and the platform's orientation had changed to east-west. This is our oldest example of the orientation later used at Monte Albán.

Prior to the building of the platform for this temple, a number of late Guadalupe/early Rosario burials had been exhumed and reburied on the spot selected for its construction. These secondary burials featured highly ranked youths, both male and female, along with their sumptuary goods.

Included among the ritual activities in the temple were feasting (with subsequent ritual burial of the serving vessels); bloodletting (with obsidian facsimiles of stingray spines); sacrifices of quail; and ritual cannibalism, presumably following acts of human sacrifice.

When this temple was burned by a rival rank society, the leaders of San José Mogote had a new one built only a few meters away. This new temple appears to have featured wooden columns with volcanic tuff bases, and it rested upon a plus-sign-shaped, limestone masonry platform. The threshold of the corridor running between the new and old Rosario temples was a carved stone depicting an elite prisoner whose heart had been removed, and whose name was given in Zapotec hieroglyphs. The streams of blood running from the victim's chest ended in stylized drops. The "circle and triangle" motif used for those drops (a symbol already present on shell ornaments of the Guadalupe phase) was designed to represent *tini*, or flowing blood, as opposed to *rini*, or dried blood. This was a crucial distinction in Zapotec world view.

Other innovations of the Rosario phase included the crocodile's foot motif, reflecting the belief that Earth was the back of a giant crocodile. Eventually, in addition to having its temple visible for great distances, the Rosario phase acropolis was given a circular platform for public dancing or oratory. This "performance platform" was reminiscent of those found in the lowland Maya region between 700 and 500 b.c.

The Abandonment of San José Mogote and the Founding of Monte Albán

Because San José Mogote was largely abandoned during the Monte Albán Ia phase (500–300 b.c.), we must turn to San Martín Tilcajete and Monte Albán itself for most of our ritual information on that period. We know that Monte Albán built at least one temple on a platform with a sloping wall (*talud*), but we have no actual plan for that temple. Tilcajete was still building one-room temples at this time, but added fire basins to them and built small storage rooms for temple paraphernalia.

During Period Ia, Monte Albán's Building L featured a gallery with hundreds of carved stones depicting slain or sacrificed captives (Marcus 1974). The goal of this gallery was clearly to communicate Monte Albán's military might, and many of the prisoner carvings have hieroglyphic captions that may indicate the victim's name. At the south end of the gallery stood two stelae with our first "pure" 8-glyph text in Zapotec writing. This text leaves no doubt that by 500–300 b.c., the Zapotec were using both the 365-day solar calendar and the 260-day ritual calendar (Marcus 2003a).

During this period, San José Mogote was briefly visited by a group of people who performed a ceremony of some kind on the highest point of Mound 1. This ceremony involved the building of a small altar, the burning of incense, and the creation of a subterranean offering box in which the incomplete corpse of a child was buried. This is our oldest example of what became a longstanding Zapotec ritual: centuries after the abandonment of an important civic-ceremonial center, the site is briefly revisited so that a ceremony can be carried out on its highest point. This behavior implies the existence of "social memory," prompting memorial rituals at places where previous generations are alleged to have done great things. In the case of San José Mogote, one of the "great things" its ancient leaders had done was move 2000 colonists from the Etla subvalley to the summit of Monte Albán.

Ritual in the Era of State Formation

During Monte Albán Ic (300–100 b.c.), two rival first-generation states were evidently forming at Monte Albán and San Martín Tilcajete. Those competing civic-ceremonial centers deliberately maintained different solar or astronomical orientations, with Monte Albán's major public buildings aligned north-south and Tilcajete's aligned 25° east of north. Each site likely created a cosmological justification for its orientation.

We are confident that both sites built palaces for their rulers and created important ceremonial plazas. Tilcajete's palace has been excavated (Spencer and Redmond 2003), but any Period Ic palace at Monte Albán presumably lies undiscovered below the North Platform of that site.

Built early in Monte Albán Ic, Tilcajete's Structure 20 was a one-room temple with rubble pillars; there were small storage rooms and cooking facilities not far away. By 100 b.c., Tilcajete had constructed its first two-room temple, Structure 16. This is our oldest excavated example of a Zapotec temple with inner and outer rooms. While the minor priests would probably have spent considerable time in the inner room, Tilcajete had also built two residences nearby to house the major priests. When one adds to this the construction of storage units in the area, we have our first example of an actual temple precinct (Redmond and Spencer 2008, 2013). "Frying pan" incense burners had also been added to the ritual paraphernalia, making the burning of copal a portable activity.

Government and Religion in an Expansionist, Militaristic State

By Monte Albán II (100 b.c.–AD 200), there can no longer be any question that we are dealing with a Zapotec state, one featuring state religion in addition to household ritual. We are now able to compare the capital of the Zapotec state, Monte Albán, with two of its secondary administrative centers, Cerro Tilcajete (Elson 2007) and San José Mogote (this volume). Both secondary centers shared Monte Albán's north-south orientation, and Cerro Tilcajete even built a road leading north toward Monte Albán.

The extent to which Monte Albán and San José Mogote reflected a common architectural template is striking. Both sites were organized around main plazas with nearly identical dimensions. Each had a governmental palace on the north, an I-shaped ballcourt on one side, and a temple-covered mound on the south. Both sites built additional temples on natural rises in their main plazas. Each site had residences for extended families of nobles who, over the course of time, changed the internal traffic routes and subdivided or enlarged the rooms as needed. At both sites, *Cociyo* (Lightning) was strongly associated with royals and nobles. Elaborate funerary urns and incense braziers were produced by the thousands.

One notable difference between Monte Albán and San José Mogote was that Monte Albán had hieroglyphic monuments during Period II and San José Mogote did not. Nor did San José Mogote have anything equivalent to Monte Albán's Building J, which once featured the hieroglyphic names of more than 40 places claimed as subjects by Monte Albán (Marcus 1980, 1992).

Despite being only a second-tier center below Monte Albán, San José Mogote has contributed to our understanding of Zapotec state and class ideology, state religion, and ritual behavior. Our data suggest that some Zapotec two-room temples were rebuilt or replaced at the end of each 52-year calendric cycle. Rituals of sanctification were carried out before construction began, and offerings were sometimes left in the debris of the previous temple. Among the rituals related to the temple were infanticide, cannibalism, beheading, and heart sacrifice. Cups filled with a ritual beverage might be left as offerings, as were incense burners.

The data from San José Mogote also make clear that nobles and commoners had their own distinct rituals. Commoners went to the spirit world of their human ancestors after death. Nobles, on the other hand, metamorphosed into cloud people and took on many attributes of *Cociyo*. Their metamorphosis might be witnessed by Clouds, Rain, Wind, and Hail, the quadripartite companions of *Cociyo*. Flutes and drums were played at their funerals.

As the gulf between nobles and commoners grew, the small handmade figurines of the Formative period disappeared. The figurines of later periods were often mold-made and mass-produced, and some may represent culture heroes (Marcus 1998). Among the culture heroes of the later Zapotec were legendary "founder couples" such as Lord 1 Jaguar and his consort, Lady 2 Maize. Drinking vessels carved with their hieroglyphic names were sometimes left behind as offerings in abandoned temples.

To be sure, the religion of Monte Albán II was not identical to the historic Zapotec religion of AD 1529. More than 1000 years intervened between the Early Classic abandonment of San José Mogote and the writings of Spanish eyewitnesses such as Juan de Córdova. That having been said, many of the principles of later Zapotec state religion were in evidence by AD 200.

By that time, the Zapotec cosmos was already quadripartite, with each world quadrant associated with a primary color. Earth was the back of a giant crocodile, and his angry movement was embodied in Earthquake. Sky's angry face was Lightning, distant kin to the Zapotec royal family. The relationship between Lightning and humans was reciprocal, with supernatural gifts such as life-giving rain requiring offerings of flowing blood in return. A deity visited his *yohopèe*, or temple, only after the secular ground had been converted to sacred ground with labor-intensive offerings, or after the sacrifice of humans, turkeys, or quail.

Among the colors we found on the walls and floors of Zapotec temples, pure white and blood red were the most important. Among the animals we found depicted in art, jaguars and bats were especially featured. One, with his fangs and claws, was a metaphor for the Zapotec ruler. The other, who emerged from the caves at dusk and returned at dawn, served as a messenger between the land of the living and the land of the dead.

Culture heroes like Lord 1 Jaguar—surely mythologized, but possibly based on an early ruler of Monte Albán—served as intermediaries between their human subjects and the supernatural forces of the Zapotec cosmos. Commoners, who once had communicated with Lightning through the ritual, now found themselves too lowly to approach a powerful supernatural that way. Instead—like the citizens of sixteenth-century Ocelotepec, who continued to pray to their ruler Petela even after the Spaniards had burned his mummy (Espíndola 1580)—the Zapotec commoner petitioned his deceased ruler for the favors he once would have requested from Lightning (Marcus and Flannery 1996:21).

Conclusions

As hoped, we can see the elements of Zapotec religion gradually coming together over thousands of years. To be sure, there were periods of stasis and periods of more rapid change. The San José phase, when hereditary inequality emerged, saw elite lineages co-opt supernatural forces such as Lightning and Earthquake and use them to rationalize their privileged status. Monte Albán II witnessed the creation of a ruling class who could metamorphose into cloud people after death, leading commoners to pray to deceased rulers rather than addressing Lightning directly.

We believe that in the future, cognitive archaeology will play an increasingly important role in the analysis and description of ancient Mesoamerican societies. We worry, to be sure, that not every archaeologist will stay within the parameters set by his or her empirical archaeological data. No scholar should believe that he or she has the "intuition" or "sensitivity" to jump from a ritual artifact directly to an ultimate sacred proposition. The success of cognitive archaeology depends on our ability to make it as rigorous and scientific as subsistence-settlement archaeology.

Appendix A | The Mound 1/Area A Step Trench

Mound 1 at San José Mogote rises 15 m above the main plaza. Its sides are so steep that when we first saw it, we assumed that it was a man-made pyramid. Not only did we assume that it was an artificial mound, we believed that it might be too recent a structure to fall within the scope of our project. Our attention at that time was strongly focused on the Early and Middle Formative periods.

It took us several seasons to work out the sequence of early houses and public buildings in Area A of the site (Flannery and Marcus 1994: Chapter 18; 2005: Chapters 12–14). As our masons worked to consolidate Structures 1 and 2 of Area A (Chapter 4, this volume), we looked up from time to time at Mound 1 and wondered about the heavy limestone slabs strewn down the east side of the mound. Many of those slabs had been seen and photographed half a century earlier by Constantine George Rickards (1910) (see Fig. A.1). It occurred to us that the source of the stones might have been a massive staircase, a guess that later turned out to be accurate (Fig. 9.2).

We had already discovered that the staircase on Structure 2 of Area A faced east (Fig. 4.21). If our guess was correct, there might also be a monumental building on the summit of Mound 1 whose staircase faced east. Soon we began to wonder whether we might have a long stratigraphic sequence of east-facing public buildings, rising all the way from Structure 2 to the top of Mound 1.

Clearly, one way to test this possibility would be to treat Mound 1 as if it were a Near Eastern *tell*, and excavate a traditional Near Eastern step trench into its east side. Such a trench would tell us whether, in fact, we had a long stratigraphic sequence of public buildings linking Area A to Mound 1.

In 1974, armed with a new excavation budget, we finally got the chance to make our step trench. The results were not at all what we had expected. First, we learned that roughly 13 m of Mound 1's height consisted of a steep natural hill. As a result, there was no connection between Structure 2 and the buildings on the summit of the mound. In addition, we learned that some of the most monumental buildings on Mound 1 were earlier than we had expected: they were Middle Formative.

Beginning the Step Trench

We selected a prominent rise on the northeastern summit of Mound 1 as the place to begin our trench. We did not know at that time, of course, that the rise had been created by a series of superimposed Monte Albán II temples. One of the most obvious features of the rise was a depression that we suspected might be an old looter's pit. We had discovered that one could often learn a lot by cleaning out old looter's pits, so we decided to do so before laying out the trench.

Above: Figure A.1. When Constantine George Rickards (1910) took this photograph, Mound 1 of San José Mogote belonged to the former Hacienda del Cacique. The owner of the hacienda had sent his workmen to pull many large limestone blocks out of the Rosario phase staircase of Structure 14. A number of these large blocks can be seen on the east slope of the mound.

Below: Figure A.2. The south profile of the Mound 1/Area A Step Trench, Squares S2W2 to S2E3 (*a*, east half; *b*, west half). These were the first five squares excavated. Once it was clear that they contained a sequence of stucco floors, including the floor of at least one two-room temple (Structure 13), we decided to try for the complete plan of each building, once the step trench had been taken to sterile soil or bedrock.

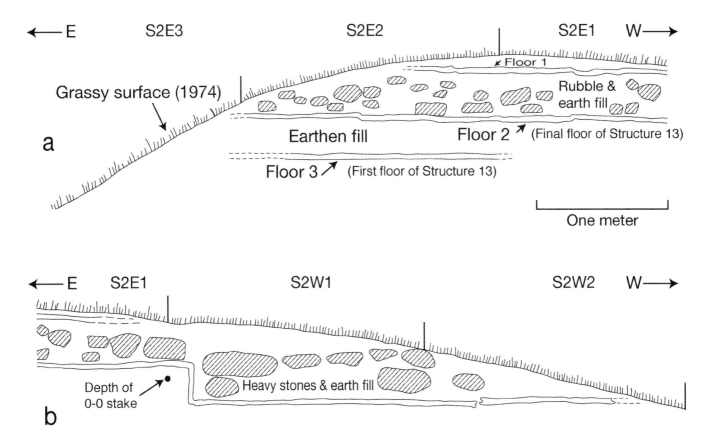

We soon found that our looter's pit had broken through a stucco floor some 40 cm below the grassy surface of the mound. While we did not know it at the time, that stucco floor belonged to a temple that we would later designate Structure 13 (Chapter 13).

The stucco floor became a convenient landmark for the start of our step trench. We cleared more of the floor to the west of the looter's hole, and found a preexisting crack where we could insert a metal stake without causing further damage to the stucco. That stake became our zero-north, zero-east datum point, not only for the step trench but also for the grid used to excavate Structures 13, 14, 35, 36, and 37 (Chapters 9, 13).

The step trench was 2 m wide and made up of Squares S2W2 through S2E12 of our grid. Our datum stake became the northwest corner of Square S1E1, as well as the point from which we calculated all depths. The stucco surface we had cleared was eventually labeled Floor 2 because the expansion of our excavation soon revealed an even higher floor, only 8 cm below the grassy surface, at the junction of Squares S2E1 and S2E2 of the grid. That stucco layer became Floor 1 (Fig. A.2).

As the step trench progressed, we were able to take a screened sample of ceramics from the fill between Floor 1 and Floor 2. The diagnostic sherds from this fill were incorporated into the list on pages 283–284, and indicate a Monte Albán II date.

At a depth of 22 cm below Floor 2 we encountered Floor 3, which later turned out to be an earlier floor of Structure 13. The diagnostic sherds trapped between Floors 2 and 3 were incorporated into the list on page 280, and indicate a Monte Albán II date.

While extending our trench west into Squares S2W1 and S2W2, we came to a place where Floor 2 abruptly stepped down 30 cm and then continued west. We had seen two-room temples at Monte Albán whose floors featured just such an abrupt step between the inner and outer rooms. Now we knew more than we had known before we began the step trench: Floor 2, in all likelihood, belonged to a Monte Albán II temple with at least two construction stages, one represented by Floor 3 and one by Floor 2.

Excavating Squares S2E3 and S2E4

In typical Near Eastern fashion, we began stepping our trench eastward and down into Squares S2E3 and S2E4. At a depth of 64 cm below datum we came upon Floor 4, the fourth well-made stucco surface that we had encountered so far (Fig. A.3). We did not know it at the time, but Floor 4 would later turn out to be the stucco floor of the inner room of Structure 35, an earlier Monte Albán II temple (Chapter 13).

Some 60–70 sherds were lying in direct contact with the Structure 35 floor; the diagnostics have been incorporated into the list on page 271. These ceramics revealed that we were still in deposits of the Monte Albán II period.

Below Floor 4 we encountered a thick layer of fill composed of stones, earth, and dozens of adobe bricks that had clearly been removed from a preexisting building. The surfaces of these adobes were coated with lime plaster and multicolored paint, and (as Fig. A.3 shows) they had often been stacked 4–5 bricks high. Eventually we reached Floor 5, a stucco surface that (in contrast to all previous floors) displayed a cream to yellowish-white color.

We did not know it at the time, but Floor 5 belonged to a brightly painted Monte Albán II temple that we would come to designate Structure 36. Floor 5 lay 2.24 m below our datum point and had suffered great damage from the massive piles of stones and reused adobes stacked upon it. At the time, we wondered why anyone would choose to pile so much fill over an old building before constructing a new one. We later realized that it had been done so that there would be space below the temple floor for a series of large, stone masonry offering boxes (Chapter 13).

Not surprisingly, we recovered hundreds of sherds from the thick layer of fill between Floors 4 and 5. The diagnostics from this fill have been listed already on pages 246–247, and indicate a Monte Albán II date.

Excavating Squares S2E5 and S2E6

As our trench stepped eastward and down into Squares S2E5 and S2E6 (Figs. A.4, A.5) we encountered a mass of stony rubble set in mud mortar. We would later discover that this rubble had been laid over the ruins of Structure 37, a Rosario phase temple, to provide a firm foundation for Structure 36. Because Structure 37 was smaller than Structure 36, the rubble extended well to the east of the earlier structure. We also discovered that with the passage of time, erosion had carried away the eastern edge of Structure 36. Square S2E6, in fact, yielded little more than slopewash.

Excavating Square S2E7

Square S2E7 (Fig. A.6) was extremely informative. The layer of slopewash encountered in Square S2E6 eventually came to rest against a limestone slab that had been partially exposed by erosion. This limestone slab was laid upon another in such a way as to suggest that they were both part of a staircase. Later we would realize that we had discovered the original Rosario phase staircase on the east side of Structure 14 (Chapter 9). Had our step trench been placed farther to the north we would have missed this staircase entirely, because the Rosario phase stage of the building was narrower north-south than the Monte Albán II stage (Fig. 9.1).

Indeed, as we later learned, we were lucky to find any part of the Rosario phase staircase. Not only had later Monte Albán II architects "borrowed" many of the Rosario staircase stones to use elsewhere, but the owner of the Hacienda del Cacique had removed more stones between 1890 and 1910. In fact, we were told by some of the older residents of San José Mogote that most of the large slabs lying on the east slope of Mound 1 (Fig. A.1) were ones the *hacendado*'s crew had pried from the staircase, then

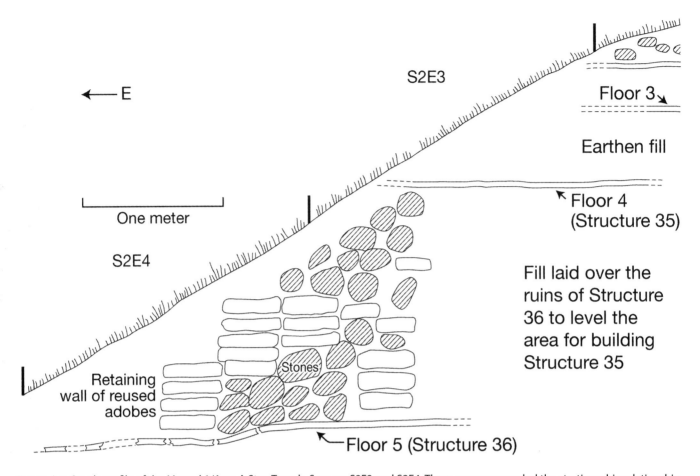

Figure A.3. South profile of the Mound 1/Area A Step Trench, Squares S2E3 and S2E4. These squares revealed the stratigraphic relationship of Structures 35 and 36.

found too heavy to carry. All this "borrowing" had left the staircase too disturbed to be reconstructed, and parts of it were full of intrusive later materials, both Monte Albán II and Colonial.

Behind the two stairway stones in Square S2E7 we found a layer of grayish brown fill and smaller stones. Below this fill was a layer of sand that seemed to us suspiciously uniform and horizontal, as if connected in some way to a structure.

We continued downward in Square S2E7 until we were roughly 2 m below the horizontal sand layer. At that point we encountered ignimbrite bedrock and realized that Mound 1 was a natural hill rather than a Near Eastern-style *tell*. To reach bedrock, our workmen had to remove three layers of the kind of sterile greenish clay that forms above ignimbrite. Resting on the uppermost stratum of sterile clay was a layer of San José phase sherds.

This layer of San José phase sherds was weighed down by a series of stony rubble and earthen fills, laid in deliberately to provide support for the staircase. We encountered the lowermost in situ staircase stone at a depth of 50 cm below the aforementioned horizontal sand layer, stabilized by a layer of hard yellow earth that resembled puddled adobe. This yellow earth, which appeared not to have been affected by the later stone robbing, yielded 10

Socorro Fine Gray sherds of the Rosario phase (featuring negative white and zoned toning); a Guadalupe phase figurine head; and 25 redeposited sherds of the San José phase. This discovery allowed us to date one of the few intact sections of the staircase to the Rosario phase.

Excavating Squares S2E8–S2E12

Once we began to step eastward and down into Squares S2E8 and S2E9, the whole nature of our trench changed. No longer were we encountering horizontal layers and traces of architecture; now we were finding only layers of slopewash, some of which descended at a 45° angle (Figs. A.7, A.8). Clearly, from Square S2E8 eastward we were dealing with a natural slope so steep that no structures could be built there without the creation of artificial terraces. In Squares S2E9 and S2E11 we reached sterile soil. After completing Square S2E11, we terminated our step trench, since there seemed little chance of finding any more buildings on the east slope of the mound.

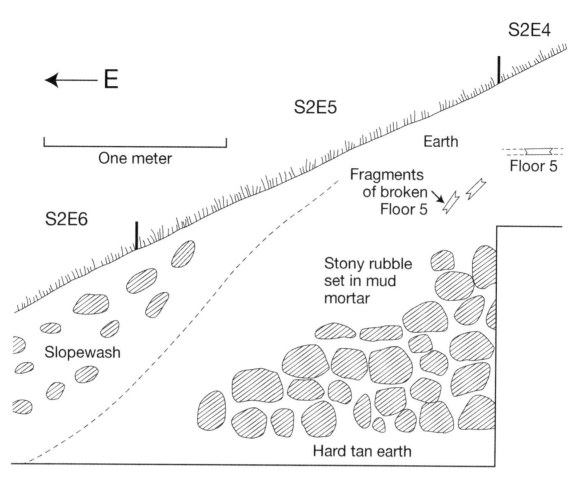

Above: Figure A.4. South profile of the Mound 1/Area A Step Trench, Square S2E5. The mass of stony rubble set in mud mortar was deliberately laid over the ruins of Structure 37 in order to provide a foundation for Structure 36. By making that foundation 1 m thick, the architects allowed room for subfloor offering boxes.

Below: Figure A.5. South profile of the Mound 1/Area A Step Trench, Square S2E6.

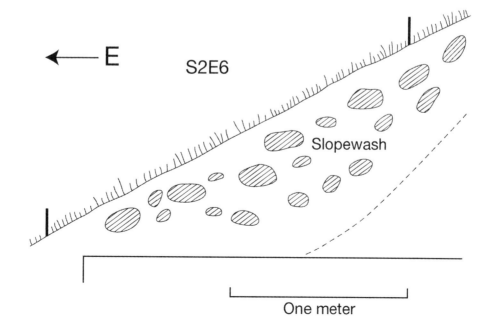

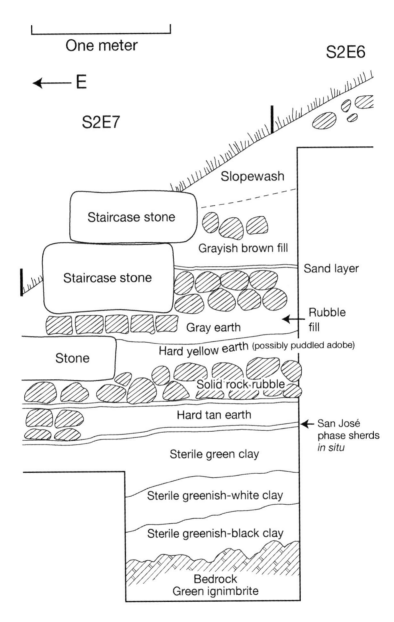

Figure A.6. South profile of the Mound 1/Area A Step Trench, Square S2E7. This square, excavated below Structure 14's eastern stairway (composed of huge blocks of Matadamas limestone) provided crucial stratigraphic information. It showed that Structure 14 had likely been built directly on sterile soil, except for an intervening layer of San José phase sherds. Later excavation of Square S9E5, on the south side of Structure 14, confirmed that the latter had been built directly atop a San José phase house (Flannery and Marcus 2005:396–399).

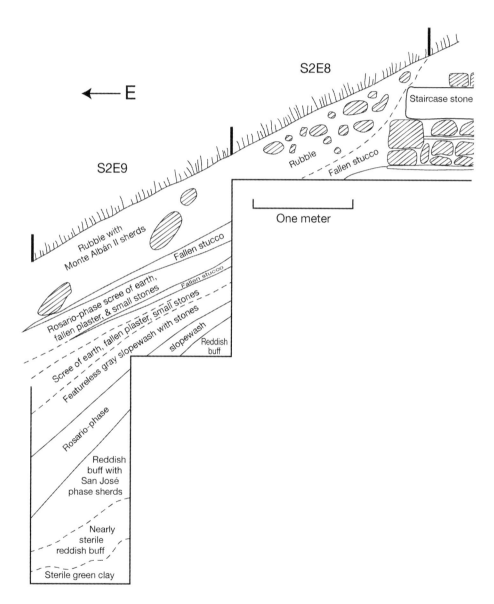

Figure A.7. South profile of the Mound 1/Area A Step Trench, Squares S2E8 and S2E9. Excavation of these squares revealed that the east stairway of Structure 14 ended in Square S2E8. Below this point the slope of the natural hill fell off steeply, and there were no more buildings of any phase.

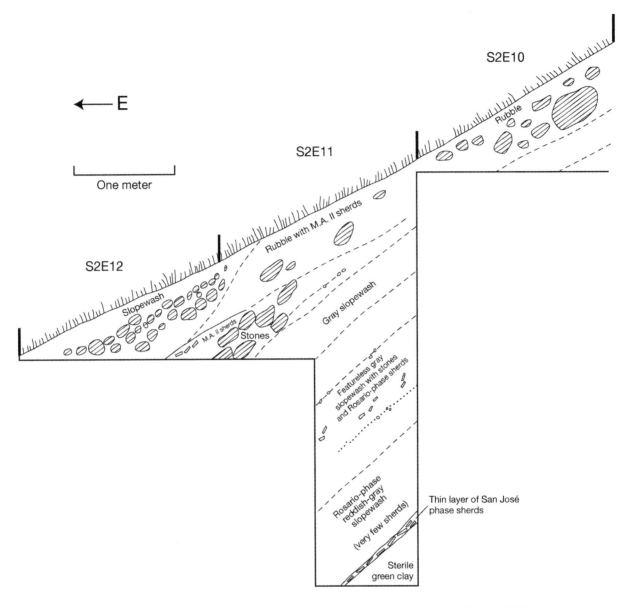

Figure A.8. South profile of the Mound 1/Area A Step Trench, Squares S2E10 to S2E12. Excavation of Square S2E11 to sterile soil made it clear that the natural slope of the Mound 1 hill was so steep that no further buildings would be found. As a consequence, the step trench was not continued beyond Square S2E12.

What We Learned from the Step Trench

1. About 85 percent of Mound 1 is a natural hill, made up of ignimbrite (volcanic tuff) covered with a layer of sterile greenish clay up to 50 cm thick.

2. The oldest sherds found on sterile soil belong to the San José phase.

3. There was a major period of construction during the Rosario phase, involving the use of limestone blocks from the Matadamas quarries. At least one Rosario phase building had a large, east-facing staircase.

4. The five uppermost stucco floors we found were associated with Monte Albán II buildings. Unfortunately, the eastern edges of those buildings had eroded down the side of the hill.

5. We realized that it would be well worth excavating the northeast summit of Mound 1, since it had the potential to reveal a stratigraphic sequence of Rosario phase and Monte Albán II public buildings.

Appendix B | Resumen en Español

En *Excavations at San José Mogote 2* se presenta la totalidad de las evidencias cosmológicas, religiosas e ideológicas prehistóricas que fueron exhumadas durante nuestras excavaciones. Dichas evidencias se complementan, en ciertas ocasiones, con datos provenientes de otros sitios del Valle de Oaxaca, tales como Gheo-Shih, Barrio del Rosario Huitzo, Santo Domingo Tomaltepec, Fábrica San José y San Martín Tilcajete. El objetivo de este libro es realizar un detallado estudio de la evolución de la religión zapoteca a lo largo de siete mil años.

Época Arcaica (8000–2000 a.C.)

El sitio de Gheo-Shih, cerca de Mitla, fue un campamento de cazadores y recolectores. En el centro de este campamento aparecieron dos alineamientos paralelos de cantos rodados que se prolongaban a lo largo de 20 m, con una separación de 7 m entre ellos. Los 140 m² de la superficie delimitada se asemejaban a las "pistas de baile" creadas por los cazadores y recolectores oriundos del occidente de los Estados Unidos. Tales espacios rituales fueron usados también para rituales iniciáticos, juegos y otras ceremonias.

El arqueólogo Richard MacNeish descubrió entierros de niños sacrificados en niveles Arcaicos de la Cueva de Coxcatlán (Valle de Tehuacán, Puebla), evidencia fundamental para documentar la gran antigüedad de los sacrificios humanos y el canibalismo en Mesoamérica.

Fase Tierras Largas (1500–1150 a.C.)

Durante la fase Tierras Largas, San José Mogote fue una aldea de 7 hectáreas; contaba con una palizada de postes de pino y algunas de sus casas de bajareque mostraban huellas de quema deliberada, muestras ellas de violencia grupal. La fase Tierras Largas fue una época de vida igualitaria en la cual hombres y mujeres praticaban rituales en forma separada. En torno a sus casas, las mujeres practicaban ritos con pequeñas figurillas que representaban a sus ancestros recientemente fallecidos. Por su parte, los hombres construían pequeñas casas cubiertas con un enlucido blanco que se asemejan a las casas rituales de varones de Polinesia, Melanesia y el sudeste de Asia. La orientación de cada una de estas casas era de 8° al Norte del Este, y el elemento más común en dichas casas de varones fue la presencia de un pozo repleto de cal en polvo, probablemente molida para mezclarla con tabaco u otra planta narcótica. En y alrededor de las casas de varones se encontraron máscaras grotescas, tal vez para ritos que invocaban a los ancestros más lejanos e inclusive ficticios.

Fase San José (1150–850 a.C.)

Entre 1150 y 850 a.C., San José Mogote alcanzó una superficie de 60–70 hectáreas y comenzó a mostrar evidencias de personas de alto rango social. Estas personas eran sepultadas con bienes suntuarios, tales como la madreperla, las conchas del género *Spondylus*, el jade, los espejos de mineral de hierro y ciertas vasijas con motivos de Relámpago y Terremoto. Los motivos de Relámpago representan la más antigua evidencia del ser sobrenatural que los zapotecas del siglo XVI llamaron *Cociyo*.

En el sitio de Santo Domingo Tomaltepec, Michael E. Whalen encontró un cementerio con 80 individuos correspondiente a la fase San José. Si bien la mayoría de las personas fueron sepultadas allí completamente extendidas y boca abajo, un grupo de seis hombres adultos estaban enterrados envueltos en fardos y en una posición sedente. Aunque estos individuos representaban sólo el 12.7% del cementerio, habían sido enterrados con el 88% de los objetos de jade y el 50% de las vasijas con motivos de Relámpago.

Durante la fase San José, las casas de varones fueron paulatinamente reemplazadas por templos propiamente dichos, erigidos arriba del nivel del pueblo y provistos de escalinatas. Este cambio arquitectónico refleja el hecho de que los ritos de una sociedad igualitaria—en la que los ancestros de todos los miembros eran importantes—habían cedido el paso a la veneración de deidades con las que únicamente la elite tenía vínculos genealógicos. Sin embargo, las escalinatas de los primeros templos de la fase San José eran estrechas—de una sola fila—cosa que sugiere que algunos ritos todavía no eran para todo el pueblo, sino para un número reducido de individuos importantes.

Los primeros templos de la fase San José fueron erigidos sobre grandes plataformas (Estructuras 1 y 2). Las paredes exteriores de dichas plataformas eran de mampostería de piedra, y algunas de las piedras provenían de canteras ubicadas en los terrenos de aldeas satélites, a 5 km de distancia de San José Mogote. Los muros de retención para el relleno eran de adobes "en forma de buñuelo" (circulares y plano-convexos). La forma de estos adobes obedece a que fueron moldeados en el fondo de cántaros rotos.

Fase Guadalupe (850–700 a.C.)

Durante el Formativo Medio varios pueblos se enfrentaron como rivales políticos de San José Mogote, entre ellos Barrio del Rosario Huitzo y San Martín Tilcajete. Tanto en Huitzo como en San José Mogote aparecieron patios ceremoniales con templos situados en varios lados. El mejor conservado de estos templos fue la Estructura 3 de Huitzo, un gran edificio de bajareque dotado de un solo cuarto, el cual descansaba sobre una plataforma con escalinata. Construida con adobes en forma de buñuelo, dicha plataforma medía 1.3 m de altura por 11.5 m de largo. Su ancha escalinata contaba con tres escalones, cada uno de los cuales iba intercalado en la plataforma a fin de fortalecerlo. La Estructura 3 mantenía la antigua orientación de 8° al Oeste del Norte, pero su amplia escalinata indica que el acceso al templo no era tan restringido como en la fase San José.

La Estructura 8 de San José Mogote era parecida a la Estructura 3 de Huitzo, pero sus adobes "buñuelos" se apoyaban en un cimiento de dos hileras de piedra.

Una de las estrategias para entablar alianzas durante la fase Guadalupe era celebrar banquetes con los vecinos. La aldea de Tierras Largas, probablemente un satélite de San José Mogote, muestra evidencias de uno de estos banquetes, en el cual se consumieron al menos 50 kilogramos de carne de perro doméstico.

Fase Rosario (700–500 a.C.)

Durante el periodo comprendido entre el 700 y el 500 a.C., al menos tres sociedades del tipo "jefatura" participaron en una competencia feroz por el control del Valle de Oaxaca. La sociedad más grande era una del subvalle de Etla; consistía en 18–23 aldeas, con San José Mogote a la cabeza. La segunda en dimensiones era una sociedad del subvalle de Zimatlán, con San Martín Tilcajete como su cabecera. A continuación, le seguía una sociedad del subvalle de Tlacolula, con Yegüih sirviendo de cabecera. Tan agresiva era la competencia entre ellas que se conformó justo en el centro del valle una "tierra de nadie."

Durante la fase Rosario los líderes de San José Mogote construyeron una acrópolis de edificios públicos en la cima del Montículo 1, una loma natural de 13 m de altura. El edificio más grande de la acrópolis consistía en un templo de bajareque y adobe (Estructura 28), erigido sobre una plataforma de mampostería y relleno (Estructura 19). La plataforma, construida en tres etapas sucesivas, llegó a abarcar 21.7 m por 28.5 m e incorporaba grandes bloques de caliza traidos de las canteras de Matadamas, localizadas a 5 km de San José Mogote y al otro lado del Río Atoyac. La primera etapa constructiva mantuvo la vieja orientación de 8° al Norte del Este; pero durante la etapa final, la orientación era Este-Oeste.

La Estructura 28 poseía un piso hundido, reforzado por muros de adobes cuadrangulares. Enterrado bajo cada esquina de este piso hundido, se encontró un gran cajete; probablemente, estos cuatro recipientes contuvieron alimentos durante un gran banquete de inauguración del templo.

En las postrimerías de su historia, este templo fue el escenario de un grave incendio que destruyó el edificio y tuvo como resultado colateral miles de fragmentos de barro vitrificado. El análisis de tales fragmentos demuestra que el fuego fue tan intenso que debió de haberse producido de manera intencional, es decir, como resultado de un ataque.

Después del incendio, los jefes de San José Mogote dirigieron la construcción de Estructura 14, una nueva plataforma de mampostería con orientación Este-Oeste. Sobre ella construyeron la Estructura 37, un templo con muros de adobes cuadrangulares sobre cimientos de mampostería de piedra; se encontraron vestigios de columnas de madera con soportes circulares de toba volcánica.

Entre la Estructura 14 y los restos de la Estructura 19 se extendía un estrecho corredor. Sirviendo de umbral a este corredor apareció una gran losa grabada, el llamado Monumento 3. La escena grabada muestra a un hombre desnudo, víctima del sacrificio, con un complejo motivo mostrando que se le había abierto el pecho para extraerle el corazón. Entre los pies de esta desdichada víctima, probablemente un prisionero importante procedente de una jefatura enemiga, aparece su nombre calendárico anotado en jeroglíficos zapotecos: Uno Movimiento (o "1 L" en el sistema de Alfonso Caso).

Estas evidencias del uso temprano de la escritura zapoteca se pueden fijar en el tiempo gracias a una serie de fechas de carbono 14. El Monumento 3 se encontró abajo de dos hogares (Elementos 18 y 19) con fechas de 560 a.C. y 630 a.C., y estaba asociado a cerámica de la fase Rosario. Podemos sugerir, por tanto, que la escritura zapoteca apareció durante el Formativo Medio, en el contexto de competencia feroz entre caciques, y que uno de los roles más importantes que jugó era el de propaganda política.

Sobre las ruinas de la Estructura 28, se construyó una elegante residencia para una familia de la élite. A poca distancia de ella se erigió también la Estructura 31, una plataforma circular de unos 6 m de diámetro. Aunque las plataformas de este tipo son raras en Oaxaca, se han encontrado docenas de ellas en el Formativo Medio de Belize. Allí se consideran plataformas para danzas u oraciones públicas.

A finales de la fase Rosario, el sitio de San José Mogote fue víctima de un abandono casi total. Se deshabitaron también la mayoría de sus aldeas satélites; la mitad de las aldeas de la fase Rosario cuya ocupación no continuó durante la fase Monte Albán I se localizan en la porción sur del subvalle de Etla.

El abandono de San José Mogote y sus satélites tuvo lugar simultáneamente con la colonización de Monte Albán, un cerro del Valle de Oaxaca ubicado en "tierra de nadie." Después de 200 años de guerra con otras sociedades de jefatura y tras innumerables templos quemados y prisioneros sacrificados, 2000 habitantes de la región de San José Mogote abandonaron sus casas y se fundieron en una nueva comunidad en la cúspide de un cerro estratégicamente situado. Pronto empezaron a construir un muro defensivo de 3 km de largo.

Fase Monte Albán Ia (500–300 a.C.)

Alrededor del 500 a.C., se produjo un fenómeno inesperado: San José Mogote, la mayor comunidad del valle durante más de 800 años, perdió la mayoría de su población. Unos dos mil habitantes del subvalle de Etla— 1000 de San José Mogote y 1000 de sus aldeas satélites—dejaron sus hogares tradicionales para fundar la ciudad de Monte Albán encima de un cerro defensible. Durante los 200 años de la fase Monte Albán Ia (Monte Albán Temprano), la población de esta ciudad creció de 2000 a 5000 individuos.

En su primera época, Monte Albán mostró varios elementos heredados de San José Mogote: edificios públicos de mampostería de piedra y adobes cuadrangulares con una orientación Este-Oeste o Norte-Sur; cerámica gris bruñido con motivos incisos; culto al Relámpago como un ser sobrenatural; escritura jeroglífica, y monumentos grabados con motivos asociados a la guerra, la conquista y el sacrificio.

Uno de los edificios públicos de Monte Albán Ia—hoy día parcialmente sepultado bajo el Edificio L de Monte Albán—conserva cuatro hileras de piedras grabadas en su posición original. Las piedras se asemejan al Monumento 3 de San José Mogote: cada una exhibe la figura de un víctima masculina, sacrificada o muerta en combate, con los ojos cerrados y en ocasiones con una voluta de sangre para indicar la mutilación genital. Es obvio que el conflicto entre sociedades rivales, ejemplificado por el templo quemado de San José Mogote, no solamente perduró durante Monte Albán Ia, sino que se incrementó.

Dos estelas asociadas a la galería de prisioneros del Edificio L presentan un texto zapoteco cuyos jeroglifos se refiriente tanto al calendario ritual de 260 días como al solar de 365 días.

Queremos comprender la naturaleza del ritual propio de esta época, pero existe un gran obstáculo para ello: los templos más antiguos de Monte Albán se encuentran por debajo de la Plataforma Norte de este sitio. Para conocer los templos de la fase Monte Albán Ia, vale la pena visitar San Martín Tilcajete, el rival político más poderoso de Monte Albán. En Tilcajete, gracias a los arqueólogos Charles Spencer y Elsa Redmond, podemos admirar un templo completo de la fase Monte Albán Ia, el cual fue denominado Estructura 1. Este templo, de un solo cuarto y con dos *tlecuiles* o hogares rituales, medía 6.7 m por 2.7 m; se encontró encima de una plataforma cuyas dimensiones eran 12.6 m por 7.6 m. La Estructura 1 formaba parte de una plaza ceremonial con una orientación de 25° al Este del Norte. Los constructores de Tilcajete, obviamente, optaron por una orientación muy diferente a la de Monte Albán, y la mantuvieron durante todo el conflicto. La Estructura 1 eventualmente fue quemada, probablemente por Monte Albán, alrededor del 330 a.C. Sin embargo, Tilcajete no se rindió, sino que persistió.

Mientras tanto, en San José Mogote las 40 hectáreas del núcleo ceremonial del sitio quedaron abandonadas. Todavía podían encontrarse algunos barrios dispersos de campesinos en los alrededores del sitio, pero San José ya no hacía las veces de cabecera para el subvalle de Etla. Sin embargo, tal parece que alguien recordaba a San José Mogote. Fue visitado brevemente durante Monte Albán Ia por una delegación de sacerdotes y sus asistentes, quienes constuyeron un altar en la cima del Montículo 1.

El altar, llamado Estructura 23, era una pequeña plataforma de mampostería como los "adoratorios" de Monte Albán. Cerca de él se halló también la Estructura 24, una caja de ofrenda que contenía dos botellas de color granate y el esqueleto de un niño de 5–8 años. Los ritos asociados al altar dejaron fragmentos de incensarios y abundante ceniza.

Aquella corta visita fue un ejemplo típico de una tradición muy larga en el Valle de Oaxaca: siglos después del abandono de un sitio importante, alguien acude a él para conducir un rito en el punto más elevado del sitio.

Fase Monte Albán Ic (300–100 a.C.)

Para el periodo 300–100 a.C. carecemos de evidencias sobre la ocupación en San José Mogote. Para conocer un poco la vida religiosa de la fase Monte Albán Ic, tenemos que regresar otra vez al sitio de San Martín Tilcajete. Durante la época Ic, el conflicto entre Monte Albán y Tilcajete continuó intensamente. Tilcajete creció en dimensiones y población, construyó muros defensivos y mantuvo la orientación de 25° en sus nuevos edificios públicos.

La Estructura 20 de Tilcajete se edificó a principios de la fase Monte Albán Ic. Se trata de un templo de 34 m por 6.75 m con cuatro pilares en la entrada. El templo propiamente dicho se limitaba a un solo cuarto, pero estaba acompañado de dos pequeños cuartos de depósito y un espacio dedicado a la preparación de banquetes.

Más tarde, en la misma fase, ocurrieron cambios importantes:

por primera vez, Tilcajete construyó un palacio real y un templo de dos cuartos. Los edificios de ese tipo normalmente son construidos por las sociedades que llamamos estados (o monarquías). En el caso de los templos zapotecos de dos cuartos, el cuarto exterior era menos sagrado y servía al público; el cuarto interior era más sagrado y era privativo de sacerdotes.

El primer templo de dos cuartos en Tilcajete era la Estructura 16, la cual formaba parte de un complejo ritual con cuartos de depósito y casas para los sacerdotes. Este templo fue incendiado, probablemente por Monte Albán, en el año 30 a.C. Los invasores quemaron el palacio real también, de manera que Tilcajete quedó abandonado. Eso fue, casi seguramente, el momento en que Monte Albán se convirtió en la capital de todo el Valle de Oaxaca.

Fase Monte Albán II (100 a.C.–200 d.C.)

Ya no puede haber sombra de duda de que la sociedad del Valle de Oaxaca estaba organizada como estado e incluso como estado militar expansionista durante la fase Monte Albán II. En el valle conocemos alrededor de 518 comunidades de aquel periodo, con una población estimada de 41,000 habitantes, si no más. Entonces existió una jerarquía política de cuatro niveles. En el primer nivel encontramos a Monte Albán, la capital, con aproximadamente 14,500 habitantes. Dentro de un radio de 14 a 28 km de la capital había seis centros administrativos del nivel 2, con 975–1950 habitantes cada uno. El nivel 3 consistía en al menos 30 "aldeas grandes" de 200–700 habitantes cada una. Finalmente, el nivel 4 de la jerarquía consistía en más de 400 aldeas pequeñas con poblaciones de menos de 200 individuos.

Durante Monte Albán II, San José Mogote fue deliberadamente reocupado, gozando de un "renacimiento" como centro administrativo del nivel 2. Sus estrechas relaciones con Monte Albán son obvias. San José Mogote fue dotado de una plaza principal con 300 m de Norte a Sur y 200 m de Este a Oeste, la cual era muy parecida a la plaza principal de Monte Albán. El Montículo 8 de San José Mogote, que forma el límite norte de la plaza, al parecer correspondía a la Plataforma Norte de Monte Albán. Cada uno de ellos sostenía una estructura gubernamental a la que se accedía al subir por una gran escalinata y pasar por un pórtico columnario: el pórtico de la Plataforma Norte poseía dos hileras de seis pilares cada una, mientras que el del Montículo 8 de San José Mogote contaba con una sola hilera de seis columnas. Los dos lugares tenían patios hundidos para reuniones de la élite.

Frente al Montículo 8 y en un lugar menos elevado, apareció la Estructura 9, un palacio amplio para una familia noble. Dicho palacio tiene una larga historia de modificaciones arquitectónicas. Muchas de ellas implicaron la división de habitaciones y patios preexistentes en espacios más reducidos, posiblemente como respuesta a un aumento del número de sus ocupantes.

El Montículo 7, en el lado oeste de la plaza de San José Mogote, contenía una cancha de juego de pelota en forma de I. Este edificio era similar al de la plaza principal de Monte Albán y contaba con dimensiones casi idénticas.

Finalmente, tanto en la cima del Montículo 1 como en otros lugares en la plaza, San José Mogote tenía una abundancia de templos con dos cuartos, todos en el estilo de Monte Albán. En la plaza de San José Mogote había al menos 10 templos de este tipo; la plaza de Monte Albán tenía el doble.

En algunos casos en San José Mogote, el templo visible era simplemente la versión más reciente en una larga secuencia de templos. Tal fue el caso de Estructuras 36, 35 y 13, una serie de templos construidos sobre las ruinas de la Estructura 14, plataforma abandonada de la fase Rosario ubicada en la cima del Montículo 1. Varios de dichos templos tenían cajas para ofrendas debajo de sus pisos originales. Las ofrendas se habían enterrado durante "ritos de consagración" que tornaron suelo secular en suelo sacro, justo antes de la construcción de un edificio religioso.

El templo más antiguo de este sitio, la Estructura 36, data de Monte Albán II Temprano. Medía 11 m por 11 m y estaba ligeramente conformado en forma de T. Las dos columnas que flanqueaban la entrada del cuarto interior y las cuatro que flanqueaban la entrada del cuarto exterior estaban hechas con troncos de ahuehuete (*Taxodium mucrunatum*). Como en el caso de todos los templos de dos cuartos, el piso del cuarto interior (el lugar más sagrado del templo) era unos 20–35 cm más elevado que el piso del cuarto exterior. Aunque los muros de adobe estaban casi destruidos, se encontraron restos de estuco con pintura de tres o cuatro colores. En el escombro de los muros destruidos aparecieron restos de codorniz, ave favorecida por los zapotecas como objeto de sacrificio. Los zapotecas consideraban a la codorniz como un animal "limpio" o "puro," debido a que bebía las gotas del rocío en vez del agua sucia.

La Estructura 35, un templo construido sobre los vestigios arrasados de la Estructura 36, databa de mediados de la fase Monte Albán II. Medía 12 por 13.5 m y tenía forma de T como su predecesora. Sus columnas —una a cada lado de las entradas interior y exterior— no fueron elaboradas con troncos de árbol, sino construidas con piedra y mortero.

El piso del templo mostraba manchas circulares de carbón en los lugares donde los sacerdotes colocaron incensarios para quemar copal. Sabemos que en el siglo XVI, los zapotecas creían que las columnas de humo aromático de los incensarios se elevaban hasta llegar al cielo y complacer a los antepasados nobles, quienes se habían convertido en "gente de las nubes."

En una esquina oscura del cuarto interior se encontraron dos cuchillos de obsidiana del tipo "hoja de laurel" para la extracción de corazones humanos y 42 navajillas prismáticas de obsidiana del tipo usado por los sacerdotes zapotecas para sacrificar codornices o extraer sangre de sus propias orejas y lenguas como forma de autosacrificio.

Las ofrendas dedicatorias de la Estructura 35 eran espectaculares. En una caja de ofrenda, debajo del piso del cuarto interior, había dos estatuas de jade, dos cuentas del mismo material y un montoncillo de pigmento bermellón. La estatua más grande mide 49 cm de altura y representa a un hombre desnudo, erguido en una posición hierática, posiblemente una víctima simbólica del sacrificio.

En otra caja de ofrenda, debajo del mismo piso, salió a luz una escena conformada por siete piezas de cerámica. El elemento central de la escena era una tumba en miniatura, cuyas paredes estaban elaboradas con adobes colocados de canto, con una losa que hacía las veces de techo.

Dentro de la tumba, en el interior de un cajete abierto, había una figurilla humana arrodillada del tipo que en Oaxaca se llama "acompañante." El cajete estaba flanqueado por el esqueleto de una codorniz sacrificada y un par de astas de venado, del tipo que los zapotecas usaban para tañer el tambor.

Tendida en toda su extensión sobre la losa que servía de techo de la tumba apareció una "figura voladora" con una larga capa sobre su espalda. La figura tenía en su rostro una máscara que representaba a *Cociyo* (Relámpago) y así con sus manos una vara y la lengua bífida de una serpiente.

Sentadas en fila detrás del volador apacerieron cuatro urnas-efigie; cada una de ellas representaba una mujer arrodillada con una máscara grotesca de *Cociyo*. Es probable que esas urnas femeninas, cada una de cuyas cabezas era un receptáculo para copal, representaran los cuatro compañeros de *Cociyo*: las Nubes, la Lluvia, el Granizo y el Viento.

Es posible que esta escena represente la metamorfosis de un señor zapoteca difunto en una "persona de las nubes," quien viviría eternamente en el cielo en contacto con Relámpago. En la figura del volador se observa precisamente la transformación parcial del hombre arrodillado en la tumba en miniatura, captado en una etapa en que su cuerpo es aún el de un ser humano, pero su rostro es ya el de *Cociyo*.

Después del abandono de la Estructura 35, un nuevo templo—la Estructura 13—fue erigido sobre los vestigios arrasados de su predecesora. Este templo, que data de Monte Albán II Tardío, medía 15 por 8 m. Sus columnas—dos en la entrada del cuarto interior y cuatro en la del exterior—eran de mampostería. Su cámara interior tenía un *tlecuil* o pila para ofrendas quemadas, el cual estaba embebido en el estuco del piso.

La secuencia estratigráfica de las Estructuras 36, 35 y 13 genera una pregunta crucial: ¿con qué frecuencia fueron re-emplazados o reconstruidos los templos del estado zapoteco? Las fechas de carbono 14 fueron las siguientes: Estructura 36, 15 d.C.; Estructura 35, 65 d.C.; Estructura 13, 125 d.C. Existe la posibilidad, en otras palabras, de que dichos templos fueran reemplazados cada 52 años, siguiendo así un ciclo que combinaba los calendarios de 260 días y de 365 días.

La secuencia de las Estructuras 36-35-13 tuvo lugar en la esquina noreste de un pequeño patio en la cima del Montículo 1. Otros tres templos ocuparon las esquinas restantes del patio: la Estructura 29 en la sureste, la Estructura 21 en la suroeste y 22 en la noroeste. De la Estructura 22 sabemos muy poco, dado que miles de las piedras de sus paredes fueron robadas durante la época colonial. La Estructura 21 era un templo de dos cuartos y típico de Monte Albán II; el piso de su cuarto interior tenía un *tlecuil* como el de la Estructura 13.

De la Estructura 29, solamente quedaron ciertas porciones del piso de estuco; la erosión había terminado con lo demás. Sin embargo, abajo de una porción del piso se encontró una caja de ofrenda con un incensario-efigie extraordinario. Representaba la cara arrugada de un hombre de edad avanzada, posiblemente un antepasado real, cubierta de pigmento bermellón. En los ojos y la boca tenía huecos que permitirían salir el humo del copal cuando éste era quemado.

Atrás de las Estructuras 21 y 22 fueron exhumadas dos escalinatas subterráneas secretas, enterradas en el lado oeste del Montículo 1. A través de dichas escalinatas, los sacerdotes de Monte Albán II podrían entrar por una puerta en la base del montículo, desaparecer en la oscuridad y aparecer de nuevo en uno de los templos en la cima. Tal recurso misterioso seguramente afirmó el poder mágico-religioso de los sacerdotes.

En otros términos, todas las evidencias de la fase Monte Albán II nos permiten señalar que la cosmología, la religión y la ideología de la sociedad de aquella época pueden ser comparadas con las de los zapotecas del siglo XVI. La gente de Monte Albán II vivía en un universo dividido en cuatro grandes cuarteles, cada uno asociado a un color. *Cociyo* (Relámpago) era la fuerza sobre-natural más poderosa, y entre sus compañeros se encontaban las Nubes, la Lluvia, el Granizo y el Viento. *Tini*, la sangre que fluía, era más sagrada que *rini*, la sangre seca. Existió un calendario ritual de 260 días, un calendario solar de 365 y un ciclo de 52 años que señalaba el momento para construir un nuevo templo. Entre las ceremonias asociadas al templo se encontraban los ritos de consagración, el uso de copal y el sacrificio de hombres, mujeres, niños y animales de diversas especies.

Los gobernantes de la sociedad de Monte Albán II estaban adscritos al estrato social de la nobleza hereditaria. Al morir, atravesaban por un proceso de metamorfosis que los convertía en "gente de las nubes." En contraste, los plebeyos simplemente morían. Como resultado, las pequeñas figurillas de los antepasa-dos de los plebeyos desaparecían de los sitios arqueológicos y eran reemplazadas por urnas-efigie de ancestros nobles, los únicos que tenían relevancia durante Monte Albán II.

En la iconografía de la fase Monte Albán II se observan pumas y jaguares, símbolos del *coqui* o rey zapoteco; el murciélago, mensajero entre el mundo de los vivos y el de los muertos; el tabaco y otras plantas rituales; el cocodrilo, cuyas placas dorsales simbolizaban la Tierra; la cabeza-trofeo, como símbolo del poder militar, y el "glifo del cerro" que era usado (en combinación con otros glifos) para indicar un determinado lugar geográfico. Por supuesto, la sociedad zapoteca del siglo II no era idéntica a la del siglo XVI, pero las abundantes correspondencias que hemos mencionado llaman la atención de los arqueólogos.

References Cited

Acosta, Jorge R.
1965 Preclassic and Classic architecture of Oaxaca. In *The Hand-book of Middle American Indians*, vol. 3, edited by Robert Wauchope and Gordon R. Willey, pp. 814–836. Austin: University of Texas Press.

Acosta, Jorge R., and Javier Romero
1992 *Exploraciones en Monte Negro, Oaxaca: 1937–38, 1938–39 y 1939–1940*. Mexico: Instituto Nacional de Antropología e Historia.

Aimers, James J., Terry G. Powis, and Jaime Awe
2000 Preclassic round structures of the upper Belize River Valley. *Latin American Antiquity* 11:71–86.

Alcina Franch, José
1993 *Calendario y religión entre los zapotecos*. Mexico City: Universidad Nacional Autónoma de México.

Anderson, David G.
1994 *The Savannah River Chiefdoms: Political Change in the Late Prehistoric Southeast*. Tuscaloosa: University of Alabama Press.

Asensio, Gaspar
1905a[1580] Relación de Macuilsuchil y su partido. In *Papeles de Nueva España: segunda serie, Geografía y Estadística*, vol. 4, edited by Francisco del Paso y Troncoso, pp. 100–104. Madrid: Est. Tipográfico "Sucesores de Rivadeneyra."
1905b[1580] El Pueblo Teutitlán. In *Papeles de Nueva España: segunda serie, Geografía y Estadística*, vol. 4, edited by Francisco del Paso y Troncoso, pp. 104–108. Madrid: Est. Tipográfico "Sucesores de Rivadeneyra."

Balsalobre, Gonzalo de
1892[1656] Relación auténtica de las idolatrías, supersticiones, vanas observaciones de los indios del Obispado de Oaxaca. In *Anales del Museo Nacional de México*, Primera Época 6:225–260.

Bernal, Ignacio
1946 La cerámica preclásica de Monte Albán. Master's thesis. Mexico: Escuela Nacional de Antropología e Historia.

Blanton, Richard E.
1978 *Monte Albán: Settlement Patterns at the Ancient Zapotec Capital*. New York: Academic Press.

Blom, Frans
1924 Report on the preliminary work at Uaxactun, Guatemala. In *Carnegie Institution of Washington Year Book*, no. 23, pp. 217–219. Washington, D.C.

Boos, Frank H.
1966 *The Ceramic Sculptures of Ancient Oaxaca*. South Brunswick: A. S. Barnes.

Broda, Johanna
1971 Las fiestas aztecas de los dioses de la lluvia: Una reconstrucción según las fuentes del siglo xvi. *Revista Española de Antropología Americana* 6:245–327.

Buck, Sir Peter H.
1949 *The Coming of the Maori*. Wellington, New Zealand: Whitcombe and Tombs.

Burgoa, Francisco de
1934a[1670] *Palestra historial de virtudes y exemplares apostólicos*...Publicaciones del Archivo General de la Nación 24. México: Talleres Gráficos de la Nación.
1934b[1674] *Geográfica descripción*. Publicaciones del Archivo General de la Nación 25–26. México: Talleres Gráficos de la Nación.

Byers, Douglas S. (editor)
1967 *The Prehistory of the Tehuacán Valley, Volume1: Environment and Subsistence*. Austin: University of Texas Press.

Canseco, Alonso de
1905[1580] Relación de Tlacolula y Mitla hecha en los días 12 y 23 de agosto respectivamente. In *Papeles de Nueva España: segunda serie, Geografía y Estadística*, vol. 4, edited by Francisco del Paso y Troncoso, pp. 144–154. Madrid: Est. Tipográfico "Sucesores de Rivadeneyra."

Carrasco, Pedro
1974 Sucesión y alianzas matrimoniales en la dinastía teotihuacana. *Estudios de Cultura Náhuatl* 11:235–242.
1984 Royal marriages in ancient Mexico. In *Explorations in Ethnohistory: Indians of Central Mexico in the Sixteenth Century*, edited by Herbert R. Harvey and Hanns J. Prem, pp. 41–81. Albuquerque: University of New Mexico Press.

Caso, Alfonso
1928 *Las estelas zapotecas*. Monografías del Museo Nacional de Arqueología, Historia y Etnografía. Publicaciones de la Secretaría de Educación Pública. México: Talleres Gráficos de la Nación.
1938 *Exploraciones en Oaxaca, quinta y sexta temporadas, 1936-1937*. Instituto Panamericano de Geografía e Historia, Publicación 34. Mexico.
1965a Lapidary work, goldwork, and copperwork from Oaxaca. In *Handbook of Middle American Indians, Volume 3, Archaeology of Southern Mesoamerica, Part 2*, edited by Robert Wauchope and Gordon R. Willey, pp. 896–930. Austin: University of Texas Press.
1965b Zapotec writing and calendar. In *Handbook of Middle American Indians, Volume 3, Archaeology of Southern Mesoamerica, Part 2*, edited by Robert Wauchope and Gordon R. Willey, pp. 931–947. Austin: University of Texas Press.
1966 The lords of Yanhuitlan. In *Ancient Oaxaca*, edited by John Paddock, pp. 313–335. Stanford: Stanford University Press.

Caso, Alfonso, and Ignacio Bernal
1952 *Urnas de Oaxaca*. Memorias del Instituto Nacional de Antropología e Historia, no. 2. Mexico City.

CBA (see Caso, Bernal, and Acosta 1967)

Caso, Alfonso, Ignacio Bernal, and Jorge R. Acosta
1967 *La cerámica de Monte Albán*. Memorias del Instituto Nacional de Antropología e Historia, no. 13. Mexico City.

Chase, Arlen F., and Diane Z. Chase
1995 External impetus, internal synthesis, and standardization: E group assemblages and the crystallization of Classic Maya society in the southern lowlands. In *The Emergence of Maya Civilization: The Transition from the Preclassic to the Early Classic*, edited by N. Grube, pp. 87–101. Acta Mesoamericana 8. Möckmühl, Germany: Verlag Anton Saurwein.

Coe, Michael D.
1961 *La Victoria: An Early Site on the Pacific Coast of Guatemala*. Papers of the Peabody Museum of Archaeology and Ethnology, no. 53. Cambridge: Harvard University.

Coe, Michael D., and Richard A. Diehl
1980 *In the Land of the Olmec*, vols. 1 and 2. Austin: University of Texas Press.

Collier, Donald
1955 *Cultural Chronology and Change as Reflected in the Ceramics of the Virú Valley, Peru*. Fieldiana Anthropology 43. Chicago: Field Museum of Natural History.

Córdova, fray Juan de
1886[1578] *Arte en lengua zapoteca*. Morelia, Mexico: Pedro Balli.
1942[1578] *Vocabulario en lengua zapoteca*. Mexico: Pedro Charte y Antonio Ricardo.

de la Fuente, Julio
1949 *Yalalag: Una villa zapoteca serrana*. Mexico: Museo Nacional de Antropología.

de Laguna, Frederica
1990 Tlingit. In *Handbook of North American Indians, Volume 7: Northwest Coast*, edited by Wayne Suttles and William C. Sturtevant, pp. 203–228. Washington: Smithsonian Institution.

del Paso y Troncoso, Francisco
1905 Relaciones geográficas de Oaxaca. In *Papeles de Nueva España: segunda serie, Geografía y Estadística*, vol. 4. Madrid: Est. Tipográfico "Sucesores de Rivadeneyra."

Demand, Nancy H.
1990 *Urban Relocation in Archaic and Classical Greece: Flight and Consolidation*. Norman: University of Oklahoma Press.

Drennan, Robert D.
1976 *Fábrica San José and Middle Formative Society in the Valley of Oaxaca*. Memoir 8. Ann Arbor: Museum of Anthropology, University of Michigan.

Drucker, Philip J., Robert F. Heizer, and Robert J. Squier
1959 *Excavations at La Venta, Tabasco, 1955*. Bureau of American Ethnology Bulletin 170. Washington: Smithsonian Institution, U.S. Government Printing Office.

Durán, fray Diego
1964 *The Aztecs*, translated by Doris Heyden and Fernando Horcasitas. New York: Orion Press.
1971 *Book of the Gods and Rites and the Ancient Calendar*, translated by Fernando Horcasitas and Doris Heyden. Norman: University of Oklahoma Press.

Ekholm, Susanna M.
1990 Ceremonia de fin-de-ciclo: El gran basurero ceremonial de Lagartero, Chiapas. In *Epoca Clásica: Nuevos Hallazgos*, edited by Amalia Cardós de Méndez, pp. 455–467. Mexico: Museo Nacional de Antropología.

Elson, Christina M.
2007 *Excavations at Cerro Tilcajete: A Monte Albán II Administrative Center in the Valley of Oaxaca*. Memoir 42. Ann Arbor: University of Michigan, Museum of Anthropology.

Elson, Christina M., and Michael E. Smith
2001 Archaeological deposits from the Aztec New Fire ceremony. *Ancient Mesoamerica* 12(2):157–174.

Espíndola, Nicolás de
1905[1580] Relación de Chichicapa y su partido. In *Papeles de Nueva España: segunda serie, Geografía y Estadística*, vol. 4, edited by Francisco del Paso y Troncoso, pp. 115–143. Madrid: Est. Tipográfico "Sucesores de Rivadeneyra."

Fernández Dávila, Enrique
1997 San José Mogote, Etla. *Arqueología Mexicana* V(26):18–23.

Ferree, Lisa
1972 The Pottery Censers of Tikal, Guatemala. PhD dissertation, Department of Anthropology, Southern Illinois University, Carbondale.

Flannery, Kent V.
1973 The origins of agriculture. *Annual Review of Anthropology* 2:271–310.
2003 Monte Negro: A reinterpretation. In *The Cloud People: Divergent Evolution of the Zapotec and Mixtec Civilizations*, edited by Kent V. Flannery and Joyce Marcus, pp. 99–102. Clinton Corners: Percheron Press.
2009a Foreword to the updated edition (2009). In *Guilá Naquitz: Archaic Foraging and Early Agriculture in Oaxaca, Mexico* (updated ed.), edited by Kent V. Flannery, pp. xix–xxii. Walnut Creek: Left Coast Press.
2009b Sampling by intensive surface collection. In *The Early Mesoamerican Village* (updated ed., with a new foreword by Jeremy A. Sabloff), edited by Kent V. Flannery, pp. 51–62. Walnut Creek: Left Coast Press.

Flannery, Kent V. (editor)
2009 *Guilá Naquitz: Archaic Foraging and Early Agriculture in Oaxaca, Mexico* (updated ed.). Walnut Creek: Left Coast Press.

Flannery, Kent, and Joyce Marcus
1976 Formative Oaxaca and the Zapotec cosmos. *American Scientist* 64(4):374–383.
1994 *Early Formative Pottery of the Valley of Oaxaca, Mexico.* Memoir 27. Ann Arbor: Museum of Anthropology, University of Michigan.
2000 Formative Mexican chiefdoms and the myth of the "mother culture." *Journal of Anthropological Archaeology* 19:1–37.
2003a The earliest public buildings, tombs, and monuments at Monte Albán, with notes on the internal chronology of Period I. In *The Cloud People: Divergent Evolution of the Zapotec and Mixtec Civilizations*, edited by Kent V. Flannery and Joyce Marcus, pp. 87–91. Clinton Corners: Percheron Press.
2003b San José Mogote and the tay situndayu. In *The Cloud People: Divergent Evolution of the Mixtec and Zapotec Civilizations*, edited by Kent V. Flannery and Joyce Marcus, pp. 289–290. Clinton Corners: Percheron Press.
2003c The origin of war: new ^{14}C dates from ancient Mexico. *Proceedings of the National Academy of Sciences* 100(20):11801–11805.
2003d The growth of site hierarchies in the Valley of Oaxaca: Part I. In *The Cloud People: Divergent Evolution of the Zapotec and Mixtec Civilizations*, edited by Kent V. Flannery and Joyce Marcus, pp. 53–64. Clinton Corners: Percheron Press.
2005 *Excavations at San José Mogote 1: The Household Archaeology.* Memoir 40. Ann Arbor: Museum of Anthropology, University of Michigan.
2012 *The Creation of Inequality.* Cambridge: Harvard University Press.

Flannery, Kent V., and Ronald Spores
2003 Excavated sites of the Oaxaca preceramic. In *The Cloud People: Divergent Evolution of the Zapotec and Mixtec Civilizations*, edited by Kent V. Flannery and Joyce Marcus, pp. 20–26. Clinton Corners: Percheron Press.

Folan, William J., Joyce Marcus, Sophia Pincemin Deliberos, María del Rosario Domínguez Carrasco, Laraine Fletcher, and Abel Morales López
1995 Calakmul: New data from an ancient Maya capital in Campeche, Mexico. *Latin American Antiquity* 6(4):310–334.

Fowler, Melvin L., and Richard S. MacNeish
1972 Excavations in the Coxcatlán locality in the alluvial slopes. In *The Prehistory of the Tehuacán Valley, Vol. 5, Excavations and Reconnaissance*, by Richard S. MacNeish, Melvin L. Fowler, Ángel García Cook, Frederick A. Peterson, Antoinette Nelken-Terner, and James A. Neely, pp. 219–340. Austin: University of Texas Press.

Furst, Jill Leslie
1978 *Codex Vindobonensis Mexicanus I: A commentary.* Institute for Mesoamerican Studies, Publication 4. Albany: State University of New York at Albany.

Goldman, Irving
1963 *The Cubeo: Indians of the Northwest Amazon.* Urbana: University of Illinois Press.

González Licón, Ernesto
2003 Social Inequality at Monte Albán, Oaxaca: Household Analysis from Terminal Formative to Early Classic. PhD dissertation, Department of Anthropology, University of Pittsburgh.

Grove, David C.
1984 *Chalcatzingo: Excavations on the Olmec Frontier.* London: Thames and Hudson.

Grove, David C. (editor)
1987 *Chalcatzingo.* Austin: University of Texas Press.

Hally, David J.
1999 The settlement patterns of Mississippian chiefdoms in northern Georgia. In *Settlement Pattern Studies in the Americas: Fifty Years since Virú*, edited by Brian R. Billman and Gary M. Feinman, pp. 96–115. Washington: Smithsonian Institution Press.

Hansen, Richard D.
1998 Continuity and disjunction: The pre-classic antecedents of Classic Maya architecture. In *Function and Meaning in Classic Maya Architecture*, edited by Stephen D. Houston, pp. 49–122. Washington: Dumbarton Oaks.

Hodges, Denise C.
1989 *Agricultural Intensification and Prehistoric Health in the Valley of Oaxaca, Mexico.* Memoir 22. Ann Arbor: Museum of Anthropology, University of Michigan.

Johnson, Scott A. J.
2014 The correlation of surface and subsurface artifacts: A test case from Late and Terminal Classic Popola, Yucatan, Mexico. *Journal of Field Archaeology* 39(3):276–291.

Kaplan, Lawrence, and Thomas F. Lynch
1999 *Phaseolus* (Fabaceae) in archaeology: AMS radiocarbon dates and their significance for pre-columbian agriculture. *Economic Botany* 53:261–272.

Keen, A. Myra
1958 *Sea Shells of Tropical West America.* Palo Alto: Stanford University Press.

Kelly, Raymond C.
2000 *Warless Societies and the Origin of War.* Ann Arbor: University of Michigan Press.

Kirkby, Anne V. T.
1973 *The Use of Land and Water Resources in the Past and Present Valley of Oaxaca, Mexico.* Memoir 1. Ann Arbor: Museum of Anthropology, University of Michigan.

Kopytoff, Igor
1987 Internal African frontier: The making of African political culture. In *The African Frontier: The Reproduction of Traditional African Societies*, edited by Igor Kopytoff, pp. 3–84. Bloomington: Indiana University Press.

Kowalewski, Stephen, Gary M. Feinman, Laura Finsten, Richard Blanton, and Linda M. Nicholas
1989 *Monte Albán's Hinterland, Part II: Prehispanic Settlement Patterns in Tlacolula, Etla, and Ocotlán, the Valley of Oaxaca, Mexico.* Memoir 23. Ann Arbor: Museum of Anthropology, University of Michigan.

Kozlowski, Stefan Karol (editor)
1998 M'lefaat: Early Neolithic site in northern Iraq. *Cahiers de l'Euphrate* 8:179–273.

Lowie, Robert H.
1915 *Dances and Societies of the Plains Shoshone.* Anthropological Papers of the American Museum of Natural History, vol. 11, pt. 10. New York.

MacNeish, Richard S., Frederick A. Peterson, and Kent V. Flannery
1970 *The Prehistory of the Tehuacan Valley, Vol. 3: Ceramics.* Austin: University of Texas Press.

Marcus, Joyce
1974 The iconography of power among the Classic Maya. *World Archaeology* 6(1):83–94.
1976 The origins of Mesoamerican writing. *Annual Review of Anthropology* 5:35–67.

1980 Zapotec writing. *Scientific American* 242:50–64.
1992 *Mesoamerican Writing Systems: Propaganda, Myth, and History in Four Ancient Civilizations*. Princeton: Princeton University Press.
1998 *Women's Ritual in Formative Oaxaca: Figure-making, Divination, Death and the Ancestors*. Memoir 33. Ann Arbor: Museum of Anthropology, University of Michigan.
1999 Men's and women's ritual in Formative Oaxaca. In *Social Patterns in Pre-Classic Mesoamerica*, edited by David C. Grove and Rosemary A. Joyce, pp. 67–96. Washington: Dumbarton Oaks.
2003a The first appearance of Zapotec writing and calendrics. In *The Cloud People: Divergent Evolution of the Zapotec and Mixtec Civilizations*, edited by Kent V. Flannery and Joyce Marcus, pp. 91–96. Clinton Corners: Percheron Press.
2003b Zapotec religion. In *The Cloud People: Divergent Evolution of the Zapotec and Mixtec Civilizations*, edited by Kent V. Flannery and Joyce Marcus, pp. 345–351. Clinton Corners: Percheron Press.
2006 Identifying elites and their strategies. In *Intermediate Elites in Pre-Columbian States and Empires*, edited by Christina M. Elson and R. Alan Covey, pp. 212–246. Tucson: University of Arizona Press.
2009 Rethinking figurines. In *Mesoamerican Figurines: Small-Scale Indices of Large-Scale Social Phenomena*, edited by Christina T. Halperin, Katherine A. Faust, Rhonda Taube, and Aurore Giguet, pp. 25–50. Gainesville: University Press of Florida.

Marcus, Joyce, and Kent V. Flannery
1994 Ancient Zapotec ritual and religion: An application of the direct historical approach. In *The Ancient Mind*, edited by Colin Renfrew and Ezra B. W. Zubrow, pp. 55–74. Cambridge: Cambridge University Press.
1996 *Zapotec Civilization: How Urban Society Evolved in Mexico's Oaxaca Valley*. London: Thames and Hudson.
2004 The coevolution of ritual and society: New ^{14}C dates from ancient Mexico. *Proceedings of the National Academy of Sciences* 101(52):18257–18261.

Marquina, Ignacio
1951 *Arquitectura prehispánica*. México: Instituto Nacional de Antropología e Historia.

Martínez Donjuán, Guadalupe
1985 El sitio olmeca de Teopantecuanitlan en Guerrero. *Anales de Antropología* 22:215-226.
2010 Sculpture from Teopantecuanitlan, Guerrero. In *The Place of Stone Monuments: Context, Use, and Meaning in Mesoamerica's Preclassic Transition*, edited by Julia Guernsey, John E. Clark, and Barbara Arroyo, pp. 55–76. Washington, D.C.: Dumbarton Oaks.

Mata, Juan de
1905[1580] Relación de Teozapotlan. In *Papeles de Nueva España: segunda serie, Geografía y Estadística*, vol. 4, edited by Francisco del Paso y Troncoso, pp. 190–195. Madrid: Est. Tipográfico "Sucesores de Rivadeneyra."

Miller, Arthur G.
1995 *The Painted Tombs of Oaxaca, Mexico: Living with the Dead*. New York: Cambridge University Press.

Parry, William
1987 *Chipped Stone Tools in Formative Oaxaca, Mexico: Their Procurement, Production and Use*. Memoir 20. Ann Arbor: Museum of Anthropology, University of Michigan.

Piperno, Dolores, and Kent V. Flannery
2001 The earliest archaeological maize (Zea mays L.) from highland Mexico: New accelerator mass spectrometry dates and their implications. *Proceedings of the National Academy of Sciences* 98:2101–2103.

Pires-Ferreira, Jane W.
1975 *Formative Mesoamerican Exchange Networks, with Special Reference to the Valley of Oaxaca*. Memoir 7. Ann Arbor: Museum of Anthropology, University of Michigan.

Plog, Stephen
n.d. The Measurement of Prehistoric Human Interaction. Undergraduate honors thesis. Department of Anthropology, University of Michigan, Ann Arbor.
2009 Measurement of prehistoric interaction between communities. In *The Early Mesoamerican Village*, edited by Kent V. Flannery, pp. 255–272. Walnut Creek: Left Coast Press.

Proskouriakoff, Tatiana
1962 The artifacts of Mayapan. In *Mayapan Yucatan Mexico*, edited by Harry E. D. Pollock, Ralph L. Roys, Tatiana Proskouriakoff, and Augustus Ledyard Smith, pp. 321–442. Carnegie Institution of Washington, Publication 619. Washington, D.C.

Radcliffe-Brown, A. R.
1922 *Andaman Islanders*. Cambridge: Cambridge University Press.

Rappaport, Roy A.
1971 The sacred in human evolution. *Annual Review of Ecology and Systematics* 2:23–44.
1979 *Ecology, Meaning, and Religion*. Richmond: North Atlantic Books.
1999 *Ritual and Religion in the Making of Humanity*. Cambridge: Cambridge University Press.

Rautman, Alison
1983 Letter to Flannery.

Redmond, Elsa M., and Charles S. Spencer
2008 Rituals of sanctification and the development of standardized temples in Oaxaca, Mexico. *Cambridge Archaeological Journal* 18(2):239–266.
2013 Early (300–100 B.C.) temple precinct in the Valley of Oaxaca, Mexico. *Proceedings of the National Academy of Sciences* 110(19):E1707–E1715.

Rickards, Constantine George
1910 *The Ruins of Mexico*. London: H. E. Shrimpton.

Ricketson, Oliver G., Jr., and Edith Bayles Ricketson
1937 *Uaxactun, Guatemala, Group E—1926–1931*. Carnegie Institution of Washington, Publication 477. Washington, D.C.

Salazar, Agustín de
1945[1581] Descripción del pueblo de Cuylapa. In *Dos relaciones antiguas del pueblo de Cuilapa, estado de Oaxaca*, edited by Robert H. Barlow. *Tlalocan* 2(1):18–28.

Sanders, William T.
1974 Chiefdom to state: Political evolution at Kaminaljuyu, Guatemala. In *Reconstructing Complex Societies*, edited by Charlotte B. Moore, pp. 97–116. Supplement of the Bulletin of the American Schools of Oriental Research, no. 20. Cambridge, Massachusetts.

Sandweiss, Daniel, James B. Richardson III, Elizabeth J. Reitz, J. T. Hsu, and Robert A. Feldman
1989 Early maritime adaptations in the Andes: Preliminary studies at the Ring Site, Peru. In *Ecology, Settlement, and History in the Osmore Drainage, Peru*, edited by Don S. Rice, Charles Stanish, and Phillip R. Scarr, pp. 35–64. BAR International Series 545. Oxford: Archaeopress.

Satterthwaite, Linton, Jr.
1944 Ballcourts. In *Piedras Negras Archaeology: Architecture*. Philadelphia: University of Pennsylvania Museum.

Shaffer, Gary
1993   Letter to Flannery.

Smith, Bruce D.
1997   The initial domestication of *Cucurbita pepo* in the Americas 10,000 years ago. *Science* 276:932–934.

Speiser, Ephraim A.
1935   *The Excavations at Tepe Gawra, Vol. 1: Levels I–VII.* Philadelphia: University of Pennsylvania Press.

Spencer, Charles S., and Elsa M. Redmond
2001   Multilevel selection and political evolution in the Valley of Oaxaca, 500–100 B.C. *Journal of Anthropological Archaeology* 20(2):195–229.
2003   Militarism, resistance, and early state development in Oaxaca, Mexico. *Social Evolution & History* 2(1):25–70. Moscow: Uchitel.
2006   Resistance strategies and early state formation in Oaxaca, Mexico. In *Intermediate Elites in Pre-Columbian States and Empires*, edited by Christina M. Elson and R. Alan Covey, pp. 21–43. Tucson: University of Arizona Press.

Spencer, Charles S., Elsa M. Redmond, and Christina M. Elson
2008   Ceramic microtypology and the territorial expansion of the early Monte Albán state in Oaxaca, Mexico. *Journal of Field Archaeology* 33(3):321–341.

Spores, Ronald and Kent V. Flannery
2003   Sixteenth-century kinship and social organization. In *The Cloud People: Divergent Evolution of the Zapotec and Mixtec Civilizations*, edited by Kent V. Flannery and Joyce Marcus, pp. 339–342. Clinton Corners: Percheron Press.

Stevanović, Mirjana
1995   Letter to Flannery.

Steward, Julian H.
1938   *Basin-Plateau Aboriginal Sociopolitical Groups.* Bureau of American Ethnology Bulletin 120. Washington, D.C.: Smithsonian Institution.

Stuart, George E., and Enrico Ferorelli
1992   Mural masterpieces of ancient Cacaxtla. *National Geographic* 182(3):120–136.

Taube, Karl A.
1988   A prehispanic Maya katun wheel. *Journal of Anthropological Research* 44(2):183–203.

Thompson, Victor D., and C. Fred T. Andrus
2011   Evaluating mobility, monumentality, and feasting at the Sapelo Shell Ring Complex. *American Antiquity* 76(2):315–344.

Tolstoy, Paul
1989a   Coapexco and Tlatilco: Sites with Olmec materials in the Basin of Mexico. In *Regional Perspectives on the Olmec*, edited by Robert J. Sharer and David C. Grove, pp. 85–121. Santa Fe: School of American Research and Cambridge University Press.
1989b   Western Mesoamerica and the Olmec. In *Regional Perspectives on the Olmec*, edited by Robert J. Sharer and David C. Grove, pp. 275–302. Santa Fe: School of American Research and Cambridge University Press.

Whalen, Michael E.
1981   *Excavations at Santo Domingo Tomaltepec: Evolution of a Formative Community in the Valley of Oaxaca, Mexico.* Memoir 12. Ann Arbor: Museum of Anthropology, University of Michigan.
2009   Sources of the Guilá Naquitz chipped stone. In *Guilá Naquitz: Archaic Foraging and Early Agriculture in Oaxaca, Mexico*, updated ed., edited by Kent V. Flannery, pp. 141–146. Walnut Creek: Left Coast Press.

Wicke, Charles
1957   The ball court at Yagul, Oaxaca: A comparative study. *Mesoamerican Notes* 5:37–76. Mexico City: Mexico City College.

Willey, Gordon R.
1953   *Prehistoric Settlement Patterns in the Virú Valley, Peru.* Bureau of American Ethnology Bulletin 155. Washington, D.C.: Smithsonian Institution.
1999   The Virú Valley Project and settlement archaeology: Some reminiscences and contemporary comments. In *Settlement Pattern Studies in the Americas: Fifty Years since Virú*, edited by Brian R. Billman and Gary M. Feinman, pp. 9–11. Washington and London: Smithsonian Institution Press.

Winter, Marcus C.
1972   Tierras Largas: A Formative Community in the Valley of Oaxaca, Mexico. PhD dissertation, Department of Anthropology, University of Arizona, Tucson.
1976   *Cerámica de la fase Rosario encontrada en dos pozos tronco-cónicos en el sitio de Tierras Largas, valle de Oaxaca, México.* Oaxaca: Centro Regional de Oaxaca.

Winters, Howard D.
1955   Excavation of a colonnaded hall at Mayapan. *Carnegie Institution of Washington, Current Reports* 31:381–396. Washington, D.C.

Woodburn, James
1972   Ecology, nomadic movement and the composition of the local group among hunters and gatherers: An East African example and its implications. In *Man, Settlement and Urbanism*, edited by Peter J. Ucko, Ruth Tringham, and Geoffrey W. Dimbleby, pp. 193–206. London: Duckworth.

Yellen, John E.
1977   *Archaeological Approaches to the Present: Models for Reconstructing the Past.* New York: Academic Press.

Zoubek, Thomas Andrew
1997   The initial period occupation of Huaca El Gallo/Huaca La Gallina, Viru Valley, Peru and its implications for Guañape phase social complexity. PhD dissertation, Department of Anthropology, Yale University, New Haven, Connecticut.

Index

limestone quarry, 63, 384; *see* Rancho Matadamas
limey whitewash, 26, 58
limpet, 141, 142
lineages, 5, 382
Loma de la Cañada Totomosle, 68
Loma los Sabinos, 68
Lorenzo, José Luis, *xxii*

M

Macuilxochitl, 381
Madera Coarse (Brown variety) pottery, 90, 93
Magdalena Apasco, 227
maguey hearts, 7
maize, early dates of, 6; productivity, 6, 13
mano, 7
Maori, 185
masks, 15, 27, 29, 382, 383
mat, reed, 47, 51; *see also petate*
mat-impressed pottery, 137, 175, 211, 284, 361
mat impression, 95; silica exoskeleton "ghosts" from patches, 51
mat motifs on pottery, 43, 382
Matadamas limestone, 123, 231, 341, 392, 394
Matadamas quarry, 63, 119, 165, 229, 394
Maya, 181, 193, 199, 219, 259, 285, 367, 384
Mayapan, 296
men's houses, *xxi*, 1, 4, 12, 13, 14, 15, 16, 17, 18, 19, 20, 21, 23, 24, 26, 27, 29, 34, 35, 36, 37, 39, 49, 50, 51, 54, 55, 56, 60, 63, 72, 89, 123, 192, 382, 383, 384
men's ritual, 49, 382, 383
Méndez, don Leandro, 315
Mesopotamia, 45
mesquite, 279, 323, 325, 351
mesquite-grassland environment, 7
mesquite pods, 7
metamorphosis, *xxii*, 4, 5; metamorphosed into cloud people, 4, 5, 271
metate, 7, 31, 32, 40, 59, 60; boxlike metate with loop handle, 17, 27, 28, 36, 382
Mexican cottontail, 7
mica, 44, 79, 80, 365, 382
mirrors, 56, 382
Mississippian rank societies, 105
Mitla, 7, 8, 381
Mixtec, 27
M'lefaat, 7
molds for round adobes, 73; *see also* broken storage jars
molluscs, 42; *see also* mussel, pearl oyster, spiny oyster, *Spondylus*
monarchy, 106, 223, 226
monkey, spider, 54–55, 382; *see also* spider monkey skull
Monte Albán, 103, 106, 218, 219, 222, 223, 224, 225, 226, 227, 228, 259, 266, 280, 322, 339, 365, 366, 367, 372, 380, 384, 385, 386, 389
Monte Negro, 185, 316, 322
Montezuma quail, 258
Monument 1 (San José Mogote), 64–65
Monument 2 (San José Mogote), 64–65
Monument 3 (San José Mogote), 177, 181, 182, 183, 184, 187, 192, 193, 202; AMS date of, 182; *see also* heart removal, prisoner, sacrificed prisoner, sacrificed victim
Morelos, 46, 88, 90, 92, 93
morning glory, 4, 13, 27, 382
mosaics, stone, 381
Mosul, 7
Motagua jadeite, *xxii*, 264, 265
mother-of-pearl, 44, 69, 332, 333, 382
motifs on pottery, double-line-break, 46, 141, 191; Earth motif, 43, 44; Earth/Earthquake motif, 141, Lightning motif, 43, 44; *see also* Sky/Lightning motif
Mountain Ok, 13, 14
mouse, 146, 147
mud turtle, 296, 297, 299, 300

multidimensional scaling, 107, 108, 202
mummy, 386
mushroom, 4
musical instrument, 259, 266
mussel, 44

N

Naga, 13, 14
Nakbe, 18
Naranjo, 181
necklace, shell, 34, 42; *see also* shell necklace
needles, 297, 301
needles, sewing, 297
negative or resist motifs, 93, 97, 102, 103, 107, 112, 132, 144, 202, 203, 205, 209, 361; *see also* zoned toning
neighborhoods, 3
net, 11
New Guinea, 13
nicotine, 13; *see also* tobacco
Nochixtlán Valley, 68, 82

O

obsidian, 3, 12, 260; obsidian blade, 75, 80, 137, 210, 211, 214, 224, 258, 260, 333, 365; daggers, 260–261, 383; lancets for blood-letting, 4, 258, 260; obsidian lancet, 4, 224, 383; stingray spine of obsidian, 153, 156, 157, 384; *see also* autosacrifice, bloodletting
Ocelotepec, 386
offering box, 242, 245, 246, 251, 258, 259, 260, 262–263, 266–267, 292, 294, 296, 385, 389, 391; *see also* dedicatory offerings
Ok, *see* Mountain Ok
Olmec, *see* Gulf Coast, La Venta, San Lorenzo (Veracruz)
oratory, 193
ore lumps, *see* iron ore, iron ore chunks, iron ore mirrors, iron ore sources
orientation of buildings, 4, 15, 18, 29, 50, 56, 58, 72, 82, 86, 87, 106, 118, 119, 141, 147, 149, 226, 383, 384, 385; *see also* "E Groups"
orioles, 147
ornament, 7, 43, 301, 332
ornament manufacture, 8, 42, 44
orthostats, 129, 130, 135, 340, 341, 343, 344, 349, 350
otoliths, 98, 99, 100; drum otoliths, 100
Otomanguean languages, 45
Otumba, 75
oven, earth, *see* earth oven
owl, 215, 217
owl pellets, 146

P

Pacific Northwest, 46
painted ritual basin, 49, 56; *see* ritual basin
painted stucco, 240, 243, 244, 248, 368, 372, 373, 374, 380, 386, 389
painted adobes, 389
paired temples, 228–229
palace, 5, 106, 219, 227–228, 339–350; governmental palace, 227, 228, 338–350, 380, 381, 382, 385; residential palace, 339, 340, 343, 351–366, 385; *see also* Monte Albán, Tilcajete
Palenque, 181
palisade, 13, 16
palm-impressed bowl, 209
paramount chiefly center, 105
parrot feathers, 381
partitioning rooms, 358, 359, 360, 362
pasillo techado, 316, 318, 322
Patio Hundido, 339; *see also* Monte Albán
pattern burnishing, 107, 113, 177, 189, 209
paw-wing motif; *see also* "crocodile's foot" motif, 93, 97, 102, 103
pearl oyster, 44, 56, 332, 334, 335, 358, 365